Steven Vanderputten
Medieval Monasticisms

Oldenbourg
Grundriss der Geschichte

———

Herausgegeben von Karl-Joachim Hölkeskamp,
Achim Landwehr, Steffen Patzold und Benedikt Stuchtey

Band 47

Steven Vanderputten

Medieval Monasticisms

Forms and Experiences of the Monastic Life
in the Latin West

DE GRUYTER
OLDENBOURG

ISBN 978-3-11-054377-3
e-ISBN (PDF) 978-3-11-054378-0
e-ISBN (EPUB) 978-3-11-054396-4

Library of Congress Control Number: 2020930331

Bibliografische Information der Deutschen Nationalbibliothek
Die Deutsche Nationalbibliothek verzeichnet diese Publikation in der Deutschen
Nationalbibliografie; detaillierte bibliografische Daten sind im Internet über
http://dnb.dnb.de abrufbar.

© 2020 Walter de Gruyter GmbH, Berlin/Boston
Satz: Integra Software Services Pvt. Ltd.
Druck und Bindung: CPI books GmbH, Leck

www.degruyter.com

Editors' Foreword

Since 1978, the series *Oldenbourg Outlines of History* has served both students and teachers as an important means of orientation, delivering what its title promises: an outline, a plan providing insights from a bird's-eye view which would be difficult to gain from other perspectives.

The series has held fast to its main purpose since its inception. In a proven three-part structure, each volume first provides an introduction to the given historic subject. The second part is devoted to a thorough survey of the research, providing newcomers with the given area an overview of current and past debates. Equally, trained historians and newcomers are increasingly challenged to keep up to date on the major ramifications of a research topic, in view of the characteristic complexity, international scope, and temporal depth of such discussions. At this point the series is a crucial aid – and this is the key feature which significantly distinguishes it from other publications of its kind. Each volume is rounded up by a third part which offers an extensive bibliography.

In the course of its own history, the *Oldenbourg Outlines of History* series has responded to the changes in research, debate, and study of history. It has gradually expanded to include new subject areas. The series overall is no longer exclusively devoted to a survey starting in Greek and Roman antiquity, scrutinizing the European Middle Ages at length, then arriving in the present, broadly understood as the modern era. While this chronological tour of German and European history remains fundamental for an orientation in relation to historic events, its scope is increasingly being broadened by volumes on special themes and non-European subjects. Thus the series documents the substantive changes that are continuously taking place in the study of history.

The *Oldenbourg Outlines of History* series presents these topics to students who want to explore not only the substance, but also the research history of a complex field. At the same time, they are intended to support teachers in their endeavours to communicate such topics in lectures and seminars. Nevertheless, the primary objective remains accurately to portray past times, the more recent as well as the more remote, not simply by representing them as events

https://doi.org/10.1515/9783110543780-202

and structures, but by showing that the scholarly treatment of them is a part of their history.

Karl-Joachim Hölkeskamp
Achim Landwehr
Steffen Patzold
Benedikt Stuchtey

Acknowledgements

I am grateful to Steffen Patzold for inviting me to write this book, to Johan Belaen, Jirki Thibaut, and Guido Cariboni for the inspiring conversations while I was drafting it, and to the countless generous colleagues with whom I was able to exchange views and ideas over the last two decades. Also to Susan Vincent, for the careful editorial work and the many difficult questions. I owe most of all to my wife Melissa, who reviewed version after version of each chapter, gave me endless encouragement, and continues to be my anchor. Finally, this book is dedicated to Hugo: *luceat lux tua*.

https://doi.org/10.1515/9783110543780-203

Contents

I Historical Survey

1 Introductory Comments

The story of monastic life in the Latin West used to have a straightforward narrative logic. As a social and spiritual phenomenon, it was said to have emerged in the desert wilderness of third-century Egypt and Palestine. Fleeing persecution and looking to escape from worldly distractions, Christian hermits withdrew there in search of communion with God through a life of austerity and self-abnegation. Over time, their example drew such large numbers of followers that it became necessary for leading individuals to establish the earliest organized communities. Cenobitism, the nature and purpose of which was first described in a rule by the Desert Father Pachomius (d. 348), shifted the focus from the spontaneous withdrawal of solitary ascetics to the deliberately structured experience of life in a monastery. Over the course of the fourth and early fifth centuries, the number of desert monasteries grew explosively, and soon the phenomenon also spread across the Mediterranean region and further into Gaul and the British Isles. In all of these places, founders established different strands of cenobitism whilst continuing to look for inspiration to the eastern cradle of monastic life. This process of expansion was driven forward by the creation of numerous written rules, each of which represented an attempt to balance the individual's quest for perfection with the needs and challenges of community life.

Traditional narratives

Origins of cenobitism

From this phase of intense experimentation and mutual influences emerged the pinnacle of early monastic rule-making, the sixth-century *Rule of St Benedict*. The *Rule*'s rise to dominance was consolidated by the Carolingian reforms of the eighth and early ninth centuries, which presented that text as the ultimate account of monastic community life. Successive 'waves' of reform in the next two and a half centuries corroborated the authority of that tradition, until various eremitical and apostolic movements post-1000 broke its normative monopoly. The charismatic founders of these movements criticized monastic prayer service as overly formalistic and insufficiently focused on the apostolic legacies of the early Church, and the lifestyle of practitioners as insufficiently committed to the ascetic ideal. They also challenged lay

'Triumph' of Benedictinism

https://doi.org/10.1515/9783110543780-001

Emergence of orders
and congregations

and clerical interference in monastic affairs, and found the unit of the single monastery lacking as an efficient organizational paradigm for the various difficulties facing the cenobitic phenomenon at that time. In order to make their ideal of a return to the authentic spirit of desert monasticism and the primitive focus of the apostolic Church a realistic prospect, this leadership gradually developed a range of supra-institutional procedures for legislation and governance: from these experiments emerged the earliest monastic orders.

Mendicant and lay
movements

By the late twelfth century, these new orders, too, faced criticism for their wealth and privileged status, and for being out of touch with the laity's then-current attitudes and expectations. They were in turn replaced at the forefront of monastic life by various mendicant orders focusing on poverty and pastoral actions. Also emerging in this period were semi-religious movements that hosted men and women who wished to pursue the monastic ideal without taking vows or becoming part of a cloistered community. Later medieval developments led to major ideological, legal, institutional, and economic difficulties in nearly all strands of monastic

Reform and decline

life. Various reform endeavours and the rise of Humanism gave some of these orders and movements a new lease of life in the late fourteenth and fifteenth centuries: but their charismatic appeal as ascetic movements was irrevocably lost. Observers sensed that they were witnessing the closing stage of a glorious epoch – correctly, so it turned out. Dissolution, Reformation, and the drastic interventions of the Catholic Church would soon fundamentally transform the monastic landscape of Europe.

New perspectives

This, in a nutshell, is how the history of Western monastic life was taught to generations of students, and how it continues to be recounted in major surveys and handbooks. Admittedly it makes for a gripping account of the resourcefulness of men and women in both their quest to achieve an ascetic identity and also to establish the modes of organization that would turn monasticism into a major institutional, socio-economic, and cultural force. Another aspect of its appeal lies in the description of the heroic, almost Sisyphean nature of these endeavours. It charts the various obstacles that made achieving the abovementioned goals difficult, the solutions charismatic reformers came up with imperfect, and the longevity of their renewal efforts doubtful. However, the sheer attractiveness of that narrative should not divert us from the fact that it is problematic as a representation of historical realities. Besides treating non-institutional and non-collective forms of monastic life as marginal phenomena, it also brings specific modes of observance and governance in and out of focus depending on later commentators' estimation of their success, at a given point in their existence, in realizing the 'authentic' spirit of the monastic ideal. To justify this mode of storytelling, the traditional account does two things. One is to define a sequence of dominant models or movements and then to fit the history of each of these into a narrative cycle of charismatic origins, blossoming, and decline. The second is to represent each of these models and movements as homogeneous in terms of their ideology, governance, and observance.

Against this approach, recently scholars have argued that the monastic past should not be studied as a continuous chain of coordinated attempts to realize a single, ahistorical ideal, but rather as a situation in which there simultaneously existed many such ideals, and many different attempts to realize them. As the study of monastic forms and experiences in late antiquity and the Middle Ages is becoming fully historicized (meaning that all aspects of monastic life are considered in terms of their historical situatedness), the awareness is growing among experts that it makes no sense to argue that the practitioners of these different ideals and realizations belonged to one and the same ideological and behavioural phenomenon, or to describe their history as consisting of a single, forward-looking movement. Through its use of the plural *monasticisms*, the title of this book explicitly acknowledges this trend.

Historicization of the field

'Monasticisms'

Deconstruction of the great master story has been useful and necessary. Besides other things, it has encouraged specialists to re-open case files they had long thought of as closed, and consider them from a less prejudiced standpoint. Some are trying out new methodologies and approaches, and exploring long-ignored sources and typologies. Others are making a case for bottom-up study of forms and experiences of the monastic life in order to capture its intrinsic diversity and make a more realistic estimation of common patterns. And others still are integrating previous research into the broader study of identity formation and historical culture in the medieval and early modern West. All of this has helped us gain a detailed understanding of how our previous story of the monastic past was formed through the prism of medieval and

New perspectives

early modern conceptions of private and organized religion, human organization, and (ethnic, gendered, social,...) identity.

New challenges   But the disintegration of the master story has also shown that the field currently faces a narrative crisis. While most experts admit that the standard account of monasticism's first fifteen hundred years does not match with the current scholarly understanding of the phenomenon, so far there has been no indication that the academic community is ready to substitute a new global narrative for the old one. Studies published over the last few decades have provided ample indications of not only the immense diversity of monastic forms and experiences, but also the substantial difficulties of reconstructing them adequately –let alone fitting them into a synthetic account that is suitable for use in classroom contexts and in handbooks. Meanwhile, research has also shifted from a chronological focus to a thematic one, a development many experts see as placing a new overarching narrative even further out of reach. Nonetheless, somehow we still need to integrate these recent approaches and findings into a chronological discussion that will give readers a first impression of the current state of knowledge on the subject.

Focus of this   The present handbook is not an attempt to provide readers
handbook   with comprehensive thematic discussions of monastic institutions, economies, spirituality, artistic and cultural life, societal impact, and so on. Rather, its aim is to focus on monasticism from a viewpoint that is inspired by sociological and anthropological perspectives, and to highlight two key features of early twenty-first century scholarship. One is the justified preoccupation of many specialists with the way in which narratives of the monastic past have been constructed over the last millennium and a half and how these have distorted our understanding of late antique and medieval realities. And the second key aspect is the abovementioned focus on the diversity of monastic forms and experiences, their continuous state of transformation, and their embedding in specific physical, socio-economic, even personal realities and experiences.

'Messy' realities and   Together these features explain why the story of medieval monas-
experiences   ticism is shaping to become far 'messier' (in the sense of diverse, non-linear, and historically situated) – and arguably also a good deal more interesting – than it used to be.

Note: The references (preceded by **S**) in Part 1 of this book are to the primary sources listed in Part 3, Chapter 1.4.

2 The Beginnings of Monasticism(s)

2.1 Earliest Monasticisms

Christian monasticism in its broadest meaning of ascetic with-   Earliest inspirations
drawal and self-abnegation manifested itself not long after the
earliest faith communities emerged. Multiple traditions set a range
of precedents. Educated Christians could refer to Stoic and Neo-
Platonist traditions in Greco-Roman philosophy that celebrated the
figure of the ascetic sage and advised that those seeking wisdom
did best both to withdraw from ordinary social interactions and
to practise chastity. They might also have had some knowledge
of Jewish traditions of eremitism and other forms of ascetic life as
evidenced through the Essenes and the Qumram community, and
the taking of temporary vows to abstain from impure activities and
contacts. More broadly familiar to early Christians would have been
the New Testament tales of John the Baptist's eremitism and Jesus's
forty-day retreat in the desert. Furthermore, on a metaphorical level
there were numerous clues in the accounts of Jesus's teaching that
provided apparent endorsement of this lifestyle. By abandoning
all that is worldly, rejecting all passions, and practising strenuous
self-abnegation and mortification, the individual – so such teaching was thought to suggest – would be led to spiritual wisdom and
insight into the very essence of divine being. As Jesus says in Luke
18:22, "Go, sell all that you have... and come and follow me".

Early accounts by Christian commentators celebrated those   Earliest testimonies
faithful who willingly renounced their former situation in life
and sacrificed their personal comfort and physical safety to find
union with God. Alongside those who perished at the hands of
Roman persecutors, others sought out an alternative, less violent
form of martyrdom. By withdrawing from the immediate demands
of family life and society in general, they pursued an existence
marked by drastically reduced social interactions, sexual purity,
and physical and psychological self-denial: they were the earliest
monastics. For the first two and a half centuries of Christian history,   Ascetic lifestyles
we find scattered references in contemporary sources to men and
women living in a state of poverty and chastity, observing silence
and strenuously fasting, and devoting their existence to the imitation of Christ's ideals. The chronographer Eusebius of Cesarea
(d. 339/340) paints a picture that seems plausible in general terms

when he describes how members of the early Church of Jerusalem had abstained from consuming alcoholic drinks and luxurious foodstuffs, never used ointments, and never took baths. According to his testimony, they had prostrated so often to venerate God and ask pardon for his people, that the skin on their knees had become raw "like those of camels". Such practices may also have been a feature of community life in first-century Corinth and Smyrna, and also in other urban contexts where Christianity gained an early

Eschatological motives

foothold. For these first generations of believers, the ambition to 'leave the world' probably had an urgency that transcended personal feelings of unease over how to reconcile one's faith with one's role in society, and related instead to the question of how to prepare for Christ's imminent second coming.

Even though eschatological concerns would periodically re-emerge over the next millennium and a half, over time their relevance as a primary focus in the faith practices of Christian communities

'Ascetic specialists'

declined. Presumably the realization set in that members had families to provide for and a role to play in public life, and that extreme practices of ascetic self-abnegation by all members would in the long term cripple a community's worship and social cohesion. Although local Churches continued to collectively practise certain ascetic behaviours (fasting, sexual abstinence, and purity rituals) at specific times of the year or for specific reasons, over time only a small minority took to a life where these and other behaviours actu-

Eremitism

ally became a determining factor in their identity. Some of these people may have chosen to walk in the footsteps of John the Baptist by opting for a solitary life situated literally on or beyond the limits of society. But presumably more numerous were those who carved out a special place for themselves within the urban context of early

Other ascetics

Christian communities. Many of the men who followed this way of life were members of the higher clergy, who served an altar and who practised chastity as a way of retaining their ritual purity. The women were mostly consecrated (or veiled) widows and virgins: the *Pastor of Hermas*, an anonymous text written probably in Rome c. 140, describes a group of twelve virgins whose main occupation consisted of worshipping God through dancing, chanting, and praying. Prominent Christian commentators of the fourth and fifth centuries noted the existence of similar groups of ascetic women and praised their lifestyle.

Numerous individuals and small groups emerge from these and other commentaries as 'household ascetics', people who pursued a monastic existence in the familiar environment of their own home or on the estate of a relative or fellow monastic. Women feature prominently in the testimonies regarding this lifestyle. In one of his letters, Church Father Jerome (d. 420) describes how a fourth-century woman named Asella spent her days inside her bedroom in the family residence in Rome, refusing all contact with other people, including her relatives, and following a strenuous regime of fasting, prayer, and psalmody. We also know of married couples, like Melania and her husband Pinianus, who withdrew for a private life of prayer and abstention to their estate outside the city. Household asceticism was relatively easy to organize, as long as its practitioners had the means to afford such a lifestyle and as long as they were able to surround themselves with servants and associates who were willing to assist them in their ascetic endeavours.

Household ascetics

It was also a lifestyle that could be pursued discretely in times of persecution: more importantly though, it echoed the Roman elites' anxiety about preserving the honour of aristocratic women. While some individuals took it as an opportunity to become 'house hermits', rejecting all direct human contact, others were more open to interactions with their fellow believers. In another letter, Jerome reports how, in the 350s, a recently widowed woman named Marcella withdrew to her parental home in Rome for a life of abstinence, charity, and the study of Scripture. She went outside only to visit churches and the tombs of martyrs, and always arranged for witnesses to be present at her spiritual conversations with monks and religious men. Despite this relatively sheltered existence, she eventually became the leading figure in a circle of virgins and widows, some of whom even moved in with her. These women were all members of the aristocracy, and would pray, study, and psalmodize together. Contemporary sources refer to similar communities in Verona, Bologna, Turin, and an unspecified location in Gaul.

Social interactions and group formation

Jerome's testimony links the activities of Marcella's informal community to other groups of ascetic women – also consecrated widows and virgins – who dedicated their lives to serving their local faith community alongside celibate clerics. Some of these groups staffed *xenodochia*, guesthouses for travellers and the poor, or organized themselves to attend to the poor and needy in other ways. In some eastern Churches, and from the eighth century onwards

Social and other roles

also in Rome, *diaconiae* occupied a distinct place or service, which mostly pertained to charity, in the ecclesiastical system. And in the Iberian Peninsula, male and female followers of the aristocrat Priscillian (d. c. 385) jointly served oratories and preached to the faithful. Others still played a role in organizing the early cult of martyrs, preparing bodies for burial, acting as a weeping choir at funerals,

Cult of martyrs and subsequently becoming guardians of martyrial graves. As these burial sites became focal points of Christian veneration, altars were erected above tombs: some of these cult sites (the earliest of which were situated in private homes or on privately owned estates, while later ones were established by lay and secular rulers to Christianize former sites of pagan worship) eventually became martyrial *basilicae*. The female monastics who staffed these places are referred to in some sources as *matronae* ("matrons") and are attested for current-day Switzerland, Rome, and other parts of the Christian world including Syria. A conjugal image was sometimes used to describe their spiritual and functional cohabitation with the clerics who assisted them in their service.

These and other testimonies allow us to glimpse the existence in some places of a division of tasks and responsibilities, and of some form of hierarchy. According to Jerome, Marcella's companions ended up referring to her as their "mistress" (*magistra*), and to

Early regulation themselves as her "disciples" (*discipulae*). Common sense also tells us that especially those groups providing a service to the Christian community must have relied on a number of informal regulations to facilitate their various operations, and to prevent outside distractions from interfering with their ascetic pursuits: but none of these were codified.

The presence of monastics at cultic sites in particular was highly charged with meaning. The North African writer Tertullian (d. c. 240) compared martyrs' graves to the prison in which they had been incarcerated prior to their death, and via that image also to the

Desert eremitism desert world inhabited by biblical prophets. Yet, in terms of their long-term impact on monastic culture and the imagination of countless readers living outside of monastic settings, the accounts of these early ascetics were no match for the heroic tales of the fourth- and fifth-century Desert Fathers of Egypt and Palestine and their struggles with physical deprivation and mental demons. Popular accounts – such as Jerome's *Life* of Paul of Thebes (d. c. 341) written in the 360s; Athanasius of Alexandria's roughly contemporary *Life* of Anthony the Great (d. 356); the *Life* of Mary of Egypt (d. c. 421); and the fifth-century *Sayings of the Fathers* [S APOPTHEGMATA PATRUM] – portrayed their subjects as heroic figures who sought out the primordial rawness of the desert, partly as a way to escape persecution and partly to attain the most perfect connection with the divine mystery. Removed from society and its temptations but still connected to it through encounters with visitors and aspiring followers, these men and women were depicted as devoting their existence to finding and subsequently rooting out the evil in themselves, thereby undoing original sin and reconnecting with Creation. For that purpose, they subjected themselves to fasting, sleep deprivation and social isolation, and risked exposure to extreme weather conditions and wild animals. As their home, they took a cell, a cave, the top of a pillar, or simply a hole in the ground, which became the place where they studied Scripture, recited the psalms, and performed repetitive manual tasks such as basket-weaving or rope-making. Silence and stability were routinely cited in this literature as defining features of their conduct, although readers were also told about ascetics who committed some of their time to teaching those who had newly arrived to the eremitical life or more generally provided moral counsel to visitors.

Representations

Just as Jesus's forty-day journey into the desert functioned as a parable for finding God by withdrawing from the distractions of everyday life and suppressing natural desires, so the accounts of the Desert Fathers functioned as literary aids for a life dedicated to ascetic pursuits. As such, they celebrated austerity, simplicity, and single-mindedness as being the only way to achieve spiritual union with the divine. But they also brought comfort to their readers: they showed that the monastic life was open to every Christian, regardless of their prior education, status, and conduct; they warned against excess in the practice of self-denial, and depicted failure, temptation, distraction, and lack of motivation as part and parcel of every monastic's heroic struggle to achieve self-knowledge; and they promoted mutual tolerance of one another's abilities and character traits. Several of these accounts soon entered into wide circulation in the Western parts of the Roman Empire, a development that was possibly helped by the fact that they were translated from the Greek, Coptic, and Syriac into Latin. Throughout late antiquity and the entire medieval period, monastics were drawn to link their own experience of self-abnegation and ascetic

Biased narratives

withdrawal to that irresistible image of the early hermits' terrifying journey into the hostile, often surreal world of the desert. Little did it matter that such texts contained anachronisms that revealed their origins in profoundly different theological and societal contexts than those they claimed to describe. For instance, Athanasius's theological discourse in his 360s account of the life of Anthony the Great referred to then-current doctrinal issues that were alien to his hero's experience of faith. Such manipulation of biographical traditions was a typical feature of early ascetic literature: in the *Life* of Pelagia of Antioch, a virgin who apparently committed suicide when persecuting Roman soldiers came to find her, she was recast as a former prostitute and cross-dresser, who withdrew to a cell on the Mount of Olives and starved herself to death in repentance for her sins.

Nuanced realities Neither did it matter that such tales drastically distorted the social realities of early monastic life in Egypt, more specifically the fact that its practitioners were far less isolated socially and far less easily distinguishable from those in other forms of religious life than is suggested in the traditional canon of literary accounts. The earliest known use of the word *monachos* or "monk" is in a 311/312 treatise known as *De Patientia* ("On Patience"), which mentions *monachoi* living alongside clerics, virgins, and widows. The next appearance is in a letter dated 324, where an Egyptian villager states that a *monachos* and a deacon had rescued him from being battered by his enemies. In both cases and in many others, these individuals do not appear as socially isolated beings or as part of a distinct community of ascetic individuals, but in conjunction with men and women belonging to (to a greater or lesser extent) organized religious groups. Yet, in the circulating accounts of desert eremitism, authors presented a world so alien to the majority of their readership, and literary themes so drenched in allegorical meaning, that their works were automatically taken as a metaphorical reflection on the nature and challenges of monastic life. As such, they acquired a meaning that was universally relevant. In creating this alien and over-determined world, these authors **Influence as inspirational literature** achieved a perfect match with their readers' expectations. For what late antique and medieval audiences of the lives and sayings of the Deserts Fathers were looking for was not an accurate reconstruction of early eremitical ideology, or descriptive accounts of the complex reality of ascetic withdrawal in the towns and countryside of Egypt and Palestine. Rather, readers wanted tales of sacrifice and reward that strengthened them in their own resolve to carry out their own ascetic sacrifice, regardless of the historicity of the events portrayed.

2.2 The 'Rise of Cenobitism'

Beginning in the latter half of the fourth century, we find the earliest formulations of a perennial narrative stating that the Desert Fathers were the founders of Christian monasticism. Although Jerome, John Cassian (d. c. 435), and other influential authors admitted that there had been individual ascetics and ascetic communities in various parts of the Empire (including the West) prior to the middle of the third century, they discussed or in some cases even dismissed these lifestyles and initiatives as being private and ephemeral. The 'real' tradition of monastic life, so they suggested, emerged in the deserts of Egypt and Palestine, first as informal gatherings of like-minded ascetics, but soon also as cenobitical communities that became increasingly institutionalized and organized through the creation and use of written rules.

> Status of cenobitism as the 'real' monasticism

The trigger for this transformation, so these commentators and many that came after them stated, was the end of Christianity as a persecuted minority religion and its gradual emergence as the principal faith across the Roman Empire. Deprived of the opportunity to be martyred at the hands of persecutors, disenchanted by the loss of an eschatological perspective in their faith and the normalization of Christian practice, and dismayed to see the Church transform into a state-sanctioned (and to some extent also state-controlled) institution, many would-be ascetics reportedly saw no other option but to renounce their place in society. This prompted growing numbers of men and women to join the original desert hermits – those individuals who had fled into the desert to escape persecution under the Emperors Decius and Diocletian in the 250s and early 300s – in their spiritual endeavours. An additional incentive for seeking the company of these hermits was their reputation as 'holy men' and their draw for the faithful who sought spiritual counsel.

> Alleged origins of cenobitism

Whether this narrative is accurate, and whether the above factors actually led to a mass exodus into the desert is difficult to say. What we do know for certain is that, beginning in the 320s,

> Realities of early cenobitical life

monastic practitioners (sometimes referred to as *monachoi*) turn up far more regularly in Egyptian sources than before, including in legal documents, letters, and other types of everyday evidence. From the onset, these hermits and other ascetics lived in symbiosis with their urban or rural environments. Their sheer numbers, their attraction to pilgrims and those seeking spiritual counsel, and their transactions with the population, made them a significant factor in the society and economy of fourth-century Egypt. What we also know is that the success of Egyptian eremitism, even though it did not in fact match the classic image of ascetics gathering in desert communities far removed from society, compelled the creation of new physical and virtual spaces, making the ideal of withdrawal from the world once again a realistic prospect.

Pachomian cenobitism One example is the foundation around the year 320, by Pachomius, of a settlement for hermits in the region of Thebes. Initially, Pachomian community life was nearly as loose as the contemporary community of hermits at Kellia, a sprawling settlement in the Nitrian Desert that according to legend was founded in 338 by a disciple of St Anthony's named Amun. At Kellia, members lived in separate cells that were situated at great distance from one another, and came together on Saturdays and Sundays only, to worship, listen to the spiritual advice of the elderly, confess their errors and receive punishment, and exchange the products of their manual labour. But over time, Pachomius intervened in his foundation to reduce the number of dwellings, introduce a division of tasks, set up a fixed routine for prayer, and surround the settlement with a high wall. Pachomius's model, which established the cenobitical community as a self-supporting economic unit with a clear hierarchical structure led by an abbot, was popular. By the time of his death in 348, it was reportedly observed in thirteen communities, ten for men and three for women.

Simultaneity with other initiatives Past historians readily accepted that Pachomius's reputation as a successful monastic organizer and his authorship of the first instructional text (better known as his *Rule*) written specifically for monastics established him as the father of cenobitism, and helped spread his model beyond Egypt's borders from the mid-fourth century onwards [S Pachomius]. But as we already saw, ascetic communities had existed for many years. And following the end of the persecutions, experiments with new forms were happening in different places too. In the 330s, Eustathius of Sebaste (d. after 377) founded several ascetic settlements in and around Armenia, his region of origin. And towards the middle of the century, John Chrysostom (d. 407) reported that he visited two communities of male monastics – which he refers to as *asketeria*, "ascetic houses" – in the Syrian city of Antioch, to learn about the spiritual foundations of ascetic life.

Although these founders and other practitioners may have been aware of what was happening in the Egyptian desert they certainly did not try to slavishly copy it, and instead relied on a range of influences to design their preferred version of community life. On his family estate of Anesi in Cappadocia, Bishop Basilius of Cesarea **Basilian cenobitism** (d. 379) founded a settlement that he organized according to principles he had interiorized as part of an education strongly rooted in Hellenistic and Christian intellectual culture, which he had further explored during his travels throughout Egypt and other parts of the Orient. As in latter-day Pachomian cenobitism, members were expected to live together, attend office together at specific hours, pray together, eat together in the refectory, and spend the rest of their time studying or performing manual labour. But Basilius's two *Rules* (which were less prescriptive documents than ad hoc responses to concrete problems, presented in the form of questions and answers) reveal that his ideal of community life was also different from that of Pachomius, in that it explicitly prohibited excessive ascetic practices, established a more rigidly defined internal code of conduct, and imposed milder punishments for errors. He also subjected all cenobites to the principle of obedience to the abbot and to the community generally, and grounded this obligation in the central virtues of humility and charity. From these principles derived other obligations, including stability, the individual's relinquishing of free will, and the idea that the abbot should represent Christ to his community.

Further afield, yet more experiments were taking place. From **Experiments in the** c. 340 onwards, Bishop Eusebius of Vercelli (d. 371) subjected the **Western Empire** clerics at his episcopal court to a form of ascetic community life. And in or around 361, a former soldier from Gaul named Martin (d. 397) gave up his life as a hermit on an island in the Ligurian sea, and established instead a community of monastics near the town of Poitiers, on the site of a Roman villa which may or may not have been abandoned at the time. This settlement, which his- **Martin of Tours as** torians have described as a hermitage, would later become the **founder** abbey of Ligugé. On being elected as bishop of Tours in 371, Martin continued to practise an ascetic lifestyle and founded a new eremitical settlement on the site of the future abbey of Marmoutier, outside of the city. If we are to believe Martin's biographer Sulpicius Severus (d. c. 425), the community there resembled some of the earliest eremitical groups in late third- and early fourth-century Egypt [**S** Sᴜʟᴘɪᴄɪᴜs].

Augustinian cenobitism

A similar figure in certain respects was Augustine (d. 430), a North African who became a Christian in 386. Soon after his conversion he withdrew, along with a group of relatives and friends, to a property in the Italian town of *Cassiacum*: together, they engaged in spiritual conversation, reading, and prayer. This ephemeral community was dissolved in the spring of 387, when Augustine was given his Catholic baptism and returned to Africa. On moving there, he re-created *Cassiacum* on a family estate at Thagaste, but in 391 he also established a more formal *monasterium* for male ascetics – the first community in North Africa to be given such a name – in a garden donated by the local bishop, Valerius, on the occasion of Augustine's ordination to the priesthood. Once made bishop of Hippo in 395, Augustine subjected his episcopal household to a quasi-cenobitical regime and also became involved in a local community of women that had reportedly been founded by his sister.

Augustine's Rules

For his latter two foundations, Augustine wrote brief admonishments that indicated in general terms how he imagined cenobitical life ought to be organized and stressed the importance of mutual love and charity as a means for enhancing the ascetic achievements of individual members. His instructions soon became absorbed in other commentaries on cenobitical life. One example is that of Bishop Alypius of Thagaste, who had preceded Augustine as founder of the earliest known cenobitical settlement in the Roman province *Africa*. Alypius worked with a number of commentaries he had brought from a journey to Bethlehem to draft instructions for the members of that community. Of this text, which much more than Augustine's own writings is focused on the practical organization of internal life, we only have a version destined for women, and another one for men in which he redrafted his original text with the aid of one of Augustine's admonishments [**S** Aᴜɢᴜsᴛɪɴᴇ]. Alongside Augustine's and Alypius's foundations there were others, including a *xenodochium* in Hippo that had been founded with

Augustine's support. And again at Thagaste, a woman known as Melania 'the Elder' in 411 established a monastery that reportedly housed no fewer than 130 women and 80 men, the latter group consisting of former estate slaves. Such undertakings by women were reported for other regions too. Late in the fourth century, a Roman widow named Paula together with her daughter moved to Bethlehem, where she created four monastic settlements, one for men and three for virgins.

By the year 400, cenobitism, although still far from a mass phenomenon, was becoming a major feature of the religious landscape in many places. Scholars are only beginning to understand the transnational dynamics that explain its rise over the course of the fourth century. Obviously, sheer demographics must be taken into consideration. While it is difficult to guess how many people became monastics out of dissatisfaction with the 'normalization' of the Christian faith and its growing integration in Roman state structures, some of them would have now found entering a community of ascetics more attractive because it no longer made them an easy-to-spot target for persecutors. For many individuals, entering a cenobitical community also promised a better quality of life and in some cases also a better intellectual training than that which could be achieved outside: it is probably no coincidence that the earliest reports of parents giving their child to a monastic community (a phenomenon known to scholars as child oblation) date from the late fourth century.

Finally, cenobitical life was attractive because of its relative blurring of social inequality. Late antique society was one where elite structures, patronage and clientelism, and wealth imposed strict limits on interactions between members of different classes. Yet, in their respective 'rules', Pachomius and Augustine insisted that all monastics were to respect each other, remain modest, and not refuse to interact with brethren of a different social background. And at Paula's community in Bethlehem, which hosted those of modest origins alongside aristocrats, there was no separation between individuals of different social origins when members gathered to pray. Augustine also made provisions for each monk to receive the same clothes, bedding, and food, and forbade all private property.

A second factor, aside from demographics and social motives, contributed to this rising status of cenobitism within the range of

Causes and dynamics

Attraction of cenobitical forms

Rising status of cenobites

monastic lifestyles. The fourth century marks the growing prominence in Catholic thought of a hierarchic view of religious attainment, where ascetics were regarded as having achieved the pinnacle of Christian wisdom, and in debates over orthodoxy were heard as the voice of authority. It is perhaps in response to this development and to protect the pastoral role of the clergy that some Church leaders became concerned about the views and conduct of 'wandering ascetics'. Augustine's interest in setting up cenobitical communities has been linked to the ongoing struggle for dominance between Catholic and Donatist Christians in North Africa. As we can infer from contemporary reports, the Donatists rejected cenobitical life as lacking any foundation in Scripture, and they travelled from one martyr's shrine to the next, seeking martyrdom through strenuous ascetic peregrination. Parallels can also be drawn with the fierce opposition of Spanish bishops to the Priscillianists, who actively included preaching in their mission.

At the same time, bishops became interested in integrating the clergy within ascetic lifestyles, and also sought to rely more heavily on monastics to promote a particular interpretation of Christian faith. It is no coincidence that Martin founded the community near Poitiers in close concord with his former patron, Bishop Hilary of Poitiers (d. c. 367): worth mentioning in this context are his frequent forays post-settlement into the countryside of Gaul, promoting conversion and turning pagan sanctuaries into sites of Christian worship. For his part, Augustine preferred his clerics at Hippo to be part of a community of monastics, and at least one of his foundations there was intended to house them. Monastic society as he imagined it in his written commentaries was an open one, where members were supposed to act as preachers of Christ's message and where laypeople looking for spiritual guidance were welcome as guests.

Finally, various observers increasingly came to regard Christian ascetics – monastics, in the broad definition used here – living outside of cenobitical contexts as problematic. Concerning women, bishops' arguments were focused on protecting them physically and guaranteeing their purity. Around 400, the first council of Toledo instructed female household ascetics to avoid all contact with men, except for their relatives: the frequency and detail of other such conciliar measures destined for women would only increase over time. Meanwhile, Christian and non-Christian commentators also

Social and other contestation

Clerical lifestyles

Negative perceptions of private ascetics

began expressing scepticism over the lifestyle and attitudes of male hermits and ascetic wanderers, calling them socially disruptive, uncivic even. Although a non-Christian himself, the fifth-century poet Rutilius Namatianus may well have echoed the views of certain members of the ruling Christian elites when he called an acquaintance of his who lived as a hermit, a "credulous exile skulking in the dark" and a "poor fool" for thinking that "heaven feeds on filth". Before him, the late fourth-century pagan teacher and author Libanius of Antioch had expressed vehement disapproval of a "black-robed tribe" of "cave dwellers" who attacked rural sanctuaries and disrupted city life during summer: against the background of this criticism undoubtedly also lay reports of violent attacks by groups of monastics against Eastern bishops and their clergy.

On a more fundamental level, Christian commentators and Church leaders also sought to redefine the monastic life as a collective endeavour by a group of like-minded ascetics. While Jerome primarily saw the *monachus* and its female equivalent *monacha* as an isolated, withdrawn individual, Augustine feared that a rise of private asceticism would create a double standard for Christian faith, with perfection being reserved for a small elite of high-achieving ascetic practitioners, and another, watered-down faith being viewed as good enough for the masses. For him, the terms *monachus* and *monacha* signified being "one-with-others", in other words part of a "holy society" (*sancta societas*) of individuals fighting for a common cause. For him, the principal purpose of the monastic life was not to preserve one's ritual purity but to free oneself from the troubles of the world to become entirely devoted to God through collective worship.

Although the focus of most modern accounts of early monastic history shifts to cenobitism post-330, the impression they create that the Christian world was now teeming with cenobitical communities and that other forms of ascetic withdrawal had become socially and spiritually marginalized is a false one. Non-institutionalized expressions of the monastic ideal were decidedly thriving. Hermits living either alone or in small groups continued to be found even in major centres of cenobitical life: while still a child, the future Bishop Theodoret of Cyrrhus (d. 449) was sent by his mother to be blessed by two solitary monastics, one living in a tomb outside the city, and one in town. Jerome and others acknowledged that eremitism and anchoritism – a form of enclosed withdrawal within the

Enduring diversity

boundaries of civic society – were permissible for the most talented among those who had previously interiorized the principles of monastic life in a cenobitical setting. And household ascetics, even though they were subject to increased clerical scrutiny, for various reasons remained a prominent and legitimate part of the monastic landscape: for instance, in 397, the third council of Carthage formally allowed female virgins who had lost their parents to live together.

Ephemeral character of cenobitism

Meanwhile, we also see that the long-term future of cenobitical or quasi-cenobitical settlements was hardly guaranteed, and that some vanished as suddenly as they were formed. Marcella in her old age dissolved her urban community and moved to the countryside, where she created a *monasterium* for herself and a single companion; when life there became too dangerous because of constant warfare, she returned to the city. The long-term future of even major cenobitical settlements was hardly assured: such was the case for those associated with Pachomian monasticism, snuffed out in the early fifth century by invasions and warfare. Likewise, Augustine's clerical monasticism foundered during the Vandal invasion of North Africa. Monasticism's status as an open experiment was far from over.

2.3 Early Cenobitisms in Southern Gaul

Former approaches

Scholars of early Christian monasticism used to argue that beginning in the later fourth and early fifth centuries, the focus of monastic reflection and innovation shifted to southern Gaul. While much can be said about the overly reductive nature of that statement, the area does provide a relatively well-documented, regional case study of the variety and the experimental nature of cenobitism in this period.

'Rustic' cenobitism in Aquitaine

Traditional accounts tend to distinguish two major strands. The first consists of what scholars have referred to as 'ascetic households', some of which were situated in rural Aquitaine. Sulpicius Severus describes how former hermit Martin of Tours (above, Chapter 2.2) undertook extensive journeys in the rural areas of northern Gaul, during which he encountered wealthy landowners and former members of the imperial administration, and that it was in the residences of some of these individuals that ascetic communities were subsequently established. Sulpicius himself exemplified this trend: inspired by his hero Martin, his contemporary and spiritual advisor Paulinus of Nola (d. 431) [S Paulinus], and an associate who had travelled to Egypt, sometime around the year 400 he abandoned his secular career and exchanged it for "the service of God". In order to do so, he whittled down his property portfolio to a single estate at *Primulacium*, where he then withdrew to a life shaped by ascetic pursuits. His mother-in-law Bassula joined him there, as did a number of close friends and also some *pueri familiares* – a term that usually refers to young slaves. The set-up of this rural villa-turned-monastery as it is described in Sulpicius's 403/406 *Dialogues* resembles a similar settlement by Bassula, first in Toulouse and then in Trier. Like Sulpicius, she was well connected, and personally knew trendsetting monastics of her time like Paulinus and the immensely wealthy Melania 'the Younger', granddaughter of the abovementioned Melania 'the Elder'.

Scholars used to see a stark contrast between the spontaneous, private settlements created by Sulpicius and like-minded aristocrats, and a second, more institutionalized and presumably also more 'worldly' (some have argued elitist) strand of cenobitical life in Provence and upwards to the Jura region. In the turbulent context of the early to mid-fifth century, many aristocrats from the Rhône River region were looking to forge an ecclesiastical career as an alternative to taking up public office, albeit without having to abandon their social standing and the lifestyle they had grown accustomed to. Prominent Church leaders and commentators responded to this trend by arguing the benefits of entering a cenobitical community, reassuring an elite readership that the impact on their lifestyle would be minimal. Bishop Hilary of Poitiers in his *Life of Honoratus* represented his hero as a builder, a benefactor, and a host capable of receiving his many guests in style. Hilary was also linked to the community of Lérins, a 405/410 foundation on a few islands on the Mediterranean coast near present-day Cannes. This kind of monasticism, designed to feature well-defined institutions, be high performing economically, and also function as a regional centre of power, presumably appealed to aristocratic recruits by proposing a form of ascetic life whereby individuals could retain their leading status in society. Over time, Lérins turned into a breeding ground for clerical talent: multiple former members ascended to the metropolitan thrones of Riez, Tours, Vaison-la-Romaine and

'Elite' cenobitism

Arles during the fifth and sixth centuries. Lérins also expanded its influence along the Rhône River, with establishments created, for example, in Vienne, Arles, and Lyon.

Recent nuancing

The contrast, so some specialists claimed, between the sophisticated, relatively comfortable elite asceticism of Lérins and its rough-hewn, loosely organized rural counterpart in Aquitaine, could not have been greater. In reality, the differences between these two strands were far less pronounced than scholars suspected, and their models of community life less rigidly defined than formerly argued. The case of *Primulacium* illustrates this well. Although Sulpicius is often depicted as a man with no affinity for Lérins's model, in his *Life of St Martin* he insists on the same idea of an ascetic life as an alternative career for members of the Gallo-Roman elite. Through his correspondence with Paulinus of Nola, we also learn that his ascetic household soon acquired institutional features: Paulinus had advised him to give up his role as *paterfamilias* and become a lodger in his own house, renounce his personal wealth, and consider himself a servant among his slaves. It is likely – as has also been observed for contemporary communities like those of Paula at Bethlehem and Basilius's sister Macrina in Cesarea – that then-current ideals of spiritual equality became reified through the equal treatment and status of former lords and slaves and the dissolution of Roman household structures.

The result was the transformation, in some places at least, of 'household asceticism' into what Sulpicius refers to as a "monastic brotherhood" (*fraternitas monacha*). Finally, given the link between some earlier household ascetics and the cult of martyrs and also charitable activities, it should not surprise us that some of the early rural estates-turned-ascetic-communities in Gaul rapidly absorbed these functions too. Underneath *Primulacium*'s altar was placed the grave of Carus, one of Martin's followers at Marmoutier. It is possible, likely even, that the site also hosted both prominent and more ordinary visitors: Paulinus's community in Nola, which is thought to have inspired Sulpicius's model, was linked to up to three *basilicae*, and hosted cells for ascetic men and women, as well as rooms and spaces reserved for distinguished guests and the poor. Overall, it seems that the institutional development and societal impact of these and other settlements have been underestimated.

Similar observations can be made for the supposed chasm between (on the one hand) Lérins's 'Rhône model' and 'Jura monasticism' as it was practised at major houses such as Condat, Lauconne, and La Balme, and (on the other) a separate strand founded by Marseilles native John Cassian. At the beginning of his ascetic career, John travelled to Bethlehem and Egypt before returning to Marseilles, where he founded one male and one female community. Presumably it was for these two settlements that he drafted his famous *Institutions* and *Conferences* [**S** COLLATIONES]: whereas the former text gave practical advice on how to organize a cenobitical group, the latter (a series of fictitious dialogues with Egyptian hermits and cenobites) sought to establish a theological foundation for monastic life. John advocated a life of withdrawal from clerical and worldly concerns, emphasizing that mutual love amongst community members was the principal means through which the journey of the individual to their inner self could be accomplished. To facilitate this journey, he proposed a specific regime – that of the canonical hours – for reciting the psalms on two set times of the day: in doing so, he took part in a broader trend, over the course of the fifth century, to consolidate liturgical practices in cenobitical communities.

John Cassian

John's call for equality and for individuals to cut the ties with their former background has been viewed as a feature that distinguished his brand of monasticism from the one practised at Lérins. In addition, it was argued that this made it unpopular with the Gallo-Roman elite. But as recent scholarship has suggested, Lérins monasticism was probably far less homogeneous than once thought, and its outlook less elitist. When in the early sixth century two brothers from the monastery of Saint-Maurice d'Agaune wrote to the abbot of Lérins to request advice on what mode of ascetic life they should follow, he forwarded their request to a monk from Condat, who reportedly sent them a copy of the *Lives* of the first abbots of his monastery and John's *Institutions*. The 'Jura monasticism' of Condat and other places in the region likewise emerges from recent studies as much more socially egalitarian than previously thought. A substantial part of the self-imposed mission of these communities, so it seems, was to reorganize rural society so as to prevent exploitation of its inhabitants, to offer help to those in need, to manage agricultural labour and production, and to intercede with various rulers and powerholders. These inclusive 'monastic societies' offered a safe haven to people (male and female cenobites, hermits, household ascetics, clerics, men and

Contrast with 'elite' forms

Inclusive monastic societies

women from the laity) from very different backgrounds and with very different lifestyles.

Episcopal interventions

Meanwhile, several generations of bishops had been working to claim supervision over what used to be strictly private settlements, and were looking to contain the phenomenon to the benefit of their own spiritual and pastoral authority and that of their clerics. The acts of the council of Chalcedon of 451 and that of Orléans in 511 illustrate a trend on the part of these leaders to assert the higher clergy's role in defining what conduct was acceptable for cenobiti-

Causes and motives

cal groups. In these definitions, the focus lay on the purity of monks and women religious as a result of their separateness from secular society and on their role as intercessors (via their prayer service) between humanity and God. In some cases, these regulations and the drastic interventions that resulted from them had an additional driver: this was the desire to counter the part played by monasteries (particularly those in the Jura region) in organizing rural society along egalitarian lines and preventing its inhabitants from being deprived of social aid and subjected to ruthless exploitation. In other cases, episcopal or royal intervention marked the end of a power struggle with aristocratic founders or their descendants for control over the latter's former estates.

Impact

Whatever the precise circumstances, the impact of these interventions was dramatic. In 515, King Sigismond of Burgundy and his son dismissed an entire group of ascetic women and their "secular servants" at a martyrial sanctuary at Agaune (now in the Valais canton of southern Switzerland), and together with the local episcopate replaced them with monks who were instructed to carry out perpetual prayers (*laus perennis*) for the benefit of the entire world

Resistance

[S Vita abbatum Acaunensium]. Monastic observers at the time were keenly aware of the potentially devastating impact of episcopal and other propaganda against the inclusive nature of their 'monastic societies': so it has been speculated that the drafting by the monks at Lérins of the fifth-century *Rule of the Four Fathers*, which tried to establish an authoritative account of local practices and attitudes, was a direct attempt to counter episcopal interference [S Regula quattuor patrum].

Outcomes for male and female groups

In and of itself, the grounding of the Agaune monks' communal identity in their prayer service for all of Christian society was highly influential. But shifting clerical expectations impacted first and foremost on the role and status of female monastics. This was the time when ecclesiastical councils began making a distinction between 'lay' and 'religious' veiled women, in which the former were allowed to consider their status temporary and live in their own house or some other private dwelling, while the latter were expected to live permanently in an enclosed communal space. In particular, clerical rulers sought to address the age-old presence in urban contexts of groups of consecrated virgins and subject these women to a regime that reflected concerns over their protection – quite literally, as many towns in Gaul were repeatedly wrecked by warfare – and discipline.

For his foundation of a female house in the old Roman city of Arles, former Lérins monk and metropolitan bishop Cesarius (d. 542) drafted a *Rule* imposing strict stability, poverty, a heavy routine of prayers and chanting (in winter, the religious were supposed to recite eighty-five psalms each day, along with responsories, hymns, lectures, antiphons, and prayers), and also strict enclosure [**S** CESARIUS OF ARLES]. Although the *Rule* heavily relies on commentaries by Augustine and John Cassian, and on various precedents of monastic practice at Marseilles, La Balme, and Lérins, its innovative significance lay first and foremost in shifting the burden of ascetic achievement away from the individual, and conceiving of the monastery as an unpolluted space where consecrated women could safely await the arrival of Christ. Cesarius's ideas represent a break with former views on how monastics could have an impact on Christian society: rejecting hospitality as a primary focus, he prohibited his cloistered women religious from hosting members of the clergy, relatives, or other laypeople.

Cesarius of Arles

The publication of Cesarius's Rule did not set monastic life for women on an entirely new footing. For instance, Merovingian Queen Radegund (d. 587) maintained a distinctly aristocratic lifestyle at her 558 foundation of Sainte-Croix in Poitiers [**S** VENANTIUS], while many women (and did men) continued to practise a noncenobitical lifestyle. Nonetheless, its text came to be relied on for inspiration in female monastic circles in Gaul and northern Spain throughout the early medieval period, alongside Cassian's works, Columbanian rules and the *Rule of St Benedict*, discussed below. Commentaries by Ferreolus of Uzès (d. 581), the anonymous author of the *Regula Tarnatensis* (sixth century), and Donatus of Besançon (d. 658) all built on Cesarius's work. At the same time, subtle and not-so-subtle changes to his original outline reveal how closely

Alternative forms

Alternative interpretations

ideals of (particularly female) monastic observance were linked to rapidly changing societal contexts [S REGULA CUIUSDAM PATRIS]. A new *Rule* by Aurelian (d. 551) [S AURELIAN], Cesarius's successor at Arles, already reveals a fundamentally different outlook of cloistered life, where the latter's focus on self-perfection is replaced, or at the very least complemented, by a strong focus on intercessory prayer for those living in the outside world. In many respects, Aurelian's text was more attuned to the expectations of royal and other lay patrons, and the emerging, 'medieval' view of monastics as professional intercessors with God.

2.4 Experiments on the Italian and Iberian Peninsulas

The written legacy of Pope Gregory the Great (d. 604), his *Dialogues* in particular, features prominently in standard accounts of sixth-century monastic life on the Italian Peninsula [S GREGORY]. Written c. 593, the second book of the *Dialogues* contains a *Life* of Benedict of Nursia (whose death is situated by convention in 547), which established Benedict's reputation as an individual who singlehandedly synthesized the legacies of late antique monasticism and managed to shape the face of monastic life for the next five and a half centuries. According to Gregory's much-debated testimony, Benedict was born in the late fifth century to a noble family in the Umbrian town of Nursia, and subsequently enjoyed a literary education, which brought him to Rome. Dissatisfied with the lifestyle of his companions and nearly killed by their attempt to poison him, he became a rural ascetic, not unlike Sulpicius Severus and his contemporaries in late fourth- and early fifth-century Gaul. In the mountainous region of Subiaco, Benedict encountered a number of cenobites. On the advice of one of them, he became a hermit, living in a cave and relying on this associate for sustenance and spiritual support. After three years, Benedict was asked by the monks of a community in the region to become their abbot. He accepted, but when his views on an appropriate lifestyle clashed with those of his subjects, and he once again withdrew to his cave, apparently to lead the Subiaco community. Widely known as a holy man and drawing numerous visitors, Benedict eventually left Subiaco and went on to establish twelve communities in the region, including Monte Cassino in 530. It was there that he allegedly wrote a *Rule*,

Pope Gregory on Benedict

and (still according to Gregory) continued to perform many miracles until his death seventeen years later.

It would surely be going too far, as some historians have done, to argue that Gregory's biography of Benedict is strictly a work of fiction, and that the abbot represents little more than the pope's attempt to create a literary ideal of combined charismatic and pragmatic leadership. But Gregory clearly did not write his text with an eye to providing his audience with an objective historical rendition of the abbot's life, and modern readers are well advised to consider the hagiographic and moralizing dimensions of the account. Against the background of ongoing discussions over Benedict's historicity and the authenticity of Gregory's account also looms the growing realization by scholars that the abbot's double achievement – the foundation and leadership of a number of monastic communities in middle Italy, and his presumed authorship of the *Rule of St Benedict* – was far from unique or exceptional. Gregory himself acknowledges that Benedict did not operate in a monastic void, and that eremitical and cenobitical experiments in the Italian countryside and also in urban contexts had been taking place on a scale large enough to generate considerable public interest.

These experiments resulted in the forming of cenobitical institutions, and presumably also led to competition between different cohorts of monastics over the favours and attention of the laity. So Gregory mentions the existence of late antique rural villas-turned-monasteries and references organized communities in a wide range of economic and social settings. Cassiodorus's (d. c. 585) foundation at Vivarium, which was noted for its vibrant intellectual atmosphere, represents but one of many possible options alluded to in the pope's text. Whilst living in Rome, Gregory also witnessed many forms of monastic community life there, some of which were dedicated to prayer and contemplation, whilst others took up an active role in urban society as hospices, pastoral centres, and suchlike. Not least important in these references is the strong presence (similar to what we already saw for Gaul) of groups of consecrated women serving sanctuaries dedicated to Christian martyrs, in some cases also providing aid to the poor and to pilgrims. Gregory himself was intimately familiar with these and other monastic arrangements, including the most private ones. In the *Dialogues*, he refers to three of his aunts, dedicated virgins who lived together as household ascetics.

Monastic life in Italy

Gregory's views Gregory's account in the *Dialogues* of Benedict's life and legacies functioned first and foremost as a means to express the author's preference for a tightly organized, communal form of monastic life with a focus on prayer, the study of Holy Scripture, and solitude. In his letters and the *Dialogues*, the pope fulminates against wandering monks and warns that some household ascetics (most notably one of his aunts) end up losing their commitment. More generally, Gregory complains about the poor material and spiritual state of many communities. All the inherent failings and deficiencies of these forms of monastic life – lack of oversight, insufficient focus on ascetic withdrawal, insufficient boundaries with the outside world, and insufficient provisions taken to guarantee an orderly and self-sufficient form of community life – are absent from his portrayal of Benedict's achievement. In the pope's account, Benedict had established the ultimate, most efficient form of monastic community life, which was based on a strictly hierarchical, tightly organized routine that laid strong emphasis on prayer, liturgy, and manual labour.

Whether Benedict himself actually had stood for these ideals, and whether he truly was the innovative individual Gregory made him out to be, remains an open question. The same is true for what Gregory says about Benedict's sister Scholastica, who supposedly stood at the beginning of 'Benedictine' monastic life for women. What we do know for certain is that prior to writing his *Dialogues*, Gregory had a track record of nearly twenty years of leading and overseeing monastic institutions, most notably his own foundation of San Andrea in Rome. It would not be overly speculative to think that his account of Benedict's legacy references his own experiences with organizing ascetic community life, and maybe also those of a number of his associates (including his friend Leander of

Implications for Benedict's legacy Seville, d. c. 600). How these various experiences related to those of Benedict himself can no longer be established: but what matters in the end is that Gregory shaped Benedict's literary persona and legacy in such a manner that he was able to express his own preferences, and that Benedict came to be regarded as one of the founding fathers of contemplative monasticism in the medieval West.

In a discussion that was initiated nearly a century ago, specialists of early monastic literature not only showed that there are no conclusive arguments to support the historical attribution of the *Rule of St Benedict* to the Benedict who is commemorated by Pope

Gregory, but also that the *Rule* itself is hardly the ground-breaking work of legislation later commentators made it out to be [**S** REGULA BENEDICTI]. Prior to its apparent canonization by Gregory in the 590s – the *terminus ante quem* of its creation – it was just one among many efforts to synthesize and adapt for local use the many circulating accounts of cenobitical life. One such attempt is the *Rule of the Master*, a text with origins either in southern Gaul or Italy. Its relationship to the *Rule of St Benedict* remains uncertain: far longer than the latter, it is conceived as a dialogue between a master (*magister*) and a number of disciples seeking spiritual instruction. Its principal chapters discuss the spiritual service of four kinds of monks, only the first two of which are acceptable: cenobites; anchorites (later also known as recluses) or hermits (former cenobites who are strong enough as spiritual beings to seek the road to salvation on their own); sarabaites (inexperienced monastics pursuing the path of salvation without any guidance); and gyrovagues (wandering monastics).

The Rule in context

These chapters also provide a detailed account of daily life in a monastery, including numerous instructions on how to enforce discipline and virtuous conduct. Like earlier rules, the *Rule of the Master* deserves to be read not as a legislative text, but as a literary representation of the ideal monastery, designed to inspire those in charge of organizing real-life communities. For its part, the *Rule of St Benedict* largely mimics the structure and overall contents of the *Rule of the Master*, but presents itself as a manual for those who are new to the monastic life. As such, it offers a deliberately simple discussion of divine service, punishments for infractions to internal regulations, the organization of a monastery, and its various roles and offices. At the heart of the text stands a strong emphasis on obedience to the abbot, the abandonment of free will, and the importance of virtues like humility, obedience, and (much less emphatically) stability. In addition, the day is strictly divided into moments that are assigned to specific activities: spiritual reading, prayer, manual labour, and sleep.

The *Rule of St Benedict* distinguishes itself from other normative commentaries written in the fourth to sixth centuries not by virtue of its originality, but by its subsequent stature. Notable is the speed with which it became known in various parts of the Latin West. Seventh-century commentators in Italy, Gaul, and the Iberian Peninsula were aware of its existence and contents, and of the fact

Subsequent stature

that it was linked *nominatim* to an otherwise unidentified abbot named Benedictus, "He who is blessed". Eighth- and especially ninth-century commentators from Francia further amplified Benedict's stature by presenting the *Rule* as the pinnacle of centuries of monastic rule-making. A masterful account of monastic community experience, and a deeply humane treatment of the challenges facing the individual's immersion in a life dedicated to the service of God, the *Rule* explicitly and implicitly referenced a number of textual antecedents and in doing so introduced them to a very large readership.

References to earlier accounts Implicitly, it adopted some of Augustine's views (as found in his *Rule* – or rather, in the collation of several texts written either by Augustine or by his associates) to promote a vision of the cenobitical community as one consisting of individuals with different needs and different backgrounds, ruled by an abbot whose virtue matches his authority. More explicit were the *Rule*'s endorsement of John Cassian's egalitarianism and its references to his work, both of which explain why Cassian's written legacy became such a prominent part of monastic reading culture in later centuries. Over time, the *Rule*'s use of these traditions helped blot out their true nature as topical (or historically situated) commentaries on contemporary issues in Christian orthodoxy and on ascetic purity and practice. At the same time, the *Rule* staked no claim to normative exclusivity, and even recommended Basilius's *Rule* (or at least its Latin version) [**S** BASILIUS] to experienced monastics. Subsequent users would take the author's invitation to heart, and read his text alongside other commentaries.

By the time the first copies of the *Rule of St Benedict* arrived on the Iberian Peninsula, monastic life in this part of the world had been the stage of intense transcultural exchange for many decades. Iberian monasticism Various sixth-century councils had picked up on conciliar legislation from Gaul, while individuals coming from that region had established a number of monastic settlements, the precise nature of which remains mostly obscured because of a lack of contemporary testimony. From Pannonia also came a preacher named Martin (d. 580), who worked on the conversion of the Sueves in Galicia and subsequently founded several monasteries near Braga: his main influence on later generations was through his involvement in translating biographies and sayings attributed to the Desert Fathers from Greek into Latin. Meanwhile, indigenous monastics also looked for inspiration to the East: one such was Egeria, a consecrated woman who reported on her travels in Judea and Egypt to an unspecified group of women she referred to as her "sisters" [**S** EGERIA]. Yet, these and other influences changed nothing about the fact that monastic experiences remained as locally situated and as heterogeneous as was the case in other parts of the Latin West. Much of the Peninsula in this period was affected by invasions and warfare, while deep social, economic, ethnic, and ideological fracture lines ran throughout the entire region.

These fractures become obvious if we look at commentaries on the state of ascetic community life from the seventh century. King Reccared's conversion to Catholicism and the organization of the Third Council of Toledo in 589 symbolically marked the end of a period of political and religious troubles, and spurred a number of authors from the higher clergy to express (as their colleagues in Gaul had done before them) their displeasure over the fact that physical and virtual boundaries between monastic groups and the outside world were practically non-existent. In his late 640s *Rule*, Fructuosus of Braga (d. 665) called out the numerous abuses and scandals that had corrupted "the regular tradition". He particularly objected to "people (who) organize monasteries in their own homes... and gather in community with their wives, children, servants and neighbours... and consecrate churches in their own dwellings with names of martyrs... and call them monasteries" [**S** FRUCTUOSUS]. Some three decades earlier, Bishop Isidore of Seville (d. 636) had already published a *Rule* in which he addressed the fact that many communities of monastics had settled in late antique rural or suburban villas of southern Spain, apparently without adopting a code of internal conduct and organization that corresponded with the bishop's ideals of ascetic withdrawal. In the *Rule*, he sketched a form of community life featuring a rigid internal hierarchy, a strict penitential tariff, and clear physical and virtual boundaries between the state of a monk and that of an outsider [**S** ISIDORE].

Seventh-century forms

Even though Isidore and Fructuosus seemingly sought to address the same issues by relying on roughly the same principles, in reality the two clergymen were working in entirely different contexts. Isidore's monastic landscape as he describes it in his *Rule* reminds us of the Aquitanian settlements described by Sulpicius Severus, where wealthy aristocrats had established ascetic communities on their own property. In contrast, Fructuosus's world,

Socio-geographical contexts

which roughly corresponds with the current-day Spanish northern province of Léon, emerges from his *Rule* as an impoverished environment without much agricultural activity. Here, institutionalized monasticism had ostensibly originated out of a need felt by local communities to sustain essential aspects of social and economic organization following the collapse of late Roman political structures. Across the region, families, perhaps even entire villages, had chosen to establish a monastery – the only available institutional paradigm at that point – with a view to addressing the challenges of a subsistence economy and possibly also the need to defend themselves. Unsurprisingly given that context, Fructuosus's text awards a great deal of attention to property conflicts, and acknowledges that various communities will be collaborating in what some scholars have referred to as a "confederation" or "pact": hence the expression *Pactual Monasticism*. Presumably, the primary purpose of such confederations, some of which lasted into the eleventh century, was not to coordinate (let alone homogenize) ascetic practice in various settlements, but to achieve other, more 'worldly' objectives, such as setting up a local system of trade and exchange, creating some degree of political security, and maintaining roads and other public facilities.

These two rules by Isidore and Fructuosus were just two out of many ad hoc responses to concrete realities that presented themselves, in very different economic and political settings, across the seventh-century Iberian Peninsula. Accordingly, the experience of monastic life, be it inside or outside of institutional settings, remained highly diverse. The reading culture within these communities further enhanced that diversity: surviving manuscript copies of commentaries by Augustine, Jerome, Cassian, Cesarius, and to a lesser extent also the *Rule of St Benedict*, tell us that local groups of monastics studied and absorbed a wide range of literary traditions. Some of the life options they distilled from these met with resistance. For instance, towards the end of the seventh century, the hermit Valerius of Bierzo (d. c. 695) bemoaned the loss of original fervour in monastic observance. But his criticism appears to us as that of an ascetic athlete, whose relationship with anything but the more extreme, individualistic forms of Christian withdrawal would have been problematic anyway [**S** VALERIUS].

Certainly Valerius would have found it difficult to accept that many cenobitical communities by that point functioned as major

Pactual Monasticism

Diversity grounded in local reading

Involvement in local societies

keystones in networks of local and regional power. Donations by noblemen and -women of considerable estates in exchange for monastics' intercessory prayers and commemorative service had turned some institutions into very large property owners. This not only generated considerable wealth but also implies that these institutions developed sophisticated administrative procedures to manage these estates, to engage in trade, and to carry out all kinds of transactions with tenants, merchants, and other agents. Unfortunately, our understanding of how these communities fared and how contemporary observers perceived them is largely obscured by the fall of Visigothic rule in 711 and its poorly documented aftermath. Still, what little we do know about the increasingly close links between aristocratic and clerical patrons on the one hand, and monastic groups on the other, echoes similar developments in seventh-century Gaul, discussed below.

2.5 Irish and 'Iro-Frankish' Monasticisms

One of the enduring tropes of monastic historiography is that Ireland in the fourth and early fifth centuries was a popular destination for hermits. Allegedly its position at the very edge of the known world and its rugged geography were an irresistible attraction to those who wished to escape from the structures and strictures of the now state-sanctioned Catholic Church. However, early testimonies contain no reliable indications of a particularly notable presence of eremitical practitioners on the island. In contrast, the Irish bishop Palladius (d. 457/461) did note that he had heard of men who had become monks and women who had chosen a life as consecrated virgins, and also of widows and celibate men who practised a life of chaste withdrawal. Considering how swiftly and seemingly spontaneously such private forms of monastic life had emerged in other parts of the Christian world, his testimony may well be accurate: but as we also see for other parts of the West, reports of these people were quickly overshadowed by those describing the earliest forms of organized community life.

Narratives of eremitism

One individual whom traditional accounts used to celebrate as a pioneering figure in the arrival of cenobitism in Ireland is Patrick, a Welsh migrant who managed to forge strong links with the local aristocracy and who used these to co-establish, in the 430s, a

Emergence of cenobitism

monastic community at Kildare. This consisted of strictly separated groups of men and women. Over the course of roughly a century, new foundations – Clonmacnois, Doire, Clonard, Clonfert, to name only the most important – were established across almost the entire island.

Early monasteries Early Irish monasteries were not as we might imagine them, as spatially and functionally distinct institutions reserved for the pursuit of ascetic life. Instead, they were multi-functional establishments that provided anchor points for organizing Irish society in a political, economic, religious, and generally also a cultural sense. Abbots and abbesses exercised far-reaching juridical and political powers, and were recruited from founding families that often retained control over the monastic estate. While our knowledge of women's communities in this period is limited, the role of monks as providers of pastoral service appears to have been extensive, thanks in no small part to their reputation as 'holy men': the nation's bishops were also recruited from this pool, and once appointed some remained by their former abbot's side. Some institutions, in addition to developing an exceptionally strong focus on learning, also set up and maintained *paruchiae*, transregional networks of what one might arguably call priories – subordinate smaller settlements – that owed obedience to a specific monastery. The success of these endeavours and the longevity of these *paruchiae* very much depended on the support and subsequent fortunes of a monastery's lay patrons.

Expansion into Scotland By the mid-sixth century, 'Irish monasticism' – an expression that should not be taken to reflect unity in observance and organization – expanded into what is now Scotland. In 563, a missionary named Columba (d. 597) founded the island monastery of Iona, which like Clonmacnois in Ireland would become one of the prime centres of learning in the British Isles. From there, it once again, gradually, expanded eastwards. In 635, an Irish monk based in Iona founded the priory of Lindisfarne on a tidal island on the Northumbrian coast. The foundation took place at the request of local royalty and also functioned as the local bishop's seat.

Ideals of ascetic conduct One of Lindisfarne's most famous inmates was Cuthbert (d. 687), who founded the abbey of Ripon. Hagiographic memory portrays him as the ultimate 'holy man', preaching, providing spiritual advice, caring for the poor, and leading a life of strict self-abnegation [**S** VITAE SANCTI CUTHBERTI]. Like a number of his contemporaries, he temporarily withdrew as a hermit to escape the demands of office so that he could focus on his spiritual journey, but he returned fully committed to pastoral mission, becoming bishop of Hexham and, later on, of Lindisfarne. Cuthbert belonged to a world of monastic learning that saw the feverish production of written accounts of monastic conduct [**S** ALDHELM]. Hagiographic narratives, including his own *Life*, served a double purpose of celebrating a subject's sainthood and communicating ideal modes of behaviour to their monastic audiences. Irish authors also composed and preserved large quantities of canonical rulings and penitentials: these taught that true monastics became such not by virtue of the physical spaces they inhabited but by a mode of conduct that was recognizably distinct from that of the laity. At the same time, such authors also insisted on the need, within monastic sites, to create spaces reserved specifically for monastics and members of the clergy in order to retain the purity of the rites executed there, and to likewise establish ritual boundaries between members of the two sexes. In that latter sense, their views come fairly close to those of fourth- to sixth-century commentators on the Continent: between the mid-eighth century and c. 900, they would be adopted and actively propagated by communities linked to what scholars have referred to as the céilí Dé movement.

Consolidation of these ideals

Beginning in the late sixth century, ascetic peregrination became a popular feature of religious life in these parts of the world. On arriving on the Continent some of these *peregrini* were met with suspicion, hostility even. But others relied on their experiences in their native country to connect with the Frankish elite and subsequently co-establish cenobitical institutions. The most famous of these was Columbanus (d. 615), who arrived in Burgundy in 590/591 and went on to assist in the aristocratic foundation there of three institutions: Annegray, Luxeuil, and Fontaines. Following his exile from Burgundy after an altercation with the king, he journeyed on to Metz, then Alemannia, and finally to the Lombard territories in northern Italy, where he founded a fourth institution at Bobbio. From a later generation we encounter both Fursa, who arrived in the 640s and helped found Lagny in Gaul, and Foillan and Ultan, who co-founded Fosses in Austrasia. Early and high medieval hagiographies retain the memories of an impressive number of other such individuals, although few of these accounts hold up against closer scrutiny. Still, there can be little doubt that

Ascetic peregrination

Columbanus

the activities of Columbanus and his associates in Gaul truly merit being called a meeting of minds with the Frankish aristocracy, and that their approach was actively emulated by indigenous founders. In exchange for allowing *peregrini* and other monastic agents to establish a 'Columbanian' community on their estate, the local elites were able to create for themselves and their relatives institutions that provided intercessory and commemorative prayer, served as a dynastic necropolis, and were available to house unmarried female relatives. Sealing the deal for many aristocrats was the fact that such sites literally and metaphorically anchored into local societies the position of regional dominance they were trying to establish for themselves. It is not a coincidence that 'Columbanian' monasticism's initial rise took place in peripheral regions of the Merovingian realms, where competition for political dominance was still strong.

Aristocratic interest [margin note]

The result of these developments was that the number of cenobitical communities in Gaul, or at least in certain parts of it, grew substantially. One estimate speaks of a jump from 220 in the late sixth century to an astounding 550 by the early eighth century, a figure that becomes even more impressive if we consider the estimated number for Italy (around 110) and Spain (around 87). Later in the seventh century, the Lombard monarchs in Italy would embrace the same principle of patronizing monastic foundations and 'restoring' existing ones in order to assert their dominance over certain parts of the realm, and to establish links with local members of the higher clergy and lay lords. Alongside numerous male communities, women staffed a significant number of seventh-century aristocratic foundations in these regions. This is not surprising when we consider the previous track record of female monastics in the service of martyrial sanctuaries and that the new foundations focused on the commemoration and burial of aristocratic founders, some of whom ended up being venerated as saints. The female religious were assisted in their endeavours by monks or clerics: such was the case at Remiremont, Nivelles [S Vita sanctae Geretrudis], Faremoutiers, Jouarre, Marchiennes, Santa Giulia in Brescia, and numerous other institutions. Prominent aristocratic women – widows mostly, succeeded in time by their celibate daughters or nieces – combined the spiritual leadership and ownership of these institutions. In some cases, like that of Aldeneik in Austrasia, these foundations had originally served

Growth of cenobitism [margin note]

Prominence of foundations for women [margin note]

Family monasteries [margin note]

as a private retreat for entire households; presumably, servants and associates were invited or compelled to join these individuals in their ascetic endeavours.

It is difficult to get a clear sense of what 'Columbanian' or 'Hiberno-/Iro-Frankish' monasticism actually stood for. In fact, both expressions are misleading, since they obscure the diversity of views and practices within aristocratic foundations in seventh-century Gaul. Perhaps the best indication of this diversity is the way in which Columbanus's ideological legacy was received following his death. His vision of cenobitical life as consolidated in his *Rule* heavily emphasizes intercessory prayer and bears distinct traces of the Irish fascination with penance and confession: in particular, it relies on a detailed list of penitential tariffs to maintain the purity of monastic inmates and sustain its code of conduct [**S** COLUMBANUS]. It is tempting to argue that many communities across Gaul that are known to have had direct or indirect links to his principal foundation of Luxeuil were influenced by its ascetic and institutional models. But as we now know, most of these links were established after Columbanus had left the abbey, and after his successor there had done away with many typical 'Irish' features of monastic life, including the emphasis on penance and the strong focus on learning.

Intrinsic diversity

Archaeological evidence, and the information that is available through various hagiographies, charters, and sundry textual materials, additionally indicates a great deal of variety in the way these communities were organized. And looking at the various monastic commentaries that have survived from this period, here too we encounter many signs of divergence from Columbanus's views. His biographer Jonas of Bobbio (d. after 659), who wrote shortly after the man's death, already sketched a profoundly different view of monastic life, and reworked versions of the *Rule* present views that strike us as being quite distinct from those of its original author [**S** JONAS]. Depending on the text and the context, we encounter commentators keen to accommodate the expectations of aristocratic patrons and recruits (emphasizing prayer service and proposing much more benign forms of austerity and self-abnegation), or those who resolutely denied the need to do so. In other cases still, we get glimpses of a trend by local commentators to substitute a focus on inner sentiments and morality in place of Columbanus's harsh, 'automated' system of penance and retribution.

Dissenting views

Presumably, it was the sheer flexibility and diversity of 'Columbanian monasticism' that explains why it was so easily exported to other places, in Gaul, Italy, and elsewhere. England in particular proved a fertile soil for such experiments, even though the ascetic landscape was already a crowded one. The earliest cenobitical foundation there had been the 598 abbey of Saints Peter and Paul in Canterbury, which scholars suspect drew its observance from that of Gregory the Great's monastery of San Andrea in Rome; and earlier, as we already saw, Northumbria had been colonized, so to speak, by Irish monastics. There also seems to have been considerable scepticism in England with regard to Columbanus's endeavours. Bede the Venerable (d. 735) speaks of him not as a monastic founder, but as a heretic [S BEDE THE VENERABLE]: his former abbot Benedict Biscop (d. 690), who travelled extensively through Gaul while researching his *Rule* for the monks at Monkwearmouth-Jarrow, appears to have avoided contact with communities linked to Luxeuil.

Still, transferral of 'Columbanian' practices and institutional models from the Île-de-France and its surrounding territories to Kent, East Anglia, and Wessex did take place: a case has been made for the role of the Merovingian queen Balthild (d. 680), an Anglo-Saxon by birth, in promoting monasticism in the Kent area, and particularly in assisting with the foundation of a number of nunneries. To explain this Continental influence, scholars have referred to the shared geographical, economic and political features of the two regions and speculated that institutional models in the former must have appeared particularly suitable to prospec-

tive founders in England. But there is also reason to think that they were drawn to the continuous process of blending normative and local traditions that occurred in 'Columbanian' houses during the second half of the seventh century, and to the way these houses adapted to local circumstances and expectations, particularly those of aristocratic founders and other patrons. Contrary to what some specialists, based on comments by Bede, used to argue, monastic life in England during this period did not take on a fairly uniform appearance. In particular, the traditional notion that England's religious landscape came to be dominated by 'minster monasticism' - a form of monastic life focused not on contemplation and intercessory prayer but on providing pastoral care - no longer appears tenable.

2.6 Monastic Experiences at the Dawn of the Eighth Century

Distilling any kind of forward-moving logic from the immense variety of monastic experiences c. 700 is neither possible nor necessary. While scholars formerly tried to identify a number of dominant institutional 'movements', ideological trends, and normative models that broadly characterized forms of ascetic withdrawal in various parts of Europe and helped them to describe 'typical' features and experiences of the monastic life in this period, more recent studies have indicated that to a significant extent local circumstances continued to shape monastic forms and lifestyles. A range of factors determined these circumstances, including geophysical location; relation to the socio-economic environment and other connections with secular society; demographics of recruitment and the social and educational background of a community's members; expectations by lay founders and benefactors; relationships with the local clergy; and the presence and nature of a saint's cult. Nearly all of these were subject to change: local societies evolved; one generation of ascetics, lay stakeholders, and clerical rulers was replaced by the next; and reflections on monasticism's ideological foundations kept evolving. Because of the distance of time, the fragmented state of the primary evidence, and the biased nature of many testimonies from the period, our understanding of these realities remains woefully incomplete.

Even though the focus on most discussions of monastic life after c. 350 lies squarely on cenobitical communities and those who inhabited them, hermits, anchorites, and wandering ascetics probably existed in far greater numbers than the sum total of those individuals whose names we can still recover from contemporary sources. And while household ascetics are attested in the primary evidence almost exclusively on an anecdotal basis, at various points in time and in various places these people and those who assisted them in their endeavours may well have outnumbered those living in monastic institutions. In fact, it may be unwise to try and strictly distinguish private from institutionalized monasticisms pre-700, as most monasteries were privately owned and boundaries between cenobitical and other lifestyles remained permeable. Practitioners of different monastic forms could often be found living in close proximity to each other, sometimes even in a state of functional and spiritual symbiosis, and many ascetic individuals seem

Former attempts at categorization

Contextual factors of diversity

Enduring prominence of 'private' forms

Functional diversity

to have been able to move from one form to another depending on their expectations and situation in life. Monastic experiences also remained highly diverse functionally, including in community settings. Alongside the contemplative communities and those created specifically to serve at a specific grave of a saint or founder, or those whom kings, bishops and other rulers instructed to pray for the welfare of sovereign and society, we also encounter 'active' groups, as for instance those in the aforementioned *diaconiae* and *xenodochia*, and the groups of ascetic clerics living in episcopal centres.

Ideological diversity

Various factors further enhanced the diversity of monastic experiences. A first one was ideological. Local communities across the Latin West voraciously consumed all kinds of rules, commentaries, and hagiographies that presented various – sometimes conflicting – views on the nature and purpose of Christian ascetic life inside and outside of community settings. Out of the comparative reading of these texts and the subsequent confrontation with the expectations of both community members and local society, emerged a broad range of local interpretations. Such interpretations could be just as fleeting as the circumstances in which they originated and the existence of the people who created them. The scant commentaries, hagiographies, and manuscripts that survive from this period, although certainly very precious, offer but snapshot glimpses of worlds of monastic thought and practice that were in constant development [S DEFENSOR]. A second factor impacting

Ethnic and cultural factors

on the diversity of monastic experience derived from ethnic and cultural interactions. An example of this is found in the various male and female Greek monasteries in Rome. Originally established in the early seventh century by individuals who had fled from warfare and political instability in their native regions, these communities were continuously replenished until the beginning of the ninth century, and had a noted influence on their monastic neighbours. Similar observations could be made for migrant communities and individuals in northern Iberia, northern Italy, Gaul, and England, all of whom brought new practices and attitudes to these areas.

Social aspects of diversity

A final factor was social. Monastics certainly did not all belong to the same class or cohort, a fact that must have caused different hierarchies and *habitus* to manifest themselves implicitly or explicitly in the morally egalitarian (but hierarchically administered) world of the monastery. We also find that individuals who had made formal vows were joined by large numbers of people whose personal connection to ascetic pursuits was indirect. Sharing in the space and at least some aspects of the monastic experience were many servants, associates, and family members who ended up living in or around monastic settlements, by their own free will or because they were told to do so by their relatives or masters. In some places, these individuals took part in ascetic endeavours: here, class differences often expressed themselves in different task assignments, rather than in views on whether or not a person was entitled to lead an ascetic life. But in other cases, this broader membership lived a life that was distinct from that of the 'real' monastics: one such example is that of the Irish *manaig*, individuals who had an abbot as lord in much the same way as a person living in the world could be the subordinate of a lay lord.

Experiences by 'non-monastics'

Finally, in relation to diversity of monastic experience, we must also think of the men, women, and even children who temporarily stayed in a monastic environment. Women's monasteries and female anchorites in some cases accepted a range of incomers: young girls who came there to be educated; women who had fled manipulative relatives following the death of their husband; widows and virgins whom their relatives wished to keep from the matrimonial market; or those who had retreated from the world as penitents. Male monastics and their communities fulfilled similar social roles. Engaging in some shape or form with ascetic withdrawal and self-abnegation must have influenced the world-view and the conduct of at least some of the individuals who subsequently returned to the world, while their presence in monastic settings surely also impacted on the attitudes and conduct of the core community. Together, they were the front-row witnesses to the profound transformations affecting monastic life in the eighth and early ninth centuries.

3 Early and High Medieval Monasticisms

3.1 Continuities and Transformations in the Long Eighth Century

The emergence of the Carolingians as the ruling dynasty in eighth-century Francia was intimately linked to the family's monastic policies. East of the Rhine, where there existed few monasteries, leading family members and their associates founded and co-founded

Insertion in Frankish rule

numerous institutions as part of the area's Christianization and as a means to integrate the area into the Frankish realm. Such establishments were key in shaping the political landscape of these territories and functioned as nodal points of a vast network linking local societies and aristocratic networks to the court. In the Western parts of the realm – where there already existed hundreds of private monasteries, hospitals, *xenodochia*, and sanctuaries served by monastics –rulers, bishops, and high-placed laymen staked countless formal and informal claims to the lordship of such settlements. This massive transferral of landed wealth and symbolic resources took place in opportune circumstances. Many aristocratic lineages of former monastic founders had died out or were in the process of doing so, leaving room for the Frankish elites to claim control over 'orphaned' communities and their assets. And as more and more such institutions fell into the orbit of these rulers, the relative proportion that was privately owned fell even more steeply. New foundations by local aristocrats had been on the decline since the final years of the seventh century, a phenomenon scholars have linked to the growing role of the Mass in lay spirituality and the corresponding rise in the significance of ordained clerics (and hence also a shift towards endowments of parish churches instead of monastic foundations). Also pertinent was the declining freedom of aristocratic women, in particular, to found and endow new religious houses.

Decline of private foundations

The process of political integration was aided by two royal practices. The first was initiated by Merovingian royals in the late seventh century and consisted of placing monasteries under the protection of the sovereign and of granting them immunity. Depending on the specific circumstances, the right of immunity liberated monastic communities from various duties and taxes and from the interference of royal agents, and recognized them in the ownership of their estate. Despite the fact that the privileges in which royals awarded these rights heavily insisted on "freedom" (*libertas*), these documents functioned in the first place as powerful signifiers of the king's authority over monastic institutions and of a relationship of mutual interdependence. By granting immunity, Merovingian royals were able to create a network of large and increasingly wealthy institutions whose faithful service to the throne was secure. These monasteries also functioned as a massive repository of material and symbolic resources. As such, they constituted a counter-

Immunities

weight to the continuously shifting aristocratic alliances on which royal authority had previously rested. The second royal practice that aided the political integration of monastic houses was to make them substantial donations. This not only allowed these places to develop into increasingly complex institutional entities and major sites of economic and cultural production, but also created a bond (or strengthened an existing one) of mutual obligation between these institutions and their new lordship.

Mutual obligations

The monastics reciprocated these transferrals of rights and properties with commemorative and intercessory prayers [**S** LIBER MEMORIALIS], the hosting of royal visitors, and by providing assistance to the exercise of sovereign power. They also complied, to a greater or lesser extent, with rulers' requests to adopt a typically 'Gregorian' vision of cenobitical practice and community life. From the middle decades of the seventh century onwards, clerical and lay rulers in Francia had indicated that their preference was for a monastic lifestyle that was dedicated to prayer, removed from all distractions of the secular world, including – crucially – pastoral work, and subject to a strictly enforced hierarchy. An early, local reference to this is in the decrees of the 663/675 synod of Autun, which stipulated that all monasteries in the diocese must observe the *Rule of St Benedict*. Further indications are in a number of royal and especially episcopal privileges, which declare the author's wish that the beneficiary communities observe the *Rule of St Benedict* and/or Columbanus's *Rule*. It is tempting, as some historians have done, to read in these and other testimonies the first stirrings of a movement that sought to reverse a decline of fervour in 'Columbanian' or 'Iro-Frankish' monasteries of the sixth and seventh centuries. But in reality, the goal of these statements was not to launch a global 'reform' of monastic observance. Rather, it was a succinct way for bishops and rulers to indicate, in general terms, what type of conduct and service they expected from their cenobitical subjects.

Focus on contemplation

Prominent eighth-century Churchmen and rulers – most notably the Anglo-Saxon Boniface (d. 754), a leading figure of the Anglo-Saxon mission in eastern Francia who became archbishop of Mainz, and his female associate and missionary Leoba (d. 782) [**S** RODULPH OF FULDA] – likewise supported a vision that reflected Pope Gregory's ideal of cenobitical life. At the 742/743 *Concilium Germanicum*, an important Church gathering dealing with the

Boniface's project

eastern parts of the realm, palace mayor Karloman and Boniface decreed that monks and women religious in Austrasia were to live according to the *Rule of St Benedict*. As with earlier such statements, the emphasis on the *Rule* was not part of a policy designed (as some historians formerly speculated) to revitalize monastic life or to promote strict observance of that text in all contemplative institutions of the realm. Instead, we must understand it as a political argument in the context of ongoing attempts to award contemplative monastic groups a specific role in the Frankish Church and establish them as distinct, functionally and in terms of their

Distinct roles of clerics and monastics

organization and observance, from the clergy. The 755 council of Ver, held just one year after Boniface's death, came to the heart of the matter when it explicitly distinguished communities of contemplative monastics from those of clerics and defined them as two separate cohorts. However, by stating that those in the former cohort could live either according to the *Rule of St Benedict* or the "decrees of the Fathers", those assembled at the council also admitted that non-clerical groups with diverse (contemplative, caritative, and other) roles and identities would continue to populate the religious landscape.

Chrodegang's cathedral clerics

Frankish rulers and churchmen also took notice of Boniface's intention to subject groups of clerics, in particular those serving cathedral sanctuaries, to a quasi-monastic form of community life. A central figure here was Chrodegang, bishop of Metz (d. 766) and a close confidante of former palace mayor and now-king Pippin III. Chrodegang founded a contemplative monastery at Gorze (748) and later took responsibility for another foundation by his relative Cancor at Lorsch (764). But his main achievement was the c. 754 *Rule for canons* that organized community life for clerics along the lines of the *Rule of St Augustine*, yet allowed clerics to own private property. The objective, so he indicated, was to bring the Metz cathedral clergy back to the path of righteous living and turn them into dignified individuals who were obedient to the bishop, dedicated to reading the Holy Scriptures and divine office, and (by virtue of their purity) credible providers of sacramental and other

Influence

ritual services [**S** CHRODEGANG]. Chrodegang did not intend his *Rule* to be observed to the letter by his Metz clerics, let alone serve as a manual for reforming the cathedral clergy in other parts of Pippin's realm. Nevertheless, the text did circulate widely and was picked up by Frankish reformers in the early ninth century. It also directly or indirectly influenced Insular commentators and Church leaders, including Archbishop Wulfred of Canterbury (d. 832), who reformed the cathedral chapter of Christ Church along similar lines, and possibly also the author of Ireland's *Rule of céili Dé*.

Frankish royal and conciliar decrees throughout the later 700s and early 800s continued to insist on the need for groups of contemplative monastics and those of ascetic clerics to fulfil different roles and live according to different standards. As in earlier decades, these texts also explicitly referenced lay and clerical lawmakers' focus on integrating monastic communities in the Frankish state and the exercise of sovereign rule. However, an actual legislative effort to ground their existence in two distinct, well-delineated lifestyles did not take place before the second decade of the ninth century. In 813, Emperor Charlemagne (d. 814) created the momentum for this major reform effort by calling five councils, the decrees of which contained recommendations on how to organize the lives of Church personnel – monks and women religious, clerics living in a community, and individual priests – and on what was expected of their respective types of leader. Considered together, these documents reveal how Charlemagne and his bishops sought to integrate a number of localized reform efforts and other eighth-century influences into official, empire-wide ecclesiastical and royal policies. They focus on the need for clerics serving major sanctuaries to live communally and to refrain from worldly pleasures whilst carrying out their ritual and pastoral tasks. In addition, the decrees explicitly centre the existence of groups of monks and women religious on contemplation, intercessory prayer, and commemoration, and keep them away from all things secular. Finally, they make the leaders of these religious communities personally responsible for instructing their subjects on how to live a virtuous life.

The 813 decrees were the basis on which Charlemagne's successor Louis the Pious (d. 840), and a number of clerical and monastic agents (including most notably Abbot Benedict of Aniane, d. 821), grounded their ambitious project for reform [**S** ARDO]. Over a series of councils held at Aachen in 816–819, the new emperor and his fellow convenors stated their intention to impose the principle of *una regula* ("one rule") on all contemplative monasteries in the realm and turn them into strictly Benedictine communities. As a template for the life of contemplative monastics, the sixth-century *Rule* had many obvious shortcomings. Not only did it leave numer-

Focus on distinct roles

Integrating local reform efforts

The Aachen reform councils

"One rule"

ous eventualities unmentioned, but its author had obviously also been unaware of things that would be of crucial significance to the identity and social position of future monastic groups, such as here, in the early ninth century, the focus on intercessory prayer, the role of monastic institutions as major hubs of economic, political, and cultural life, and the expectations of the Frankish sovereign with regard to monastic support of his rule and the welfare of his subjects. To address that problem, Benedict of Aniane assembled various explanations, adjustments, and then-current practices into *una consuetudo* ("one custom(ary)") and published it under the title *Regula sive collectio capitularis* ("Rule or collection of chapters").

"One custom"

Likewise, the reformers agreed to create a new, consolidated set of regulations (a text known to scholars as the *Institutio canonicorum*) for all communities of clerics. And although the functional distinction between groups of monks and those of clerics was not supposed to exist for communities of women religious – lawmakers and Churchmen insisted that veiled women were to be excluded from any sacramental or pastoral tasks – the reform councils nevertheless decreed that all female communities in the empire were to choose between a lifestyle based on the *Rule of St Benedict* and one that was outlined in a new text, the *Institutio sanctimonialium* [**S** INSTITUTIO]. While both female cohorts were subject to strict enclosure and although the reformers indicated their preference for the former lifestyle, the *Institutio* was designed to avoid alienating the aristocracy by providing an alternative to the Benedictine model. For the latter (in theory at least) wiped out class distinctions inside a convent and negated the strategic and financial motives that a family might have for one of their members to enter the monastic life. Accordingly, the non-Benedictine women religious (sometimes referred to in the literature as "canonesses") were explicitly allowed to own private property, in some cases live in their own homes within the monastic enclosure, and sometimes even wear secular clothes. The reformers' pragmatic view on organization, recruitment, and interaction with the social environment would prove vital to the survival of institutional monastic life for women over the next two and a half centuries.

Rules for "canons" and "canonesses"

Contrary to the claims of traditional historiography, the reforms under Louis did not engineer a fundamental paradigm shift in the observance, organization, and societal embedding of monastic

Continuity

community life. As far back as the late seventh century, the trend in many communities focussing on prayer and contemplation across Francia had been to follow a mode of life that echoed the ideals and behaviours outlined in the *Rule of St Benedict* and in various other rules with a similar emphasis. And as we saw earlier, clerical and lay rulers had been corroborating this trend through various decrees and charters and through supporting with donations and protective measures communities that had committed to adopting such a lifestyle.

Another misconception in these former discussions is that the reformers of the early ninth century sought to establish a situation where the organization and observance of all contemplative monasteries (for men or for women) and those of clerical communities would henceforth be identical, and strictly in accordance with a written rule. As more recent studies have shown, the written accounts of monastic life emanating from reform councils and reformist circles of the early ninth century were hardly the comprehensive descriptions they were once made out to be. They also do not represent the different steps of a carefully planned trajectory for reform. Rather, they are revealed to us as created in order to push forward an ongoing debate over how to realize the *correctio* ("correction") of the Frankish Church. Another objective behind their creation was to provide input for reflections, likewise ongoing at the time, regarding the precise role of different forms of ecclesiastical community life and on how to make each of these forms as efficient as possible in their distinct service to the Carolingian ruler and his subjects. Since the objective of reformers was for groups of ascetic practitioners to represent and support ruler and realm in vastly diverse parts of the empire, they considered diversity – in the sense of adaptedness to local circumstances and traditions – in monastic organization and practice a strength rather than a weakness. As we shall see further (below, Chapter 3.2), they responded favourably to the notion that, within certain boundaries set by consensus, individual communities and their diverse stakeholders (bishops, lay lords, patrons) could carve out a distinct identity.

Variations

Diversity as reform principle

As scholars now see it, the reform decrees of the early ninth century belong to the political and ideological context of the second half of the 810s. The transient nature of that context explains why post-819, there is little indication of a debate over strict application of these texts. For instance, conciliar and royal

Negotiated nature of local forms

decrees stopped making any meaningful distinction between the two forms of female religious life. Henceforth, the view was that *all* women living in a cloistered community setting were expected to provide intercessory and commemorative services, live in a state of enclosure, remain chaste, and provide support to ruler and empire. Whether individual members of these communities practised poverty or not, or whether their status was permanent or not, or even how these communities defined their own identity as ascetics, were issues that Carolingian lawmakers saw as a matter for negotiation between the local bishop, a community's abbess, and the lay stakeholders. For groups of monks and those of clerics (commonly referred to as *canonici*, "canons"), the rulers' emphasis lay not on homogenizing observance, but on identifying the cohorts as two distinct functional entities in the Frankish Church. How and in what measure that distinctness played out in real life, and to what extent it was enforced, was left to those in charge of things 'on the ground'.

3.2 Ninth-Century Monasticisms

Building on arguments first formulated at the 742/743 *Concilium Germanicum*, the 816–819 reform decrees bookended rather than started a transformative phase in the development of cenobitical life across various parts of the Frankish Empire. They sanctioned an existing situation where many such monasteries functioned as political and economic relays between the court and local societies, and as institutions that offered support to the ruler and his associates: essential logistical help; financial aid; and even (by furnishing troops recruited from the laity of their estate [S IRMINO], or providing arms, supplies, or money) military support. The reform decrees also reinforced the status of institutions as ideological and educational centres, as well confirming a number of prominent individuals from these places as 'influencers' at the court and in other elite circles, and as active participants in the ongoing reorganization of the Frankish Church [S DISPUTATIO]. Finally, they strengthened a growing trend to envision contemplative monasteries as privileged sites of interaction with the divine, where cohorts of highly trained men and women could dedicate their lives to intercessory prayer and commemorative service, and by doing so provide an essential

Ongoing integration
in the Frankish realm

service to ruler and empire. While it is easy to be distracted by the confident rhetoric of decrees that were issued in the early reign of Louis the Pious, their principal impact was that of consolidating processes and transformations that had been happening over many decades.

During that time, monastics' experience of life in many places had changed, sometimes gradually and sometimes more abruptly. Over the course of the previous century and a half, the emphasis in thinking about life in contemplative communities had shifted from the ritual purity of the individual to creation of unpolluted spaces where highly trained ascetics could pursue their purpose in life without undue distraction or risk. This created a momentum for reimagining monastic space, which in the early ninth century resulted in the creation of the first true examples of the cloister as an architectural concept. Architecture was now the means by which the principles of active and passive enclosure were more strictly imposed. Within the reimagined world of the cloister, groups of monks and those of women religious spent a substantial part of their time praying and chanting. To meet the various needs caused by the growing emphasis on liturgy and prayer service, a growing number of monks were trained for the priesthood: at ninth-century Fulda, up to seventy per cent of the monks were ordained priests, while women's communities recruited substantial numbers of clerics to support them in their liturgical service, say Mass, and fulfil other roles that were now off limits to women.

Inner transformations

Cloistered space and pursuits

All of these activities – to a greater or lesser extent depending on local circumstances and arrangements – came at the expense of any former roles held by a community, whether running a hospice for the poor, the sick, or for pilgrims, or teaching young children, or carrying out various pastoral duties. Manual labour, insofar as the members of a given community still practised it, was now replaced by work in the scriptorium. On an individual level, women religious in particular were subject to royal and conciliar decisions that excluded them from participating in Church governance, carrying out sacramental tasks, preaching, or providing assistance to fellow Christians. Outside defined circumstances (for instance, when an abbess was called to the court), access by outsiders was also severely restricted and closely monitored.

Still, local realities post-reform never literally reflected any of the decrees, rules, and other normative commentaries that were

Local variations

issued over the course of the eighth and early ninth centuries. Although it may sound paradoxical, the reformers' promotion of the *Rule of St Benedict* in particular, actually stimulated localized cultures of reflection on monastic tradition. Many groups of monastics, by becoming involved in institutional and intellectual networks linked to court and other elite circles, gained access to an unprecedented range of late antique and early medieval commentaries on the nature and purpose of monastic life. For instance, Benedict of Aniane in his *Codex regularum* collated no fewer than twenty-four rules for male monastics and six for female ones, eight of which are known only through this collection. Just as ground-breaking was Benedict's *Concordia regularum*, a handbook that placed "sentences" from each of these rules next to the corresponding chapters in the *Rule of St Benedict* [S CONCORDIA]. The underlying ambition of both of these projects was to demonstrate, once and for all, the status of the *Rule* as the culmination of late antique and early medieval experiments in monastic rule-making: but at the same time, these texts stimulated awareness of the existence and intrinsic value of alternative accounts of monastic life.

Diverse reading cultures

Diverse interpretations

Various commentaries on the *Rule of St Benedict* – including Benedict of Aniane's above-mentioned *Regula* and those by his contemporary Smaragdus of Saint-Mihiel (d. c. 840) [S SMARAGDUS] and Hildemar of Civate (d. c. 850) [S HILDEMAR] – reveal to us just how little consensus there existed over how to apply the *Rule* in a manner that reflected local needs, expectations, and traditions, yet that still remained faithful to the spirit of that text. It might not be a coincidence that Smaragdus - like Benedict of Aniane - originated from northern Spain, a region where monastic culture was a true melting pot of diverse literary and normative influences, and where blending of such influences was the norm rather than the exception. The diversity of ninth-century interpretations of the monastic life is additionally revealed in a mass of written, material, architectural, and archaeological evidence that shows significant discrepancies between (on the one hand) reformers' written decrees and (on the other) local experiences. The women of Remiremont, for instance, in the 820s declared that they had adopted the *Rule of St Benedict*: but they continued to practise the non-Benedictine *laus perennis* (perpetual prayer service) and actually publicized it as a key feature of their contribution to ruler and society [S THIATHILDIS]. As long as the expectations of authorities regarding

Diverse experiences

the monasteries' function in the Frankish Church were met, local stakeholders could make their own arrangements for many things that pertained to the internal workings and societal embedding of these communities.

In return for interweaving their interests with those of the ruler and his associates, monastic communities reaped significant rewards. Royal patronage and protective measures, backing from clerical and lay elites associated with the court, and all the benefits that came from integration into a range of regional and empire-wide networks, led to an upswing in the fortunes of many institutions. Besides the fact that some individual monastics became influential ideologically and achieved prominent positions at the court or in ecclesiastical centres, many monastic estates were now reorganized and expanded, recruitment improved in numbers and in the social status of new members, intellectual and spiritual life flourished, and new architectural projects and artistic work were undertaken.

Beneficial effects of integration

The expansion of many institutions, particularly those that ended up with highly dispersed estates (one example being Lorsch), led to the accumulation of knowledge on how to manage institutional entities, carry out complex transactions (including property transfers and moneylending), and function as a conduit between different levels of society and between different local societies. Some institutions, particularly those that enjoyed the special favour of rulers, relied on prayer fraternities to establish beneficial connections with religious institutions in other parts of the Empire, creating in the process wide-ranging networks in which social and cultural capital could be exchanged. On a local level too, relations with the social environment changed. Especially the former aristocratic foundations became more involved with the lay population than in earlier times: among other things, the cults of saintly founders were now being promoted to pilgrims, formerly private churches were opened to the public, and subsidiary institutions and local sanctuaries were created to manage the expanding monastic estates. In other places, monastics continued to exercise the former social role or roles of their community – aiding the poor, nursing the sick, teaching children, preaching and offering pastoral services – sometimes personally, but often also through proxies such as local clerics, servants, and lay officers.

Expertise and networking

Impact on local societies

It would be reductive of contemporary realities, though, to argue that the Carolingians' push for integration of monastic communities in the exercise of sovereign rule and the reorganization of the Frankish Church had strictly positive outcomes. Enclosure definitely had an adverse impact on the opportunities for individual monastics – women in particular – to make their own choices in pursuing ascetic ideals, and made them more reliant on the support and oversight of clerical and lay agents. We also see how the identity and social profile of monastic groups was now subject to the approval of clerical and lay lords, and that in the process of reform former such identities and profiles were often suppressed, and their memory erased. Many communities that showed reluctance to accept the strict division of pastoral and intercessory roles for monastics were forced to either turn their institution into a house of clerics or split into two separate communities, as was the case in Saint-Denis, Saint-Bertin, and Marmoutier. Such interventions had a destabilizing effect, among other things because they compelled the break-up of complex estates, and because they drastically affected the personal situation of members and their relatives. In local societies where monastic groups with different roles complemented each other functionally (for instance in Rome), the pressure to turn into a contemplative institution was seen as an attack on a community's historical roles and consequently met with much resistance. Other communities faced the fact that their location, the size of their estate, or some other factor meant that their continued existence held no interest for the ruling elite. We know of efforts, or at least plans, by Carolingian royalty and bishops to abolish houses that were found to be economically unsustainable and merge their estates with more viable ones, in the process erasing or transforming whatever spiritual, cultic and other traditions had existed in these places.

Absorption of monastic institutions into the exercise of Frankish rule also meant that stakeholdership of these places had turned into a complex and potentially contested issue. Royal monasteries – monasteries directly owned by the sovereign – in particular had become major keystones in the Carolingian state system, and the functions and roles of these settlements now far exceeded their original purpose. As a result, rulers and their associates became increasingly concerned over how to harness the growing status of these institutions as major landowners, and how to retain control

Adverse effects

Resistance

Royal oversight

over their massive, and growing, material and symbolic resources. In his 819 *Notitia de servitio monasteriorum*, Louis the Pious listed all the services to which these institutions were subject: military service, taxes, and prayers for the ruler, his offspring, and the Empire. Like his royal predecessors since the later seventh century, Louis also tied monastic houses to his authority by granting them immunity privileges. In these, he guaranteed the *libertas monas-* "Liberty" *ticae religionis* ("freedom of the monastic religion"), meaning that the members of a community would be able to pursue their ascetic *propositum* ("purpose in life") under a regular leadership (an elected abbot or abbess) in the Benedictine tradition without undue disturbance or financial worries. Above all else though, the privileges functioned as signifiers of the ruler's commitment to the *correctio* ("correction") of the Frankish Church, his role as *tutor et defensor* ("protector and warden") of monastic houses, and also his ambition to claim the institutions receiving these privileges. Local rulers, bishops in particular, acted similarly with monasteries that fell under their direct authority.

Louis and his associates further consolidated the status of Lay abbots and monasteries as sites of sovereign authority by putting lay represent- abbesses atives in charge of their external affairs and their protection. Terms like lay abbot or lay abbess (prominent aristocrats who acted as *de facto* lords and caretakers of monastic institutions) and lay advocate subsequently gained a sinister meaning of abuse of power and resources. However, there is little to suggest that lay lordship and the various institutional and financial arrangements that came with it (among other things, the allocation of part of the incomes from the estate of a monastery to the *mensa abbatialis*, literally the "table of the abbot") were by definition detrimental to the situation of the monastics, or were initially perceived as such. Many such individuals acted as intermediaries between monastics and the secular world, defended the community's interests in cases of conflict over property or income, interceded with the court, activated their networks in favour of their institutions, and acted as prominent patrons in their own right, donating manuscripts and art objects, commissioning building works, and transferring various properties to a monastery's estate. Their involvement in these places also did not exclude the presence there of an individual, sometimes also referred to as abbot or abbess, who took charge of the internal affairs of the community and acted as its spiritual and moral leader.

Negative perceptions The negative representation of these lay agents originated when the focus of territorial power began shifting away from the court to local societies in the mid- to later ninth century. With royal authority progressively weakening and monastic lordship being transferred to the local and territorial elites, traditional stakeholders more and more relied on a discourse that referenced a state of acute crisis and rampant lay encroachment, to help them reclaim some of their former ground. Sovereign rulers and bishops began issuing charters and other decrees that emphasized their continued interest in these places and in monastic governance generally, and that made provisions to protect groups of monks and women religious from the excessive demands – whether real or imagined – of local lay agents.

Accounts of encroachment To give additional credence to the purported need for protection of these places, these agents also extrapolated anecdotal reports of violence, theft, and interference, and presented these as generally relevant to the situation of a specific institution or sometimes even to all monasteries in a particular area. In 909, for instance, the participants of the Western Frankish council of Trosly complained that lay lords had been taking over monasteries as places of private residence, and were now living in them with their wives, children, and dogs. They expressed horror at the fact that some monks and women religious at the time were seeing no other option but to break enclosure and search for employment to provide for their most basic needs. Alarmed by the signs of an impending power struggle over their institutions and resources, monastic authors too began committing to memory incidents that had adversely affected their interests. In a more general sense they complained about the excessive demands of lay abbots and officers, the threat of warlords and brigands, and the difficulties communities experienced when they tried to reclaim what was rightfully theirs.

Biased nature of these accounts There are many reasons why we should not take these testimonies for granted, not the least being that commentators were looking to claim a dominant stake in these monasteries and their resources. Nevertheless, many testimonies of the period do refer to real, widely held fears of impending societal collapse. Viking raids that had been plaguing the Carolingian realms and their neighbouring regions for several decades had become more intense, with a peak in the 880s. Magyar, Hungarian, and Muslim attackers would cause a great deal of additional disturbance across large parts of the Latin West well into the tenth century. In the meantime, royals and their aristocratic competitors waged war against each other in an attempt to claim parts of the crumbling Frankish realms. These incursions and other violent episodes certainly caused major disruption to secular and ecclesiastical governance, trade and agriculture, and more generally also to the day-to-day existence and livelihood of countless communities across the Latin West [S REGINO]. People in the monastic life were not exempt from these dangers. Some private practitioners – hermits, anchorites, recluses, and household ascetics – are known to have suffered from violence and societal disruption. One of a handful of known examples is that of Wiborada, an anchoress who lived near the abbey of St Gall in current-day Switzerland, who was killed in 926 when Hungarian warriors broke through the roof of her cell [S EKKEHART]. Presumably, some hermits and anchorites fled to safety in fortified monasteries and towns, or in sparsely inhabited regions where the attackers were less likely to venture.

Looking at the impact on monastics living in institutional settings, what little reliable evidence we have suggests that short-term, nearly every surviving institution faced problems in maintaining beneficial links with lay patrons, in collecting donations, rents, and loans, and in retaining control over remote estates. They might also have found it hard to broker advantageous property deals or to attract new recruits, particularly child oblates. And in many places, liturgical routines must have been difficult to maintain; the organization of proper education challenging; and the time or leisure to study or to practise a life of contemplation lacking. In the longer term, the effects were more diverse. Some communities simply ceased to exist, often because of a combination of factors: in these cases, the only remaining trace might be a parish church staffed perhaps by a handful of clerics, a chapel, a farm, or perhaps just a place name referring to a former monastery's patron saint. Other institutions did suffer badly from pillaging, destruction, hostage-taking, or other forms of violence, but bounced back quite rapidly, as did their secular environment. Others still were spared the worst disruptions because they were situated in a region relatively unaffected by incursions or because powerful rulers singled them out for special protection.

Whatever their precise situation, the surviving monasteries' very status as beacons of stability in a world in turmoil will have

Impact of disruptions

Impact on communities

exposed them to danger. As major economic and political hubs, repositories of enormous wealth, and finally also as assets of huge symbolic value, these houses risked becoming prime targets whenever a struggle broke out for dominance in regional politics, as happened in many parts. Although they were in theory removed from worldly distractions, monastics and those who lived alongside them once again had no choice but to experience the consequences of a society in profound transition.

3.3 Restorations, Reforms, and the Problem of Monastic Lordship

The former narrative of reform

For a very long time, commentators of the monastic past described the tenth and early eleventh centuries as an era in which lay, clerical, and monastic agents in different regions of the Latin West worked to undo the precipitous decline of monastic institutions and spirituality. On the one hand, it was argued, monastic groups across the Latin West had been struggling to address the catastrophic impact of invasions, warfare, the collapse (in some regions at least) of royal power and the resulting disruption of social order. A cohort of lower aristocrats and local warlords who were keen to claim monastic offices and properties had risen to prominence (a hotly debated phenomenon that used to be described as the "feudal revolution"), and patronage links, trade networks, and communication lines were all disrupted. On the other hand, monasticism was also facing an internal crisis, with monks and women religious becoming increasingly lax about maintaining a lifestyle and performing a number of duties as outlined by the Carolingian reformers of the early ninth century.

Former views on methodologies

To resolve these issues, it was said, bishops and secular rulers recruited a number of energetic monastics and set about founding or 'restoring' a number of institutional centres where the principles of reform could be put into practice and from where these principles and practices could then be propagated. Over the course of the early to mid-tenth century, various such institutions in northern Spain, France, Lotharingia, England, and the Empire subsequently took the lead in pursuing the restoration of monastic properties and buildings and the emancipation of monastic institutions from secular lordship and interference. They introduced in these places a rigid observance according to the *Rule of St Benedict*, rationalized and established common standards for government, liturgical practice, and other aspects of monastic life, and finally also subjected all of these things to (first rudimentary, then more sophisticated) forms of coordinated governance and supervision. To back up this assessment, medieval commentators and modern historians alike pointed to the rise of various 'reform movements'. Those of Cluny, Gorze, and the English Benedictine Reform, to name but three, 'restored' the *Rule* as the authoritative paradigm for community life and institutional organization. They established strict behavioural, physical, and legal boundaries between monastics and secular society; created the conditions for economic viability; and also promoted freedom and immunity for monastic institutions, and their integration into networks and congregations. In many places, so it was said, this entailed a return to a monastery's historical origins as a Benedictine (or at the very least contemplative) community.

And on outcomes

Yet, as the scholarly understanding of realities and experiences in the tenth century becomes increasingly complex, our appreciation of the precise nature of these 'reforms' has likewise become more nuanced. As we saw earlier (Chapter 3.2), it is crucial to realize that the traditional narrative of decline, rampant encroachments, and subsequent resurgence in the context of reform conflates an immense variety of experiences on the part of communities living in areas affected in vastly different ways by the above turmoil. It also condenses hard-to-reconstruct developments over several decades into tales of catastrophic disruption, and overly relies on the biased accounts of contemporary commentators. Studies carried out in the last few decades concerning the circumstances and implications of various 'restorations' and 'reforms' have likewise yielded a more nuanced understanding of what these supposedly paradigm-shifting events entailed. In particular, they reveal to us that the programmatic nature of various such endeavours and of the 'reform movements' from which they were said to derive are in fact anachronistic projections by later commentators.

Recent criticism

Lack of reform 'programmes'

The creation of Cluny by Count William of Aquitaine is one such example of a 'reform event' that was far more ordinary than specialists used to think. The new monastery, in the heart of the former kingdom of Burgundy, was established on an estate that had formerly belonged to William's recently deceased sister Ada, who had lived there as a household ascetic. In a 910 charter, he staked a claim to the title of protector of monastic life and forbade

Origins of Cluniac monasticism

any lord – including the local bishop of Mâcon – from harming the monks' interests through invasion or the alienation of their property. In addition, he commended the monastery to the protection of the apostles and the pope. By declaring it free of any form of secular lordship, so scholars used to argue, William launched a reform dynamic that would lead to the emancipation of countless houses over the next two centuries, and had paved the way for the emergence of an independent federation of monastic houses centred on
Political background Cluny. In reality, the count's charter and the liberties it referred to were not much different from those granted by ninth-century sovereigns and bishops (above, Chapter 3.2). Instead, what made the transaction so fundamentally different were the political circumstances in which the charter was issued. Territorial power in Burgundy c. 900 had fractured to the point that no single individual could securely claim control, as lord, over major monastic institutions and their resources. Realizing his weak position politically, William transferred control over Ada's former estate and parts of his own to a newly established monastic community, thus retaining an informal controlling stake in the abbey's affairs while preventing his competitors from claiming lordship.

Unforeseen developments It was a combination of unforeseen events, not a deliberate reform effort, that subsequently elevated Cluny's first abbot Berno (d. 926) to a unique position among his monastic peers. William's premature death in 917, his lack of progeny, and the fact that there were no lay or clerical claimants who could secure control over the abbey, enabled Cluny's elected spiritual leader to take on the role of lord of the monastic estate. Berno soon started behaving in much the same manner as his aristocratic neighbours, treating his abbey's properties as his own. During the remainder of his tenure at Cluny, he also established a small number of new mon-
Berno's 'multi-abbacy' asteries, each time adding them to his personal lordship. In this 'multi-abbacy', no formal ties were established between different institutions: the only two things that bound them were Berno's ownership and the fact he acted as abbot in each of these places. The personal nature of his lordship was made plainly obvious at the time of his death. In a move that went unchallenged at the time, he bequeathed the monasteries of Gigny and Baume to his brother, a layman. The rest of Berno's properties fell to his successor Odo (d. 942), who adopted Berno's multi-abbacy without changing its conception or structure.

Odo styled himself as a major spiritual leader, on a double Berno's successors
mission to keep his own subjects on the path to salvation and to
promote his views on Christian ascetic virtues to other monastic
communities, and even the laity. Over the course of his tenure, he
worked hard to expand his multi-abbacy: but he also introduced
Cluny's liturgy and observance to a substantial number of other
monasteries across Western Francia and on the Italian Peninsula.
Cluny's fourth abbot, Maiolus (d. 994), aimed to award a deeper
meaning to Cluny's moral leadership, enhancing it by forging links
with the papacy. The 981 consecration of Cluny's second, grand
abbatial church (also known as Cluny II) and the placing there of
relics of Sts Peter and Paul, marked the beginning of the abbey's
self-identification as a 'little Rome', a centre from which a superior
form of monastic observance was disseminated.

Odo's interventions in communities other than those that Cluny as 'reform centre'
belonged to his multi-abbacy, and those of his successors Aymard
(d. 954), Maiolus, and Odilo (d. 1049), took place in a wide range
of circumstances [**S** Jotsald]. In a minority of cases, we see that
the move to call on their assistance came from inside, often in the
context of a crisis of abbatial authority. In the northern Italian
abbey of Farfa, for instance, the 998 election of a monk named Ugo
as abbot was marred by accusations of simony. In order to validate
his new standing, Ugo called in Odilo to introduce the customs of
Cluny: he also challenged the aristocratic controlling stake in a
number of the abbey's estates, and reshaped narratives of historical identity to generally depict his rule as a major improvement
[**S** Ugo] .

More numerous were those instances in which the abbot of Interventions by invitation
Cluny intervened at the invitation of a monastery's lay or clerical
lordship. Such invitations must be understood as part of a trend
among these local and regional lords to claim political prominence
and assert their dominance over religious institutions by styling
themselves as the 'protector' or 'defender' of contemplative communities, or by founding new ones. They typically launched these Methodology of reform
'restorations' by returning lost and alienated properties: they also
typically granted to communities the *libertas*, which comprised
freedom from various types of secular and episcopal interference,
and the right to elect a regular abbot or abbess. In addition, these
agents usually imposed an observance with strong Benedictine
overtones (including, crucially, the principle of individual poverty),

removed any individuals who were unwilling to accept it, and brought in monastics from a 'model community' or 'reform centre' to teach the local inmates how to organize their lives. The justification for labelling these interventions as 'reforms' lies not in the objective improvement of the institutions and observance of these places. Rather, it lies in their drastic nature and equally drastic (but not necessarily positive, see Chapter 3.4) consequences, and in the double rhetoric of new beginnings and a return to a more 'authentic' past.

Other 'reform centres' Although it was definitely the most prominent such 'reform centre', Cluny was not the only one; nor were the abbots of Cluny the only charismatic agents that were sollicited to assist clerical and lay lords in their reform endeavours. In the former middle kingdom of Lotharingia and its neighbouring region of Flanders, Duke Gislebert of Lotharingia (d. 938) and Count Arnulf of Flanders (d. 965) recruited former nobleman and monastic founder Gerard of Brogne (d. 959) to assist them with 'restorations' of various key institutions on their territories. These were sites that they were seeking to claim as dynastic sanctuaries, centres from which to control a certain region politically or economically, or simply as bargaining chips with which to secure the support of powerful allies. In implementing these interventions, they asked for, and received, the endorsement of the Ottonian or Western Frankish rulers, who although wary of Gislebert and Arnulf's quasi-regal ambitions were keen to retain a measure of influence in the region.

Relying on the assistance of individuals from other 'reform centres' such as Fleury (reformed with the aid of monks from Cluny around 930), Saint-Evre (reformed from Fleury in 933), and Gorze (in 934 [S JOHN OF SAINT-ARNOUL]), other bishops and lay lords across Lotharingia and parts of Western Francia likewise intervened in a substantial number of existing male and female institutions, and founded many new ones. With interruptions and variations depending on the region, the 'reforms' and new foundations continued into the eleventh century, albeit in different contexts and undertaken by different actors. A second 'wave' must be situated between the 990s and the 1020s/30s, with leading individuals from (among other places) Saint-Bénigne in Dijon and Saint-Vanne in Verdun acting as 'multi-abbots' and disseminators of their principal institution's practices and attitudes. And in England, the 960s saw the launch of the so-called English Benedictine reform, a movement spearheaded by prominent clerical and monastic leaders, along with prominent lay supporters, that claimed to have as its primary mission the observance of the *Rule of St Benedict* by all communities of monks and women religious in King Edgar's realm. Here too, major institutions such as Abingdon and Glastonbury functioned as places from where reformed ideals and practices were disseminated and where a new generation of monastic leaders received its training. Other such regional 'clusters' of reform activity could be mentioned here.

For a long time, historians held these and other 'restorations', 'reforms', and foundations to reveal a selfless drive by monastics, bishops, and lay rulers to rescue religious communities thrown off course by invasions, civic warfare, and societal disruption. But the chronology and implications of interventions in religious communities in various parts of the Latin West tell us a different story. To begin with, interventions of a similar nature and with similar objectives had been happening for several decades. On the Iberian Peninsula, the *Repoblación* – a lengthy process of conquest, resettlement, and restoration of power structures and religious infrastructures – of territories formerly 'lost' to Muslim conquerors had led to a flurry of late ninth- and early tenth-century foundations. Those responsible for the creation of these contemplative monasteries – particularly bishops with close links to the royal houses of Oviedo-León and Navarra and their aristocratic allies – helped redesign the Christian landscape to assist these rulers in their efforts to create a representative network of monastic houses to span the entire region. Meanwhile, a number of emerging territorial lords in late ninth- and very early tenth-century Lotharingia and eastern France had seized the opportunity to style themselves as lords and protectors of former royal monasteries and in doing so claim, symbolically and otherwise, control over the surrounding territories.

Like their 'reformist' successors of the 930s and onwards, these individuals had carried out restitutions of lost properties, intervened on behalf of the monastics in the context of juridical disputes, and bestowed on them various gifts and benefices. Even in Normandy, which at the time was ruled by Scandinavian occupiers, the new political elite was quick to recognize the symbolic, economic, and political advantages of pursuing a policy to 'restore' and patronize monastic communities, and within the space of two

Continuities (margin note)

Similarities and differences (margin note)

generations engaged in a privileged relationship with several key such institutions on their territories. What set all these and other rulers apart from the later 'reformist' lords and bishops is that they rarely framed – at least, that we know of – their actions as part of a broader attempt to 'renew' or 'restore' monastic institutions and spirituality. And although some did express a preference for an observance grounded in Benedictine tradition, as far as we can tell these individuals typically refrained from disparaging the conduct of former monastics.

Political motivation

A further observation is that the key trigger of the 'reforms' and 'restorations' of the 930s onwards was not (or not in the first place) the actual situation of the monastic communities involved, but political opportunity. Many bishops and lay lords who initiated such interventions and founded new Benedictine houses might have sincerely believed their actions of benefit to monks and women religious, and we can assume that many also sincerely hoped to reap spiritual rewards. But their focus was first and foremost on establishing a solid institutional, financial, and symbolic power base, and creating representative religious institutions for themselves and their aristocratic relatives. This explains, among other things, why rulers often only restored part of a monastery's lost estate and kept the rest for their own purposes, and why some abolished the lay abbacy but kept using the title anyway. In the Empire, too, monastic policies were driven in first place by political, dynastic, and representative concerns. Members of the Ottonian dynasty and their aristocratic associates throughout the tenth and early eleventh centuries founded a high number of new monasteries and 'reformed' existing ones as part of a policy to consolidate their control over certain territories. They subsequently relied on these places as representative institutions of royal power, centres where intellectuals, artists, and educators would work in support of imperial rule and its underlying ideology, and as 'model communities' from which other institutions could be established or reformed [S RATPERT]. The first emergence of cenobitism in the tenth- and eleventh-century kingdoms of Hungary and Poland followed a strikingly similar logic.

Support for 'unreformed' places

The political and dynastic motivations for reform also explain why many 'reformist' clerics and laymen left countless 'unreformed' communities undisturbed, for instance when their status in these institutions was already secure, or when rival aristocratic groups held too firm a grip. In some cases, they actually supported these rivals, for strategic reasons. For instance, aristocratic foundations and support of 'non-Benedictine' women's monasteries allowed the German elites to perpetuate existing family structures (with daughters investing their inherited wealth in a monastic foundation) and to prevent young women from marrying below their rank, which likely explains why these institutions were founded in such great numbers and enjoyed vigorous support by clerical and lay rulers. Their subsequent reform into 'Benedictine' houses, particularly in the eleventh century, can often be explained as an attempt to adjust the aristocratic networks in which these places were implicated or, conversely, adjust the status of these places in light of shifts in aristocratic power. The same strategic motivations clarify, too, why 'reformist' rulers apparently ignored communities that were in need of an intervention but that lay beyond their reach politically or held little interest.

Still, the memories of Carolingian *correctio* as an underlying principle of reform were not forgotten. Propaganda coming from Cluny and other places in the early decades of the tenth century led to broad support for the idea that there was a need to create stricter physical, and especially virtual, boundaries between the secular world and the servants of the Church. Abbot Odo of Cluny in his writings bitterly complained about the worldly conduct of many monastics (also below, Chapter 3.5), whom he denounced for their inappropriate delight in secular clothes, for dyeing their habits in fanciful colours, and in some cases for even carrying weapons. He also accused impure religious men – married and otherwise sexually active clerics, and those who owned private property – of polluting holy places. By contrast, he presented Cluny as an unpolluted environment in which sinful behaviour was actively rejected and deliberate steps had been taken to make such errors impossible. And beginning in the 930s, clerical rulers at Metz, Reims, Cologne, and various sees in England promoted the notion that groups of clerics who served major sanctuaries (cathedrals in particular) ought to remain strictly celibate; live in communal buildings; and had to observe an austere lifestyle that reflected their purity and elevated moral stature. Along with monastic agents recruited from major 'reform centres', these leaders additionally argued that the *Rule of St Benedict* was the best guide for contemplative monastics living in a community setting.

Physical and virtual boundaries

Relationship with reform interventions

If and to what extent these concerns and criticisms actually inspired various lay lords and bishops to intervene in specific religious communities is nearly always impossible to tell. What we do know, in contrast, is that these men had discovered that disparaging the conduct of clerics and monastics as 'dishonest' or 'impure' was a highly effective rhetorical weapon in the struggle for control over the destiny of religious institutions. Likewise, presenting their own interventions in these institutions as part of a global project of "correcting" the (regional) Church likewise helped both justify these actions and boost their own authority as Christian rulers.

Discourses of laxity

From the 930s onwards, sources routinely cite these concerns and objectives as a key motivation for interventions in individual communities, typically leaving the burden of disproof for their accusations of sexual incontinence, gluttony, and other vices to the (soon to be) former members and their supporters. In doing so, they helped shape a lasting image of a late ninth- and early tenth-century clerical and monastic cohort that had veered off course but that had been rescued, in the nick of time, by the intervention of these reformers [**S** CHRONICON MOSOMENSE].

Regional revivals of *correctio*

For a short period in the 960s and early 970s, a handful of lay and ecclesiastical agents from interconnected regions and networks in north-western Europe went one step further, and actually proclaimed a global "correction" of all monastic (and in some cases also clerical) communities in their territories. The first of those we know about was Archbishop Bruno of Cologne (d. 965), brother of Emperor Otto I. According to his biographer, he urged "the multitudes from different congregations that belonged to his honourable see" to be of "one heart and mind" and live "according to the fixed rule". Doing so would ensure they avoided both disrepute and the dangers of inappropriate dress. Better known is the council of Winchester (965/973). At this gathering, a coalition of reformist leaders led by Bishop Æthelwold of Winchester and Archbishop Dunstan of Canterbury ordained that all monasteries in King Edgar's realm, whether of men or of women, were to observe the *Rule of St Benedict*. To aid the organization of liturgical practices in these institutions, the English reformers issued a set of guidelines known as the *Regularis Concordia* [**S** REGULARIS CONCORDIA].

Finally, in 972/974, Archbishop Adalbero of Reims called a synod at which he and a number of abbots from the region debated the lack of unity in monastic observance. The synod reportedly denounced the scandal caused by monks' illicit relationships with both men and women, their loose attitude to enclosure and obedience, and their penchant for luxurious and frivolous clothes [**S** RICHER]. But none of the three projects led to a regional homogenization of monastic observance. Indeed, these initiatives served first and foremost as a means through which rulers could claim the title of *corrector* of the Church and implicate the targeted institutions in their various strategies. Nor did these rulers apparently see any objection against patronizing 'non-reformed' communities when this suited their interests, or against leaving numerous others on their territories undisturbed. If there was indeed such a thing as a 'renewal' of monastic life in the tenth and eleventh centuries, as many older studies opined, it was certainly not as a result of a global project for Benedictine reform.

Lack of homogenizing effect

3.4 (Un)Reformed Experiences at the Turn of the First Millennium

Although the pre-intervention situation of 'restored' or 'reformed' monasteries in the tenth and early eleventh centuries eludes even partial reconstruction, post-intervention many of these emerge as flourishing. In some regions at least, the often violent restructuring of the political landscape eventually settled down, creating a calmer environment for reorganizing and consolidating the monastic landscape. Through patronage networks and through the recruitment as abbots and abbesses of charismatic, well-educated, and well-connected individuals, the conditions were created for the opening or strengthening of exchange routes for know-how, cultural capital, and expert personnel. Educators, architects, artists, and scribes travelled from one community to another, disseminating their respective skills and knowledge [**S** BYRTHFERTH].

Networking implications

These personal exchanges facilitated communities of practice that held common views on monastic governance, daily life in the cloister, spirituality and liturgy, and commemorative practice. The close involvement of abbots and abbesses with various elite circles was significant too. Combined with their public persona of ascetic restraint and Christian virtue, it meant that these individuals and their associates often gained a prominent voice in public debate, thus helping to shape ideals of clerical and lay rulership. In post-reform northern Spain, England, the Empire, Western Francia, and

'Communities of practice'

Lotharingia, we see regular abbots ascending to high clerical office or holding key positions at lay courts. The regular leaders of many 'reformed' women's houses in Saxony and northern Italy, too, maintained links with sovereign or lower aristocratic courts, and directly or indirectly played a prominent role in contemporary politics.

Local implications   These abbatial connections also helped communities organize and finance major architectural campaigns. Such projects (which often involved rebuilding and redecorating abbatial churches and redesigning the layout and interior of other parts of the monastic complex) made it possible to turn these sites into visually impressive beacons: a witness both to the presence of monasteries in the social and religious landscape and to the standing and political allegiance of their aristocratic and episcopal lords. Through textual and archaeological records, we also get a sense of how new revenues, protections and immunities allowed for substantial investment in the economic infrastructure of these institutions, including in bridges, mills, and canals. Some rulers and a number of clerical lords also granted economic privileges, such as market, toll, and minting rights. All of this, in tandem with growing populations and trade across many parts of the Latin West, increased the social and economic footprint of monasteries.

Appreciating their situation at the heart of a rapidly expanding, complex secular environment, monastics also actively promoted their institutions and relic treasures as a draw for pilgrims and a religious focal point for locals. Hagiographies, hymns, and other texts and chants in honour of patron saints, solemn elevations and translations of saintly bodies, newly constructed relic shrines and tombs to house them, and artwork all helped celebrate the importance of monasteries in the experience of Christian faith – for insiders and for those living in the world. Over time, these tokens of the global relevance and spiritual authority of communal monasticism would be translated into a campaign, by a number of prominent abbots and their subjects, to 'convert' the world (below, Chapter 3.4). Monastic groups also took the opportunity to drastically revise their collective memories, creating new narratives of institutional origins, reorganizing archives, and in some cases also producing forgeries that anchored their then-current situation in a legitimizing past. Such 'reform memories' were instrumental in committing to long-term memory the double argument of a restoration of old realities and a drastic 'renewal' of monastic observance and spirituality.

Besides all these gains, however, many things were lost. Some of the institutions that had been severely affected by the development around the year 900 now suffered additional alienation of estates and relic treasures at the hands of 'reformist' lords, faced being incorporated into the estate of another monastery, or were simply left to die. Numerous other communities of male and female monastics were compelled to accept drastic rearrangements of their estates and of their patronage networks, even if this worked to their disadvantage. Governance procedures were also dramatically revised, and a new, sometimes foreign leadership, imposed. The regular abbots and abbesses of these communities were compelled to take the utmost care in dealing with the expectations of their lay and clerical lordship. Although the lay abbacy was formally abolished, rulers often continued to take key decisions or even increased their direct involvement in institutional governance.

Bishops and lay lords were also seldom inclined to take local sensitivities into consideration, which no doubt caused a good deal of resentment and trauma, within and outside of these communities. Unfamiliar customs and liturgies were foisted on the inmates of these places – that is, if they were allowed to stay – along with a devastating discourse that denounced their pre-reform conduct as irregular and their former leadership as ineffective or morally corrupt. The shock must have been particularly severe for former groups of canons, and those men or women religious living a quasi-eremitical or other, 'non-Benedictine' lifestyle, as many of them were made to choose between accepting a drastically different observance (with profound consequences for their personal situation and self-understanding) or being evicted. Whatever choice they made, they faced a future in which their former lifestyle would be the subject of criticism and ridicule.

Against the background of these transformations and transitions, diversity remained a defining feature of tenth-century monasticism. Many individuals continued to pursue non-institutional forms of monastic life, including hermits, (urban) anchorites, and household ascetics: these people often lived alongside cloistered monastics and intensively interacted with them. And although reformers were active across the Latin West and heavily publicized the universal ambitions of their endeavours, there was not a single region where *all* religious institutions (except for cathedral chapters) were turned into contemplative monasteries where the obser-

Adverse effects

Local experiences

Enduring diversity

vance was modelled on the *Rule of St Benedict*. In England, for instance, only a small fraction of such settlements were implicated in the reforms of the 960s/970s onwards; the rest simply continued to function as 'minsters', with a strong pastoral role in the local community, or as communities with another role [**S** ÆLFRIC, S ÆTHEL-WOLD]. Due to the political backgrounds of reform, it is not all that surprising that some 'unreformed' communities of the period experienced beneficial changes that are strikingly similar to the ones we have observed in reformed contexts. This was presumably because rulers did not need the ideological and political weapon of reform to incorporate these institutions within their authority. A good case in point are the women religious (later described as "canonesses") of Nivelles in current-day Belgium, who enjoyed vigorous support from the Ottonian rulers, and in the mid to later tenth century obtained market, toll, and minting rights, reviewed their hagiographic legacies, initiated massive building campaigns, and stimulated pilgrimage to the burial site of patroness St Gertrudis. And for tenth- and early eleventh-century groups of canons too, recent studies have done much to adjust the common perception of these as overly secular and badly organized, and as lacking support from the clerical and lay elites.

Within the reformed landscape too, we encounter a wide range of views and practices. Certainly there was a great deal of mutual influence between individuals and networks of people inspired by the observance in prominent 'reform centres', such as Cluny, Fleury, Gorze, Sankt Maximin in Trier, and Saint-Albans. However, there is little indication of a systematic effort in these networks to work towards a common interpretation. Looking at some of the 'multi-abbots' of the tenth and early eleventh centuries, we find that they fully expected the governance and observance in their various monasteries to be different from that of their home institution. Abbot Odilo of Cluny famously expanded his influence and range of action into England, the Iberian Peninsula, and other parts of the Latin West: but in each of these regions, he was compelled to negotiate separate arrangements on governance and observance with the local ecclesiastical and lay rulers who had invited him there.

The situation was no different for other 'multi-abbots' such as William of Volpiano, also of Saint-Bénigne in Dijon and Fécamp (d. 1027 [**S** RADULPH GLABER]), Dominic of Sora (d. 1031), Richard of

'Unreformed' groups [margin]

'Reformed' diversity [margin]

External causes [margin]

Saint-Vanne (d. 1046 [**S** HUGO OF FLAVIGNY]), and Poppo of Stavelot (d. 1047) (below, Chapter 3.6). Because of the way in which new modes of observance and monastic practice were introduced in reformed communities *verbo et exemplo* ("through word and exemplary deed"), diversity only grew as time progressed. This is a phenomenon we can witness, for instance, in the archdiocese of Reims, where half a dozen Fleury-influenced reforms in the 940s to 970s failed to result in a unified regional observance, and indeed triggered the above-mentioned attempt in the early 970s to impose one (above, Chapter 3.3). In England too, we find substantial evidence of diverging liturgical practices and of the influence of continental models on the observance of certain communities post-reform. And even in Odilo's Cluniac 'multi-abbacy', authors from different institutions who worked on customaries (accounts of local customs) and hagiography expressed distinct views on life in a contemplative community.

At the same time, the diversity we can see in the primary sources was also quite deliberate, and driven by a centuries-old tradition of adapting monastic identities to local circumstances and expectations. For instance, in the Iberian Peninsula, many 'restored' or 'reformed' communities set out to acquire a broad range of texts, including works by John Cassian, Gregory the Great, Isidore, Fructuosus, and of course also the *Rule of St Benedict* itself. Based on a comparative reading of these traditions, commentators shaped localized accounts of the monastic life [**S** SALVUS]. These local accounts actually allowed for the revival in the tenth century of former institutional paradigms, including *Pactual monasticism* (above, Chapter 2.4). Another example is the female monastery of Niedermünster in the German city of Regensburg. On being turned into a house of Benedictine women in the 990s, the community acquired a handsome manuscript with a version of the *Rule of St Benedict* adapted for use by women and Cesarius of Arles's *Rule*. Investigation of the two texts reveals that the sisters cross-referenced them to shape their own, unique interpretation of cloistered life, presumably in an effort to mitigate some of its less desirable implications and to award greater freedom of action to the abbess.

We can find many examples of how this normative diversity (or 'ambiguity') and persistent culture of localized interpretations played out in real life. In some 'Benedictine' monasteries

Internal causes

Normative 'ambiguities'

of Lotharingia and Saxony the women religious owned prebends (incomes reserved for the personal use of an individual sister) with the explicit approval of the local clergy; and in England, some monks went out preaching with the approval of none other than Bishop Æthelwold of Winchester, one of the principal figures of the English Benedictine Reform.

Transcultural factors

Transcultural exchanges, forced or voluntary migration, and the resumption of trade and other long-distance communications further enriched monastic diversity. Over the course of the late tenth and early eleventh centuries, contacts with the papal court in Rome led a number of communities in the Iberian Peninsula to adopt Roman liturgical practices. Monasticism in the kingdom of Léon was a melting pot of diverse, indigenous but also Mozarabic and Carolingian influences. And in southern Italy, we encounter communities practising a 'mixed' form of Latin and Greek monasticism; for the eleventh century, we have substantial evidence of interactions between monastics and practitioners of the Jewish faith. Meanwhile, the Italian Peninsula, southern France, and Istria were teeming with wandering hermits, many of whom helped disseminate practices and ideals from one cultural context to another. One such individual was Romuald of Ravenna (d. 1027), who during his travels witnessed cenobitical traditions and devotional practices in Byzantine Ravenna, Italy, and in the Iberian Peninsula [**S** PETER DAMIAN, VITA ROMUALDI]. He in turn transmitted his experiences to the communities he visited or founded in these regions (below, Chapters 2.5–2.6).

Migration

Greek hermits and ascetic wanderers criss-crossed the Latin West, and many were temporarily or permanently hosted in monasteries and at the courts of bishops, including at Monte Cassino, Rome, Gorze, Dijon, Toul, Liège, Trier, and Reichenau. They were joined, from the 920s onwards, by a new wave of 'Irish' or 'Scottish' religious migrants [**S** VITA CADDROE]. Some were allowed to continue practising distinct rites (as was the case with some Greek priests at Toul, and with Insular migrants in the so-called *Schottenklöster* of Germany). Others received training in continental centres and were absorbed into indigenous monastic communities; others still became anchorites living in close proximity to monastic houses.

Interest in eremitism

Along with a revived interest in the life accounts of hermits from late antiquity and the early Middle Ages, in the Latin West these men and possibly also women inspired a notable reappreciation, in literature and in real life, of eremitism and ascetic peregrination [**S** GRIMLAICUS]. Perhaps more so than their personal achievements, their mere presence in local settings stimulated awareness of the historical and transcultural diversity of monastic experiences.

3.5 The Conversion of the World

A notable feature of monastic discourse around the year 1000 is the frequent reference to lay conversion. Already at the beginning of the tenth century, Abbot Odo of Cluny (above, Chapter 3.3) had announced this new development by presenting to his readership an unusual exemplar of lay ascetic virtue. In his *Life* of Gerald of Aurillac (d. c. 909), he described a man who had taken to sexual abstention and other forms of self-abnegation, emotional restraint, and strenuous devotion, all without abandoning his divinely ordained role as a lay lord. Perhaps in response to feelings of unease over this impractical vision of lay sainthood, in his later work Odo emphasized the need for a strict divide between secular and monastic moralities. But at the same time, he continued to believe that individual members of the laity, and human society in general, would benefit from adopting at least some of monasticism's core values. During Odo's frequent forays into the world, so his biographers tell us, he took to teaching his lay audiences "through word and example" that observance of certain principles of conduct – particularly charity, peace, and humility – would make them better Christians.

Via the testimonies of hagiographers and other commentators, we know that he was not the only one to use the secular world as a stage for the representation and dissemination of ideals of Christian virtue. Beginning in the 930s, we hear about monastics in West Francia and Lotharingia who assisted lay and clerical rulers to pacify local societies and encourage lay acts of redemption, and deliberately organized their public appearances in order to demonstrate acts of Christian virtue. Over the course of the tenth and early eleventh centuries, many abbots – and quite possibly also some abbesses – followed in their footsteps. Supporters and subsequent biographers celebrated them as, in the German sociologist Max Weber's phrase, "active extraworldly ascetics", individuals of exceptional ability who did not need the protective walls and rigid

Odo's Life of Gerald

Promoting monastic morals

Abbatial charisma

hierarchies of the cloister to retain their moral integrity. But their detractors accused them of standing (as one of William of Volpiano's critics claimed) "above the *Rule*", and of allowing lay and clerical rulers to use them as the respectable figureheads of politically motivated interventions in the governance and inner experience of monastic communities. Some clerics also viewed these leaders and their associates as overstepping the boundaries of their assigned role in the Church. During his career as abbot of Saint-Riquier, the former cleric Gerwin (d. 1075) faced severe criticism for preaching to the laity and offering sinners reconciliation, and eventually had to appeal to the pope to validate his efforts.

Pastoral traditions
Such personal criticism was hardly justified. On entering the monastic life, Gerwin and other future leaders had encountered a flourishing tradition of preaching via word and deed to the laity. Among the most remarkable testimonies to survive are those that concern cloistered women who instructed young girls and adult women on how to lead a virtuous life, and urban anchoresses who provided spiritual counsel to whoever came to visit them. Meanwhile, there had emerged a strand of hagiographic and biographical literature designed to entice members of the laity to practice certain forms of devotion and ascetic self-abnegation while insisting that they would be able to continue functioning in their roles as rulers, warriors, or spouses. In the late tenth-century *Life* of Mathilda (d. 968), the wife of German King Henry the Fowler, an author working at the female monastery of Nordhausen in Saxony joined a standard vision of Ottonian queenship and matrimonial unity to an ideal of discreet asceticism drawn from late antique and early medieval literary exemplars. Substantial evidence survives that a similar message was communicated to men and women from lower strata of the laity too, and the trend would only become more prominent following the turn of the first millennium.

Literary strands

Focus on personal piety
Roughly around the time the hagiographer at Nordhausen was broadcasting her or his message, attempts to make those living in the secular world more spiritually responsible for their actions were enhanced by the addition of a Eucharistic message focussing on Christ's sacrifice. Growing attention in the run up to the millennial anniversaries of His birth and death and an increased focus in monastic spirituality on His suffering – the most emotive expressions of which are found in the writings of John of Fécamp (d. 1079) [**S** JOHN OF FÉCAMP] – galvanized this propaganda. From the

immense range of artistic, literary, and other testimonies emerges a range of objectives by monastic agents. One was to deepen the religious experience of the laity, by inviting them to take a more active part in expressions of faith and devotion and to become more invested in securing their soul's fate in the afterlife. Beginning in the later tenth century, cenobitical institutions across the Latin West acquired and founded parish churches and decorated them so as to reference Christ's sacrifice and the need for each individual to pursue their own salvation. They also invited the laity to take a more active part in devotional practice: by teaching them new prayers and urging them to attend Mass; by encouraging various acts of piety such as pilgrimages and lay processions around towns and villages; and by promoting certain saints as a focus of local urban and rural identities, or as exemplars of virtue for men or women in different walks in life. Numerous anecdotes survive of prominent abbots preaching awareness of Christ's suffering and the need for the individual to honour His sacrifice through their own conduct, particularly through acts of penance. In doing so, these preachers instilled equal measures of hope and fear within their lay audiences.

Focus on accountability

A second objective pursued by monastic agents, which becomes prominent from the beginning of the eleventh century, was to promote acts of conversion. Building on a discourse of lay encroachment that went back to the latter half of the ninth century (above, Chapter 3.2), monastics who quarrelled with their lay neighbours over properties and rights frequently criminalized their adversaries, and called on them to repent for their 'sins' [S MONASTIC MALEDICTIONS, S BERNARD OF ANGERS]. In exchange for a confession of guilt and a (complete or partial) reparation of goods or a negotiated settlement, they promised to these people a rosier outlook on their fate in the afterlife, inclusion in intercessory prayers, and the creation of an *amicitia*, or a privileged association with the monastery based on reciprocal gift-giving. Some such conflicts concerned very small matters and involved laypeople of very minor stature: but the same approach was taken for much weightier issues and with members of the higher elites too. In a 1012/1013 letter "to all the sons of the Church", the abovementioned Richard of Saint-Vanne offered one of the most unsettling accounts of the afterlife to survive from the medieval period. Among other things, it predicted a miserable post-mortem fate for the count of Flanders, for refusing

Conversion as reparation

Gift-giving relations

(on the grounds that Richard's patrons were his political enemies) to let Richard intervene in several monasteries within his territory [S RICHARD OF SAINT-VANNE]. And just over a decade earlier, Romuald of Ravenna had shocked his contemporaries by convincing Emperor Otto III that performing penance would not harm his authority as a sovereign ruler.

Promotion of donations

But reconciliation between monastics and their former lay enemies was not the only type of lay conversion promoted at the time, and not the only way in which new *amicitiae* were forged. Promoting pious donations as an instrument of redemption, abbots and their subjects transferred considerable wealth out of the hands of secular owners and into their own institutions in return for intercessory prayers, burial on or near their sites, commemoration of deceased donors and their relatives, and (particularly in societies that were facing a political or economic crisis) in a number of cases also legal and material support. Several driving factors could be cited for this development, but two appear as the most significant. One is the decline (at a different pace and to varying degrees depending on the region) of royal patronage in exchange for intercessory prayers for ruler and society. And another is the strategy by monastics and their regular leadership to link their fortunes not to a single major patron and his relatives or associates, but to as many laypeople as possible, offering these individuals a minor, non-controlling stake in a monastery's spiritual capital. Because of this quasi-economic logic of (material) gift and (spiritual) counter-gift, it is no wonder that many communities in this period began keeping detailed records of their expanding roster of benefactors and associates [S CARTULAIRE-CHRONIQUE].

Adult Conversion

Total conversion, that is the act of entering the monastic life, was also favoured by prominent abbots of the tenth and early eleventh centuries. In a development that is often overlooked in discussions of the later eleventh century and beyond, these leaders actively pursued a situation where a sizeable number of their monastic subjects were people who had made a conscious decision to enter conventual life. Contemporary sources indicate a steady increase, beginning around the turn of the millennium, of conversions in old age or *ad succurrendum*, that is by lay individuals on the brink of death. But there are indications that monastic leaders admitted growing numbers of other converts too, and that in some places former oblates (monastics whom their parents had offered to a community as children) no longer constituted the majority of monks and women religious. Just as significantly, some abbots are known to have deliberately recruited adolescents and adults with a background in the clergy or the ruling lay elites to join an elite circle of administrators and intellectuals around them.

In a development that reminds us of the propaganda aimed at members of the old senatorial elite in fourth-century Gaul (above, Chapter 2.3), we may suspect that some of these clerics and noblemen were drawn to conversion not just by the redemptive promise of life as a monastic, but also by the prospect of trading their clerical or worldly position of responsibility – often an insecure one in times of political turmoil – for a more stable monastic equivalent. The former experiences and connections of these adult recruits surely made at least some particularly suited to lead recently reformed communities (many of which consisted at least in part of former canons and other clerics, members of the lower nobility, and a host of individuals who had converted in adulthood), and possibly also better prepared than ex-oblates to engage with secular audiences.

Career prospects

As a result of these transformations and this self-styling as privileged sites of interaction with the divine, monasteries transformed, literally and metaphorically, into refuges where laypeople could find solace and the strength to pursue redemption, be it through permanent conversion, giving property to the monks in exchange for their intercessory prayers, or merely listening to the abbot, one of his monks, or a local priest sermonizing. This intertwining of monastic and lay spiritualties had clear advantages for the self-perception of communities as providing a crucial service to each individual Christian. Through it, they wove increasingly complex webs of mutuality and interdependence with secular society, and saw monastic values gain increasing prominence in accounts of public morality. But this interweaving also brought with it criticism, which soon elicited a strong response (below, Chapter 3.7).

Focus of local societies

3.6 Cluniac and Other Nebulas

In the century covered by the long abbacies of Odilo (994–1049) and Hugo (1049–1109), the Burgundian abbey of Cluny mutated from a 'reform centre' into a 'congregational' or '(con)federational' one. This process entailed a shift in abbatial focus from disseminating

The ecclesia Cluniacensis

local practices to other communities (and in some cases also adding these to a personal 'multi-abbacy'), to instead integrating these other communities into a system of houses that were affiliated to the main institution of Cluny. Four years after coming to power, Odilo received two charters by King Rudolph III of Burgundy and one by Pope Gregory V (the first document to use the expression *ecclesia Cluniacensis*, literally "church of Cluny"). These privileges recognized Cluny's endowment as a form of ecclesiastical lordship, and enabled the abbot to exercise a form of justice similar to his seigniorial peers. The privilege issued by Gregory, besides listing all of the abbey's properties, additionally established Cluny as completely liberated, legally and spiritually, from the oversight of the local *ordinarius*, the bishop of Mâcon. Obtaining these documents certainly qualified as a major achievement on Odilo's part. With his main institution now freed from episcopal control and with his position as lord of its estate now formally recognized, over the course of his abbatial career he was able to add twenty-three new institutions to his multi-abbacy.

Expansion of the multi-abbacy

Meanwhile, Cluny's status continued to change. In 1024, Pope John XIX issued a privilege stating that, henceforth, the abbey's exemptions – liberty from local juridical power – applied to all Cluniac monks regardless of their station and their previous membership of non-Cluniac institutions. It is this document, so some specialists have argued, that marks the birth of the idea of the *ecclesia Cluniacensis* as a (con)federation of institutions under Cluny's leadership. Post-1024 documents show how Cluniac commentators actively nurtured feelings of unity across institutional boundaries, and sought to address the problem of the confederation being still essentially held together by a single individual – the abbot – and his private lordship, with no guarantees that it would be passed on to his successor. In his early 1030s *Life of St Maiolus*, for instance, Odilo attributed the special status of the *ecclesia Cluniacensis* to the fact that the Cluniac abbots were part of a charismatic genealogy of monastic leaders, and also to Cluniac monasticism's status as a new stage (*ordo*) in the development of the Christian faith. In doing so, he placed his main institution's form of cenobitical life above all others and situated it at the end of a legitimizing genealogy of monastic experiments. But more importantly perhaps, he also established the idea of Cluny's foundation as the starting point of a major reform of monastic life in the Latin West.

Various commentaries from Odilo's tenure further explored his arguments about the existence of a Cluniac 'brand' of monasticism and a corresponding (con)federation of affiliated institutions. A contemporary miracle collection refers to the institutions involved in Odilo's multi-abbacy as an "army" (*collegium*), while charters from various monasteries under his rule indicate that he was no longer regarded as the abbot of multiple separate institutions, but simply of Cluny. Odilo himself also took further steps to consolidate these notions by commissioning the first of a series of cartularies, each of which built an argument in support of the notion that the spiritual and institutional unity of Cluniac monasticism was historically grounded. Measures were also taken for all associated communities in the *ecclesia Cluniacensis* – certainly for those legally connected to Odilo himself – to project a shared corporate identity to the outside world. Across the (con)federation, monks were instructed to present themselves as providing a highly efficient, 'professional' service in commemorating the dead and in offering intercessory prayers, to the point that the liturgical cycles of Cluniac monasticism became almost as intensive and time-consuming as the *laus perennis* of some late antique and early medieval communities [**S** DEATH RITUAL]. To underscore this intercessory identity, in 1030 Odilo created the Feast of All Souls, while lay patrons were targeted with a seductive rhetoric encouraging redemptive donations. The returns, in terms of prestige and property, were significant.

'Corporate branding'

As the (con)federation was rapidly expanding, around Cluny there also emerged a network of lands, churches, castles, and mills. These institutions, which ended up being inserted into a complex network of obediences and deaneries, anchored Cluny's power locally, and simultaneously functioned as agricultural centres, retreats for the monastics, and also destinations for pilgrims. From the middle decades of the eleventh century onwards, various literary, iconographic, and architectural projects (the most famous example of which was Cluny III, the new and massive abbatial church that was designed to accommodate a community of approximately three hundred monks) additionally sought to define the Burgundian abbey and its associated institutions as sanctified spaces and sites of privileged access to the divine. Always out to see these ideals translated into legal terms, in 1080 and 1098 Odilo's successor Hugo additionally obtained papal privileges that created the abbey's 'sacred ban', the first of a series of concentric circles

Transformation of Cluniac space

Cluny's 'ban'

of security and immunity around the monastery. An 1107 privilege added another: the freedom from tolls and castles, which thus enabled pilgrims, traders, and other travellers to gain unhindered access to Cluny. Elements of these policies, with minor or more substantial differences depending on the context, were repeated in other parts of the (con)federation too (below, Chapter 4.1).

Superficial inspection of the evidence suggests a striking contrast between (on the one hand) the coherence, spiritually and institutionally, of Cluny's eleventh-century (con)federation and (on the other) the local paradigms in which the rest of the monastic world continued to operate. However, a closer look at the primary sources, particularly those that originated at affiliated houses outside of Cluny's own region of Burgundy, indicates that the *ecclesia Cluniacensis* was very diverse and to an extent also very disorganized. Many newly established or newly incorporated institutions in this period entertained relations with lay and clerical rulers that differed significantly from Cluny's own situation. Particularly in England and the Iberian Peninsula, expansion was possible only because of Odilo and Hugo's preparedness to accommodate the preferences and interests of these rulers. But elsewhere too, these abbots were always thinking of how the creation of Cluniac houses might be presented as an attractive prospect to potential aristocratic founders, and they adapted their approach accordingly. Because of the variety in the legal, economic, and social situations of Cluniac houses, contemporaries for a long time continued to perceive the *ecclesia Cluniacensis* as what one scholar described as a "nebula", a disorganized, formless entity of communities centred on Cluny's abbot, rather than as an actual, legally consolidated federation of institutions. As late as the reign of Pope Gregory VII (d. 1079), papal privileges still addressed the free status of Cluny as a form of ecclesiastical lordship, making no distinction between affiliated institutions and other properties, including chapels, estates, and other immobile goods.

Variety also applied to the internal organization of monasteries. Throughout the late tenth, eleventh, and even into the early twelfth century, the Cluniacs continued to transmit their views and practices primarily through word and deed. This approach, which relied on the charisma of the abbot and the various abilities of his proxies to spread the Cluniac interpretation of monastic community life, by definition left much room for local adaptation and for

Other multi-abbacies

Cluny's 'nebula'

Diversity in the ecclesia

change over time. Although a growing body of written commentaries argued the shared ideological origins and spiritual identity of Cluniac communities, no significant effort was made to create written manuals prescribing to other communities the typically Cluniac approach to governance, liturgy, and daily life. The mere sixteen abbatial statutes that survive from Odilo and Hugo's combined tenure all concern specific liturgical matters, and like various rules and other commentaries of late antiquity and the early Middle Ages strike us as ad hoc responses to specific problems, rather than deliberate acts of monastic legislation.

Even Cluny's famous customaries, such as the 1030s *Liber tramitis* and the two customaries by Ulrich and Bernard (both from the 1080s) functioned as part-commentaries on the ideal monastic observance and part-records of actual practices. Ulrich's customary was written specifically for inspiration by Abbot William of the Black Forest monastery of Hirsau [S ULRICH]; that by Bernard, the far more successful of the two, was originally destined for use by the novices at Cluny. Neither of these documents was intended as a normative instrument of governance; nor did they provide an accurate insight into how life at Cluny was organized. Rather, they must both be viewed, much like late antique and early medieval rules, as topical commentaries in an ongoing discussion on how to realize the monastic life.

Contemporaries definitely took notice of Cluny's meteoric rise. Prominent abbots of the late tenth and eleventh centuries, such as the above-mentioned Ugo of Farfa, William of Volpiano, Richard of Saint-Vanne, and Poppo of Stavelot, forged personal and in some cases also institutional links with the Burgundian abbey and its affiliated houses. And even though they were in no position to pursue a similar legal autonomy, in their approach we can see parallels with Cluniac governance practices, such as a growing emphasis on redemptive donations, the active promotion of monastic values to lay audiences [S ODO], and a more systematic approach to commemorating deceased patrons (above, Chapter 3.5). Already since the eighth century, monasteries had relied on *libri vitae*, manuscripts in which the names of community members and important associates of their own and affiliated institutions were recorded, as tools of community-building across institutional boundaries. These evolved from the tenth-century onwards into necrologies, which were more directly focused on liturgical commemoration and listed

Customaries

Parallel trends

the names of individuals by the day and month of their death. Like the abbots at Cluny, several of these prominent leaders also sought to make monastic clothing and diet distinct from that of the laity, and limited the involvement of lay aristocrats in monastic governance. The results were far from identical to those achieved at Cluny: but from a local perspective at least, they set lordship relations and abbatial governance on a new footing.

Multi-abbacies and 'nebulas' Cluniac monasticism's rise also inspired later multi-abbots and multi-abbesses in other places to try to establish their own 'nebulas'. Over the course of the later tenth and early eleventh centuries, multi-abbatial leaders in northern Spain (various institutions implicated in the *Repoblación*), southern France (for instance Saint-Victor in Marseille and Gellone), other regions of France and Lotharingia (Fleury [**S** ANDREAS OF FLEURY], Saint-Bénigne in Dijon, Gorze, Saint-Vanne, and Sankt Maximin in Trier), England (Glastonbury and Abingdon), and the Empire (Stavelot, the female houses of Quedlinburg, Essen, and Gandersheim [**S** HROTSVIT]) took a number of steps in this direction. They acquired dependencies such as priories, cells, and chapels; visited other monasteries to instruct the members on the customs of their home institution; and they sent out their disciples and associates to take up leadership roles elsewhere.

Institutional networks Thanks to this fostering of 'communities of practice', the conditions were created for a situation where transfers of monastics from one institution to another became a routine part of governance. Such transfers were key to bringing specific expertise from one community to another, a process that led to a certain degree of integration in governance, liturgical practice, and daily routine. In some places, the ties that made these exchanges possible were consolidated in a formal confraternity agreement (*fraternitas* or *confraternitas*). At the time of their emergence in the eighth and ninth centuries, such agreements had merely implied that two or more communities exchanged the names of each other's members (and sometimes also lay patrons and associates) and promised to include them in their commemorative and intercessory prayers. But over time, those actions were additioned with a range of measures to make it possible for participating institutions to host each other's members, provide support in the administration of these places, and so on.

Enduring local factors The increasingly formalized nature of institutional collaborations did not, however, conceal the fact that most monasteries remained essentially in the hands of non-monastic lords. Furthermore, the death or removal of a secular lord or 'multi-abbot' often cut preferential links between two institutions, as did warfare, shifts in the distribution of territorial power, and any other circumstances beyond the control of monastic agents. And in spite of trends toward greater integration, regular leaders and their associates tended to be protective of local traditions and practices. For the time being, the single monastery remained firmly in place as the key paradigm of monastic organization.

3.7 The 'Quest for the Primitive'

At the turn of the first millennium, people from all walks of life relied on monasteries as reference points for organizing their lives. Although traditional discussions tend to focus on those spaces that were inhabited by cloistered men or women, typically monastic sites included a wide range of buildings that encompassed many different purposes: workshops and barns; a guesthouse and sometimes also a hospital or poorhouse; dwellings for use by lay or clerical lords and others housing local clerics; multiple churches for use by the monastics, the local clerics, and parish members; fortified walls and towers; mills, brew houses and fish ponds. All of these contributed to religious and cultural expression, modes of production and trade, political relations, and experiences of secular and sacred space that stretched far beyond the cloister walls.

Multifunctionality of monastic sites

The same can be said about subsidiary institutions, such as rural priories, churches and chapels, and hospitals: even the routes that connected these places to the motherhouse shaped the lives of those who travelled them. In some regions, a process known as *inecclesiamento* – sacralization of the area around certain monasteries and their dependencies (above, Chapter 3.6) – turned entire sections of the urban or rural landscape into places that contemporaries associated with the presence of monasticism in society. Meanwhile, a phenomenon in France, Italy, and other parts of the Latin West that is known to scholars as *incastellamento* – the emergence of concentrated rural settlements, either as fortified villages or near fortified sites – resulted in an explosive growth of the number of (mostly small) religious communities in or near these sites. These included independent monasteries; monastic dependencies such as cells or priories; and also many communities of canons, because these typically combined commemorative and intercessory services with pastoral care directed at the local population. Economic growth, demographic expansion, and urban development further enhanced the need and opportunities for the mutual integration of secular and monastic spaces.

Presence of the laity   The draw of monastic institutions for the lay population was significant. Clerical and lay lords paid regular visits, including to those parts that were usually reserved for cloistered monastics. Along with them they brought their retinue of servants and aides, and left behind numerous markers of their patronage. They arranged for family members to be buried there and also for relatives to become monastics; in some cases they even built a residence on the premises. In order to sustain these complex institutions and the various social and religious roles they fulfilled, scores of lay servants and artisans were also needed. Many lived on or in close proximity to these sites, and many others visited periodically to pay rents, carry out seasonal tasks, or undertake jobs that required a specific skill. New individuals were also drawn to these places because of the favourable legal or fiscal status that resulted from donating oneself and one's descendants to a monastic community. We also know of people who took such a step in order to find protection in times of warfare or invasion, or to avoid starvation following a bad harvest, epidemic, or natural disaster. The rest of the lay presence was made up by visiting relatives of monastics; aspiring converts who came to discuss their intentions; and lay donors who came to ritually seal a gift transaction. Others visited to bury a deceased relative in the local cemetery, and the faithful went regularly to the parish church to attend Mass or receive the other sacraments. Merchants attended the market held on the patron's feast day; pilgrims visited the graves of saints. Through all of this ran the to and fro of messengers sent by lay and clerical rulers.

Involvement with local societies   These and other functions required that the monastics living in these places – clerics, but also cloistered monastics – maintain a high level of interaction with their secular environment. Abbots and abbesses frequently ventured outside of the cloister walls to conduct business, preach, or carry out diplomatic missions. On these journeys one or several of their community always accompanied them. And individual monastics and small groups were frequently sent out to other sites – to monasteries, priories and other dependencies, secular courts, agricultural centres, and emerging urban hubs – for a wide range of reasons.

Inevitably, questions were raised over the maintenance of physical and virtual boundaries with the secular world. Some also voiced their unease over the wide array of secular interests in which these institutions were implicated, and the various obstacles some monastics reportedly encountered in their pursuit of personal ideals of ascetic withdrawal. Numerous accounts survive of individuals who struggled to reconcile their personal expectations of monastic life with the demands and circumstances of an existence inside cloistered communities. One example is that of former nobleman Romuald of Ravenna (also above, Chapter 3.5), who on joining the community of monks at San'Apollinare in Classe in Rome sometime in the late tenth century was disappointed at the prayer-focused, spiritually undemanding Cluniac discipline. With the approval of his abbot, Romuald left the monastery to become a hermit in Venice. A German woman religious named Adelheidis provides another example. Formerly of the monastery of Gandersheim, in the 1070s she became a recluse near Huyseburg, in the German diocese of Halberstadt. In the words of a local chronicler, her reason for this radical change was that she "deplored vehemently the fact that the fervour of divine love had become tepid and that the study of holy religion had fallen into ruins". *Criticism*

But besides these concerns and criticisms, there were many other factors too that drove people to other forms of monastic life: decades of monastic propaganda in favour of penance and notions of personal accountability (above, Chapter 3.5); a growing focus on Christ's suffering in contemporary spirituality and a likewise growing admiration for wandering preachers; rising population numbers; changing socio-economic conditions, including in some places urbanization; shifting family structures and inheritance customs; a decline in some parts of the royal and aristocratic patronage of monastic houses; growing pressure by the higher clergy on such institutions to subject to their oversight and juridical authority; increased trade and mobility, and the resulting cultural contacts between different parts of the Latin West and regions beyond; and finally also a growing fascination with the literary legacies of early Christianity and the Desert Fathers. *Contextual factors*

Testimonies from the eleventh century indicate a steep rise in the numbers of monastics living outside of institutional settings, *Eremitical and apostolic trends* whether wandering hermits and preachers, or anchorites and anchoresses living in urban contexts. For the first time in centuries new commentaries on eremitical life were published, the most notable of which is Goscelin of Saint-Bertin's *Consolation for the Anchoress Eva* [**S** GOSCELIN]. At the same time, numerous monastic and clerical authors celebrated the lives of male and female hermits and anchorites in biographies, hagiographies, chronicles, letters, and poems. But in institutional settings too, the quest for a more 'primitive' ideal brought to prominence several strands in the ideology and practice of monastic life, such as eremitism, apostolic agency, and the quest for an 'authentic' experience of the *Rule of St Benedict*. The above-mentioned Romuald, after spending some time as a hermit in Venice, eventually moved to Catalonia. Here he became involved with the abbey of San Miguel de Cuxa, establishing a hermitage nearby. At San Miguel he encountered and absorbed a spiritual and intellectual tradition founded on a mixture of Benedictine and Visigothic inspirations, and combined it with meditative techniques drawn from Byzantine asceticism, which he may have acquired during his time in Venice. On his return to Italy, he became a wandering preacher, gaining admiration for his zeal in promoting lay acts of repentance and for founding communities that maintained looser links with local rulers than was the case in other places. Following an ill-fated tenure as abbot at San'Apollinare in Classe – the local monks rebelled against his severe regime – in 1012 he was gifted land in Camaldoli, in the diocese of Arezzo. Here, he founded a community of five hermits, each living in his own cell, high in the hills. It soon entered into a joint living arrangement with a contemplative settlement at Fontebuono, which subsequently served as a training ground for future hermits. Combining multiple typologies of eremitical and cenobitical life, and marrying ascetic traditions from different cultural contexts, spiritual practice at Camaldoli was marked by its focus on the individual's quest for redemption and spiritual perfection.

Romuald and Camaldoli

Peter Damian (d. 1072/1073), Romuald's biographer, deliberately situated his efforts in the context of the then-emerging Church reform. Like his hero, Peter played an active role in public life, but focused his energies on campaigning against married clerics and simoniacs. His savage attacks against dissolute clerics earned him a prominent voice in early reform circles at and around the papal court [**S** PETER DAMIAN, LIBER GOMORRHIANUS], and after his

Peter Damian and John Gualberto

appointment in 1057 as cardinal-bishop of Ostia he demonstratively continued to practise an austere, contemplative life. In the intervening period, he had founded a double community of monastics and hermits at Fonte Avellana, members of which were encouraged to emulate their founder's austerity and penchant for self-punishment [S PETER DAMIAN, LETTER]; later on, he acquired several other institutions, ruling over them as a multi-abbot. Like another of his biographical subjects, Abbot Odilo of Cluny, he also spread his views on monastic practice to other communities, creating in the process a small Avellanite 'nebula'. While Peter's monastic policies merely aimed to promote ideals of austerity and self-abnegation to what were in essence conventional groups of contemplative monastics, former Camaldolese monk John Gualberto (d. 1073) sought to create an institutional environment where ideals of solitude and private devotion could be realized for an entire cloistered community. In his foundation of Vallombrosa, a community of contemplative monks was kept entirely separate from the outside world and from any secular duties. For that purpose, he supplemented them with lay brothers, who did not participate in the choir service but carried out all the community's administrative and menial tasks.

Austerity, private devotion, seclusion from worldly influences, and a tendency to absorb these ideals in a model of community life that remained recognizably 'Benedictine' in inspiration, characterized a number of contemporary foundations in France. Stephen of Muret (d. 1124), a nobleman from Auvergne, during a penitential pilgrimage had encountered many eremitical practitioners in southern Italy. On his return to France in the late 1070s, he established a hermitage in the Limousin region, rejecting the customary estate formation and management procedures of 'traditional' communities. Following his death, the hermitage was turned into the more conventional, semi-eremitical settlement of Grandmont, where members were subjected to a regime marked by austerity and strict seclusion: here too, all administrative tasks and manual duties were delegated to lay brothers. But in contrast to Vallombrosa, the strict division of tasks in the Grandmont community did not translate into a segregation of choir monks and lay brothers. All these people shared the same communal rooms, were all part of the same chapter, and were led by one and the same prior.

There were many other initiatives, each of which spoke in its own way to realizing a more 'authentic' ideal of monastic

Proliferation in France

Variations

community life. These included the achievements of Abbot Robert of Molesme (d. 1111), who along with a handful of monks left his home institution and founded a new settlement in Cîteaux near Dijon (1098); Bernard of Tiron (d. 1117) [**S** GEOFFREY GROSSUS] in the Poitiers region; Vitalis of Savigny (d. 1122) on the border of Normandy and Maine; and Stephen of Vielzot (d. 1154), who c. 1130 established the abbey of Obazine, a settlement for strictly separated groups of men and women, in Limousin. Likewise, a little earlier, in 1084, Bruno of Cologne (d. 1101) had created an alpine hermitage, which later became the valley monastery of La Grande Chartreuse [**S** GUIGO].

Women's
communities Women's monasticism was implicated in these developments too. In the early 1050s, Abbot Hugo of Cluny established, via the foundation of Marcigny, the first female branch of his movement. Here, enclosure was strictly enforced in order to create what has been described as a "communal experience of the life of a recluse" (*kollektives Reklusentum*) [**S** LE CARTULAIRE DE MARCIGNY]. In the next half century, four female priories were added to the *ecclesia Cluniacensis*, and in many other places Marcigny was subsequently used as a case study for how to (re)organize female communities. Meanwhile, in western France wandering preacher Robert of Arbrissel (d. 1116) gained such a large female following that he was able to found a monastery for contemplative women religious at Fontevraud. Established shortly before 1100, the community was soon expanded with a subordinated, strictly segregated group of monks, clerics, and lay brothers, whose main purpose was to serve the women in their liturgical and administrative needs [**S** BAUDRI]. Earlier we already saw how Stephen of Vielzot established the abbey of Obazine: this had originally grown from a small settlement of male hermits, around which a community of women had formed under the direction of Stephen's mother. Although the two groups lived separately, fulfilled different roles (the men worked on the land while the women performed various domestic tasks) and saw each other only for religious services, Stephen in 1142 created two cloistered communities where interactions were kept to a minimum and were strictly regulated [**S** VITA STEPHANI]. And over in England, parish priest Gilbert of Sempringham (d. 1190) in the 1130s founded a community comprising a group of cloistered women supplemented with another group of canons, each of which had its own written rule. To this double community were added separate cohorts of lay sisters and lay brothers: the model subsequently spread to other parts of England, and was echoed in similar initiatives in Thuringia and the Rhineland.

The above experiments in community life seem unconventional, revolutionary even on first inspection: scholars coined the term 'New Monasticism' to suggest that they were all part of a fundamental, paradigm-shifting effort to revitalize monastic life. But that impression is only sustained if we refuse to peer past the deliberate efforts by later biographers and other commentators in these places to present the 'Old Monasticism' – monastic community life as it was practised and experienced in the ninth to early eleventh centuries – as monolithic and thoroughly secularized, a stagnant movement against which these individuals and their supporters of the New Monasticism had supposedly reacted. For instance, at the abbey of Le Bec in Normandy, generation after generation of chroniclers and biographers praised their founder, the former knight Herluin (d. 1078), for declining to copy monastic practices from elsewhere, fostering instead a home-grown observance, based on local study of the *Rule of St Benedict*, a few office books, and his own teaching through word and deed. But as we now know, neither were other communities at the time slavishly copying their observance from major centres like Cluny, Gorze, or anywhere else. What is more, the organization of monastic life as it is described in the earliest customary of Le Bec scarcely strikes us as particularly unconventional. This is probably a consequence of the fact that the chronically absent Herluin, who spent a great deal of his time tending to his foundation's material interests, left much of the training of his monks to his more conventional prior, the Italian Lanfranc [**S** LANFRANC].

In their role as monastic administrators, several abbots of the New Monasticism also adopted modes of conduct that strikingly remind us of those of contemporary abbots in the 'old' monasticism. For instance, Peter Damian may have been a major proponent of ecclesiastical reform and an eremitical and ascetic thinker of the first order, but at Fonte Avellana he pursued an abbatial policy that was nothing much out of the ordinary. And in his dealings with other communities, he distinguished between the institutions that fell directly under his control and those where his role was strictly that of a spiritual instructor – just like many abbots before him had done. Although it is beyond question that he and others cited in

Nuancing the 'New Monasticism'

'Ordinary' forms and experiences

Familiar approaches

this chapter were charismatic individuals, with a keen awareness of current needs and expectations in religious life, their revolutionary impact on monasticism in the eleventh and early twelfth centuries is largely a fiction of later commentators. Eremitical, apostolic, and 'traditionalist' trends are noticeable in many older foundations too, provided one is willing to look for subtle shifts in the members' experience and spirituality over the course of the later tenth to early twelfth centuries.

'Emergence' of canons regular

The eleventh century also marked the rise to prominence, perhaps more so in the perception of contemporaries and later commentators than in reality, of groups of clerics as a major ecclesiastical cohort. For several decades, lay and clerical rulers in various parts of the West had been switching from founding Benedictine houses to creating houses of canons, presumably because this was a convenient and cost-effective option for combining patronage of religious community life with the provision of pastoral care within their territories. But soon, criticism arose against the various arrangements for life in these institutions. The most notable among these attacks is contained in a speech at the Lateran council of 1059 by Hildebrand, the future Pope Gregory VII, in which he infamously denounced the ninth-century *Institutio canonicorum* as a corrupt interpretation of the Church Fathers' vision for the community life of ascetic clerics, promulgated against ecclesiastical custom by the lay ruler Louis the Pious [**S** HILDEBRAND]. Soon afterwards, the papacy began supporting various institutional initiatives to establish what it framed as a more 'authentic' and legitimate observance.

Long-standing diversity

Contrary to what scholars previously believed, the *Rule of St Augustine* did not instantly become the standard observance in these institutions of clerics: nor did principles such as common property and a strict devotion to the shared experience of community life. C. 1100, there was still a great deal of variation between different institutions, among other things in how the canons were organized, what practices they observed, and whether they focused on pastoral tasks, eremitical withdrawal, or were more occupied with ecclesiastical governance. Far beyond the turn of the eleventh century, locality, patronage, and other variables continued to have a major impact on these internal matters. Still, the success of the revised life for canons regular – as they were now known – was unmistakeable. In the second quarter of the twelfth century, houses inspired by the customs of Saint-Ruf (near Avignon) had become established throughout France (with the abbey of Saint-Victor in Paris functioning as a major centre of intellectual and spiritual life), Italy, England, the Iberian Peninsula (including Spain and Portugal), the Empire, and Scandinavia. Meanwhile, a cleric named Norbert of Xanten (d. 1134) had established a house of canons regular at Prémontré (1120). Having adopted the *Rule of St Augustine* as its handbook, the community was designed to provide to active clerics a place to withdraw for ascetic and contemplative purposes, so as to guarantee that their service was grounded in a true monastic experience and their involvement in the world would not likely compromise their purity. Prémontré would soon grow to become the centre of a multi-abbacy and (following Norbert's departure) congregational structure (below, Chapter 4.1). Prémontré

Beginning in the later decades of the eleventh century, many newly established and reformed houses of canons received papal privileges and exemptions that were drafted with an eye to including these foundations in an international network of centres from which the papacy's ecclesiological views – particularly the call for reform and emancipation from lay investiture – could be disseminated. One notable example is the Flemish abbey of Watten, where in 1077 the canons received a papal privilege that referred to their institution as a "place of refuge" (*refugium*), an expression that referenced the pope's intention of turning religious institutions into places of moral and legal exception, free from secular interference. More so than monks, canons were ideally placed to preach principles of ecclesiastical and religious reform to lay audiences: on that basis, some began to argue that cloistered monastics had no business venturing into the world. An anonymous treatise from the late eleventh century, titled *On the difference of the life of canons and monks*, makes a clear distinction between the two groups. Monks, according to the author, had nothing to look after but their own salvation, whereas canons, whose concerns extended to the salvation of all of humanity, were expected to lead simultaneously active and contemplative lives. Involvement in Church Reform

But in real life, even the papacy was not very strict about drawing binding behavioural and functional boundaries between monastic cohorts. In a 1092 privilege for Saint-Ruf, Pope Urban II stated that the canons were expected to live in a state of eternal merit and individual poverty, a monk-like ideal he would repeat in his privileges for other houses too. And conversely, an impressive 'Conservative' vs. 'Progressive' number of 'old-style' contemplative monasteries across the Latin West (for example Cluny, Hirsau, Saint-Victor in Marseilles, San Salvatore of Fucecchio, Sahagún in León, Bury St Edmunds, Christ Church in Canterbury, and Saint-Etienne of Caen) received exemption privileges that strikingly resemble those issued to houses of canons regular. No informed reader would have missed the implication in these documents that contemplative monastics, too, were expected to proselytize in support of the papacy's reform ideals (also below, Chapter 4.1).

Military movements

Meanwhile, a number of founders and emerging movements had responded to then-current trends in views on Christian warfare and knightly piety, and became implicated in expanding Christian territories [**S** HYSTORIA]. Adelelm, the founder of the abbey of La Chaise-Dieu in c. 1080, participated as a military leader in the Spanish *Reconquista*. His involvement in warfare set a precedent to the emergence of the military orders in the twelfth century. Several of these movements originated with a distinctive caritative focus. Established over the course of the early to mid-twelfth century, the Hospitallers and Lazarenes originally provided aid to pilgrims, wounded soldiers, and other Christians (the former as a hospital, the latter as a leprosery) in the recently formed Crusader territories. Established in the later twelfth century the Mercedanians and the Order of St James (in Spain [**S** RULE OF THE ORDER OF ST JAMES]) and the Trinitarians (in the eastern Mediterranean) focused their activ-

Observance

ities on ransoming and recovering captured Christians. Although the function and scope of action of these and other emerging military movements (such as the Knights Templar and Knights Hospitaller) was distinct from that of contemplative monastics and even the canons regular, their observance was routinely modelled on existing templates. Most eventually adopted the *Rule of St Augustine*, while the twelfth-century Knights Hospitaller had a dedicated rule that nonetheless derived from that authoritative text; only the Trinitarians kept their own rule. The odd one out was the Order of Calatrava, a military movement that was formally established in 1164 and that modelled its observance after the Cistercians' regulations for lay brothers (on these, see below, Chapter 4.2).

Shift in role and geographical focus

Over time, several of these movements became involved in active warfare. The Teutonic movement, which originated as a hospital in the city of Acre, in 1198 would be recast as a military order whose primary task was to defend the position of Western rulers in the region and actively engage in battle with Muslim adversaries. In the thirteenth century, they and others would gradually move their action to Europe. As early as the late twelfth century, the Knights Templar were already represented in Western Europe, and were shifting their energies to the support of papal reform and fiscality (below, Chapter 4.3). Upon the fall of various Crusader territories in the later thirteenth century, the Knights Hospitaller moved, first briefly to Transylvania and then definitively to the Marienburg area. Here they were set to work by German rulers to conquer and maintain territory against the non-Christian Prussians. In the late thirteenth century, the Lazarenes shifted their action and establishments entirely to the West. What these groups encountered on moving there was a drastically shifted monastic landscape.

4 Later Medieval Monasticisms

4.1 Transformations in Monastic Governance

Following the turn of the first millennium there were two key changes in institutional monasticism. One was a gradual shift from authority based on an individual leader's personal morality, connections, and lordship, to a form of authority that derived from the leadership office itself – or what the German sociologist Max Weber referred to as *Amtscharisma*. Presumably this shift was a consequence of a number of factors: the growing complexity of the abbatial role; a related concern over the continuity of governance models; and a particular anxiety when these models depended on a single individual's charismatic leadership, abilities as a networker, and impeccable reputation. In a lengthy, sinuous development that took place over many decades and in different contexts occurred at a different pace and via different means, regular leaders across the Latin West delegated some of their personal responsibilities to 'objective' instruments of monastic governance.

Rise of Amtscharisma

Written instruments

    Abbots and abbesses at various places ordered a whole range of documents in which the identity and organizational principles of a community were consolidated. These included redacted foundation stories, *Deeds* of abbots, and chronicles [**S** LIBER ELIENSIS, **S** RODULPH OF SANT-TROND], cartularies [**S** CARTULARY OF HESDIN], customaries (above, Chapter 3.6), memorial handbooks, and lists of professed monks or nuns. None of these typologies were new, and initially none of the documents possessed any normative value: yet the difference with past uses lay in the fact that, over time, they would function as a (partial) substitute for a leader's verbal instructions, memories, and personal connections. One, presumably apocryphal, anecdote stands as an emblem of this shift. It concerns Richard of Saint-Vanne (above, Chapters 3.4 and 3.6), who towards the end of his life wrote a letter urging his monks to record the names of *familiares* – patrons and other associates – in a *liber memorialis* (literally a "book of memory"). In this way, they would no longer have to rely on his personal recollections and that of his closest associates to maintain the monastery's beneficial connections with these people and their relatives. Also from his tenure dates Saint-Vanne's earliest cartulary, a monumental record of the monks' legal memory.

Transformations of abbatial lordship

The second development in institutional monasticism was that of a shift from multi-abbatial networks to congregational ones. Up until the mid-eleventh century, not a great deal changed in the legal status of various multi-abbacies and associated 'nebulas'. But towards the end of his life, Abbot Odilo of Cluny gradually abandoned the practice of adding new monasteries to his multi-abbacy, and instead switched to accepting the investiture of the abbots of these places. These actions, which could not have happened without the support of a number of key lay agents, were a precursor to a call to end lay investiture at various reform councils, held from the 1060s onwards and triggering a series of similar transferrals in other places (including Saint-Victor of Marseille, Sauve-Majeure, and Charroux, to name but three): the resulting institutional associations were consolidated via confraternal agreements.

These processes were driven forward by a number of ecclesiastical reform trends in the second half of the eleventh century. To begin with, the Lateran synod of 1065, after much debate, had supported the notion of monastic institutions being liberated from episcopal oversight and fiscal control, triggering a spate of attempts to realize that goal. Among many initiatives, scribes at Fécamp and Fleury in the next decades would forge late tenth-century charters that referenced Cluny's status as described in Pope Gregory V's late tenth-century privilege (above, Chapter 3.6). A second reform trend of the time we have already seen (above, Chapter 3.7). Various successive popes of the later eleventh century issued privileges that

'Roman liberty' and reform

awarded the *libertas Romana* (literally the "Roman liberty") to a number of major monastic centres in an attempt to insert these places and their network of affiliated houses in a broad project of ecclesiological reform. Among the more notable recipients were Cluny; Cluny-influenced Hirsau in the Black Forest region of Germany; the nearby abbey of Sankt Blasien, which had adopted the customs of the Cluny-influenced house of Fruttuaria in northern Italy; and the Italian houses of Vallombrosa and Fonte Avellana. In all of these places, monastics realized the significance of being included in the popes' reform effort. Bernold of Constance (d. 1100), a former monk of Sankt Blasien who spent his final years at Schaffhausen, described the purpose of Sankt Blasien's movement as being that of restoring "the common life to the image of the primitive Church" (*vita communis ad formam primitivae ecclesiae*). Finally, a third reform trend was a papal policy that, via a number of confraternal and (con)federational networks, pushed for the creation of a hierarchical system of governance. In this system, one 'arch-abbot' would henceforth appoint and subsequently preside over a number of subordinate abbots.

The responses to and outcomes of these trends were diverse, and as such are revealing of the experimental nature of this transitional phase in the development of monastic confraternities and federations. At Cluny, the local monk Ulrich in the 1080s drafted a customary specifically to inspire the community of Hirsau. In it, Ulrich included various passages to indicate that reflections were taking place locally on how to extend Abbot Hugo's governance over the *ecclesia Cluniacensis*, so that it included monasteries that did not technically lie under his abbatial lordship. Abbot William of Hirsau (d. c. 1091) picked up on these hints, and in his own customary (a text known as the *Constitutiones* [S WILLIAM OF HIRSAU]) described a federation of monasteries that was centred on his main institution but was based on neither Hirsau's nor his own lordship of these places. Instead, the relationship was grounded on a confraternity agreement that allowed the monks from the participating communities to join in each others' choir and cloister activities, with the exception of participation in chapter meetings.

The arrangement as William proposed it rested on the assumption that monks from various places in the 'Hirsaugian nebula' would have no difficulties integrating into other communities.

Hirsau

The *ordo Hirsaugiensis*

Accordingly, his text instructed that all affiliated communities were to follow the *ordo Hirsaugiensis*, or in other words, the "observance of Hirsau". Crucially, it also reserved to William and his successors the right to intervene in other places in the federation to ensure that communities followed this principle, even to the point of designating a suitable abbot who could be relied upon to implement it. The customary additionally distinguished between three types of associated institutions: priories, which were completely subject to Hirsau; a group of monasteries whose abbot was always a former monk of Hirsau and who had sworn obedience and subjection to William; and affiliated institutions that had merely accepted Hirsau's customs. Yet, even though the distinction between these three types of community had concrete implications for their governance, William asserted that they were all joined in the confraternity and therefore were all subject to his oversight as warrantor of

Written agreements
and instruments

the *ordo Hirsaugiensis*. Although not a new phenomenon in practice, William's conceptualization of Hirsau's network was new in that it relied not on the lordship of a lay or clerical ruler, the abbot or abbey's ownership of other monasteries and priories, a papal privilege, or even personal charisma, but on a written agreement entered into by the participating monasteries (consolidated in the above-mentioned confraternity) and on a written instrument of governance (the *Constitutiones*).

(Re)structuring the
ecclesia Cluniacensis

Meanwhile, Abbot Hugo of Cluny had also been working to re-organize the Cluniac (con)federation and transform it from a relatively unstructured combination of personal lordship and 'nebulous' affiliations into a hierarchical, three-tiered congregational system consisting of abbeys, priories, and cells or obediences. Bernard's 1080s customary echoes these transformations where it mentions, for the first time, priories, and also where it makes a distinction between Cluny as "head monastery" (*capitale monasterium*) and the federation's other "members" (*membra*). It was the monastery's close links with Rome that allowed Hugo to turn these ideas and projects into legal reality, as the papacy at the time was also experimenting with ways to restructure the relations between institutions in various emerging confederations. In 1097, Pope Urban II – a former prior of Cluny – issued a privilege that made explicit some of the promise contained in Pope John's bull of 1024. Henceforth, all institutions in the (con)federation would have key rights that only Cluny itself had previously enjoyed: exemption

from episcopal taxes, immunity from excommunication and inter-
dict, right of burial, and status as an asylum for those seeking
justice or protection.

Then, in 1100, Pope Paschalis II acknowledged that the federation's monasteries were not mere properties of Cluny and its leadership, but actual members of an ecclesial 'system'. He also provided
security for the coherence and integrity of that system by making a
formal distinction between priories and abbeys, and establishing
that institutions belonging to the former category could never be
turned into those belonging to the latter. This allowed for monasteries to rely securely on priories without fearing a catastrophic loss
of property, personnel, and patrons in the event of a separation.
Similarly, it allowed lay patrons to trust that nearby priories would
be stable as sites of dynastic remembrance and representation. For
the first time, the *ecclesia Cluniacensis* had a definite, more or less
transparent institutional structure.

A third, presumably more 'progressive' variant on congregational development occurred within Camaldolese and Cistercian
federations. In 1072, Pope Alexander II formally recognized the
existence of a *congregatio* of eleven institutions linked to Camaldoli.
In the early twelfth century, Paschalis II consolidated the situation
by describing the Camaldolese (con)federation as an autonomous
union of monastic communities led by the mother house of Camaldoli, and which consisted of two branches, one contemplative
and another eremitical. Then, in 1113, he merged the two branches
and dictated that the abbots, priors and hermits of the *congregatio* were to jointly elect as their head a prior general. Henceforth,
the movement reconciled a vertical governance model present in
Cluniac monasticism with a horizontal one. Paschalis's bull and
its reference to "brotherly love" (*caritas fraterna*) as a principle of
governance puts into perspective the long-presumed revolutionary
nature of early Cistercian development. Under Robert of Molesme's
successor, Stephen Harding (d. 1134), the Cistercians had gone
through a whirlwind expansion. Four new monasteries (La Ferté,
Pontigny, Morimond, and Clairvaux) had been founded, and from
1118, each of these had started both to create their own subordinate
institutions and take under their wing existing communities that
wished to join the movement. It was Harding and the leaders of
the four other abbeys that struck a confraternity agreement – by
then a thoroughly conventional model for forging institutional alli-

Emergence of an
ecclesial system

Camaldoli

Cistercian
transformations

ances – which was then consolidated in the *Carta Caritatis*, traditionally dated shortly before 1119 and subsequently ratified by Pope Calixtus II. In this document, which lacked any reference to a superior, the participants laid out the principle of decision-making by consensus, stating their intention to prevent the "future shipwreck of their mutual peace". They also announced the future creation of a methodically constructed common observance, to be shaped and upheld by a corporate government structure consisting of two parts: the General Chapter, an assembly with legislative powers of all the abbots of all institutions in the confraternity; and yearly visitations to the member communities by representatives of the five mother abbeys [S STATUTES OF THE CISTERCIANS]. In 1147, the movement pulled off a spectacular coup by admitting the congregations of Savigny and Obazine to its ranks: such integration involved, as had been the case for centuries, the sending of monks from the integrating institution(s) to teach its customs and other practices *verbo et exemplo*. Many other communities joined on an individual basis, and others still were founded by patrons impressed by Stephen Harding's leadership and the fierce rhetoric of Abbot Bernard of Clairvaux (d. 1153) [S BERNARD OF CLAIRVAUX].

General chapters and statutes

It is difficult to decide at what point the Cistercians' confraternal federation made the transition into being a monastic order. Towards the middle of the twelfth century, in his *Dialogus duorum monachorum* ("Dialogue of two monks"), the Cistercian Idung of Prüfening boldly stated that all monasteries of the Cistercian *ordo* constituted "one body" (*unum corpus*), led by one head in the form of the yearly General Chapter. "This", he wrote, "is what makes the form of life of our *ordo* durable" [S IDUNG]. Yet, the meaning of *ordo* as used by Idung does not correspond with the modern usage of the word, which refers to a federation of monastic communities featuring consolidated central institutions and routinized procedures for legislation and supervision. Since the 1120s, the General Chapter had been issuing fairly formless statutes; and on two occasions (dated by most scholars to 1123/1124 and 1152), the *Carta* had been adapted to changed circumstances. But both of these features could not disguise the fact that the movement's integration in a legal, institutional, and procedural sense had been tentative at best, and that it barely even featured a common sense of spiritual identity.

Emergence of the Cistercian order

Indeed, contemporaries of Idung were probably less struck by the alleged institutional or spiritual cohesiveness of the

Tentative developments

movement than by its rampant expansion, spanning a region from northern Spain to eastern Europe. It was only following the middle of the twelfth century, in a context of a steady decline in the number of new (male) communities joining the movement, that the Cistercians' shared customs were finally amplified with a shared spirituality [**S** ECCLESIASTICA OFFICIA]. This focused on the idea that to achieve understanding of the divine, the individual should rely on a combination of scriptural reading and their own sensory and somatic experience [**S** CESARIUS OF HEISTERBACH]. A second and definitive phase of integration occurred in the 1170s and 1180s. In this, the movement finally established a consolidated General Chapter that came together and issued statutes on a regular basis and oversaw systematic visitations of all its member institutions [**S** NARRATIVE TEXTS FROM EARLY CÎTEAUX]. The key event triggering this development may well have been a 1169 papal privilege that awarded full exemption to all member institutions.

The tendency to experiment with new governance models and the slow emergence of order-like structures and procedures in the modern sense of the word was not limited to the Cistercians. In 1126, Norbert's abrupt abdication as abbot of Prémontré, a house of canons regular, had plunged the abbey and its system of affiliated houses into existential crisis. Not only had the emergent Premonstratensian (also known as Norbertine) movement been entirely focused on his leadership, but the abbey of Prémontré had also been his private property. His successor, Hugo of Fosses (d. 1164), clearly had been taking notes from the Cistercian example when he declined to follow in Norbert's footsteps as an autocratic lord. He submitted to his fellow abbots a proposal for a new regime, one founded on a model of consensual government by the leaders of all the monasteries that had previously adopted Norbert's 'primitive' customs. After the first gathering of these leaders in 1130, it was decided that as a General Chapter with legislative powers, meetings would take place at Prémontré on 9 October each year. This body, like the Cistercians' General Chapter, also began issuing statutes almost immediately after its creation and arranged for oversight of its member communities per *circaria* ("province"). But, as in the case of the Cistercians, it would take nearly half a century before these legislative and supervisory procedures became routine parts of Premonstratensian governance.

Emergence of the order of Prémontré

Further
transformations Soon, the fledgling Carthusians, Grandmontines, Arrouaisians (a small order of canons regular), and various other movements followed suit and established their own General Chapters. And in England, the Gilbertines mixed Cistercian legislative structures with a hierarchical executive branch. Less conventional strands of organized monastic life took part in the trend too. The Knights Templar ended up adopting a quasi-Cistercian form of governance, albeit presided over by a Grand Master who was assisted by a range of officials (on this and other military orders, see above, Chapter 3.7). The trend even extended to corners of the monastic landscape where former historians least expected to encounter it.

Trends in
'Benedictine'
monasticism In the archdiocese of Reims, at least two regional confraternity networks of contemplative, 'Benedictine' monasteries, held together by a shared interest in Bernard's Cluniac customary, struck an alliance to establish their own, regional Chapter and to issue statutes. The first meeting, which was held in late 1131, took place under the auspices of a number of clerical rulers who had been promoting Cistercian and Premonstransian foundations in the region and probably also involved Abbot William of Saint-Thierry (d. 1148), a future figurehead of the Cistercian movement. Over the next four decades, the Reims abbots would continue experimenting: such experiments included (among other things) the striking of a confraternity agreement with the Premonstratensians around the year 1140, the appointment of a 'prior' in the late 1160s, and (on the same occasion) a self-fashioning as a cohesive entity by issuing charters with a custom-made seal.

Cluniac
developments While the papacy's reponse to the Reims initiative was muted and participating abbots seemed unsure about the implications of their actions, the Cluniacs were quick to pour scorn on the initiative. For one, the meeting and its written output challenged their inclusive view on the status of monasteries situated at the outer fringes of the Cluniac 'nebula'. And secondly, the Reims meeting was also the last in a series of setbacks for Cluny's abbot, Peter the Venerable (d. 1156) [S PETER THE VENERABLE]. Although the *ecclesia Cluniacensis* had been at the height of its powers and expansion at the time of Abbot Hugo's death in 1109 – his successor Pontius in 1116 referred to himself as *abbas abbatum*, "abbot of abbots", and to his abbey of Cluny as *monasterium capitale* and *caput ordinis* – to most observers it had now become obvious that the 'charismatic genealogy' of Cluniac abbots had come to an end. It was clear to

them that the federation had changed to the point that a drastic rethink of its governance model was urgently needed. In circumstances that largely elude us, a 'schism' took place under Pontius, and following his abdication in the 1020s, his successor Peter struggled to keep his priors in check, who grumbled about his hierarchical style of governing.

Contributing further to a sense of crisis were Bernard of Clairvaux's savage criticisms of the Cluniacs' spirituality, wealth, and focus on liturgical service. Various developments, like the 1131 General Chapter meeting at Reims, further challenged the traditional interpretation of the *ecclesia Cluniacensis*. In 1132, Peter organized the first General Chapter of his own movement, and over the course of the next fourteen years he also issued a series of statutes. In these, he defiantly justified a range of adjustments to customary practices and created a permanent record of his efforts to redirect legislative powers in his movement whilst retaining the supremacy for his office. Peter's embattled governance did not stop him from being an energetic abbot and churchman: among other things, he successfully reorganized Cluniac finances and administrative processes, and had the Koran translated with a view to engaging in intercultural dialogue. Cultural production at Cluny was still flourishing too [**S** RELATIO]. Still, it was clear that Peter's new governance model was a transitional one, and that momentous changes in the leadership status of Cluny's abbots were bound to take place sooner or later.

Crisis of Cluniac leadership

4.2 Monastic Experiences in the Long Twelfth Century

Sometime in the early decades of the twelfth century, Orderic Vitalis (d. c. 1142), an English monk at Saint-Evroul in Normandy, noted that "a swarm of cowled monks is spreading all over the world" [**S** ORDERIC]. Monasteries, he said, "are founded everywhere in mountain valleys and plains, observing new rites and wearing different habits". Various factors – the recent reform movement within the Church, rampant demographic growth and economic expansion, the changing nature of political power, the changing legal status of monastic institutions and their estates, new expectations regarding the laity's involvement in religious practice, and of course also developments in ascetic spirituality – had combined

Expansion of institutional monasticism

to drive change. Monastic groups over the course of the previous century had responded in a number of ways. They had adapted their recruitment policies, modified their attitudes towards interaction with secular society, and in some cases had also established large confraternity networks, vastly enhancing the mobility and exchange of expertise, personnel, and objects. The sheer institutional and geographical scope (but not necessarily the coherence ideologically or practically) of these networks can be reconstructed through study of mortuary rolls, which were sent around communities implicated in a confraternity on the death of an abbot or abbess [**S** MEMORIAL ROLLS].

Emergence of 'corporate cultures'

The gradual decline of monarchic abbatial rule over the course of the eleventh century and the equally gradual changes in the legal status of congregational networks further accelerated the formation of 'corporate cultures' across institutional boundaries. Subsequently, a trend slowly emerged to promulgate principles of governance and modes of conduct as law. The legitimacy of these was established not by tradition or by the authoritative instructions of a single abbot, but by consensus among the leadership of all the communities associated in a particular movement. Monastics

Arguments of distinction

across these different movements took pride in claiming that their liturgical practice, observance, and even their outward appearance, derived from legislative acts designed to reflect the *caritas* – mutual love and support – among their membership.

Proliferation of forms

Having been born in the later eleventh century, Orderic was well placed to express the wonder many of his contemporaries felt at how rapidly institutional monasticism was expanding and evolving, and how centuries-old forms and views appeared to have changed drastically in the space of just one or two generations. An 1130s/1140s treatise titled *Libellus de diversis ordinibus et professionibus qui sunt in ecclesia* ("Booklet on the diversity of orders and professions that exist in the Church") distinguished no fewer than seven categories of ascetics. It described hermits; monks living close to the laity; monks living far from the laity (the Cistercians); canons living far from the laity; canons living close to the laity (in three groups, namely contemplatives living in a cloister, those living in a cloister but occupied with the care of guests and pilgrims, and those living outside the cloister in dependencies and parishes); secular canons; and finally also "secular monks". For the first six, the anonymous author recognized biblical precedents, and on that basis stated they were legitimate. Only the last, of which he had nothing to say but that they did not live under the authority of an abbot and therefore inevitably showed dissolute behaviour, he found to have no legitimacy [**S** LIBELLUS].

In some ways the testimony of the *Libellus* is misleading, in that it creates a false impression that the turn of the twelfth century had witnessed the spectacular, kaleidoscopic diversification of a formerly monochrome, primarily Benedictine, monastic landscape. As we have seen throughout the preceding chapters of this book, an incredible diversity of monastic experiences, inside community settings and out, can be detected throughout Christianity's first eleven hundred years. Be that as it may, it is true that there had been significant pressure from inside and outside the monastic sphere to channel that pre-existing diversity into a range of well-defined functional, behavioural, and social identities. Church leaders were eager to establish which groups of monastics ought to fulfil which roles and services and award them a specific role in the ecclesiastical system. The result was a trend towards integration and incorporation, and towards establishing stricter boundaries between movements – institutional boundaries, but also legal, ideological, and performative. Over the course of the late eleventh and early twelfth centuries, many group hermitages and ascetic households were turned into cloistered communities, while women's houses across the Latin West were being pressured by Church administrators to adopt a 'Benedictine' observance, practice strict enclosure, and subject themselves to supervision by members of a nearby male institution. Meanwhile, male communities faced growing pressure to define their identity in a specific manner, commit to a specific functional interpretation of their monastic community life, and link their destinies to that of a specific congregational or other movement.

With ecclesiastical structures and hierarchical relations increasingly consolidated in frameworks of canon law, and with institutional identities bearing increasingly on individual monastics, these expectations grew as the twelfth century progressed. Stricter differences were thus established in how monastics from different observances and movements dressed, what they ate, in what spaces they lived, how they celebrated the liturgy, what books they read, and what art they produced or commissioned. These arrangements were designed to reflect specific emphases in the

Trends for integration

Modes of distinction

functional self-identification and spirituality of these movements. Most famous is the example of the Cistercians, who took great pride in the supposed austerity of their church buildings and cloisters: but there are many other examples, such as that of the Grandmontines, who relied on a deliberately out-dated architectural style for their churches and in doing so became instantly distinguishable from their peers. The possible circumstances in which an individual might cross from one movement to the next were also limited. Such measures were needed (or so Church leaders, specialists of canon law, and polemicists argued) to maintain the integrity of communities, and to retain the relevance of their membership's vow of stability in a world where various strands of monastic life were vying for secular favours and the prize of being known as the most authentic of all.

However, various indicators help us to nuance the former image of a dominance in this period of rigidly defined, strictly delineated, 'corporate' or 'congregational' identities. To begin with, sources on the composition of monastic communities and on the life trajectory of specific individuals tell us that in this period intra-religious mobility remained high, possibly even increased. A well-known example is that of Adam of Perseigne (d. 1221), who over the course of his life adopted three different monastic identities [**S** ADAM]. Originally trained as a canon regular, he then entered the Benedictine abbey of Marmoutier in Tours, and after that became a Cistercian monk at the abbey of Perseigne, where he eventually became abbot. His life trajectory and that of countless other individuals reveals that differences in the experience of life in various movements were not as pronounced as various apologists and polemicists of the period liked to suggest.

We also need to hold in mind the fact that contemporary sources contain few references to any difficulties canons and monks might have experienced when trying to adjust to another observance. Confraternity agreements between communities from different movements and within movements do not dwell much on such issues either [**S** CONFRATERNITY AGREEMENT], and seem to build on the assumption that visiting monks or canons would have no major difficulties adjusting to local routines and rites. Despite the drive to establish distinct corporate identities, and despite the growing significance of customaries, statutes, and other written instruments, many aspects of cloistered life across different observances con-

'Intra-monastic' mobility

Enduring similarities

tinued to be rooted in a shared literary, normative, and practical tradition. In addition, we have substantial evidence of the mutual influence that existed between individuals, institutions, and communities, even across different strands of cenobitical life. Throughout the twelfth century, for instance, Cistercian communities relied on their non-Cistercian peers while building their libraries and in sourcing other forms of cultural capital. One among many examples is that of the northern French abbey of Clairmarais, which in the late twelfth century obtained numerous manuscripts that came not from the mother house of Clairvaux, but from 'traditional' houses at Anchin (where abbots in earlier decades had keenly studied then-emerging Cistercian spirituality) and Marchiennes.

Mutual influencing

And finally, we also see that numerous communities ended up situating themselves in a 'nebulous' area around certain movements. In 1120s–1130s northern Spain and the Low Countries, many 'traditional' cenobitical communities adopted quasi-Cistercian liturgical practices and modes of conduct (including an emphasis on silence and individual prayer) without joining the Cistercian movement. And towards the end of the century, numerous female communities in different parts of the Latin West also sought recognition as Cistercian monasteries, but not because they were looking to align their internal practices with that order or actually join its institutional structures. Rather, it was because they sought to benefit from various Cistercian privileges, including exemption from tithes.

'Nebulas'

Besides the numerous indications of permeable boundaries and interactions between different monastic forms and experience, and of communities that deliberately situated themselves in a 'nebulous' area around certain movements, we also find that localized interpretations of monastic tradition to a significant extent continued to shape the experience of life in the cloister. Twelfth-century communities of canons regular affiliated to the southern French monastery of Saint-Ruf used liturgical manuscripts that reveal strong adaptations to local circumstances and expectations. And when Cluniac or Cluny-inspired communities obtained a copy of Bernard's customary, they either adapted the contents to reflect their own situation or left it completely untouched, including the passages that were only relevant for application at Cluny itself, presumably to indicate that the text was to be used as a source of inspiration rather than a blueprint for (literal) application.

Enduring role of local factors

But the variations extended beyond liturgical practices and internal codes of conduct, and also included how certain groups of monastics envisioned their role in society. For example, life in communities of canons regular could be focused either on pastoral tasks, eremitical withdrawal, or on involvement in ecclesiastical governance, depending on the specific situation of the community in its social environment. Generally speaking, the overall picture is that despite a clear trend towards integration into various movements, life in cloistered communities continued to be shaped by local factors, such as the demographic of its recruits and the educational profile and former life experiences of community members; the geophysical and geopolitical location of a monastery; the nature of its estate; and its integration into the surrounding lay society.

These observations have significant implications for the way in which we understand the expansion of certain movements and the stagnation of others in this period. It is true that the newer ones owed some of their success (in recruiting and with lay patrons) to their reputation for spiritual excellence, austerity, involvement in pastoral work, and for contributing to technical, agricultural, and other innovations. However, it is equally true that an individual founder or donor's decision to promote or even join a specific strand of monastic life derived primarily from complex negotiations and deliberations in which various interests and expectations were weighed against each other. For instance, the Cistercians' success in the twelfth century must be linked not (or not only) to the powerful appeal of its spirituality, but to the attractive possibilities the mostly small foundations offered patrons from the lower lay elites to establish a site of commemoration and symbolic representation of power.

Similarly, traditional accounts explain the rapid expansion of the Cistercians into Eastern Europe by way of their superior modes of estate management, technological know-how, and experience with making previously uncultivated lands suitable for agricultural use. However, the idea that the movement systematically sought to establish itself in remote, 'wild' parts of the world is largely a literary myth; so is the view, held by a number of economic historians, that their movement was a quasi-entrepreneurial entity, always looking to seize on investment opportunities. In reality, we see that Cistercian expansion in 'border regions' (eastern Europe, but also Scotland, Wales, and the Low Countries) was driven primarily by their willingness to come to attractive mutual arrangements with the local elites – elites who sought to ground their authority using the cultural capital brought in by these communities. Across the entire Latin world – an area that now included significant parts of eastern Europe, Scandinavia, and even Iceland – corporate identities, structures, and actions continued to be shaped by the relationship with, first, major patrons (particularly aristocratic founders and benefactors), and, second, with countless minor donors. Both supported monasteries in the hope of establishing a mutually beneficial relationship, in ways that remind us of how aristocrats and monastic agents had cooperated since late antiquity. Whoever could offer them the most attractive deal – with 'deal' being used here in the least cynical sense possible – was likely to obtain their support.

Returning to Orderic's testimony, cited at the beginning of this chapter, we find that it not only refers to narratives of identity and outer forms of monastic life, but also to inner experiences. As a former child oblate [**S** GUIBERT], he would have been particularly sensitive to the fact that over the course of his lifetime, admission to the diverse forms of monastic community life had shifted decisively in favour of adult conversion. The Cistercians famously abrogated any form of child oblation, as did several other movements of the time. At the recent foundation of Hirsau, which was modelled after Cluniac exemplars, Abbot William was strict in accepting adult converts only. He denounced the common practice among the lay elite of burdening monastics with the care and education of their children, in particular those with disabilities or illnesses. Yet, we should guard against seeing the decades around 1100 as a time of drastic rupture. The ratio of oblates to adult converts had been shifting since the later tenth and early eleventh centuries, in part because monastic leaders of the period had been actively recruiting former clerics and lay adults (above, Chapter 3.4). And for the period that concerns us here, we know that an exclusive focus on adult conversion was not universally practised or maintained, not even by Cistercian communities. However, it is true that a trend was definitely set: over the course of the twelfth century canon legislation was drafted that instructed all abbots to reconfirm former oblates, and that these were transitional measures.

From now on, monastic communities where the majority of members were converted adults were the rule rather than the exception. As a consequence of this, the noviciate in many places

Decline of child oblation

Novice education

became a central feature of community life, while educators were compelled to drastically revise their approach to educating and training future monastics. Different strategies for instructing these new recruits on the basic tenets of ascetic life – teaching them Latin, liturgies and chants, and various other competences – had to be created and rolled out. That process, along with the previously mentioned shift to *Amtscharisma*, a progressive standardization of liturgical practices, and intensive cultural exchange within various movements, led to a massive literary output. There was a proliferation of texts on the education of novices [**S** HUGO OF SAINT-VICTOR], ritual handbooks [**S** MONASTIC RITUAL OF FLEURY], commentaries on various rules, and exhortatory (or parenetic) treatises. The notion of adult conversion as a consciously made, penitential act also invited prominent authors to call on their readership to consider the meaning of Scripture not simply through the commentary of Church authorities, but also through their own experience. Abbot Bernard of Clairvaux crucially contributed to bringing to the mainstream a tradition of documenting the individual Christian's journey into the deeper recesses of the mind: among the more famous texts are those by William of Saint-Thierry and Aelred of Rievaulx (d. 1167).

Changing spirituality

Monastic space

The reality that post-1100 monastic houses were now increasingly populated by former laymen or -women sharpened concerns over ritual purity, especially in contexts that were implicated in the ongoing Church reform [**S** GEOFFREY OF VENDÔME, S RUPERT]. New architectural templates began circulating that were specifically designed to shield monastics from unwanted contact and disruption. Although these built on a conceptualization of monastic space that dated back to the ninth century, the drive in many movements to establish a distinct identity led to the emergence of new arrangements [**S** SUGER]. But local models and traditions for organizing monastic space also continued to influence architectural and artistic expressions, including within the Cistercian movement, which accounts for the fact that none of the new movements succeeded in imposing an absolutely uniformous style.

Lay converses

Another way of creating ramparts against secular influence and also of addressing the various capabilities and inclinations of the large numbers of people who were looking to take part in the monastic life (or simply sought refuge in the comparatively benign lordship of a monastic house) was the position of the converse.

William of Hirsau's *Constitutiones* refer to "bearded", "exterior", "illiterate" or "converse brothers", non-consecrated laymen who had converted to a life of sobriety, prayer, and celibacy alongside consecrated monks, and who worked in the stables and work-shops, on the fields and meadows, and carried out construction and various other duties. Similar (but not identical) arrangements are attested for the Vallombrosans, Gilbertines, Cistercians, and a host of communities belonging to 'traditional' strands of monastic life. We may wonder if the individual experiences of lay converses would have been all that different from the scores of laypeople in earlier centuries whose fate and lives were bound with groups of vowed monastics: some arrangements remind us of much earlier ones in Jura, Visigothic, and Carolingian Monasticism (above, Chapters 2.3, 2.4, and 3.2). But the later eleventh century definitely marks the moment when commentators – not the least of which was Pope Urban II – for the first time described them as experiencing a distinct form of monastic life, and delineated in detail their legal status, role in monastic institutionalism, and spiritual aspirations.

Over time, the life and activities of lay converses became subject to strict regulations, particularly by the Cistercians, who created extensive sets of written guidelines. For them, the division between choir monks (or nuns) and lay brothers (or sisters) was not merely a functional one, or one that related to the occupation of different spaces by these cohorts, but also reflected an economic logic: many lay brothers lived far away from the monastery, in granges or amongst the sheep they tended, and in doing so allowed the monks in the main institution to acquire and manage complex, labour-intensive estates [**S** CISTERCIAN LAY BROTHERS]. In contrast, in the movements of Hirsau and Cluny, interactions with the choir monks were a great deal more intensive. In the former, the emphasis for lay brothers was more on work than prayer, but they still participated in evening offices. And at Cluny, a number of lay brothers were even more involved in the choir monks' liturgical practices, but always separately. Not all observers at the time approved of these arrangements, and lay brothers were often the focus of satire and reproach. And within communities too, tensions arose over class differences, with converses occupying separate spaces and contributing much of the labour: the latter half of the twelfth century was witness to a number of confrontations, revolts

Roles and social tensions

even, over these issues. The Cistercians, Gilbertines, and especially the Grandmontines would suffer significant damage to their reputation, their perception by the papacy, and (in the latter two cases) also their destiny as monastic movements, as a result of scandals and internal disputes over this issue.

Male–female interactions

As we saw earlier in this chapter, the second half of the eleventh century had witnessed the reformation of large numbers of female monasteries – ones that had previously featured an observance 'ambiguously' situated between several different written templates. Together with a considerable number of newly founded houses, many of these were inserted into male monasticism's emerging congregational structures, or at the very least were closely linked to a nearby house of monks or clerics. Such developments faced monastic administrators with practical and moral challenges. This was particularly true in cases where founders had established institutions (so-called 'double monasteries' like that of Admont and Fontevraud) that were inhabited by segregated groups of men and women. Although these communities were institutionally and functionally symbiotic – among other things, the women produced textiles and manuscripts for use by their male counterparts, while the monks or clerics often took care of spiritual guidance and administrative matters – across various movements, architecture and regulations evolved to make the two sexes in these places otherwise strictly separate. Similarly, the spiritual guidance of women by monks and clerics (also known as the *cura monialium*) in these and countless other places was subject to rigorous and detailed regulation. Such were the efforts required to keep this 'cohabitation' afloat that tensions soon arose. Polemical and normative sources from the twelfth century suggest a progressive marginalization of women in several movements. Cistercian texts refer to the pastoral involvement by monks in female communities as a burden and a cause of mental distress for these men, a great obstacle to their personal asceticism, and a severe risk to their integrity. The Premonstratensians too voiced objections against living with women, but their complaints may have been more about functional disparity – the men, who were canons regular, were expected to carry out a diverse range of pastoral tasks, whereas the women were strictly confined to contemplative roles. Also of consideration was the economic strain of maintaining two communities on the income from a single estate: already in the 1130s–1150s, various

'Double monasteries'

The cura monialium

Marginalizing trends

male communities had to be reminded by papal order to provide for their female sisters. Although the Premonstratensian movement would continue to host women religious into the thirteenth century, they formally ceased to be part of the order by virtue of a papal decree that was issued in 1198.

This trend against the presence of women in certain movements used to receive a great deal of attention from scholars of twelfth-century monasticism. But it is important to realize that it was not a universal phenomenon and that negative voices nearly always resonate far more loudly than positive ones. The biographer of Stephen of Obazine (whose movement was absorbed by the Cistercians in 1147), in his text rejected the notion that such institutional cohabitations were inappropriate, and proposed viewing nuns not as a group of (sexually threatening) women, but as a spiritual sisterhood [S VITA STEPHANI]. And in the Empire, we find   Symbiotic relations
that far fewer objections were voiced against mixed gender institutions than in France and in England. Here, as in various other parts of the Latin West, groups of male and female monastics continued to engage in intensive collaborative relationships, fostering a shared spiritual and intellectual culture and a sense of shared purpose, sometimes even emotional attachment. In some cases, including in regions where the debate raged most fiercely, issues arising from male–female cohabitations were resolved when sisters living at a certain monastery were transferred to a separate institution, which then made new arrangements with male monastics – for example, for the provision of pastoral care, and the exchange of goods, manuscripts, and liturgical items. It is rather telling that these male monastics were often the same as those with whom the women religious had previously co-existed.

Plenty of indications survive, also, of exchanges between indi-   Female monastics as
vidual male and female monastics, enough in fact to speak of highly   'influencers'
complementary, mutually reinforcing spiritual cultures in this period. In particular, the role of women in the transformation of ecclesiastical structures and ideologies has been underestimated, except for contributions by major 'influencers' such as Elisabeth of Schönau (d. 1164), Hildegard of Bingen (d. 1179) [S HILDEGARD], and Herrad of Landsberg (d. 1195). Here, as in other areas of the monastic experience in the long twelfth century, physical and virtual boundaries were often a good deal more permeable, experiences and attitudes far more flexible, and forms and expressions

far more responsive to local and personal circumstances than normative accounts appear to suggest.

4.3 Law, Custom, and the Early Thirteenth-Century Papal Reforms

The transformation of monastic institutions and (legal, socio-economic and moral) identities in the long twelfth century was not uncontested. Although numerous bishops and archbishops actively supported old and more recent strands of organized monastic life, like many lay lords they also had concerns over the way monasteries and their federations were seeking exemption from the over-

Episcopal resistance sight of rulers, from juridical control, and from fiscal obligations. In response, the episcopacy armed itself with an arsenal of juridical, ritual, and political weapons to defend – and where possible also reclaim or even expand – its prerogatives. Beginning in the late eleventh century, prelates in northern France and England asked that each abbot and abbess submit a written promise (*promissio*) of subjection and obedience to the bishop and his successors at the time of their ordination. The new rite was highly contested. Writing in the 1130s, an anonymous author from the Norman abbey of Le Bec described the *promissio* as an "unmerited novelty", and argued that it transformed the abbot's traditional promise of duty and of obedience to the *Rule of St Benedict* into something akin to secular homage and an obligation of service [S THREE TREATISES FROM

Ordination BEC]. Neither he nor other critics were far off the mark: bishops were seeking to stem the erosion of their power over monasticism by creating a cohort of regular leaders with a personal obligation of obedience and service to their direct ecclesiastical superior.

Meanwhile, clerical rulers and lay lords also sought for ways to make the expansion into their territories of recently emerged congregations and orders subject to negotiations in which their own political, familial, and other interests prominently featured.

Lay responses Aristocratic founders too tailored the creation of new communities to their personal expectations, a fact that is especially noticeable in the evidence relating to the organization, recruitment patterns, and corporate identity of female Cistercian and Premonstratensian groups. Such arrangements resulted in an experience of life in and around monasteries that never precisely matched the normative descriptions in rules, statutes, and other commentaries.

As the twelfth century was drawing to a close, it also became apparent that institutionalized monasticism's keystone status in shaping the lay experience of Christian faith was eroding. The papacy, even though it had often sided with individual monasteries in their struggles with the higher clergy, over the previous century had also been actively promoting the clergy as the frontline of its ecclesiological project. This gave clerics and groups of clerics in particular an advantage over contemplative monastics when seeking support from founders, donors, and lay agents. Also contributing to this advantage was the rising importance of the Eucharist in lay spirituality, the need for priests to cater to a rapidly growing population, and the emphasis in reformist discourse on clerical purity through celibacy and overall restraint. From the 1120s/1130s onwards, many cenobitical institutions, including some Cluniac ones, experienced a steep fall in donations, dwindling incomes from parishioners and pilgrims, and growing pressure on their estates from lay stakeholders, emerging urban societies, clerical groups, and various local competitors. Others were able to maintain a gift-giving relationship with lay patrons, but soon noticed that the relative size and value of donations was in decline. These issues only added to the difficulties many older monasteries experienced in keeping viable an estate consisting of highly diverse and often very dispersed properties, and in dealing with the transformations brought along by an emerging market economy.

Papal promotion of the clergy

Fall in institutional fortunes

Frequent episodes of warfare and social disruption, failed harvests, misjudged investments, inflation, and the expansion of international trade (and its concurrent impact on local economies) created catastrophic tipping points, putting numerous monastic economies in a perilous situation. In some places, abbots and abbesses were compelled to sell off parts of the estate, take out loans, and even send members out to live in other communities because there were no resources to provide for them. Not all of these leaders, so contemporary sources tell us, had the necessary experience or foresight to enable them to do this without harming the long-term prospects of their institution. The impact of ill-judged governance decisions was profound. Many houses were compelled to reduce the number of incoming monastics, and after the middle of the twelfth century, 'traditional' cenobitical groups in particular hosted few well-known intellectuals, lost their prom-

Crises

Loss of intellectual and spiritual prominence

inence as centres of schooling, delivered fewer future bishops or other leaders, and faded from the forefront of religious reflection and debate. Not all institutions were affected by the above challenges in the same manner and with the same intensity. Indeed, many continued to have a major impact on their social and cultural environment and enjoy the vigorous support of lay patrons and clerical rulers throughout the twelfth century. However, in the view of contemporary Church leaders, something had to be done to replicate these local success stories in communities that were doing rather less well.

Perceptions and realities of contraction

The newly emerged movements of the later eleventh and twelfth centuries were not immune to these various negative trends either. In the first half of the twelfth century, the Cistercian confraternity had expanded massively, but by the time of Bernard of Clairvaux's death in 1152, that expansion was already becoming burdensome to its institutions. In his later years, Bernard and others had become aware of criticism against the movement's economic activity, wealth, and political influence, and the fact that its service to society fell short of lay expectations. Accordingly, the number of new male foundations plummeted, as did the number of existing communities that sought to join the movement. In contrast, that of women's houses rose sharply: but this seems to have occurred because that branch of the movement was more inclined than its male counterpart to make various concessions to lay patrons.

Criticism of pastoral role

Meanwhile, the reputation of male monastics as purveyors of pastoral services to the laity was called into question. While the Cistercians faced criticism for their ineffective efforts against the Cathars (below, Chapter 4.4), the Premonstratensians bore the brunt of these attacks. They struggled to face competition from various eremitical communities and those of the Knights Hospitaller, all of whom claimed to build on the same Augustinian tradition of monastic life and whose loose organizational structures were a good deal more adaptable to changing lay expectations. Even the Carthusians, although much admired for their austere lifestyle, were now criticized for being too disengaged from lay needs and expectations.

Papal fiscality

At the time of his election in 1198, Pope Innocent III (d. 1216) was witness to a highly fractured monastic landscape. For several decades, papal officers had been pressing monastic communities to pay the tax they had been levied in return for the benefits of various privileges and exemptions. In 1192, the Roman curia assembled the *Liber censuum*, the first systematic survey of all "monasteries, hospitals... cities, castles, manors... or those kings and princes belonging to the jurisdiction and property of St. Peter and the holy Roman church and owing census and how much they ought to pay". As an instrument of financial administration, it encouraged systematic efforts to establish precisely which communities were willing and able to pay the *census*, and (more importantly) how different stakeholders handled their governance. These investigations, which took place over a number of years, revealed with even greater clarity than before the challenges facing monastic institutionalism at that point in time. An early opportunity to intervene presented itself shortly before Innocent's election. In 1196, Abbot Hugo IV of Cluny (d. 1199) had asked Pope Celestine III to endorse his plans to correct in all institutions of his movement "what ought to be corrected and regulate what ought to be regulated" (*corrigenda corrigere et ibidem statuere statuenda*).

Abbot Hugo's petition triggered the newly installed Innocent to instruct Cluny's new abbot, Hugo V (d. 1207), to "reform what was deformed by lack of care" (*per incuriam deformata reformare*) and issue the first systematic collection of Cluniac statutes. In this statute collection, Hugo V declared himself subject to "the law", that is the *ecclesia Cluniacensis*'s internal procedures of governance and the outcomes of its decision-making processes. To make this governance model possible, the statutes established a yearly General Chapter – in other words, no longer one that was held at the abbot's whim – and decreed that all members, including himself, were subject to visitation and correction. These events set in motion a rapid process of institutional change. By 1205/1206, the new statutes of the Cluniac General Chapter were codified not by the abbot of Cluny, but by *definitores*, officers with a designated role who were appointed as representatives of the assembly. From this point onwards, the General Chapter was responsible for instructing the abbot and his successors on how a good leader ought to conduct his business, and what kind of leadership profile was expected of him. Further provisions issued in the early thirteenth century made him entirely dependent upon the approval of his assembled priors: by that point, the abbot of Cluny no longer functioned as a source of monastic values and law but as a monas-

Transforming Cluniac governance

Cluniac 'law'

tic official with well-defined tasks and prerogatives, appointed to carry out a consensus-based view of his leadership role.

Papal reform   Innocent, a law specialist by training, subsequently extended his reorganizing action to other monastic movements and to non-affiliated institutions. Various strands of reformist policy were eventually anchored in the decisions of the Fourth Lateran Council (1215), which itself had been preceded by a series of regional councils that had investigated the challenges facing ecclesiastical life in various parts of the Latin West. It put a temporary stop to the creation of new orders, and decreed that in every Church province, a triennial general chapter of abbots and priors of non-affiliated (as in not belonging to a specific order or congregation) institutions was to be held "according to the manner of the Cistercians" (*iuxta morem Cisterciensium*). Presided over by two 'Benedictine' and two Cistercian abbots, these meetings were intended to discuss the life of 'traditional' monks and women religious (increasingly identified as *nonnae*, "nuns"), and to appoint officers who would carry out visitations of all communities, whether these were exempted from episcopal visitations or not.

Precedents   Contrary to what has often been argued, the decisions of the Council did not mark the birth of a Benedictine order. In fact, the organizational paradigm (consisting not of one General Chapter, but of many provincial chapters) proposed in 1215 strongly resembled one that had already been announced in the 1130s/1140s "Booklet on the diversity of orders and professions that exist in the Church" (above, Chapter 4.2). This, indeed, had been realized, with varying degrees of success, at regional chapters held in Reims (1130s–1160s) [**S** STATUTES OF REIMS], Saxony and Thuringia (c. 1145), Rouen (c. 1190), central Italy (by papal command, 1203), York (for canons regular, 1206), Lund (1206, at the initiative of the archbishop of that place, who controlled Denmark and large parts of Sweden), Rouen again (1210), and very likely **Effects** in other places too. And although 'Benedictine' and 'Benedictine *ordo*' would gradually come into use as terms to designate a specific cohort of monastic communities, the various chapters of this vaguely defined cohort of 'traditional', non-affiliated communities never coalesced into anything resembling the General Chapters of movements like the Cistercian or Premonstratensian, with their centralized system of legislation and supervision. For Innocent's reign and those of his immediate successors, there are no indications in the sources of any efforts to establish a common observance or to root out all local customs: nor is there clear evidence of an attempt to discourage Benedictine communities from appealing directly to the papacy in the case of conflicts with clerical superiors. And crucially, the Lateran Council did not exempt (as was the case for the Cistercians) the participating institutions from episcopal authority and visitation either – probably to avoid alienating the local clerical elites and to normalize the turbulent relations between certain houses and their bishops. In this, scholars have seen the influence of a range of university-educated theologians, such as Robert Grosseteste (d. 1253), Gerald of Wales (d. c. 1223), and Philip the Chancellor (d. 1236), all of whom felt far removed, both morally and intellectually, from traditional cloistered life, and who objected to the idea that monastics be exempt from clerical oversight.

Innocent's successor Honorius III (d. 1227) oversaw the implementation of the Lateran Council's decisions. It was during his tenure that the first Benedictine chapters convened and issued the earliest sets of statutes. Honorius also carried out his predecessor's plans to finance what would be known as the Fifth Crusade, through a three-year tax of a twentieth part of ecclesiastical income. As part of this massive crowdfunding campaign and of the reorganization of papal finances, the Knights Templar and Knights Hospitaller of Paris were enrolled as bankers, which led to a fundamental transformation of their corporate identity and societal impact. In contrast, Honorius's successor Gregory IX (d. 1242) focused on establishing consolidated modes and structures for supervision, and also on creating a papal legislative framework for streamlining the organization and the observance of monastic groups. To realize the first objective, Gregory relied on the higher clergy to inspect and correct life in monastic houses, particularly those of women; he also used mainly Dominican friars and Cistercians to carry out visitations of Benedictines, canons regular, and Hospitaller monks. The new pope also instructed the Cluniacs to reorganize their General Chapters to the Cistercians' example, and with regard to the Premonstratensian order, he imposed visitations and a drastic revision of the statutes.

Continuity

Gregory IX's reforms

The watershed year of Gregory's papacy was 1235, when he stated that all exempt monasteries (including those belonging to the Cistercian order) were now subject to visitations too. Around the same time he also issued a set of statutes for all Benedictine houses (revised in 1237) that imposed yearly General Chapters, encouraged these assemblies to issue their own statutes, rolled out various measures to regulate internal discipline, and reiterated the need for visitations [**S** POPE GREGORY IX]. Gregory's reform was a deliberate rupture with his predecessors' policies, in that it took the unprecedented step of legislating the daily lives of monks and women religious via a set of consolidated written instructions. The famous *Register* of the Franciscan Bishop Eudes Rigaud (d. 1275), which records over a thousand visitations he carried out in one hundred and fifty institutions across Normandy, reveals Gregory and Eudes's belief in a strictly regulated monastic landscape consisting of more or less uniform cohorts belonging to various orders and congregations [**S** EUDES].

Many local leaders – abbots and abbesses – took offence, and rejected the notion that the pope's statutes were authoritative enough to replace local custom. Compounding factors to their resistance were Gregory's authoritarian stance and his customary reliance for the visitations on individuals whose background and training made them ill-prepared to empathize with the traditions of life inside a typically 'Benedictine' convent. In an attempt to preserve a centuries-old tradition in which communities had consciously shaped their own, localized observance, abbots at Bury St Edmunds, Westminster, St Augustine of Canterbury, and Saint-Vaast in Arras defiantly issued their own customaries or sets of statutes. A much greater number of communities took the alternative road of petitioning the papacy for exemption. The English chronicler Matthew Paris (d. 1259) speaks of a 1253 attempt by "French monks" to buy themselves out of the obligation to follow Gregory's statutes [**S** MATTHEW]. That such attempts carried a fiscal subtext is revealed if we consider a move by the Benedictine abbots of the ecclesiastical province of Canterbury. In 1240 they approached the king of England and the papal legates to negotiate a lower taxation rate with Rome. Facing the rising tide of requests for exemptions and better fiscal rates, in 1254 Pope Alexander IV bestowed on a large number of male communities in France and the Low Countries privileges that did not literally say the monks were exempt from following Gregory's statutes, but nevertheless acknowledged that the statutes were not central to Benedictine tradition. Many abbots took Alexander's words as an invitation to

Legislating monastic conduct

Visitations

Resistance

Exemptions

return to localized modes of governance and observance. Various abbesses, some of whom appear to have acted collectively under the aegis of a male chapter, likewise successfully petitioned the papacy for exemptions.

Other institutions still, took a more subtle approach, incorporating elements of Gregory's directives but fiercely protecting their specific identity. In 1235, the General Chapter of the Le Bec congregation issued lengthy statutes on such topics as the management of monastic institutions, the private morality and behaviour of monks, their diet, their clothing and that of the novices, and the issue of access by women to the monastery and the abbatial church. It also decreed that the abbots or priors of participating institutions had to read these statutes to their community three times a year, and that yearly visitations organized by the general chapter were to be carried out: those appointed to undertake the visitation would each time leave a written record of their findings for next year's delegation, and five-yearly summaries on each institution would be sent to the pope. Although these decisions broadly matched Gregory's intentions, the Le Bec General Chapter was also claiming freedom to issue its own legislation, determine the content, supervise the implementation, and finally also organize visitations on its own terms and by its own membership. In a separate clause, Le Bec even arranged for itself to be exempt from the obligation to follow the pope's statutes, and placed itself above the principles of shared governance it promoted through its General Chapter.

While the various existing orders continued to rely on their Chapters for legislative and governance purposes, in contrast the frequency of the meetings of Benedictine abbots dropped dramatically following the pope's death. The 1262 provincial chapter of Trier would be the last there before the fifteenth century. At the 1274 meeting in Salzburg, the participants literally stated that their joint efforts to regulate monastic life had borne "no fruit" (*nullus fructus*). And in the few regions where these groups remained operative, as was the case in England, the collaboration of monastic leaders was driven not by a desire to comply with papal reform principles, but as part of a strategy to stand stronger as a collective in their interactions with the higher clergy and royalty. Evidently Gregory's programme had vastly overstretched the willingness of Benedictine abbots and abbesses across the Latin West to participate in papal reform.

Coordinated counter-measures

Decline of Benedictine Chapters

4.4 Emergence and Integration of the Mendicants

Shifting lay
expectations

By the time the papal reform of institutionalized monasticism was first deployed, lay interest in the religious life had risen to unprecedented heights. At the basis of this phenomenon was a penitential trend in eleventh- and twelfth-century spirituality, decades of intense monastic and clerical preaching, and profound transformations taking place in contemporary society (such as demographic growth, urbanization, the growth of the urban middle classes, and the rise of the communes). Most men and women found an outlet for these sentiments in their everyday experience of Christian faith, but others were drawn to making radical life choices. Towards the middle decades of the twelfth century adult conversion had definitely replaced child oblation as the primary method for recruiting cloistered monastics, while the life of many laypeople living in the orbit of these communities also became increasingly subject to (quasi-)monastic regimes (above, Chapter 4.2).

Growing prominence
of private forms

But outside of these institutional settings too, numbers were growing. Some took to practising 'private' or semi-organized forms of ascetic withdrawal that were situated beyond the institutional reach: these included individuals and couples living as 'household ascetics', but also loosely organized settlements with a semi-eremitical character. Late eleventh- and early twelfth-century commentators noted the existence of various such groups of celibate couples, and even entire families. Earlier we already saw how Obazine in the 1120s originated as a settlement of hermits around which a group of religious women had spontaneously formed (above, Chapter 3.7): significantly, many of those who lived at 'primitive' Obazine were related, including 'founder' Stephen and the original founder of the female community, his mother [**S** VITA STEPHANI]. Besides such arrangements, which we can observe for Italy, France, the Low Countries, and Germany, we also have reports of growing numbers of anchorites or recluses found in both rural and urban settings [**S** ANCRENE WISSE, S LIFE OF CHRISTINA OF MARKYATE, S PHILIP OF CLAIRVAUX]. Many of these gained wide notoriety for their ascetic practices and wisdom. A much-noted example is that of Mary of Oignies (d. 1213), a woman of some means who dedicated her life to penance, prayer, manual labour and charitable works whilst living in a chaste marriage among her relatives.

Meanwhile, observers in (among other regions) northern Italy and the broad area between the Loire and Rhine rivers also noted the rising prominence of a miscellaneous cohort of people known to specialists as "lay penitents". These were typically small, informal urban communities of men and women who practised various forms of self-abnegation, believed in the importance of on penance, and in a number of cases also looked to take up an active pastoral role. Observers likewise took note of the increased visibility and social significance of groups of women led by a mistress, who practised chastity and lived a life of devotion and restraint. Members – of whom those in the Low Countries, northern France, and Germany became known as Beguines – remained in control of their assets and supported themselves through manual labour (textile production in particular). Besides praying and other devotional practices, these women provided support to the sick and needy, sometimes ran small schools, and functioned as an accessible female conversation partner for those seeking spiritual counsel or moral support. Much smaller in numbers and recognition was a male counterpart, whose practitioners became known as Beghards.

Initially, ecclesiastical and lay observers failed to grasp the significance of these trends and developments. This was partly because all of the above forms in some way or other recalled practices of private withdrawal that had existed for many centuries, or were at least familiar from narrative accounts. But also, too, the tendency was to underestimate the sheer demographic scope of recent trends. Contemporaries were at first unaware of the extent of the social and economic impact, and of the potential threat that such private asceticism held for the existing political and moral hierarchies, including those of the Church and its servants. The term 'Beguine' originated as a derogatory nickname, coined by late twelfth-century observers who apparently failed to detect the sheer social impact of, and secular support for, this emerging urban phenomenon. And in the 1180s, Pope Alexander III reportedly rejected as heresy claims by the *Humiliati* and the Waldensians (two movements of ascetic men and women in northern Italy) that they could preach penitence and conversion in public. But soon, Church administrators and lay authorities across various parts of the Latin West realized that these movements had become so prominent that dismissing them as irrelevant or outlawing them would seriously imperil not only the institutions of the Church, but also orthodoxy, and public order as a whole.

Initial response

Criticism of existing
orders

Meanwhile, various observers expressed dissatisfaction about the ability of institutionalized monastics to absorb the various lay ascetic trends and bring individuals who were suspected of unorthodoxy back to the Catholic faith (also above, Chapter 4.3). The Cistercians, that most prestigious of orders, may have commanded respect for their spiritual leadership and organizational qualities, but when the papacy sent out a number of their abbots to confront the Cathars in southern France, it quickly transpired that they were ill-equipped to bring their message to the common man. And as we already saw, the Premonstratensians too faced criticism for being too set in their institutional ways to address the above concerns effectively (above, Chapter 4.2). More generally speaking, there was a growing call for new forms of monastic life that would help contain various cenobitic and social experiments by the laity. They also, it was felt, needed to engage more actively with defending the Christian faith, with providing various forms of pastoral and social care, and with representing an apostolic ideal of preaching and poverty.

The 'Crusade at
home'

One of several responses to these concerns and challenges – besides attempts to integrate some 'lay' and 'semi-religious' forms and outlawing others (below, Chapter 4.5) – was the campaign for what might be called a 'Crusade at home'. This consisted of setting in place cohorts of highly trained, charismatic ascetics to provide spiritual guidance to the laity and maintain their orthodox belief.

Tentative beginnings

Reconstructions of how this Crusade was initially realized suggest there was a great deal of uncertainty among the principal actors over how to proceed. Over the course of the late twelfth and early thirteenth centuries, a number of individuals gained prominence and a following on the basis of their strenuous asceticism, their understanding of the spiritual concerns and social needs of the lay population, particularly in urban settings, and in some cases also their oratorial talents. Members begged for alms (hence the fact that they are generally referred to as Mendicants), ostensibly in an attempt to avoid the criticism levelled at the Cistercians and

Condemnation or
integration

Premonstratensians. Some of them ended up being condemned as heretics, but others obtained official endorsement from the ecclesiastical hierarchy and ascended to a position of high influence in the Church. In the latter category, we encounter major figures like the Spaniard Dominic Guzmàn of Caleruega (d. 1221), a canon from Osma, and the Italian Francis or Francesco Bernardone (d. 1226), a merchant's son from Assisi.

Dominic was the more conventional of the two. As a canon, he accompanied the local bishop on a mission to convert the Cathars in southern France. From this experience grew his plan to create a movement, soon to gain papal recognition as an order, of preaching canons. In a sense the Dominicans (also called the Order of the Preachers), whose observance was modelled on St Augustine's *Rule*, represented a new interpretation of the Premonstratensian model, with one very notable difference. Dominican monks dedicated a significant portion of their time in the convent to studying in private, with strict limits imposed on their involvement in matters of administration and hours spent in church. The Dominicans were learned men, highly trained communicators, and able administrators, and it is no surprise that the papacy welcomed them with open arms. They soon replaced the Cistercians as the principal persecutors of heresy and promoters of orthodoxy [**S** BERNARD GUI], and became involved in visitations of 'traditional' monastic groups – male and female – and gained a prominent role as papal legates.

Dominican origins

Profiles and impact

In 1228, the movement created a sophisticated set of statutes that laid out a vision of legislative and executive procedures [**S** STATUTES OF THE DOMINICANS]. Soon, a Dominican order was established featuring a General Chapter led by a Master General, assisted by a prior for each of the provincial chapters [**S** JORDANUS]. By that time, they were at the top of their game, claiming (together with the Franciscans) prominent chairs in theology at the University of Paris and eminence in Church affairs: inevitably, this created a great deal of resistance, particularly from the clergy, who saw their monopoly on university education challenged and their parish incomes dwindle. Women joined the movement too, but because of the prohibitions against preaching by female individuals their life experience would be vastly different from that of their male counterparts. The profound contradiction between the experiences of male and female Dominicans was not lost on observers, nor were the considerable differences in the various logistics. It was a logical development that, over time, boundaries between female Dominican communities and various 'semi-religious' forms of women's monasticism (many of which were subject to visitations by male Dominicans; below, Chapter 4.5) would become increasingly blurred.

Institutional expansion

Involvement of women

In comparison, the early Franciscans (or Friars Minor) must have come across as borderline fanatics. Like many before him,

Franciscan origins

their founder Francis had gone through a lengthy process of conversion, exploring different forms of ascetic life before settling on the one he was ultimately remembered for: that of a poor, begging monastic who preached to the laity, urged the repentance of sins and conversion to a truly Christian life, and who took nature as his cloister. Gifted with a deeply charismatic personality, he adopted a quasi-messianic identity and closeness to Creation that baffled his contemporaries. Yet he was also wise enough to realize that his followers (which included men and women) would need some form of regulated life to gain official acceptance and be allowed to function according to his ideals. In 1209, he sought and received papal approval of this movement, ostensibly with the support of the bishop of Assisi.

Efforts at regulation

Negotiating
Franciscan identity

Early Franciscan texts allow us to reconstruct the various stages of transformation from that point until Francis's death. In his original account from 1209, the movement – or at least its male wing – essentially emerges as a brotherhood of individual preachers. By 1218, it had received written approval from the papacy for its mode of life: this was then encoded in a 1221 rule by Francis himself that took stock of the movement's explosive growth and acknowledged the need for institutions. By then, Francis had already handed over his leadership to Peter Catanii (d. 1221) and his successors, quite possibly as a response to his feelings of unease over the institutional direction in which the Franciscans were heading. There followed an intense phase of negotiations with the papacy, and in 1223 a third version of the rule, once again written by Francis himself and approved by Pope Honorius III, eventually established the Franciscans as a monastic order featuring a General Chapter, a Master General, and provincial Masters. Although each friar would be attached to a specific house, his main affiliation would be to the province to which he belonged. The 1223 rule also explicitly outlined modes of conduct and interaction between members, and foresaw a noviciate, signalling the definitive transition from an open, charismatic movement to one with consolidated institutions and specific modalities and procedures for joining it.

Action and impact

From that time onwards, the Franciscan friars rapidly increased in numbers, rivalling or even surpassing the other orders and spreading throughout Europe. They often settled in towns but preached in rural areas too, and additionally sought to bring the Christian faith to non-believers: such forays into non-Christian worlds included several famously documented journeys to the Great Khan and to the inhabitants of Northern Africa in the thirteenth century, and to China in the fourteenth. The Friars also engaged with a 'Franciscan nebula' consisting of groups of laypeople who entered in a confraternity with their order while staying in the world: while something similar is documented for 'traditional' cenobitical communities and their social environment, arrangements involving the Franciscans do seem to have been exceptionally popular.

Meanwhile, the female branch of the movement, which had presumably been founded by a woman named Clare (or Ciara) Offreduccio (d. 1255), established an enclosed lifestyle for women. This was focused on contemplation rather than study or pastoral or caritative action. The Clarisses' observance, which was consolidated in a 1219 rule by a cardinal associated with Francis, distinguished itself from others by its strict dedication to poverty, and a spirituality deeply imbued with notions of humility and dedication to Christ's suffering. Later on, in 1227, they were placed under the authority of the Franciscan Master General: but Clare herself fiercely resisted papal pressure, and ended up having the rule she had written for her own monastery of San Damiano approved in 1253 [**S** CLARA]. Inevitably, the experience of life in female Franciscan convents was profoundly different from that in the male branch of the movement.

The Clarisses

The integration of the Franciscan movement was fraught with difficulties. In 1228 Pope Gregory IX declared Francis a saint and in 1230 decreed that members were not bound by the severe lifestyle outlined in his *Testament* (which called for an extreme form of poverty). These interventions essentially divorced Francis's charismatic legacy from his persona as an institutional leader, which Gregory considered irrelevant for emulation by the order's current membership. Gregory's successor, Urban IV, would likewise disconnect Clare's memory from her institutional achievement, creating an order of Clarisses based on a newly fashioned rule. By 1245, the Franciscans were allowed to accept gifts of buildings and estates on behalf of the papacy, which became the formal owner of the properties. The order could then use them to establish a monastery, church building, or other religious institution. A testimony to the uneasy relationship of the Franciscans with their founder's legacy following his death is the fact that an official account of Francis's life was a long time in the making. Thomas of Celano (d. c. 1260)

Reception of Francis's and Clare's legacy

made three different versions, each one striking a different tone in describing the man's character and achievements [**S** Thomas], but the order's Master General Bonaventure (d. 1274) found all of them unsuitable. He went to great lengths to have them destroyed, and produced yet another version.

Tensions in
Franciscan ideology

Behind this process of drastic *réécriture* of the founder's life and legacies, loomed large, divisive questions over poverty. Franciscan ideology advocated complete renunciation of all worldly goods: but many groups received substantial gifts from local benefactors and ended up living in established houses with estates, stirring controversy with hardliners in the movement. The question would split the Franciscan order into two factions: the Spirituals, who advocated the strictest poverty in all respects; and the Conventuals, who stood for absolute poverty of the individual, but lived in institutional settings that were formally owned by the papacy and that accumulated wealth in order to support their membership's subsistence, education, and ministry.

Further successful
experiments

The Dominicans and Franciscans were but two exponents of the Great Mendicant Experiment of the early to mid-thirteenth century. The Carmelites originated as a group of contemplative hermits who settled on Mount Carmel in present-day Israel: in 1206/1213, they received a rule from Patriarch Albert of Jerusalem. Subsequently, some members transferred to small settlements on Cyprus and Sicily, then to England, and eventually also to other parts of Europe. Over time, the movement's eremitical identity evolved into a pastoral one that featured an observance that bore strong resemblance to that of the Dominicans and Franciscans. In 1256, the pope also brought together a number of hermit groups from Italy to form the missionary Order of the Hermits of St Augustine (also the Augustinian Friars or Austin Order). Like the Carmelites, they were relatively successful in spreading their model across regional and political boundaries. The Hungarian Pauline Order similarly originated as a conglomerate of eremitical communities. It was given various sets of statutes by papal legates and local bishops from the 1260s onwards, in the fourteenth century eventually receiving papal approval, a consolidated set of statutes and a rule, and various exemptions. Although technically mendicants, the eremitical Celestines – who practiced a variant of Benedictine community life and emerged in the mid-thirteenth century in the Abruzzo region of Italy – stood closer to these strands of monastic life than to cenobitical ones. Thanks to the support of Pope Gregory IX, their movement rapidly acquired order-like features and subsequently established communities in France, the Low Countries, and parts of Germany.

These orders were the fortunate ones, for by the mid-thirteenth century, Church leaders were becoming increasingly reluctant to recognize movements that bore little promise of being self-sufficient and of contributing to papal finances. The Sack Friars, who had recently originated near Marseilles, initially proved very popular with patrons, which led to the establishment of settlements in France, Italy, the Iberian Peninsula, and England. But it fell victim to a cull of supposedly redundant orders that was instigated by a 1274 council held in Lyon. Likewise directly affected by the cull, or the subject of papal or episcopal interventions that in the decades around 1300 caused them to fade into obscurity, were: the Servants of Mary (established in 1233 near Florence); Poor Catholics (consisting of former Waldensians); Friars of Our Lady of Areno (in southern France), Augustinian Servites (in urban contexts in Italy, and later in France and Germany), and the Friars of the Cross (Low Countries and later on England). The Spiritualist Franciscans and similar variants of mendicant spirituality in subsequent decades would be targeted by papal inquisitors, who suspected them of heresy (below, Chapter 4.5). And in the same time period, another strand of 'religious Crusaders' came under attack. At the beginning of the fourteenth century, the Knights Templar were accused of malversations and criminal conduct, and violently dissolved: fiscal and other considerations, as well as growing resistance from French royalty and the papacy played a significant role in this. As we shall see in Chapter 4.5, however, the loss of diversity in organized strands of monasticism was more than made up by the rise of 'semi-religious' movements.

Suppression of mendicant movements

4.5 'Semi-religious' Movements in the Later Middle Ages

By the turn of the twelfth century, even the greatest sceptics realized that lay monastic groups had become far too prominent a phenomenon, spiritually and socially, to make either suppression or their absorption into institutionalized monasticism a realistic prospect. Pope Innocent III in particular understood that his

Challenges of integration

reign was to be one of major transitions in the religious landscape, whether he and his clerical associates liked it or not. He decided that the wisest option by far was to incorporate lay monasticism as a separate monastic cohort. The resulting dialectic between these lay groups, the ecclesiastical authorities (both local and supra-local), and secular patrons and supporters, gave rise to the emergence of what scholars tend to refer to as 'semi-religious' or 'lay' movements.

Formation of distinct movements (margin)

Many of these movements were the result of church leaders assigning communities that featured a roughly similar lifestyle to a single, regulated strand of monasticism with a distinct legal status, mode of governance, and customs. While this worked well in theory, in practice we see that lay monastic experiences to a significant extent continued to be shaped by local circumstances and expectations, and that throughout the later medieval period their treatment by secular and clerical agents remained highly dependent on the context. On paper at least, incorporation was a relatively straightforward process. In 1201, Innocent addressed the 'Humiliati problem' by decreeing that there was room to organize a "Third Way" or "Third Order" (*Via tertia*), consisting of laypeople who enjoyed licence to preach about moral issues – not about dogma – and in specific localities only. He also prescribed that members organize themselves according to the governance model (a General Chapter, visitation, and the use of statutes) he was about to impose on all cloistered monastics. A similar thing happened to the Waldensians, who were allowed to resume their activities, albeit under strict conditions, from 1207/1208 onwards.

Approaches (margin)

The 'Third Order' (margin)

While Innocent's decrees illustrate how the papacy tried to address the phenomenon of these lay movements in the short term, case studies for the Brothers and Sisters of Penitence and for the Beguines illustrate best how the process of awarding loosely organized lay monastic phenomena a distinct legal and institutional identity unfolded in the longer term. The Brothers and Sisters of Penitence, one of many northern Italian groupings of 'lay penitents', first acquired a distinct identity when a papal decree of 1221 awarded them a set of customs. From this point onwards, member communities were subject to supervision and visitations by the higher clergy and by various monastic orders, including the Cistercians and Mendicants. Over time, the movement became increasingly implicated in the 'Franciscan nebula', and eventually evolved

Brothers and Sisters of Penitence (margin)

into what became known as the Third Order of St Francis [S Documents on the Third Order].

However, it never achieved a unified institutional, legal,
or functional identity, with the exception of a cohort of quasi-
institutionalized communities of women. These female Third Order
communities proved particularly attractive to urban patrons and
recruits because of the extraordinary flexibility of their status:
in 1289 Pope Nicholas IV awarded them a set of regulations that
allowed each community to choose between a wide range of activities, including care for the sick, teaching, and contemplation. The
later fourteenth century would also see the rise of a Dominican
Third Order for women, which received papal approval in 1405. The
profound contradiction between the Dominicans' focus on pastoral work [S Hugo of Saint-Cher] and their female counterparts'
contemplative and enclosed lifestyle was not an issue to Church
leaders: presumably, their main aim was to answer a perceived
need to allow women to participate in Dominican spiritual culture,
and to also capitalize on the Dominicans' extensive experience
with supervision and visitations of female communities.

In contrast to this fairly swift action by church leaders to inte-   Beguine integration
grate the Penitents and similar movements, the Beguines only
gained recognition as a distinct lay movement in the Church by
the mid-thirteenth century. This 'delay' was chiefly because the
practitioners did not actually see themselves as part of a cohesive movement operating across community boundaries, but
founded their identity entirely in local circumstances. It is also
likely that the difference from 'household asceticism' and other,
non-institutionalized forms of community life for women was not
always easy to discern, especially for outsiders. And initially at
least, members had no specific interest in pursuing institutionalization or integration with other groups. This changed when, beginning in the 1230s, some groups of Beguines under the leadership
of an elected mistress – a first sign of institutionalizing trends that
were happening on the local level – began acquiring communal
properties and subsequently set out to secure their legal interests.

In the following two decades, we can see several of them
making various arrangements with the local clergy and accepting
regulations as part of these deals. Some petitioned the papacy for
recognition in order to consolidate their institutional and legal   Negotiated
interests. In 1233, Gregory IX recognized all the Beguine commu-   outcomes

nities in Germany, on condition that they lived under the authority of a mistress – effectively meaning that informal, non-hierarchical groups of 'household ascetics' were once more forced into the margins of lay monastic life for women. They also had to agree to supervision and visitations by Cistercian and mendicant monastics. In recognition of the fact that the Beguines' shared identity across group boundaries was still mostly a matter of outside perception, Gregory did not require them to hold a General Chapter, accept new statutes, or relinquish the autonomy of each individual community. His liberal attitude was no doubt inspired by the lobbying of clerical supporters, including a number of prominent theologians and hagiographers, while secular patrons had also resisted the imposition of overly restrictive sets of rules.

Diverse roles and identities

Diverse local preferences and expectations, patronage arrangements, recruitment patterns, and the overall need for differentiation in the dense lay monastic landscape of late medieval towns, together explain the contrasts in the observance of neighbouring communities. The more contemplative ones leaned towards spatial and other arrangements that were not a great deal different from that of cloistered nuns, with a strict internal hierarchy and a tendency to shield individual members from interactions with the secular world. But in other places, the women enjoyed substantial freedom to orient their religious vocation according to their own judgement – whether teaching, caring for the sick, performing manual labour, or providing spiritual assistance – whilst retaining a great deal of control over their personal situation. Their status at the interface between the secular world and that of monasticism may be one of the explanations for the mystical tradition that flourished in their midst, and produced some of the most enthralling spiritual literature of the later medieval period [S MECHTILD].

Flexible identities

The flexibility of Third Order and Beguine identities explains the movement's enduring popularity with local patrons. A mass of primary sources – statutes, charters, various other archival texts, and a modest number of ego documents and other narrative accounts – bears witness to the embedding of communities in urban and aristocratic patronage networks. Financially, socially, and spiritually, the mode of life they offered was an attractive package for women from the urban middle classes who were drawn to the monastic life. At the same time, patrons and other local agents were keen to protect and expand the communities' role in urban environments as purveyors of a wide range of services. In consequence, towns in northern France, the Low Countries, and parts of Germany ended up featuring up to several dozen Beguine communities, in some cases occupying large sections of the urban space and representing a very sizeable percentage of the total population; Third Order communities were less widely represented, but numerically and otherwise significant nonetheless.

Popularity of Beguine lifestyles

The backlash in the late thirteenth and fourteenth centuries against Beguine lifestyles in particular was likewise inscribed in the relative freedom these women had previously enjoyed. Numerous Beguines in the Languedoc region had become involved in personal and ideological networks with Spiritualist Franciscans, whose pauperism and millenarian expectations, inspired by the work of theologian and monastic founder Joachim of Fiore (d. 1202), ended up drawing the attention of the inquisitors. Here and in other places, Church leaders persecuted the women who were implicated in these radical ideologies, focussing in particular on those who had gained a reputation as visionaries and prophets: one was the French mystic and author Marguerite Porete (d. 1310), who was burnt at the stake. Shortly after her death, the 1311/1312 Vienne Council launched a general attack on the Beguines, denouncing the fact that they did not take vows, refused to renounce all private property, and even declined to strictly follow a written rule – all privileges that had been granted to them by papal decision less than a century earlier.

Suppression by the Church

The council's invective echoed declining support for the movement in regions where urban economies were struggling and Beguines were increasingly regarded as unwanted competition to the local workforce. In these places, Beguines often lost their former exemptions from guild regulations and their ability to set their prices and other income according to the market. Their overall presence faded in favour of more strictly regulated, cloistered forms of monastic life. However, there were other regions where urban economies proved far more resilient and support for Beguine practitioners and communities remained strong: here, local supporters as well as lay and clerical rulers were much less inclined to accept clerical criticism of the Beguines and their communities. In the Low Countries and in Paris in particular, the contribution of Beguine women to lay spirituality and the embedding of their communities in family strategies, patronage networks, production chains, and

Declining lay support

Enduring support in some regions

education provision, continued to be highly valued. On being confronted with resistance from local lay society and powerful aristocratic patrons to plans to suppress the movement altogether, Pope John XXII (d. 1334) accepted that the communities that had survived the culls would be allowed to continue operating. The proviso was that male orders (particularly the Dominicans) would henceforth oversee members' orthodox views and conduct. In these regions, Beguine communities flourished throughout the later medieval period, and continued to have a major impact on local society via their devotional practices, informal preaching, labour, teaching, and finally also their participation (along with male preachers and monastics) in cultures of spiritual and intellectual debate.

Enduring support for other forms

Local support explains why other variants of lay monastic life likewise stayed comparatively intact in the face of high-strung condemnations by Church leaders and councils. These variants included groups of poor women, often widows, who cohabited in town houses (some German sources refer to these as *Gotzhusen* or *Seelshuzen*), married couples living in ascetic households, and other forms that we have already encountered in this book. As they did with the Beguines, mendicant agents visited many of these informal communities, relaying in the process admiration for the members' commitment to the ascetic life and their contribution to

Interactions with established orders

local affairs. In carrying out these duties, some of these men forged intense, long-lasting spiritual and emotive relationships with lay monastics. Countless testimonies relating to these interactions reveal that the various boundaries between lay and vowed monastics often remained highly permeable, and that real-life relationships – be they emotional, intellectual, or strictly spiritual – were far less hierarchical than one might suspect. One example for Italy is that of Veronica da Binasco (d. 1497), a poor woman who lived as a converse sister in the 'open monastery' of Santa Martha in Milan: the Benedictine nun Benedetta of Vimercate, who recorded Veronica's ecstatic visions, also tells us of her engagements with mendicant preachers as well as her deep understanding of the content of their preaching.

Devotio Moderna

Although Veronica's biography has a distinctive anecdotal quality, it exemplifies a broad push in the fourteenth and fifteenth centuries to reconcile lay and monastic spiritualties. So the Low Countries movement of the Modern Devotion (*Devotio Moderna*), in the early stages of its existence actively fostered intense interactions within a 'nebulous' cohort of lay and regular monastics. Its founder, Geert Grote (d. 1384), was a university-trained merchant's son from the town of Deventer, in the current-day Netherlands. He immersed himself in contemporary mysticism (in the first place influenced by Jan van Ruysbroeck, d. 1381) and eremitical life (as practised by the Carthusians at Monnikhuizen near Arnhem). Although he spent much of his later years at Monnikhuizen, he would also invest a great deal of energy directing and counselling a small, ascetic community of lay women living at his ancestral home in Deventer. These so-called Sisters of the Common Life, who sustained themselves through manual labour, lived under the direction of a prioress, and practised a lifestyle that reconciled contemplation with conduct and action in a way that reflected each individual's personal dedication to her own spiritual goal. From around 1380, Grote also established a community of laymen and clerics, the Brothers of the Common Life, who supported themselves primarily through the production and copying of manuscripts.

> Sisters of the Common Life

> Brothers of the Common Life

Grote was a controversial figure in his own time. He denounced simoniac clerics and wealthy monks and rejected the need for monastics to take vows, arguing that a personal commitment to the authentic spirit of the Gospels was enough to reach unity with the divine. However, the final years of his life would see him creating a rule drafted after that of the canons regular of Groenendaal near Brussels. And following his death, his associate Florens Radewijns (d. 1400) founded the monastery of Windesheim near Zwolle, which soon created a series of daughter houses in the Low Countries and neighbouring parts of France, Germany, and Switzerland, and established the so-called Windesheimer congregation [**S** CONSTITUTIONES WINDESHEMENSIUM]. The Council of Basel, which began its sessions in 1431, sanctioned the congregation's interventions in communities of canons and canonesses in Germany. In doing so it also gave the impetus for the formation of an additional Windesheimer 'nebula' of non-affiliated houses; the influence was felt in Italy too, where a congregational movement emerged around the Windesheim-influenced abbey of San Salvatore in Laterano, in Rome.

> Controversy and consolidation

> Windesheim

> Expansion of the congregation

Windesheimer monastics were highly regarded for their personal piety, their dedication to private works, and their outstanding spiritual achievements. The most notable example was Thomas a Kempis (d. 1471). Thomas's handbook of spiritual instructions, *The*

> Impact

Imitation of Christ, was an immediate success with monastic and lay audiences, and qualifies as one of the bestsellers of the medieval age. As such, it also testifies to the fact that achieving the full potential of the monastic experience was no longer – or had never been – exclusively associated with a cloistered existence, or with individuals who had drawn strict boundaries between themselves and the secular world. The monastic experience was now thought of as attainable by all the Christian faithful.

4.6 Late Medieval Challenges and Experiences

Traditional interpretations

Until recently, specialists of monastic history generally viewed the period from the later thirteenth century until the end of the medieval period as an era of contraction. To back this up, they provided what appears to be irrefutable evidence of internal decline, persecution, and social, religious, and intellectual marginalization. Contemplative groups could no longer boast prominence as a centre of education and learning; their membership no longer stood at the forefront of the intellectual and literary elites; and their devotional practices and claimed service to society seemed out of touch with the expectations of would-be recruits and the laity in general. Against the background of major disruption in society and in the Church (including epidemics, protracted warfare, civil insurgencies, and the Great Schism), numerous communities went through episodes of institutional crisis. Estates and incomes were destroyed or appropriated, conflicts erupted over episcopal ordination of abbots and abbesses, and debates over visitations and taxes were fraught. In some regions, the Black Death not only decimated monastics and their lay servants, but also caused a precipitous drop in tithes and other incomes. Among other things, this compelled the remaining groups to switch from the direct cultivation of land to the leasing out of property at prices that allowed lay farmers to make a profit. In the meantime, lay and clerical rulers were looking to claim the resources of communities via taxation and (towards the end of the medieval period) the appointment of commendatory abbots.

A compounding factor to the difficulties experienced within those strands of monastic life with a focus on prayer service, which affected both recruitment numbers and patronage, was the competition from regular canons, mendicant and eremitical orders, and

Declining influence

Disruptions

Secular interference

lay movements like the Beguines, Third orders, and Penitents. But several of these 'newer' movements were facing serious difficulties too. Soon after their establishment as orders, the Dominicans and Franciscans lost favour with the secular clergy for their prominence – or as the clergy saw it, their interference – in university settings, their incursions into the sphere of parish priests, and their gaining of key positions in the ecclesiastical hierarchy. The dispute between the Spiritualists and Conventualists additionally damaged the Franciscans' reputation, while the popularity of millenarian ideas and texts in Spiritualist milieus alerted Church leaders to the risk of heresy. Difficulties in 'newer' strands

After nearly eight decades of inactivity, the papacy made a first attempt to resume its monastic reform policies. Between 1332 and 1342 Pope Benedict XII, a former Cistercian monk, issued a series of decrees that stated his intention to reform the governance and financial affairs of the Benedictines, Cistercians, Franciscans, and canons regular, with a view – so he said – to restoring the ideals of the original founders. His criticism that male monastics had lost sight of their ascetic calling had a precedent in the 1294 papal decree *Periculoso*, which stated that the licentious conduct of vowed nuns and canonesses required the imposition of strict enclosure on all female communities. Yet, the response to this comprehensive reform effort was tepid at best. When Benedict sent out his decrees, each order acknowledged then shelved them. The reform the pope had additionally planned to roll out for the Carthusians and Dominicans faltered on the outright refusal of their General Chapters to cooperate with what they saw as an illegitimate attempt to intervene in their autonomy as a legislative body. And although Benedict's decrees for cloistered women did impact on the experience of life in some communities – for instance, via the introduction of barred windows, locked doors, partitions, and strict regulations on the separate use of spaces the women shared with male religious – in many other places *Periculoso* remained a dead letter. Papal reform attempts Tepid response

In part also because the success of these top-down reforms was so limited, there was a growing sense that the proliferation of institutionalized monastic lifestyles had passed beyond the point of diminishing returns. One example is that of the abbey of Chalais [**S** CHARTERS OF CHALAIS], an 1124 foundation in the Isère region of France, and its corresponding movement. Situated in close Decline of movements proximity to the Carthusian motherhouse of La Grande Chartreuse, Chalais housed a semi-eremitical community that practised an observance inspired by the *Rule of St Benedict* and over time established a small regional congregation. But by the early thirteenth century they were outflanked by the Carthusians, who by then boasted far more developed institutional features and had been far more successful in promoting their 'brand' of monastic life and services to the outside world. Soon, the Chalaisian order disintegrated and its founding abbey was turned into a Carthusian convent. Another example is that of the Grandmontines, which as we noted above (Chapter 4.2) suffered instability from c. 1200 onwards, and saw their membership dwindling rapidly: many former houses in the movement were subsequently turned into small communities of clerics, parish churches, or estates belonging to another monastic institution.

Meanwhile, mendicant movements of the mid to later thirteenth century struggled to obtain papal recognition because their poverty ethos made them potentially unsustainable and definitely unattractive for papal finances (above, Chapter 4.4). More generally speaking, the growing number of movements and communities, some of which were very small, put growing strain on the few orders the popes and other clerical rulers still trusted to carry out visitations, while clerical rulers themselves likewise struggled to carry out their duty of oversight effectively. Visitation reports complained about the lax conduct of cloistered monastics, their sexual improprieties, the many apostates who fled the monastery for a secular life, and the all-too-casual attitude of abbots, abbesses, and other leaders with regard to the involvement of the laity in monastic affairs. Lay commentators, although they were often supportive of specific older and newer forms, were sceptical of the possibility that such large numbers of monastics in such a broad range of movements could all be sincerely dedicated to their purpose in life. Even though satirical depictions of religious were hardly a new phenomenon in the fourteenth and fifteenth centuries [**S** Bernard of Morval, **S** Concilium], the genre and its tropes now flourished. Monks and nuns were routinely cast in the role of gluttonous buffoons who cared nothing for the ascetic ideal; sinning against humility, chastity, and poverty, they forgot their promises in their eagerness to seek out the pleasures and distractions of secular life.

Negative reports from visitations

Lay commentaries and satire

These and other reports of institutional and spiritual crisis, failed attempts at restoration, and absorption into other movements make for a compelling story of contraction and decline. But as we already saw for earlier phases in the medieval monastic past, we must be wary of collating individual instances of crisis into a general picture, or indeed of seeing a binary divide between 'conservative' and 'progressive' movements in this period. Both of these traditional approaches are based, we must remember, on the above-mentioned clerical criticisms, lay satire, polemics between monastics, and on early modern assessments by (mostly Protestant) critics of monasticism pre-1500. It also draws on former historians who were looking to postulate the eleventh and twelfth centuries as the 'golden age' of medieval monastic life and the following period as one of global institutional decline, growing moral laxity, and contraction.

Nuancing arguments

In contrast, more recent studies have pointed at the need for multiple modes of differentiation. A first such mode is regional. For instance, we see that the Dominicans and Franciscan expansion in south, west, and central Europe diminished greatly by the early fourteenth century. But in Poland, Lithuania, Hungary, Dalmatia and other parts of northern and eastern Europe this expansion continued far longer. And while Benedictine leaders on the Continent showed a lack of interest post-1270 in holding regional Chapters, in England such gatherings remained operational because abbots relied on them to join forces in the struggle with local adversaries and competitors, and to raise the profile of their communities as intercessors for the welfare of the state. In other places, abbots (and presumably also abbesses) relied on more conventional instrument of confraternity agreements to facilitate collaboration across institutional boundaries and pool human and other resources.

Regional differences

A second mode we need to differentiate within our analysis is the local – in other words, the level of single communities. Investigation of what happened in such individual institutional settings likewise yields a far more complex picture. Admittedly, many communities and even entire congregations throughout the Latin West faced financial, legal, and spiritual crises. Some experienced a substantial drop in new recruits, clashed with local society, monastic competitors, lay and clerical rulers, visitators, and sometimes even the Inquisition. Others were unable to compete with institutions and entire movements that were better developed, had a more

Local and institutional differences

precisely defined corporate identity, and enjoyed a greater impact on contemporary lay spirituality. But not all institutions experienced the above challenges at the same time, for the same reasons, and with the same intensity.

Indications of flexibility

Evidence of communities' flexibility in adapting to changing circumstances is plentiful. Numerous Benedictine, Cistercian, and other monasteries retained a major footprint on the religious, cultural, and social landscape. These institutions and their membership continued to hold very significant estates and urban properties; retained the favour of a sizeable portion of the local population and of major patrons; and continued to invest in infrastructure and technological innovation. Many monastic groups also carried on their hospitality and aid to the poor and to pilgrims; their functional and spiritual relationships with non-cloistered and lay monastics; and their engagement with the laity through preaching and sermon-writing. Finally, they continued to produce significant works of theology, hagiography and historiography; made and acquired major works of art and pieces of music; amassed considerable libraries; and oversaw major architectural projects. Cultural activity was still considerable, if often less noted outside of cloistered contexts: among the more exotic examples is that of a fifteenth-century Benedictine – a man or woman – who turned Benedict's life story as told by Gregory the Great into an Icelandic saga [**S** SAGA]. Over the course of the later thirteenth and fourteenth centuries, French and English Benedictine houses began to seek permission to reduce their intercessory prayer service and increase their involvement in secular schooling, ostensibly in an attempt

University training

to enhance their social impact. Numerous contemplative monastics also found their way into university contexts, a process that was aided by the creation of colleges where young monks received training in theology and canon law. Benedictine, Cistercian, and Carthusian scholars also adapted their written output and thematic scope to reflect ongoing intellectual and spiritual developments. In the process, they developed a broad range of intellectual interests that blossomed in Humanistic circles of the fifteenth and early sixteenth centuries.

Negotiated measures

Some abbots also sought to counter adverse trends and circumstances by tightening links between their institution and powerful members of the lay elite. Such was the case in France, where many houses joined the *garde royale* to enjoy the king's special legal protection and financial aid in return for certain concessions: the king's right to name a commendatary abbot, claim certain incomes from monastic estates, and use a monastery's facilities. Here and in other regions, numerous individual communities and their leadership also actively worked to establish long-term functional and spiritual relationships with a host of urban and rural stakeholders, deeply entrenching themselves in the surrounding society in order to weather the worst social and economic shocks. The carefully negotiated nature of these arrangements and the enduring shaping of monastic experiences by local circumstances sheds different light on the question of why there was so much resistance to various reform attempts by the papacy and other ecclesiastical agents.

The staunchest critics of reform were often those individuals with a deep, first-hand understanding of the daily experience of monastics and the embedded nature of this experience in the local environment. No less than Humbert of Romans (d. 1277), the Master General of the Dominicans, himself argued that enforcement of strict enclosure would overburden female houses with the expense of rearranging monastic space and obtaining additional supervision. To explain his point, he indicated that it would compel certain communities to reduce their numbers to keep them viable and also require them to relocate to urban settings to make supervision and provisioning practicable. Humbert and subsequent critics of *Periculoso* also opined that putting women religious literally behind bars was hardly an effective way to persuade outsiders of their ritual purity, and that successful adaptation to changing circumstances almost always happened via a bottom-up process.

Defending local realities

'Trans-monastic' exchanges were also frequent, deliberate, and far less counter-intuitive than historians have sometimes suspected. They were the basis on which subsequent reform trends and approaches grew, providing a grassroots counterweight to ill-received top-down initiatives. Ecclesiastical rulers of the later fourteenth and fifteenth centuries (including those associated with the reform councils of Constance (1414–1418) and Basel (1431–1449)) likewise favoured a bottom-up approach to reform. In this approach, the impetus for change came from heterogeneous circles of monastics, members of the (local) clergy, lay rulers and their advisors, university theologians and intellectuals, city councils, and finally also members of the urban and rural lay population.

Bottom-up reform

Role of the Carthusians

Carthusian agents frequently played a central role in these initiatives. Their order's rise to prominence had been driven by its combination of a strict, eremitical lifestyle with a spiritual culture deriving from an attractive blend of mysticism and (from the fourteenth century onwards) Humanistic study. This gave them an authoritative voice in various debates over how to 'renew' monastic observance. A few individuals became abbots of Benedictine and Cistercian houses that had either been just reformed or were considered in need of reform, but far more numerous were those who coached and facilitated the initiatives of local leaders. Meanwhile, Dominican and Franciscan theologians laid the groundwork for a return to their respective movements' ascetic origins. In the case of the latter, this led to the rise of the so-called Observants: they were represented in many corners of the Latin world, including in Portugal, Spain, Italy, Poland, Germany, and France [S BERNARDINO]. As with the Carthusians, individuals from both orders influenced and assisted with a range of local initiatives by leading agents in other strands of organized monastic life. And beginning in the later fourteenth century, the same was also true for the Windesheimer movement.

Other influences

Observant Reform

The late medieval push for a return to a stricter, more 'authentic' monastic observance – a phenomenon that is aptly referred to by historians as the Observant Reform – extended into the Benedictine and Cistercian movements. Here too, we see a distinct tendency not to work with instructions coming from a clerical authority, but to pursue the reform of monastic observance on the ground. Beginning in the later 1340s, Swedish noblewoman Brigitta (d. 1373) established a quasi-congregational, regional movement of observant Benedictine nuns (and a brief-lived one for monks) from her foundation of Vadstena in Sweden. Further congregations and 'nebulas' of similarly organized communities for Benedictine men arose in Padua, Bologna, Valladolid, and Montserrat. Of particular note is the Italian house of Subiaco, which in the 1360s issued a set of customs that functioned to spread a more austere mode of life to other communities, giving the abbey a role of 'reform centre' that reminds us of Cluny in the tenth and early eleventh centuries.

Brigittines

Male initiatives

Monastic leaders north of the Alps soon learned of this trend in Italian Benedictinism, and with the support of the reform councils and a number of lay and clerical rulers revived the long-dormant provincial Chapters. Some of these Chapters promoted a combination of the austere lifestyle practised at Subiaco with elements from the Carthusians' observance. The abbeys of Melk (now in Austria), Kasti (Palatinate), and Bursfeld (Lower Saxony) became prominent centres where these views were turned into real-life practices [S STATUTES OF BURSFELD]. In the process, they influenced other communities in their orbit [S CONSUETUDINES SPRINGIRSBACENSES-RODENSES]. Bursfeld became the centre of a congregational movement (sanctioned by papal decree in the 1450s) that based its activities on the principles of unanimity and mutual aid, and featured legislative procedures as well as a system of visitation: numerous female monasteries also joined its 'nebula'. Bursfeld

Other institutions were influential in an indirect sense, in that 'nebulas' centred on their observance formed spontaneously. In 1284/1287, Abbot Guillaume de Julémont of the Benedictine house of Saint-Laurent in Liège drafted a customary that provided detailed instructions on how to reform the observance of his subjects' life. In it, he acknowledged the influence of Bernard's Cluniac customary, the "older customs" of the Cistercians and the Premonstratensians, the work of the above-mentioned Humbert of Romans, but first and foremost that of a local Carthusian theologian named Godefroid of Fontaines. Although the direct impact of Guillaume's efforts must have been strictly local, in later centuries his customary was copied and used in several of the area's major Benedictine houses. Meanwhile, the Cistercian General Chapter launched several of its own attempts to reform the movement, with mixed success. Possibly in response to this, the Cistercian congregation of Sibculo (1418) took inspiration from the Benedictine bottom-up approach. Sibculo's movement inspired the emergence of a gathering of about twenty predominantly male communities that practised a very strict observance and were situated mostly in the Low Countries and northern Germany. Another such congregation was that of Castille, which ended up clashing with the Cistercian General Chapter over its ambition (approved by the pope) to become independent. Other conflicts arising over such 'bottom-up' or 'grassroots' movements within the Cistercian order, including a number in Italy, reflect negative views held by some concerning the General Chapter's ability to understand local needs and circumstances. 'Nebulous' movements Cistercian reform initiatives

Despite these reform efforts, globally speaking organized monasticism faced a major backlash in the sixteenth century. Various trends had resulted in a considerable growth in the number Expansion of monastic movements of new foundations and that of new congregations, the like of which had not been seen since the twelfth and early thirteenth centuries. Along with the expansion of lay monastic movements, this led to considerable density in the monastic landscape, in some regions of Europe at least. Such developments created various pressures on local and regional society, and made it plainly obvious to clerical and lay rulers, city governments, and other stakeholders, that there were massive cultural and material resources held in these institutions. At the same time, reformed communities were also becoming more active in asserting their claims on various rights and resources than they had been in a long time. Reorganization of monastic estates and the redirection of economic ventures confronted the rural population with heavier taxation and less freedom in their agricultural activities. Deliberate attempts to maintain and enforce monastic privileges, exemptions, and other claims to independence led to further confrontations with lay and clerical stakeholders.

Lay resistance

In some parts of Europe, such local confrontations over time created the momentum for much bigger ones. These include most famously the Dissolution of the Monasteries in England during the 1530s, which must be considered alongside various smaller initiatives in Protestant, and even some Catholic, regions on the Continent. Such drastic transformations obviously had complex roots in late medieval religion and politics. However, the fact that monasteries, priories, friaries, and subsidiary institutions at the time held almost half of the ecclesiastical revenues and a third of all benefices of the parishes was clearly a major factor in King Henry VIII's push for an outright suppression of institutionalized monasticism. In other contexts too, concerns grew among the nobility and the other lay elites over whether the tighter administration of rights and privileges and a more distant relationship with patrons would mean a loss for them of any meaningful return. In other words, would their investments – donations, the awarding of certain privileges and rights, sending their sons and daughters to become members, having their relatives buried in an abbatial church, patronizing art and music – still result in influence, symbolic prestige, and a privileged relationship with the monastics? As an alternative, some enthusiastically supported communities that pursued strict individual and communal poverty. But others did not find that an attractive option either. Many of the wealthy must have recoiled at

Dissolution

Declining attraction for the laity

the idea of seeing their adult offspring enter a life of austerity or even deprivation, and even more would have viewed the insistent call for austerity and strenuous devotion of certain movements as socially disruptive, possibly even sectarian.

Perhaps the greatest problem of all, though, was that it had become hard for observers and even for practitioners to discern a monastic cohort that was still somehow unified in its ascetic mission. Already in the twelfth century, the Premonstraten- Criticism of diversity sian Anselm of Havelberg (d. 1158) had written that the diversity of lifestyles and rules was causing people to lose their trust in institutionalized monastic life as something that was God-given rather than a human creation. Developments over the course of the later Middle Ages did nothing to assuage these sentiments. Things were not helped, also, by the fact that polemics between pro-reform groups and those that stood for a *status quo* created deep divisions within various movements and across movement boundaries. Many monastics resisted reform not out of principle, but because they realized that subjecting entire communities to a harsh ascetic regime marked by strenuous devotional practice and self-abnegation would put excessive strain on those members who were less (or not at all) prepared to deal with the physical and psychological consequences. And as we saw above, those who resisted reform also appreciated that the deleterious consequences for individual members would jeopardize both the recruitment of new personnel and the routine functioning of these communities. Many critics also realized that stripping the monastics' physical environment – the abbatial churches, the monasteries themselves, the goods and artefacts – of a former lustre might also deter wealthy patrons who wished to see their high status adequately represented in these places.

But perhaps worse than these internal rifts was the fact that Polemics and their impact various disputes spilled into public awareness, with consequences that were far more serious than any of the participants would have anticipated. By publishing all the dirt (and more) they could find on their adversaries, monastic polemicists inadvertently fed growing public sentiment against institutionalized forms of ascetic withdrawal. Intellectuals and social commentators, most famously Desiderius Erasmus (d. 1536) and Martin Luther (d. 1546), watched with a mixture of dismay and glee as some of these polemics descended into vulgar shouting matches. It did not help that many key contributors were educated in circles linked to international networks of university educated theologians, law specialists, courtiers and counsellors, and that their enthusiastic use of the newly invented movable print spread any major argument without much time for criticality or reflection on the consequences.

Loss of charisma
All these things gave rise to the idea that a great chapter in the history of Christian monasticism was closing. At the beginning of the sixteenth century, the Benedictine abbot and chronicler John Trithemius (d. 1516) wrote about the later Middle Ages as a time when the apostolic fervour of the founders of the eleventh and twelfth centuries had been either squandered or lost [**S** JOHN TRITHEMIUS]. Along with many others, he looked forward to new beginnings but was unable to provide a realistic scenario. As it turned out, it would take another a century and a half before the Catholic Church came up with a cohesive and strategic vision for the future. In the meantime, diversity and a high degree of experimentation remained defining features of Western monastic life.

II State of the Art

1 Introductory Comments

Over the last half-century, the study of medieval monasticism(s) has been utterly transformed. Beginning in the 1960s, for the first time lay scholars began to outnumber monastic and clerical ones, a development that loosened the ties that had previously existed between discussions of monastic life as a historical phenomenon and the identity narratives of various orders and religious movements. These historians challenged the standard notion that the changing face of monasticism throughout Christian history was symptomatic of three things: one, humanity's never-ending quest to realize an original, ahistorical ideal of unity with God; two, recurrent attempts to return to monasticism's 'authentic' roots as established by the Desert Fathers and to the 'primitive' ideals of the early apostolic Church; and three, the cycle of charismatic origins, blossoming, and decline that apparently characterized all movements that tried to realize these two goals. Instead, secular scholarship pushed for a thoroughly historicized approach, in which all forms and experiences of the monastic life would be explicitly linked to broader demographic, social, cultural, and other developments in contemporary society.

Transformation of the field

Historicizing perspectives

As a result of this, multiple new research strands emerged. In a first, specialists became interested in dissecting past narratives of monastic history in order to understand the circumstances in which these narratives originated, and how they shaped subsequent reconstructions of the phenomenon's emergence, nature, and social impact. A second strand drew on the vast body of primary sources – written, iconographic, material, and even geophysical – to develop a continuously expanding range of thematic interests. Initially these interests were driven either by developments in other fields of historical research or in order to study specific types of text so their interpretations could be refined and adjusted. But from the late 1980s onwards, research became increasingly informed by the many and various 'turns' that have shaped historical scholarship since then, whether literary, linguistic, archaeological, material, iconographic, semiotic, sociological, anthropological, affective, biographical, gendered, or spatial. Not all of these brought questions to the table that were new to the field: but they did inject it with new lines of enquiry

Implications

https://doi.org/10.1515/9783110543780-002

and new approaches. Importantly, they also stimulated exchange with colleagues in other fields of historical research and in non-historical disciplines too. Over time, scholars started combining multiple thematic interests deriving from these 'turns', for instance by looking at spatial experiences in monastic settings from a gendered perspective, or studying the affective implications of material objects such as artworks and manuscripts. To these sophisticated, multidisciplinary interests were recently added those deriving from both network and queer theory; approaches that considered monasticism's situatedness in natural and human landscapes; and ones that focused on the role of inter- and transcultural exchange, particularly in so-called frontier and border regions. In the meantime, developments in Digital Humanities and the recent breakthrough of social media as a vehicle for collaborative study and exchange of ideas have accelerated the ongoing transformation of the field.

Multi-perspective research [margin note]

Without a doubt, these are exciting times to be working on medieval monasticisms. The sheer rate at which paradigm-shifting studies are currently being published, methodological frontiers broken, and new research interests explored is unprecedented. But at the same time, it has become difficult for any individual scholar to appreciate the full scope and implications of these developments, as the field remains fractured in countless methodological strands, thematic and period-bound discussions, and national and linguistic research traditions. The following pages are an attempt to succinctly tie together key strands, discussions, and traditions, and arrange them in a chronologically organized overview of the current state of the art. Their purpose is twofold. One, to offer some guidance to novice students as they take their first steps in the verdant fields of monastic history. And two, to stimulate reflection for more seasoned experts.

Challenges [margin note]

Purpose of Part 2 [margin note]

Note: The references in Part 2 are to the corresponding bibliographical sections in Part 3.

2 The Beginnings of Monasticism(s)

2.1 Earliest Monasticisms

Origins of former narrative [margin note]

Traditional accounts represent the emergence of the earliest cenobitical communities in late third- and fourth-century Egypt as the 'birth' of monasticism or (as it is sometimes referred to) the *vita reli-giosa*. In its essence, this view derives from a cumulative narrative of monastic beginnings that was established over the course of five centuries in late antiquity and the early Middle Ages. At its origin stood a number of tendentious statements by commentators such as Jerome, Augustine, and John Cassian, who viewed wandering ascetics and other, non-institutional practitioners as a potential threat to Catholic orthodoxy and an undesirable competition to the clergy [CANER 2002]. These authors were also aware that late antique culture and society viewed private ascetic withdrawal as problematic, and that observers (including some Christian ones) accused hermits, anchorites, recluses, and other individual ascetics of anti-social or even uncivic behaviour. Even Jerome's positive account of female 'household ascetics' in late fourth-century Rome likely met with criticism from the elite, who feared that the religiously positive view of the couple and of the married woman would be undermined by such praise [COOPER 1996].

Late antique perceptions

Various developments from the fifth century onwards supported the prominence in normative accounts of the notion that non-cenobitical forms of ascetic life were essentially private pursuits with no historical ramifications or clear benefit for society. It was felt that such a lifestyle jeopardized the moral integrity of all but the most talented ascetics because it did not provide a distinct, clearly defined spatial, disciplinary, and hierarchical environment in which to pursue the spiritual quest. From the ninth century onwards, the argument became even more precisely articulated. On the one hand, commentators insisted that the two key features that distinguished monasticism from other ascetic lifestyles were the creation of physically separate spaces in which groups of ascetics could withdraw from the secular world, and the use of written rules. And on the other hand, they claimed that the origins of both of these distinctive features could be traced back to the earliest cenobitical settlements of fourth-century Egypt. Because the story of monasticism's origins in the desert and its subsequent spread through the Christian world made for a highly attractive, linear narrative, this version was also adopted by chroniclers of the monastic orders and, later on, by historians of the nineteenth and twentieth centuries.

Later developments

Place in modern discussions

Current interpretations, by contrast, tend to consider as monastics *all* individuals and communities pursuing a lifestyle defined

Current views

by religiously motivated ascetic withdrawal and self-abnegation. Considered together, they make for a "dizzying range of ascetic professions", as one author described it [DEY 2008]. Specialists increasingly think of as irrelevant any attempts to exclude certain categories of Christian ascetics based on the terminology of the sources, the social and spatial settings of their withdrawal, the nature of their self-abnegation, and the degree to which their lifestyle was regulated or not by written texts [HELVÉTIUS 2015, BROOKS HEDSTROM 2017]. Just one way in which they have come to this conclusion is by looking at the terminology in documents from late antiquity. Focussing on descriptors such as "monk", "veiled" or "consecrated virgin/widow", "matron", and "monastery", scholars have discerned that these refer to a reality far more variegated and far less easy to categorize than former generations used to suspect [ELM 1994]. There has been the realization, too, that traditional views of the paradigm-shifting impact of early Egyptian cenobitism and its lasting influence on ascetic community life were based on anachronistic assumptions. Likewise flawed are conclusions about its rational and forward-looking nature, and its grounding in written rules designed to function as normative instruments for monastic governance and discipline [RAPP 2017]. On this basis, most specialists now reject the former distinction between 'primitive' and more 'advanced' forms of ascetic withdrawal [RUBENSON 1998]. Also rejected is the traditional evaluation of early monastic lifestyles from the perspective of the institutional templates and ideological movements they developed into [DIEM/ROUSSEAU 2020].

As a result, the definition of 'monasticism' as currently used in many studies is deliberately less precise than it used to be. Whereas previous work used to focus almost exclusively on the circumstances that led the so-called Desert Fathers to establish the earliest cenobitical communities, more recent discussions emphatically cover the broad range of ascetic lifestyles that are known to us through a variety of testimonies. They revolve around three major interests. The first considers the physical, social, gendered, and memorial spaces monastics inhabited. Following an initial phase in which a great deal of effort went into reconstructing the spatial dimension (location, structure, layout) of ascetic settlements from a formal standpoint, the focus in recent years has been informed by sociological and anthropological research. Among the more notable approaches is that of engaging with 'taskscapes'. This

Multiplicity of forms *(margin note)*

Open definitions *(margin note)*

Non-linear approaches *(margin note)*

Non-hierarchical perspectives *(margin note)*

Current approaches *(margin note)*

Space *(margin note)*

entails looking at the interaction between monastics, their spaces, the sensory experiences generated by this reality, and the movement of people and objects [BROOKS HEDSTROM 2017; also the comments in Chapter 2.2]. Another approach looks at hagiographic and other written commentaries as biased, but nonetheless significant, witnesses to the social and gendered space these people inhabited pre- and post-conversion.

Numerous such accounts are illuminating when scrutinized for the impact of social status and gender on an individual's options when pursuing a monastic life. They also speak to the consequences of conversion for a person's gendered identity, social status, access to various resources, and also access to varied networks [DOSSEY 2011]. And in a further aspect to this spatial turn, scholars have been looking at the spaces early monastics *metaphorically* inhabited, retrieving this through narrative descriptions, through their reading practices, and through the life experiences of monastics in later times [COOPER 1996]. Comparison of these more recent testimonies with late antique and early medieval accounts indicates that aspects of ascetic conduct as reportedly practised by early monastics continued to be reproduced in real life for a very long time – in fact, throughout the medieval period – by hermits, anchorites, and various other practitioners [Magnani 2020]. While the focus of many of these investigations has been on Egypt and its neighbouring territories, there remains much room to expand these geographically to other parts of the Mediterranean world, including also substantial territories in the Latin West.

In a second major research approach today, specialists have been reassessing the role of monastics in shaping their cultic, social and spatial environment during the first centuries of the Christian era. Renewed attention to martyrdom, the literature that celebrates it, and its *lieux de mémoire* has brought to prominence the intimate spatial and functional association between the cult of martyrs and the groups of "matrons" who served the sites where these saints were buried [HELVÉTIUS 2017]. In a similar fashion, scholars have been paying more attention to the groups of men and especially of women that provided shelter and assistance to the poor, the sick, and to travellers. While some of the work has been done for the eastern Mediterranean and North Africa [DOSSEY 2011], relatively few such studies are available for the Latin West. This is chiefly because it is difficult to distinguish these early ascetic

Environment

communities, particularly when they were staffed by women [DEY 2008, HELVÉTIUS 2017]. The reason for this is that, following the end of the persecutions, control over martyrial sanctuaries, *xenodochia*, and other places of Christian worship became the subject of intense competition [BOWES 2008]. On gaining hold of such sites, members of the higher clergy (many of whom rejected the former involvement of female ascetic communities [CANER 2002, DOSSEY 2011]) and lay rulers often removed the groups of women from them, and in some instances even transformed their institutions, for instance into a community of monks performing the *laus perennis* [ROSENWEIN 2001]. Such interventions were routinely accompanied by efforts to either disparage the 'pre-reform' presence of monastics at these places, or outright suppress its memory. Study of written sources, but especially also the archaeological record; geosocial analysis of the location of early *basilicae* and *xenodochia*; and GIS-based reconstructions of these sites in their regional and international networks: all of these things will assist future scholars in their efforts to shed new light on the nature of monastic settlements and their impact on the social and physical environment in the earliest stages of their existence.

Idealized landscapes   The third and final research strand comprises studies that identify and describe idealized monastic landscapes in literary accounts and confront these with the realities of early cenobitical life as reconstructed from written and archaeological sources [DOSSEY 2011]. The growing prominence of Coptic studies and papyrology [WIPSZYCKA 2009], and a number of archaeological campaigns in the deserts of Egypt and Palestine [BROOKS HEDSTROM 2017], have created substantial new opportunities for testing these literary accounts (also below, Chapter 2.2). Meanwhile, renewed interest in the written legacies of Egyptian monasticism has revealed that former readings of these texts often adopted an anachronistic perspective on their nature and purpose [HARMLESS 2004]. And, as has been pointed out, much of the late antique narrative of cenobitism's emergence in the Egyptian desert was created by outsiders for outsiders. For instance, late fourth- and early fifth-century authors insisted that the Desert Fathers belonged to a world of heroic pioneers far removed from the one inhabited by their readership [CANER 2002]. Some commentaries were even tailored to shape the expectations of contemporaries who travelled as pilgrims to Egypt and the Holy Land. The texts, furthermore, determined the way in

which these travellers decoded the foreign realities of desert eremitism and cenobitism and then applied them upon returning home
[FRANK 2000]. They projected onto the desert environment of Egypt
then-current views on the organization of monastic life: that it be
situated in cenobitical settlements, overseen by a designated superior, and regulated by means of a set of oral or written rules. This,
along with the authors' emphasis on the economic self-sufficiency
of a monastery and on the members' confinement to its physical
space, would have seemed highly attractive to contemporary clerical and lay rulers [HELVÉTIUS 2017]. At present, scholars are still in
the process of unravelling the biased discourses of these accounts,
placing them in their chronological, institutional, and ideological contexts, and of testing the old narrative of monastic origins
against the latest findings.

2.2 The 'Rise of Cenobitism'

An enduring trope in medieval and modern discussions of monastic history is that the emergence and subsequent 'triumph' of Egyptian cenobitism in the fourth century fundamentally altered the
paradigm of Christian ascetic life. In order to distinguish it from
earlier forms, these traditional commentaries refer to the members'
strict separation from the secular world, achieved by walled enclo-
sures, cells and a range of conceptual boundaries. However, recent   Experiments
work on contemporary documents and on archaeological evidence
has led to the conclusion that fourth-century cenobitism remained
an open experiment [BROOKS HEDSTROM 2009, 2.1 RAPP]. Various
studies have also cast doubt on the notion that physical separation from the secular world was as strict and interactions with
non-monastics as limited as former commentators had imagined.
Archaeological research on various sites in Egypt and analysis of   Permeability
the monastic landscape there has led scholars to conclude that   of boundaries
measures to create physical boundaries were neither universal nor
absolute. Instead of turning their backs on life, whether rural or
urban, monastic communities actually helped shape it [2.1 BROOKS
HEDSTROM]. For other regions too, scholarship has increasingly   Societal embedding
acknowledged the need to situate the various forms of early cenobitism as precisely as possible in their sociological, ecological, and
physical settings (also above, Chapter 2.1). For instance, specialists

now have good reason to suspect that in the fourth-century province of *Africa*, cenobitical communities were architecturally open to city life, and that few efforts were made to maintain any conceptual separations [DEY 2004, DOSSEY 2011]. There is a need for further case studies that identify and describe idealized monastic landscapes as found in literary accounts, and then confront such idealizations with the realities of early community life as we reconstruct them from written and archaeological sources.

Topical nature of rules — Traditional historiography additionally argued early cenobitism's paradigm-shifting nature by claiming that its organization and ideology were grounded in written rules from early in its existence. In recent years, however, the towering reputation of these normative commentaries has been gradually eroded. In particular, Pachomius's *Rule* emerges from scholarship as being a mixture of responses to, and retrospective commentary on, past achievements. This is fundamentally at odds with its reputation as a forward-looking masterpiece of monastic legislation: but the precise stages through which the text evolved and the exact way in which its content was applied continues to elude us. What is obvious, though, is that Pachomian cenobitism did not emerge fully formed from its inception, but went through a succession of trial-and-error stages. Reconstructing this process of community formation and institution-building remains difficult, and certainly we must not use the *Rule* as an objective testimony of what the life of monks and women religious in these foundations would have looked like [ROUSSEAU 1985, FINN 2009].

In a similar fashion, studies of the last few decades have deconstructed Basilius of Cesarea's reputation as a 'founder' and key legislator of Eastern cenobitism. His *Rule* – by which is often meant Rufinus of Aquileia's Latin translation of Basilius's *Shorter Rules* – now emerges not as a deliberate foundational document of Cappadocian and, later on, Eastern cenobitism, but as a selection of ad hoc responses to concrete issues that were submitted to him as life in these communities was unfolding. What is more, Rufinus's text seems to have been fairly popular in the West, whereas traces of its direct or indirect influence in the East are few and far between. Even in Byzantine times, each institution had its own written rule (*typikon*), a reality that tells us of the need to abandon the idea that a single text by a single author might have changed the face of cenobitical life, even in a specific region of the Empire [2.1 RAPP].

Further on (Chapter 2.4) we shall be making similar remarks about the *Rule of St Benedict* in the Latin West.

More generally speaking, since the 1990s the realization has grown among specialists that fourth- and fifth-century rules and other normative commentaries must be read not as normative instructions designed to consolidate the organization of cenobitical communities, but as topical commentaries that were written in response to then-current concerns and debates [2.1 HELVÉTIUS 2017]. On that basis, scholarship has also established that the qualitative distinctions between different categories of monastics (made by authors like Jerome, Augustine, John Cassian, and later on the author of the *Rule of St Benedict*) by no means reflected a consensus among contemporaries or even a gradual consolidation of lifestyles into distinct, well-delineated categories. Instead, these statements must be understood in two ways. One, they were arguments in broader debates on the place of celibate clerics, lay monastics, and consecrated women in the Church, and on the degree to which the individual Christian could influence his or her own salvation [2.1 RAPP]. And two, they were responses by individual commentators – members of the higher clergy in particular – to what they saw as a challenge to their religious and social authority. So Augustine's comments that lay men were allowed to become cenobites and his efforts to strictly separate men and women in such contexts must be read against the double background of tensions between Catholics and Donatists in North Africa, and his actions against a monastic tradition established in the context of the earliest Christian *basilicae* [LEYSER 2000, DOSSEY 2011]. Presumably it was fear of social disruption that led other clerical rulers to make complaints: about late third-century wandering monks attacking sanctuaries around Antioch; about 'debauched' Priscillianists in fourth-century Spain; and about wandering male and female ascetics in Egypt [2.1 ELM, FINN 2009, SANCHEZ 2009].

In the turbulent context of the fourth and fifth centuries, some bishops were forced to accept responsibility for urban society, and on that basis some of them raised concerns over the impact of monastics on the local economy. Basilius's model of cenobitism may have been intended as a response to that of Eustathius of Sebaste, which combined ideals of ascetic withdrawal with caritative action (providing aid to the poor) and social protest. Clerical leaders accused Eustathius's followers of celebrating the liturgy

Relation to then-current debates

Promotion of cenobitism

without the aid of priests, refusing communion from married clergy, rejecting traditional gender roles and family structures, and of dressing in an outlandish, inappropriate manner [CLARK 1998].

Opposition An important realization in recent studies is that statements like this from the time likely stirred opposition, and not just from dissident preachers, ascetic wanderers, and other individuals and groups operating on the fringe of ecclesiastical society. So Augustine's views may have led to accusations that he sought to devalue the sanctity of the clergy and to disrupt an ascetic space formerly reserved for celibate clerics and consecrated women [2.1 LEYSER, DOSSEY 2011]. For instance, we know that Emperor Theodosius (d. 395) at the end of the fourth century suspected that some bishops were looking to claim the assets of existing urban groups, particularly those of women [2.1 CANER]. It is likely that some communities of ascetic women harboured similar suspicions, as did their relatives and patrons [ELM 1994, 2.1 HARMLESS].

'Private' forms Although from the mid-fourth century onwards non-cenobitical individuals and groups fade to the background of general accounts of monastic life, we know that a huge variety of practitioners continued to populate the monastic landscape in considerable numbers. Among them were hermits, anchorites, "choirs of virgins", groups of ascetic women serving the graves of martyrs or running *xenodochia*, small groups of hermits gathered informally around a master, and wandering ascetics [ISTRIA/PERGOLA 2013, 2.1 HELVÉTIUS 2017]. There is much suggestive evidence of symbiotic relationships between the practitioners of various forms of monastic life in local contexts, of permeable boundaries between lifestyles, and of the fact that individual monastics frequently moved between them. Such observations have been made for Palestine [PATRICH 1995], Antioch, and Cappadocia, where fourth-century cenobitical settlements co-existed with female household ascetics, male hermits, and a range of other monastic lifestyles. In Italy and North Africa too, multiple forms of ascetic life co-existed, in some cases peacefully and in others in a state of competition, hostility even [JENAL 1995, DOSSEY 2011]. John Cassian and several other influential commentators after him actually pointed out that they saw cenobitical life as a training ground for eremitism, which they thought of as the most perfect form of ascetic withdrawal. So it has been suggested that John, in making his statement, was actually thinking of a number of specific eremitical settlements on islands in

the Mediterranean where his followers would be able to withdraw
[RIPART 2017]. There remains much room to expand these observations and speculations with a systematic study of sources that bear
witness to 'intra-monastic' exchanges and mobility, and a detailed
analysis of the nature and implications of these phenomena.

'Intra-monastic'
exchange

2.3 Early Cenobitisms in Southern Gaul

The intense production of monastic rules and commentaries in
fifth-century southern Gaul has been a long-time focus of interest
[ALCIATI 2009]. Initially, specialists saw in analysis of these texts
and reconstruction of their circulation an opportunity to chart the
rise and geographical distribution of specific 'strands' of cenobitical life. These research endeavours would eventually make it
possible, so they hoped, to assign each individual monastery in
pre-650s Gaul to one of three such strands: Lérins's aristocratic
'Rhône valley' monasticism, a private and more egalitarian 'Aquitanian' counterpart, and John Cassian's model as represented in his
writings and in his foundations at Marseilles [PRINZ 1988].

Nature and purpose
of monastic rules

These putative strands are now regarded as historiographical
constructions [VON DER NAHMER 1987, 2.2 RIPART]. According to the
current view, normative monastic literature was highly amorphous
and functioned in ways that modern perceptions have still not adequately appreciated. Important in that respect is the observation,
by a number of authors, that the idea of a written rule as a monastic
law-text is a notion that dates back only to the Carolingian period
[DIEM 2011]. In addition, studies have found that the oppositional
stance modern observers used to discern in certain rules does not
seem to have registered in the same way with contemporaries. For
instance, John Cassian's *Institutions* and *Conferences* have long
been held to represent a view that radically opposed Lérins's 'aristocratic' brand of monastic life [GOODRICH 2007]. But Lérins and
several of its associated communities were actually one of the principal conduits through which Cassian's work was disseminated
across the Rhône valley and further north [ALCIATI 2009].

On realizing that rules were written to inspire rather than
dictate, scholars also began looking more attentively at early hagiographic material, which reflected and presumably also informed
monastic attitudes in much the same manner [DIEM 2005, ISAIA/

Other genres

GRANIER 2014, 2.1 HELVÉTIUS 2017]. One example is the *Lives of the Fathers of the Jura*, a 530s text that explicitly addresses such key issues as obedience, poverty, and community life [2.2 RIPART]. Later on, in the sixth and seventh centuries, this hagiographic corpus was expanded with the so-called *joca monachorum*, where aspects of monastic observance were discussed in the form of questions and answers. Also appearing then were florilegia of patristic and other texts covering a wide range of thematic and moral issues. Long overlooked, these and other accounts set templates for discussing the nature and purpose of cenobitical life for centuries to come; they also deserve to be included in any discussions of how monastic commentators of the period tried to shape their fellow ascetics' attitudes and conduct. Considered together, they reveal a constantly shifting world of ideas and practices that eludes strict categorization in discrete strands or movements.

In the older literature, specialists backed up their reconstructions of normative 'strands' of cenobitism with late antique and medieval accounts of paradigm-shifting foundations and 'restorations' or 'renewals' of existing ones. More recently, scholars have tried to offset these biased narratives against historical and archaeological sources that offer direct (if highly fragmentary) insight into the realities of monastic community life [FIXOT/PELLETIER 2009, 2.1 HELVÉTIUS 2015, 2.2 RIPART]. The results of these investigations allow us to argue that previous interpretations of cenobitical experiences in this period are overly reductive of complex, continuously evolving, often highly localized realities. Various 'Aquitanian' monasteries, which used to be viewed as private, rural counterparts to Lérins's aristocratic, politically oriented model, now emerge from the evidence as subject to rapid institutionalization, featuring strong connections with elite patrons interacting intensely with local and regional society [ALCIATI 2011]. Similarly, Lérins's paradigm-shaping role in Rhône monasticism has been called into question, the evidence pointing instead to substantial diversity between, and even within, communities that supposedly belonged to its movement [CODOU/LAUWERS 2009].

It is also becoming increasingly clear that former interpretations of ideology and practice in certain monasteries have overly focused on cenobitical groups whilst disregarding other ascetics living in these places. The Lérins islands, for instance, hosted not just a group of monks, but also other individuals who felt drawn to the

[margin note:] Evolving forms and experiences

[margin note:] Multiciplity of forms

sanctifying power of that place: hermits, married men, couples even, who came to live in close proximity to the monks and sometimes even formed small communities of their own [KASPER 1991, 2.2 RIPART]. Such diversity of ascetic identities at a single monastic settlement undoubtedly called for adaptations and variations in lifestyle, prayer routines, and modes of governance that are not inscribed in (quasi-) normative commentaries and narrative testimonies.

Although the idea of homogeneous normative strands of cenobitism in fifth- to early seventh-century Gaul is thus no longer tenable, many monasteries did take part in informal networks for the exchange of personnel, texts, and other forms of social and cultural capital. The precise implications of these exchanges for the development of monastic thought and experiences are yet to be fully understood. Just one of several ideas that appear to have spread rapidly through such networks was the notion promoted from Lérins that entering the monastic life constituted an accession to a "clerical militia" (*militia clericalis),* whose mission it was to lead the Christian people. There is now sufficient evidence to argue that this idea was promoted not simply to fulfil the internal liturgical needs of the Lérins community, but to actually ground sacerdotal authority in ascetic practice [HELVÉTIUS 2012, 2.2 RIPART].

Dissemination of ideas

Typically for this period, other communities adopted, and then moulded these ideas to reflect their own views. Sixth-century texts from Saint-Maurice d'Agaune insist, like those from Lérins, on the monks' participation in celestial powers, but they indicate that this is only so because of the monks' *laus perennis* and their rejection of all manual labour. As a practice, the *laus perennis* was soon exported to other places, including such major institutions as Remiremont, Saint-Denis, and Laon. But here too, adoption and transformation went hand in hand, as prayer service in these places was toned down, ostensibly in response to episcopal concerns about orthodoxy [HELVÉTIUS 2009].

Adaptation of these ideas

Another key notion that was transmitted through these informal channels is that of the monastery and its immediate environment as a sanctified, but also sanctifying, space [LAUWERS 2016]. Hilary of Arles's assertion in his 430s *Life of Honoratus* that the Lérins monks took the place of angelic choirs [SCHERLIESS 2000] resonated in the monastery's fifth- and sixth-century literary output. These texts speak of the islands that housed the community as "castles of God" (*castra Dei*), a "haven of quietness" (*portus quietis*), and a

Notions of space

"paradise" (*paradisus*) [2.2 RIPART]. Perhaps because of the specific genre in which Hilary announced these views, they quickly began circulating outside of Lérins too, surfacing time and again in commentaries on monastic space right up to the end of the medieval period.

Not coincidentally, this is the period also when monastic commentators began to push for the creation of legal ramparts to protect the physical and virtual space of cenobitical communities. In the 510s or 520s, Cesarius of Arles obtained a papal privilege for his women's monastery in Arles [RUDGE 2011, DIEM 2014], limiting the power of the local bishop to visitations only and preventing him from exercising his juridical *potestas*. In 595 Pope Gregory the Great would grant a similar exemption to Saint-Cassien in Marseilles [2.2 RIPART]; Saint-Maurice d'Agaune almost certainly had one in the early seventh century; and exceptions for Lérins and Luxeuil are attested from c. 700 onwards [HELVÉTIUS 2009]. As part of the same movement of protection from undue episcopal interference, some monastics sought royal status for their institution, leading various Merovingian rulers to award protection from various types of episcopal and lay interference. Study of the precise circumstances and contents of these privileges has long remained difficult because many key documents have been the subject of forgery or interpolation. A compounding factor has been the tendency of historians to apply the practical and legal meanings of exemption from the eleventh and twelfth centuries onwards, back onto early medieval realities, an approach that has led to anachronistic interpretations. Current scholarship, in contrast, prefers an approach that emphatically situates these documents and their legal implications in the context of their own time [RENNIE 2018].

Protection of monastic space

Anachronistic views

2.4 Experiments on the Italian and Iberian Peninsulas

Multiplicity and notions of decline

The monastic world Pope Gregory the Great describes in his *Dialogues* and his *Letters* was crowded and very diverse, a fact that former discussions of fifth- and sixth-century religious life on the Italian Peninsula either ignored or cast (as Gregory himself did) in a narrative of laxity, unclear boundaries with the secular world, and precipitous decline. The situation is one that study of written [2.1 JENAL] and archaeological sources [STASSOLA 2017, BULLY/DESTEFANIS

2020] has rendered even more complex by uncovering the multi-functional nature of many settlements and the fact that various types of ascetic practitioners co-existed in a state of social and spiritual symbiosis. This complexity has inspired new questions about Benedict of Nursia's place in this world, and about Gregory's reasons for presenting him as a monastic founder and legislator who fundamentally transformed the nature and organization of cenobitism [2.1 LEYSER, WOLLASCH 2007].

A major issue that has not been resolved and probably never will be concerns Benedict of Nursia's historicity and legacy. Since the early 2000s, the only near-contemporary testimony of his life, found in Book 2 of Gregory's *Dialogues*, has come under intense scrutiny. A fairly heated debate was ignited when one scholar speculated that this particular part of the *Dialogues* was not written by the pope himself but by a late seventh-century forger at the papal court, and is therefore untrustworthy [CLARK 2003]. Most specialists reject these arguments and accept that Gregory was indeed behind the abbot's biography. At the same time, however, they admit that accessing the historical Benedict, in particular his ideas and personal achievements, is exceedingly difficult [WOLLASCH 2007]. There is no way around the fact that our understanding of the man, his activities, and his legacy is strictly based on the accounts of authors working from the late sixth century onwards. Given this, at least one historian has therefore been tempted to argue that none of these testimonies can help us to reliably reconstruct the man's life and actions, let alone his views: indeed, that Benedict is most likely entirely fictional [FRIED 2004].

Historicity of Benedict

However, the broadly accepted view today is that Benedict most likely did exist as a historical figure and that the rough outlines of Gregory's biography are probably based on authentic memories. Still, it is quite clear that Gregory used Benedict's persona to reflect his own views, not all of which derived from what he had heard about Benedict's achievements. Between the 570s and 590s, the future pope had keenly studied early accounts of the monastic life, including the *Life of the Fathers* and the *Life* of St Anthony. He had also spent time in Constantinople, where he undoubtedly had the opportunity to observe Eastern monastic realities, and had come into contact with bishops with a similar interest in asceticism. No less important is the fact that Gregory had immersed himself in a culture of reflection that envisaged the ideal ecclesiastical leader as

Influence of Gregory

primarily a contemplative and a preacher combined [MÜLLER 2013]. All these inspirations, influences, and contacts deserve further investigation.

Benedict's status

Speaking from a long-term viewpoint, Benedict's main significance surely lies not in what the man did or did not achieve during his lifetime, but in how later commentators – Gregory in particular – cast his abbatial persona and especially his legacy as a monastic founder. And looking at Gregory's monastic policies during his tenure as pope and at his strong preference for governance rooted in written law, there is reason to suspect that his reference to Benedict's authorship of a rule is likewise rooted in his own personal experiences and expectations [MÜLLER 2013]. A thorough, contextualized reconstruction of the relationship between Gregory's 590s biography of Benedict, his involvement in monasticism prior to and during his papacy, and the promotion from c. 600 onwards of the *Rule of St Benedict* as a major, authoritative commentary on monastic life would help clarify that issue.

Rule of St Benedict

But the *Rule of St Benedict* itself also raises a number of important questions. To begin with, the text elevates certain topical commentaries from earlier centuries (those by John Cassian in particular) to a status of permanent relevance in monastic reading [2.3 GOODRICH]. At present, the true implications for monastic ideology and practice of these explicit and implicit references to various older rules and commentaries remains ill-understood, as some of these texts also appear to have reached a broad monastic readership independently of any mentions in the *Rule*. Comparative study of the manuscript transmission of key texts might help towards resolving this. A second question raised by the *Rule* is its relationship with that other monument of sixth-century rule-making, the *Rule of the Master*. Although the matches between the two texts make a close (if not necessarily direct) kinship obvious, it is unclear which came first. Since the 1930s, most scholars have been inclined to think that the *Rule of the Master* preceded the more concise *Rule of St Benedict* [DE VOGÜÉ 1992, DUNN 2000]. But the former might contain elements – particularly its emphasis on the distinction between monks and laymen – that point to a more 'modern' view of monastic identity than is found in the *Rule of St Benedict* [DIEM/

Need for further study

RAPP 2020]. A thorough re-investigation of the authorship, content, structure, and early manuscript tradition of the two texts by means of computer-assisted methods (such as stylometric analysis and database-driven applications) might provide new answers to these questions.

Although the *Rule of St Benedict* swiftly achieved prominence in the canon of late antique and early medieval rules and was frequently referenced in seventh-century sources from across the Latin West, its progressive 'triumph' post-600 as a template for organizing monastic life now appears to us as doubtful. Like the *Rule* itself, Gregory's *Dialogues* soon became a staple of monastic reading across the Latin West: but in Rome at least, his views met with hostility or indifference, particularly, one imagines, from those monastics who were involved in caritative and pastoral action [LEYSER 2003]. Here, as in many other places, the pope's contemplative ideal as reflected in the *Rule* and the *Dialogues* was still far removed from becoming the dominant paradigm of institutionalized monastic life.

Enduring normative diversity

Scholarship for seventh- and eighth-century Italy provides strong indications of this heterogeneity (below, Chapter 2.6). However, arguably there is no better example than the Iberian Peninsula, with its urban communities of clerics, rural villas-turned-monasteries, and 'monastic villages' – all striking evidence of how wildly diverse monastic experiences would remain for hundreds of years to come [Díaz 1999], and how grossly past generations of scholars have overestimated the homogenizing power of written rules and putative 'movements'. One of the key features of recent scholarship for the region is the linkage of monastic forms and experiences to regional identities and power blocs [WOOD 2012]; economic and social structures [DÍAZ 2011]; and (particularly for southern Spain] the development of urban societies under episcopal governance [GARCÍA MORENO 1993]. Under the influence of the recent 'spatial turn', a number of regional case studies have looked at evidence for how monasteries in some parts of the Peninsula helped organize political and economic landscapes [LÓPEZ QUIROGA/MARTÍNEZ TEJERA/ MORÍN DE PABLOS 2007]. Other studies have reconstructed how then-current debates on observance and the use of space impacted on the views of commentators such as Isidore and Fructuosus [DÍAZ 2011, LÓPEZ QUIROGA 2016]. Although very active in recent years, archaeologists have yet to formulate a synthetic interpretation on these issues [DÍAZ 2015]. Relevant to our understanding of monastic diversity are also those works that have used a fresh perspective to look at Valerius of Bierzo's commentary on the state of monasticism during his lifetime [SALGADO RAFFAELI 2013], and also the place of

Iberian forms

Societal embedding

Commentaries

eremitism in the Iberian religious landscape generally [García de Cortázar y Ruiz de Aguirre 2011].

2.5 Irish and 'Iro-Frankish' Monasticisms

Much work remains to be done in revisiting the hagiographic testimonies of major figures in early Irish monastic history, including Patrick, Columba the Elder, and Brigida of Kildare [Dawson 2014]. As the *Lives* of these saints were written from a considerable chronological and in some cases also a cultural distance, sifting authentic memories from the rubble of literary invention is a challenging exercise. The question is how, from this compromised kind of evidence, do we reconstruct the life paths of these individuals and the experiences of the island's earliest monastics [Kehnel 1997].

To provide some help with this problem, archaeologists in particular have tried to shift attention from the subjects of hagiography to the physical settings of monastic life, including such things as the organization of monastic space and the multifunctional nature of monastic sites [Herity 1995, Etchingham 2014]. These studies show a significant discrepancy between the material record and various narrative and normative commentaries, and invite a more diverse understanding of early realities for groups of men and women than the one we find in the traditional account of early Irish monasticism [Collins 2015]. For instance, various scholars have pointed out that strictly localized testimony concerning Irish bishops' subordination to abbots and the relatively insignificant role of bishops in ecclesiastical organization and leadership has been injudiciously extrapolated to all of Ireland, despite a lack of corroborative evidence [Haarländer 2011]. In particular, this shows the danger of relying on biased commentaries, such as those by authors from the *céilí Dé* movement in the later eighth and ninth centuries, about the lack of boundaries in early Irish monasticism with the outside world.

Specialists have also become a great deal more cautious in speculating on the typically 'Irish' views and practices of the *peregrini* travelling to England and the European Continent from the late sixth and early seventh century onwards. These individuals are certainly no longer seen as all having the same views on monastic ideology and practice [Blair 2005, Wood 2016]. Advances in the

Revising classic accounts

Shift to non-literary sources

Significant diversity

'Irish' monasticism on the Continent

understanding of hagiographic traditions have also revealed some saintly biographies (such as Jonas's *Life* of Columbanus) reflect views that were at least one step removed from those held by their subject [Fox 2016]. In a similar fashion, the cohesiveness of 'Columbanian' monasticism has been called into question: as one commentator recently stated, "'Columbanian' and 'iro-frankish' should... be regarded as no more than terms of convenience" [WOOD 2017]. Former reconstructions of a vast network of 'Iro-Frankish', 'Columbanian' institutions in seventh- and eighth-century Gaul [2.3 PRINZ] now appear to us as erudite instances of wishful thinking, as their basis in the primary evidence has turned out to be thin. In a number of cases, for instance, scholars assumed a monastery's allegiance to Columbanian ideals strictly on the basis of its links with Merovingian court circles [WOOD 2016]. And although the connections of Luxeuil post-Columbanus with numerous other communities in Gaul are well established, very little that was typically 'Irish' (besides a moderate emphasis on penance and a far greater one on learning and book production) travelled from there to these other institutions. Furthermore, the suspected distinctiveness of 'Columbanian' observance has also been called into question: while former studies saw a deep ideological chasm between 'Columbanian' views and that of monastic communities in southern Gaul, that view no longer holds currency [RICHTER 2008].

Constructed notions of cohesiveness

Adaptations

Recent re-readings of 'Columbanian' rules and other commentaries additionally speak against uniformity in monastic ideals and practices. Modes of observance and governance as they circulated in 'Columbanian' or 'Luxovian' circles were subject to considerable adaptation and reinterpretation. Besides the notable differences between Columbanus's *Rule* and Jonas's account of monastic life, all other known rules in this tradition reflect some degree of localized reinterpretation. For instance, the eighth-century *Regula cuiusdam ad virgines* heavily borrows from the *Rule of St Benedict*, creating a hybrid text that emphasizes the need to discipline not just one's outward behaviours, but also one's inner attitudes. Donatus of Besançon's rule for women shows an author who is even more deeply preoccupied with the need to control one's inner feelings, thoughts, dreams even. Another example is the *Regula cuiusdam patris*, which implicitly rejects Columbanus's reliance on the support of mighty patrons and founders. It rejects, too, the role played by monastic institutions – male and female – in political

Reinterpretations and dissent

networks of the time, and the emphasis in some places on prayer service. There may be links between these altered perspectives and a number of conflicts that, following Columbanus's death, erupted over monastic discipline at major institutions like Bobbio and Luxeuil, possibly in the context of attempts to turn the latter into a training ground for lay members of the aristocratic elite [Diem 2016]. Key to recent discussions of these rules is the realization that they all constitute topical commentaries written in response to particular issues. These issues, in turn, arose in a particular religious, social, and political environment. The rules, therefore, cannot be taken as evidence of views widely held in a supposed 'Columbanian' movement.

Situating monastic life in local contexts has invigorated the study of early cenobitism on the Continent and on the British Isles. For the former, much scholarly effort has gone into reconstructing the contextual variables – particularly the expectations of the Frankish aristocracy – that determined the nature and purpose of new communities [Gaillard 1990, Fox 2014, Bully/Dubreucq/Bully 2018]. There has also been investigation of the striking similarities between 'Columbanian' foundations in Kent, East Anglia, and Wessex and earlier ones in Île-de-France. The results appear to suggest that lay founders in England imported the specific modes of cenobitical organization that best suited the socio-economic and political circumstances in their own territories [Wood 2017] and that also best reflected their personal interest – for instance, in supporting female monastic communities [Yorke 2017]. Ongoing strands of archaeological and geophysical research corroborate the now-standard view of sixth- and seventh-century monasticism as highly diverse, contextualized, and responsive to external (particularly aristocratic) impulses [Thomas/Knox 2017].

England

2.6 Monastic Experiences at the Dawn of the Eighth Century

The central narrative thread running through the discussion so far has been about the diversity of monastic experiences: regionally, generationally, between the practitioners of various forms of monastic life, and finally also between individuals and groups who belonged to what scholars used to think of as fairly homogeneous 'strands' of cenobitical life. Time and again, studies belonging to a wide range of disciplines and covering an equally broad array of interests bring to the fore the need to step away from a narrative that squeezes highly changeable and contextualized realities of monastic life into normative schemes and templates.

Diverse forms and identities

This diversity continued into the eighth century, and is expressed in the significant variety of terms used in contemporary documents to reference monastics and the spaces they inhabited [L'ORIGINE 2016]. Manuscript copies of rules and other commentaries likewise offer precious testimonies of the creativity of male and female monastics in adapting normative traditions to local circumstances and expectations [for an overview, DE VOGÜÉ 1991–2007; on adaptations, 2.3 DIEM 2014]. Renewed attention to the hagiographic legacy of monastic communities from the sixth, seventh and early eighth centuries (and the echoes we find of lost such narratives in rewritten saint's *Lives* from the ninth century onwards) has additionally yielded a complex, variegated understanding of an ascetic reality that was very much shaped by local circumstances and was highly susceptible to change over time.

Written evidence

To the paucity of detail that we are able to glean from written records, archaeological evidence offers some relief. Just one among many relevant case studies is that of Hamage, a women's monastery in northern Gaul, which over the course of two centuries following its foundation in the late 600s evolved from a motley collection of separate dwellings, to buildings with communal rooms and individual cells, to an actual cloister in the early ninth century. Archaeological study of this and other sites shows that the former image of, especially, rural monasteries as deliberately removed from secular activity is incorrect. As it turns out, many foundations – including that of Hamage – were established close to burgeoning centres of rural, proto-industrial, and also commercial activity [LOUIS 1999]. Others, including Annegray, Columbanus's first foundation on the Continent, appear to have been situated near and closely involved in important communication networks [MARRON 2012]. Likewise subject to profound changes in structure were prominent urban monasteries such as Santa Giulia in Brescia, which was founded on the site of a former Lombardic palace [ANDENNA 2011]. Undoubtedly, the physical and social environment of such communities profoundly impacted on their organization and identity [WEST-HARTING 2019].

Archaeological evidence

Diversity of roles   Even though communities with a focus on contemplation and prayer are those that we hear the most about in the written sources, various recent studies have made a strong case that there still existed numerous groups with an explicitly caritative, pastoral, or educational profile, particularly in urban settings. These are generally hard to distinguish in the primary evidence, partly because of historical revisionism by commentators from the ninth century onwards, and partly because many such communities were subsequently turned into contemplative monasteries or clerical institutions. Only in rare cases do we get a clear view of the diverse cohort of contemplative monasteries, *diaconiae*, and *xenodochia* that were found in a number of urban societies. Likewise, it is only in glimpses that we see how contemporaries viewed this diverse presence as useful and even necessary. However, eighth- and ninth-century Rome is an exceptionally well-documented case: here, the papacy fostered specialization within the diverse cohort of the city's ascetic communities in order to meet the varied needs of the Roman population and those who visited the city [DEY 2011]. For smaller towns and rural societies too, we encounter occasional references in contemporary sources to the continued presence of groups of celibate clerics living in episcopal centres; ascetic communities living in or near small oratories on private estates; *diaconiae* and *xenodochia*; and finally also urban "choirs of virgins" [2.1 HELVÉTIUS 2017].

Normative distinctions   At the same time, it has also been pointed out that attempts to establish a normative distinction between 'active' and 'contemplative' monastic groups only date back to the Carolingian period. Similarly, in places where there were insufficient resources or motivation to establish multiple institutions with distinct functional identities, monastic communities routinely fulfilled a range of roles (contemplative, pastoral, educational, and caritative) [2.1 DEY]. Unfortunately, material and written sources offer us but scant glimpses of how this multifunctional identity worked in practice, or more generally how it impacted on life in and around these settlements. Ethnic and cultural diversity further enhanced the diversity of the monastic landscape and experience. While the Greek monasteries of eighth-century Rome have been relatively well studied [SANSTERRE 1993], more generally speaking the entire issue of migrant communities in various regions of the Latin West is an underdeveloped but promising area of interest (for Irish migrants, FLECHNER/MEEDER 2016). So, too, is the presence of individual migrants in indigenous communities,

Ethnic and cultural diversity

and also the evidence of various types of cultural transfer – for example, in reading culture and manuscript production [McKITTER-ICK 1992, Richter 2008], and governance and economic management [WOOD 2017].

Increasingly, scholars are also acknowledging that we need to award a more prominent place in the narrative to the many people we do not usually think of as monastics, but who were nevertheless in close proximity to monastic practitioners. These included orphaned children; boys and girls who spent time at a monastery being educated; widows and unmarried women; exiles and those seeking sanctuary from their enemies; and various serfs and servants [FELTEN 2005, FLECHNER 2017, 2.1 HELVÉTIUS 2017]. We must add to these the numerous pilgrims, wandering ascetics, hermits, anchorites, and other people who had committed to some form of monastic life and often interacted intensively with cenobitical groups, temporarily joining them or at least participating in their cultic and other activities. Our understanding of these interactions and symbiotic relationships remains incomplete, and would most assuredly benefit from further study.

Involvement of 'non-monastics'

3 Early and High Medieval Monasticisms

3.1 Continuities and Transformations in the Long Eighth Century

The traditional notion of eighth- and early ninth-century reform as a premeditated strategy to redesign the organization and observance of religious communities is now viewed as an anachronism [BARROW 2008]. Whereas older scholarship leaned towards a narrative that described the progressive elaboration of a cohesive masterplan, the current majority approach sees the reform of the Frankish Church as a more ad hoc and improvised development, driven forward by continuous debates and periodic compromises in broad circles associated with the Carolingian court [KRAMER 2019].

New perspectives

Against the background of these debates and compromises, we can observe how rulers and their clerical associates gradually developed a triple agenda for religious community life, each part of which has been the subject of intense study over the last two and a half decades. One aim was to create functional and behavioural boundaries between the clergy and cloistered monastics [CHOY 2016].

Triple objective

Another was to turn monastic houses into physical spaces where the polluting world had little chance of penetrating, creating in the process a privileged sphere of interaction with the divine [DE JONG 1995]. And a third was to implicate monastic communities in the exercise of sovereign rule and its ongoing mission to "correct" the Frankish Church [CONTRENI 2014, KRAMER 2019, and below, Chapter 3.2]. Yet, views on how to realize these three objectives were never universally agreed upon, and were prone to change over time. Accordingly, recent scholarship tends to highlight the historical and local situatedness of various reform endeavours [CLAUSEN 2004, AIRLIE 2007].

Surely the most significant of all the recent reinterpretations concerns the reform councils of 816–819. According to the traditional view, these operated a paradigm shift in ecclesiastical organization by establishing a comprehensive framework of written rules for monks and women religious living according to the *Rule of St Benedict*, canons following the *Institutio canonicorum*, and so-called canonesses following the *Institutio sanctimonialium*. For a long time, scholars took the proclamation of the reform decrees and the comprehensive nature of related commentaries as indicating that strict legal, functional, and behavioural boundaries between different categories of organized monastic life were established post-819 [KOTTJE 1965, SEMMLER 1983, SEMMLER 2005]. Yet, if we confront these claims with what we know about the status of individual groups of monks, clerics, and women religious post-reform, it quickly becomes obvious that no single community followed any of the above rules literally and that functional and behavioural boundaries between various cohorts in many places remained fluid at best.

Looking first at women religious, older studies postulated that the reformed female monastic landscape consisted of two distinct categories: Benedictine nunneries, and houses of canonesses (or, in German, *Kanonissenstifte*). In each of these categories, it was thought, the communities were organized strictly according to the reformers' written edicts. But more recent enquiries have established that any attempts to strictly classify women's monasteries in these two normative categories are basically futile. Based on what we know about daily practices, internal organization, the status of members, and even the terminology in the sources, it seems safe to say that observance in all these communities was 'ambiguously'

Former categorizations

Real world applications

'Ambiguous' forms and experiences

situated – that is, real life fell between the two different rules, written for Benedictine women religious and canonesses respectively [SCHILP 1998, FELTEN 2005, VANDERPUTTEN 2018]. Revealingly, post-819 royal and conciliar legislation, too, fails to make a clear distinction between cohorts of women religious, preferring instead to focus on the service (intercessory prayer for ruler and Empire) and ascetic behaviour (obedience, enclosure, stability, observance of the basic principles of monastic life) that was expected from cloistered women regardless of their legal or institutional status [PARISSE 2011]. For monks and canons too, there are abundant indications that the life experiences and functional roles of these cohorts remained diverse, and that these were less literally dictated by written regulations and reformist commentaries than historians formerly suspected [RAAIJMAKERS 2012, SCHNEIDER 2016; also further, Chapter 3.2].

Some older studies interpreted these findings as revealing the failure of the early ninth-century reforms. They offered a variety of explanations for this, including the incomplete and inconsistent nature of various reform decrees and the lack of legal and other means to enforce them; resistance by monastics and their lay patrons; and finally also the political instability and various contestations that plagued Louis the Pious's reign in the last two decades of his life [SEMMLER 1983]. But more recent publications have tended to reject the notion that the reform decrees and related commentaries from the early ninth century constituted an attempt to establish legally binding blueprints for the organization of every monastic and clerical community in the Empire [RAAIJMAKERS 2012]. Instead, researchers have argued that we must think of these documents as ambitious, but topical, attempts to outline the service of these communities to ruler and Empire, delineate the forms of observance and community life that were held to be legitimate, and suggest where the boundaries of legitimate experimentation in each of these were situated [VANDERPUTTEN 2018].

Former notions of failure

Reform texts as topical commentaries

Pertinent here is the insistence in contemporary legislation on guidance by regular leaders, whose task it was to interpret monastic tradition for their subjects and provide them with a template of conduct through word and exemplary deed [2.4 MÜLLER]. The legislation likewise stressed the need for clerical rulers and even secular lords to be involved in the governance of monastic institutions to hammer out the finer details of how reform would be implemented in

Transmission and reception

each individual community [VANDERPUTTEN 2018]. While detailed reconstructions of the form, nature, and especially also the manuscript transmission of various rules, decrees, and other commentaries on monastic life are now available [2.5 GAILLARD, SCHMITZ 2012, ENGELBERT 2015], a systematic effort to identify and analyse various ninth-century redactions of these texts will shed important new light on their reception and assimilation in local narratives of monastic identity and observance [BODARWÉ 2011, VANDERPUTTEN 2018; also below, Chapter 3.4].

Recent reinterpretations of early ninth-century reform decrees also help us to revise the traditional understanding of lawmakers' insistence, from the late seventh century onwards, that one or multiple rules/*Rules* be observed. In earlier scholarship, these references in charters, conciliar acts and royal decrees constituted evidence of a progressive 'triumph' of the *Rule of St Benedict*. Alternatively, they were taken as an indication of the growing normative value of written rules generally [SEMMLER 2005]. But more recently, this corpus has been reinterpreted as being (besides those aspects discussed in the paragraph above) a strategy designed to force individual communities into submitting a cohesive account of their ascetic identity and observance for testing against ruler expectations. This self-appointed prerogative to evaluate what one might call the 'rule-narrative' of monastic groups was first and foremost a political act to claim legitimate authority over the destinies of monastics and the nature of their service to society, as part of a broader discourse outlining rulers' intention to "correct" the Frankish Church [CLAUSEN 2004, 2.3 DIEM 2011].

Negotiated nature of forms and experiences

We can observe – especially for the immediate aftermath of the 816–819 reform councils – how the ensuing confrontation between local interpretations and those of the reformers described a dialectic or a negotiation between different stakeholders. Case studies of a number of major 'reform centres' have revealed that local communities and their leadership (on the one side) and various agents pursuing reform (on the other) sought to negotiate modes of monastic governance and observance that met the general expectations of rulers yet were also grounded in local circumstances. These local circumstances included the social status of monastics, their relationship with their secular environment, cultic identities, and other specific local traditions [VANDERPUTTEN 2018; KRAMER 2019; for parallels with the playing out of different views between monastic communities and their regular leadership, BOOKER 2016]. Future studies should offer us a fuller picture of exactly how these negotiations played out in various local settings across the Empire, and how we can detect their outcomes in sources detailing the daily experiences and organization of individual communities post-reform. As mentioned earlier, study of various redactions of written rules and other commentaries will also offer us more insight into the various local 'rule-narratives' that emerged in the context of reform.

Scholars have also become more interested in how monastics, as individuals and sometimes also collectively, tried to steer expectations of their mode of life and its role in Frankish society. Case studies detail how influential thinkers such as Theodemar of Monte Cassino [MEEDER 2016], Walahfrid Strabo [PICKER 2008], and Smaragdus of Saint-Mihiel [PONESSE 2006] actively engaged with reform circles. But there remains ample room for investigation of how these and lesser-known figures, including a number of abbesses [VANDERPUTTEN 2018], sought to promote their views and influence then-current reform policies.

Monastic 'influencers'

The need for such studies gains pertinence in light of recent research that has shown Benedict of Aniane's reputation as principal mastermind of the reforms derived in fact from his biographer Ardo. In his text, Ardo claims that Benedict managed to turn the practices at his home institution of Aniane into the golden standard for all monastic communities in the Empire [CUSIMANO 2012]. But as is now firmly established, the biographer grossly overstated the role of his hero in order to justify a prominent biographical memory and to bolster his institution's self-confidence whilst competing for prominence with other houses, such as Gellone and Corbie [GEUENICH 1998, KETTEMANN 1999]. A new approach that takes into account multiple, possibly competing monastic 'influencers', and considers their presumed role in shaping rulership's reform policies, has begun to yield promising results [KRAMER 2016].

Legacy of Benedict of Aniane

3.2 Ninth-Century Monasticisms

According to the traditional interpretation, the transformations of the eighth and especially the early ninth centuries fundamentally changed experiences of life in and around monastic sites across the

Implications of
integration Frankish Empire. Some specialists pointed to the massive expansion of monastic institutions and their estates. They noted the fact that numerous monastic sites acquired a multifunctional identity that helped reshape local economies and societies, and elevated agricultural production and trade to a more sophisticated level. These expanded institutions also facilitated communication with other parts of the Empire through their networks, and served as representative sites of sovereign power [REUTER 1994]. Other scholars emphasized the drastic impact on (especially post-819) of experiences inside the cloister, citing such key aspects of reform programmes as strict enclosure, the homogenization or integration of ritual and daily practices across institutional boundaries, and the massive increase in exchanges of social and cultural capital between communities that were implicated in the reforms [3.1 DE JONG]. Finally, there were those who insisted that these transformations (or 'reforms') made the ascetic and devotional practices of contemplative monastics for the first time socially relevant, in that these practices were explicitly framed as a redemptive and intercessory service to the ruler and to society as a whole [SULLIVAN 1998]. While these interpretations remain relevant today, over the last twenty-five years it has become clear that we need to both expand and in some cases also adjust them.

Integration of monasteries into the Frankish state definitely transformed experiences in and around monastic institutions. Multiple functions of
monastic sites Recent studies have brought into focus the relationship between the reorganization of monastic compounds and the growing complexity of these sites in a political, economic, and symbolic sense. Functional and representational needs explain why some monastic sites were transformed to include significant areas reserved for access and use by the laity [BULLY/SAPIN 2015]: in some cases they even ended up resembling palatial complexes [HEITZ 1980, BOTO VARELA 2006, MARAZZI 2014, PAIN 2015]. These and various other interventions were designed to reflect the multiple contributions monastic institutions were expected to make towards the exercise of Carolingian rule, by providing prayer service and dynastic legitimation, acting as repositories of wealth and other resources, and functioning as centres from which the political landscape could be managed. That there was extensive theoretical reflection behind these interventions is revealed in the famous Plan of St Gall, which has recently been reinterpreted as a theoretical representation of the Reichenau abbey's functional multiplicity [LAUWERS 2014].

In a similar fashion, specialists have been looking at the impact of this integration process on local economies. According to the former view, it was part of a deliberate effort to transform local economies and revitalize trade (thanks to far-reaching monastic networks and intensive consumption of luxury goods) [LEBECQ 2000]. To some extent, this view was shaped by the production (beginning in the 780s) of comprehensive inventories (also known as polyptychs) of monastic properties, rights, and other economic resources. But more recent work on these and other documents indicates that the (re-)organization of estates and management procedures was less a deliberate plan to boost the Carolingian economy, and more an effort to sustain the individual monastic economies, maintain the position of sovereign rulers and their associates, and more generally insert these institutions in the exercise of sovereign power [DEVROEY 2020].

Impact on economy

Finally, the involvement of individuals from the local and regional aristocracy in the governance of monasteries (and a concomitant division of incomes in a *mensa abbatialis*, literally "table of the abbot", and a *mensa conventualis*, literally "table of the convent") is no longer strictly viewed as a symptom of growing political instability and of the decline of central authority's grip on local societies in the mid to later ninth century. Instead, it is now increasingly understood as a phenomenon that reflects the growing complexity of monastic governance and the Carolingians' reliance on these institutions as relays of political power between the court and local societies [FELTEN 1980, 3.1 DE JONG, HELVÉTIUS 1998, 2.6 ANDENNA]. A recent study insisted on the fact that many such arrangements were introduced as far back as the reign of Louis the Pious [CALVET-MARCADÉ 2015].

Involvement of lay agents

Reorganization of monastic sites, estates, economies, and governance, exposed monasteries to significant long-term risks. Groups of monastics were often mere stakeholders in these processes, and sometimes resented, even resisted, the costly transformation of their environment into a multifunctional site [3.1 RAAIJMAKERS]. Specialists have additionally drawn attention to the fact that the sheer size and complexity of some institutions, their reliance on long-distance trade networks, their sometimes scattered estates, and their transformation into regional hubs of political and economic life, all made them vulnerable to societal shocks and shifts in the distribution of political power [3.1 DE JONG]. This

Risks

Responses

vulnerability raises questions over the complex dynamics behind the disappearance of numerous, mostly smaller royal monasteries post-850 and the possibility that some did not suffer from catastrophic attacks or depredations, but were dissolved to reflect the changing scale of political life and monastic patronage in this period [3.1 VANDERPUTTEN].

There are indications, also, that a number of regular leaders tried to counter some of the potentially adverse effects of the shift in political life from the court to the local level by diversifying their roster of aristocratic and clerical patrons [BUTZ 2015]. To consolidate these alliances, they relied on the exchange of symbolic and material goods in gift-giving relationships: this same process also drove child oblation, which in the course of the ninth century had become the predominant mode of monastic recruitment [DE JONG 1996]. Also noticeable is a trend whereby some communities now actively promoted a deceased founder or saintly patron as lord and proprietor of their estate, ostensibly to make their institution less reliant on a secular lord [JOYE/BERTRAND 2014, 3.1 VANDERPUTTEN]. Some also explicitly began claiming certain (sometimes all) properties and incomes for the exclusive use of the vowed monastics and attacking lay lords and officers for abusing resources (below, Chapter 3.3). All these issues require further attention from scholars.

Inner experiences

Shifting our attention to experiences of life within monastic communities, we find that the emphasis in Carolingian reform policies on active and passive enclosure of male, and especially female, monastics has likewise been the subject of reinterpreta-

Space

tion. Indicating the importance that was awarded to creating separate, strictly enclosed spaces is the emergence, in the late eighth century, of the earliest examples of what we tend to recognize as cloisters: quadrangular open spaces bordered by a church, a dormitory, refectory, and a fourth building used for varying purposes. This architectural development was coupled with the elaboration of a liturgy to sanctify (and thus also distinguish from the secular world) the interior spaces of the cloister. Yet, although lawmakers and reformist commentators issued a number of instructions on how to (re)organize monastic space(s), there are no indications that there was an attempt to systematize these normative instructions [LAUWERS 2014]. The circulation and adoption across different parts of the Empire of certain architectural templates and other spatial arrangements is well attested: but these do not as such derive from a systematic effort to redesign monastic space in accordance with a cohesive normative account.

Here, as in other areas of the monastic experience, the focus of reformers lay on realizing a basic ideal of monastic distinctiveness in different contexts and through different means depending on a given institution's historical situation, its geophysical embedding in the landscape, and a range of other variables [PAIN 2015]. Former studies also viewed spatial transformations and various other arrangements of the period [for instance stricter arrangements for hosting visiting monks and clerics from other communities, JORDAN 2007] as designed to realize three objectives. The first was to keep contemplative religious away from ecclesiastical governance and pastoral and sacramental services; the second, to protect them from undue interference in their activities and their status as vowed monastics; and the third, to shield them from worldly temptations [on theoretical reflections, MATIS 2016]. But more recently, it has been argued that we also need to understand the focus on enclosure as part of a strategy to transform monasteries into meeting points for political networks and into representative institutions for sovereign authority – the authority of emperors, kings, and (from the mid-ninth century onwards) also queens. As a consequence, their integrity as religious communities was linked to the stability of the political system [MACLEAN 2003]. Preserving these places as privileged, unpolluted points of access to the divine indicated a ruler's ability to manage the multifunctionality of monastic sites and sustain a professional cohort of ascetics whose service to society required such an environment.

Needless to say, the massive amount of time spent by monks and women religious praying for the ruler and his subjects must have deeply impacted on their understanding of self, individually and as a community. It must also have influenced their reflections on the purpose and forms of their liturgical and other ritual services [on commemoration and prayer fraternities, ALTHOFF/ SCHMID 1978, WOLLASCH 1994, GEUENICH/LUDWIG 2015]. Among other things, transformations in the liturgy and commemorative practices have resurfaced in recent years as a significant focus of scholarly interest [BUTZ 2015, BILLET 2019]: the fact that there was a definite tendency for 'clericalization' of vowed monks surely was a significant factor in these transformations [OEXLE 1978]. Yet,

Focus of reformers

Relation to stability of the empire

Roles and occupations

while it is true that the Carolingians awarded special significance to the intercessory prayers of cloistered monastics and the purifying meaning of their devotions and liturgies [3.1 CHOY], we must not forget that contemplative communities represented but a fraction of monastic lifestyles at this time.

Enduring diversity

Our knowledge of the enduring diversity of the period, however, is somewhat limited by the lack of a comprehensive discussion of newly established or reformed communities of clerics, their organization, liturgical practices, pastoral roles, and other aspects of their existence. Although a number of regional case studies have shed important new light on the modalities of new foundations and of the splitting up of a number of monasteries into two distinct institutions – one for canons and one for monks [2.5 GAILLARD, KURDZIEL 2015] – the question of the extent to which the lifestyle [3.1 SEMMLER 2005] and property status [TRUMBORE JONES 2016] of canons was truly distinct from that of monks currently lacks a satisfying answer. Further development of a narrative that views monastic community life in the eighth and ninth centuries as a collaborative project involving different individuals and communities with different statuses and tasks, might help us nuance the view that contemplative monasteries came to be regarded exclusively as sites of intercession and commemoration, and that houses of canons acquired a fundamentally distinct role, focused on pastoral service.

Diverse monastic landscapes

There is, in fact, substantial evidence to argue that former notions about distinct identities and roles are problematic. In some parts of the Empire, groups of monks fiercely resisted the reformers' call to withdraw to a cloistered life of contemplation and prayer. They sought instead to maintain functionally diverse monastic landscapes that included contemplative and 'active' communities [2.4 LEYSER, 3.1 DEY]. In other locales, contemplative monastics relied on a diverse cohort of clerical and lay proxies to provide pastoral care, aid to the sick and needy, and other services traditionally associated with monastic life. Not enough attention, for instance, has been awarded to the 'shadow communities' of clerics that served male and especially female monasteries across the Empire. An investigation that evaluates the phenomenon in institutional and financial terms, but that also pays attention to the relationships involved, is urgently needed [3.1 VANDERPUTTEN].

Significance of 'private' forms

To these 'shadow communities' we must also add a substantial cohort of anchorites, hermits, consecrated virgins and widows, and household ascetics. Many of these maintained a symbiotic relationship with cloistered communities, producing small goods (for example, pigments and textiles) for use inside the cloister; educating young recruits; and offering spiritual counsel to the monastics and lay visitors [GARVER 2007]. While the individual liberties and life choices of cloistered monastics were drastically reduced in this period [WEMPLE 1981, SCHULENBURG 1984], for these other categories we find that their legitimacy and contribution to monastic spirituality, including that of cloistered communities, was widely acknowledged. This is attested in various sources, including commentaries by Benedict of Aniane and Smaragdus of Saint-Mihiel [COON 2011], by Grimlaicus [FRANK 1999], and also in the numerous copies from this period of late antique and early medieval rules and ascetic texts. Because specialists still tend to focus primarily on institutional forms of monastic life and the limitations these imposed on its practitioners, the substantial dimension of private ascetic practice and its place in contemporary monastic ideology both remain to be fully understood.

3.3 Restorations, Reforms, and the Problem of Monastic Lordship

Traditional discussions viewed the tenth and early eleventh centuries as a radical departure from the heterogeneous, secularized realities of late Carolingian monasticism. Over the last three decades, it has become apparent that there are fundamental issues with this approach [WOLLASCH 1999, VANDERPUTTEN 2013]. In particular, its set of arguments concerning a state of spiritual and institutional crisis are flawed. So, too, are those relating to the restoration efforts by various secular and clerical rulers (discussed here) and the programmatic approach, emancipatory goals, and unifying impact of various so-called reform movements (discussed below, in Chapter 3.4).

Most commentators today accept that the traditional view of a near-collapse of monastic institutions and spirituality is no longer tenable. Indisputably, a considerable number of monasteries in different parts of the Latin West were affected, in one way or another, by warfare and invasions, the destruction and alienation of estates and rights, and the displacement, abduction, or murder of personnel, both monastics and their lay servants. Many communities also

Impact of societal disruptions

experienced one or multiple phases of economic hardship, and the reduction of long-distance communication and trade [WOLLASCH 1999]. Yet, to collate (as historians used to do) the contemporary mass of anecdotal and often incomplete evidence and the biased reporting of later commentators into a generalizing narrative of decline is methodologically problematic. A host of case studies show us that the nature, intensity, and long-term impact of adverse circumstances could be very different from one region, locality, **Responses** even monastic settlement to another. We can also discern that the responses to these challenges could be very different from one institution to the next [2.5 BLAIR]. Even seemingly objective indications, such as the disappearance of monasteries from the written and archaeological record, cannot be taken for granted. We must be open to the possibility that some communities ceased to exist not because of some catastrophic circumstance, but as a result of a deliberate intervention. So it has been suggested that some smaller communities and their estates were merged with others to create a more robust institutional environment for members to pursue the ascetic ideal and fulfil their service to society [3.1 VANDERPUTTEN]. Further research will establish the extent of this phenomenon, and reconstruct the various dynamics behind the transformation of numerous contemplative institutions into rural sanctuaries served by small groups of clerics.

Biased accounts Scholars have also become more sensitive to the biased nature of late ninth- and early tenth-century statements on the perilous situation of organized monastic life. Such is the case with Carolingian royal diplomas that denounce the excessive demands of lay officers and proclaim the rulers' protection of communal assets [KOZIOL 2012]. Similarly, conciliar decrees and episcopal 'reform charters' that attack lay interference in monastic affairs and decry a breakdown in the observance of monks and women religious we now read as signifiers of an episcopal intention to claim a controlling stake in the governance of these institutions, or to justify actions taken to that effect [3.1 VANDERPUTTEN]. A biased approach is also revealed in a broad range of monastic texts (including charters, but also hagiographies, and biographies), some of which have been re-read as belonging to a wider range of adaptations to increasingly changeable political circumstances [IOGNA-PRAT 1992, 3.1 VANDERPUTTEN]. By the late ninth century, some communities also began deploying what eventually became a veritable arsenal of oral, written, and ritual weapons designed to ward off unwanted competition over monastic assets [LITTLE 1993, MAZEL 2005]. The tales of chroniclers and hagiographers that related stories of destruction, theft, and monastics left as the innocent victims of godless attackers and amoral laymen, perfectly complemented these tactics. While it would be unwise to dismiss them as fictional, much remains to be understood about why they were recorded at a specific point in time and in a specific genre, and how they might have served various purposes, such as self-defence, the construction of communal identities, and historical revisionism.

Much could be said about vibrant intellectual and spiritual cultures [3.1 VANDERPUTTEN], manuscript and art production, and other indicators that organized monasticism c. 900 was by no means on the brink of extinction, either institutionally or spiritually. But perhaps the best proof is that lay and clerical rulers, including those that had forcibly established their power base, viewed at least some of these sites and communities as worth preserving. They quickly re-established these institutions as multifunctional sites from which local politics and economies could be controlled, and where their personal and dynastic interests could be represented [2.5 BLAIR, KEATS-ROHAN 2005, VANDERPUTTEN 2013]. As a range of studies have demonstrated, such rulers also symbolically claimed lordship over these sites by staging highly publicized restitutions of property to the community living there, and by demonstratively taking measures they presented as critical to the continuation of monastic life in these places [BOSHOF 1989, PARISSE 1989]. Unquestionably, many communities benefited from this renewed interest in monastic lordship and patronage, even if it interrupted a trend towards greater self-control in some places, and even if the vocal assertions of support by local rulers often implied an unequal partnership with considerable mutual obligations [VANDERPUTTEN 2013, 3.1 VANDERPUTTEN].

Continuities in secular patronage

Older scholarly discussions often looked to the revival of the Carolingian *libertas monasticae religionis* and the renewed promotion of Benedictine observance. They implied that these constituted evidence of a selfless devotion by rulers to 'restoring' or 'reforming' monastic institutions and spirituality. Certainly there is no reason to doubt that most lay and clerical rulers involved in these various 'restorations' and 'reforms' were linked to transregional networks where the legacies of Carolingian reform were actively studied and

Nuancing views on 'liberty'

transmitted [SEMMLER 1989, STECKEL 2010]. However, the various privileges that awarded 'liberty' (*libertas*) need to be understood not as a ruler's attempt to emancipate monastic communities from all secular interference, but as signifiers of an intention to appropriate for themselves the role Carolingian sovereigns had formerly occupied with regard to these communities [MAZEL 2011].

Implications at Cluny
As an extensive bibliography now reveals, the granting of *libertas* had different implications depending on the social and political context. In regions where there were no lords who could dominate their immediate peers, for instance at Cluny, such acts signified a ruler's ambition to reap at least the redemptive and commemorative rewards from taking protective measures as *tutor et defensor* of a monastic community. It enabled them to remain at least symbolically implicated in a monastery's affairs, and prevented local competitors from the lay and clerical elites from claiming a controlling stake [CONSTABLE 2010]. But the long-term implications of Cluny's exceptional situation were by no means apparent in the early 900s [NEISKE 2005]. Rather, studies have shown, its position resulted from a process of gradual accretion driven by persistent political fractures in Burgundy; the diplomatic and leadership skills of Abbots Berno and Odo; and the implications of various papal, royal, and other privileges granted over the course of the tenth century [CONSTABLE 2010, ROSÉ 2013]. At the heart of these developments stood that of the Cluniac 'multi-abbacy', which throughout the eleventh century remained central to all of Cluny's claims on property and on control over other institutions [MÉHU 2010]. A similar situation has been described for other contexts too, including that of the *incastellamento* in France and Italy [ANDENNA 2007, DELL'OMO 2007].

Implications in other settings
In other regions where local rulers were able to secure their lordship status over monastic houses, the various 'liberties' and proclamations of 'restoration' or 'reform' were part of a double strategy. First, it was a demonstrative expression by these individuals of their self-assumed status as heir to the Carolingian sovereigns in their role as protector of monastic institutions. It enabled these rulers to symbolically establish their dominant position in local and regional elite circles. Second, they were also able to thus claim the governance and resources of monastic institutions, except for specific areas of abbatial governance as described in the *Rule of St Benedict* [NIGHTINGALE 2007]. A number of Ottonian and

West Frankish royal charters from the mid-tenth century occupy a middle ground between these two approaches. In these documents, we see how sovereign corroboration of a recent 'restoration' of a royal monastery on the part of lay or clerical rulers facilitated the transfer of control to faithful local allies (particularly key institutions in politically disputed regions, Lotharingia and Flanders being two good examples), whilst indicating that they themselves remained the legitimate proprietors of these monasteries [VANDER-PUTTEN 2013]. Further study is needed to verify if the donations and rights that are included in these royal and imperial charters were intended to strengthen the position of the monastics against the personal interests of their local 'restorer' and his associates. This is especially pertinent for regions and institutions where the patronage of monastic communities reflects a complex web of aristocratic alliances and rivalries [NIGHTINGALE 2007]. Although it is often difficult to reconstruct these continuously shifting realities, case studies suggest that we need to consider the lordship of monastic houses as a mode of governance that was subject to ongoing negotiation [ROSENWEIN 1989].

Negotiated nature of monastic lordship

For some parts of the Latin West, the source record allows us to observe in considerable detail how aristocratic rivalries and opposing interest groups were represented in the membership and patronage of certain communities [NIGHTINGALE 2007, D'ACUNTO 2018]. In others, a more focused approach is discernible: but here too patterns in patronage depended heavily on political circumstances and alliances. East of the Rhine, so a wealth of scholarship reveals, the early Ottonians continued a tradition established by their Carolingian predecessors of relying on monasteries as political, economic, and representative hubs of sovereign power, using them also as a means to connect and communicate efficiently with local aristocratic networks. Here, we also see monastic foundations – especially of female houses – taking place on an impressive scale. This phenomenon has been linked to processes of territorial expansion; the itinerant nature of royal governance in this period; and the representative needs of the Ottonian and early Salian rulers. However, it also ties in to expectations of female commemorative service and a demographic trend whereby women who had accumulated wealth were keen to keep this out of the hands of distant relatives [LEYSER 1979, BERNHARDT 1993, ALTHOFF 2003]. The deliberate policy of monastic patronage by East Frankish rulers – which abruptly ended in the second quarter of the eleventh century, when they began to rely more on bishops and transferred the lordship of many monasteries to these individuals [SEIBERT 1991, VOGTHERR 2000] – finds many parallels on the Iberian Peninsula. Here, members of the royal houses of León and Navarra and their lay and clerical aristocrats were extremely active in the patronage and (re) foundation of monasteries during the *Repoblación* [LORÉS 2013]. The East Frankish example is also paralleled in the earliest monastic settlements in the kingdoms of Hungary and Poland [BEREND/ LASZLOVSKY/ZSOLT SZAKÁCS 2007].

Role of abbots and abbesses

It is no wonder, given these circumstances, that lay and clerical lords were keen to appoint as regular leaders individuals with good connections and especially also highly developed diplomatic skills. As a range of recent work has shown, many abbots from this period deftly navigated complex aristocratic networks and connections and were willing to adapt their governance to patronal expectations [BULST 1973, PARISSE/OEXLE 1993, CUBITT 2018, REGLERO DE LA FUENTE 2018]. But more still could be done to precisely reconstruct the networks of these individuals, their social and educational profiles, and their public activities. Less noticed by scholars are the female leaders who developed a prominent public profile as capable administrators and charismatic religious figures. For Saxony, we know that abbesses were often recruited not only on the basis of their familial connections to the imperial court, but also because they were prominent members of the political elite in their own right. They were able to mobilize major networks and resources for the benefit of both their relatives and their monastic subjects [MÜLLER-WIEGAND 2005, THIBAUT 2018]. With the exception of a handful of high-status abbesses in northern Italy [2.6 ANDENNA] and northern Spain [JARRETT 2003] our understanding of the extent and limits of female leadership agency in other parts of the Latin West remains limited.

3.4 (Un)Reformed Experiences at the Turn of the First Millennium

Notion of 'reform monasticism'

The traditional view of the tenth and early eleventh centuries is that of an age in which Benedictine monasticism triumphantly rose from its ashes. Although scholars conceded that monasticism had always been subject to subtle and more drastic transformations, in their view the two centuries on either side of the year 1000 witnessed an incremental process of deliberate change that had more profound implications than anything attempted before or since. To argue their point, they did three things. One was to coin the term 'reform monasticism' (*Reformmönchtum, monachisme réformateur, monachesimo riformatore*) as a shorthand descriptor, to which they added subsidiary ones, like 'Cluniac reform' or 'Gorze reform' [SACKUR 1892–1893, HALLINGER 1950–1951]. The second was to conceptualize 'reform monasticism' as a movement that pursued an agenda (on the one hand) of restoring an authentic experience of the monastic ideal, and (on the other) of radically altering the ways in which it was organized and how it related to the secular environment. And finally, scholars also developed a tendency to call just about every positive change in monasticism a reform, whether in the domain of governance, estate management, observance, liturgy, spirituality, literature, art, or architecture.

This approach is now thought by most scholars to be a historiographical construct. It relies, firstly, on the idea that claims regarding the catastrophic decline of monastic life c. 900 are globally relevant, and that there was an objective need for drastic intervention to 'restore' and 'reform' it. Second, it recognizes in these restorations and reforms a deliberate attempt to break away from the situatedness of monastic institutions and spirituality, to establish instead autonomous, quasi-congregational structures in which the member communities would follow the same principles of governance, liturgical practice, and organization of daily life (see the nuancing discussion above, Chapter 3.3). And finally, the traditional view of this renewal considers the survival of 'non-reformed' monasticism, the discrepancies between life in various reformed communities, and the unchallenging spirituality of monks and women religious as revealing the presence of societal obstacles that ultimately prevented the merging of these movements and the flowering of a homogeneous Benedictine 'order' (see the discussion below, Chapter 3.7).

Former views

Emerging in the late 1960s but becoming prominent only in the early 2000s, critical testing of this broad narrative revealed that it rests on layers of biased interpretations by medieval and then early modern commentators, who were looking to project current concerns and expectations onto a legitimizing past. This traditional narrative was further compromised by studies that pointed out

Critical testing of these views

various problematic assumptions: about reform's rooting in opposing 'movements' that featured pre-set reform programmes; about the role of 'reform centres' as catalysts of spiritual and institutional integration; about the normative intent of early customaries; and, too, about the use of necrologies to reconstruct institutional networks [WOLLASCH 1973, SCHMID 1959, KOTTJE 1989, 3.3 WOLLASCH, VANDERPUTTEN 2020]. Determining how historical views and interpretations have shaped the modern understanding of monasticism in the tenth and eleventh centuries has now gained wide recognition as being essential in building a new, more accurate narrative. Specialists have particularly called for greater awareness of the historical semantics, and current use in scholarship, of culturally loaded terms such as 'reform', 'restoration', and 'renewal' [TELLENBACH 1988, 3.1 BARROW, 3.3 VANDERPUTTEN].

New approaches

A further corollary is that the above lines of enquiry have brought into focus the enduring diversity of monastic life. Indisputably there are signs of a trend towards greater integration of monastic governance, written practices, architectural design, liturgical rites, and so on. But the scope of this trend clearly surpassed the action range of specific reform 'movements' or agents. It must instead be attributed to broader policies: the transregional networks of intellectuals and elite figures, in which theoretical and practical models of ascetic withdrawal were compared, discussed, and transmitted; economic growth, with increased trade and mobility of goods and people; and a shift in the social embedding of monastic communities and in cultural expectations of monastic life generally.

Trend for integration

Looking at various reform 'movements' or 'networks' as we find them reconstructed in the older scholarship [3.3 HALLINGER, KNOWLES 1966], here too we see definite signs of integration of monastic institutions and practice. Confraternity links between monastic institutions may well have been one of the principal vehicles of such integration processes: their precise nature and implications in the later tenth- to mid-eleventh century definitely deserves closer attention. However, the cohesion and homogeneity of these networks and their shared sense of identity has been vastly overstated. Specialists of Cluny have long abandoned the notion that the abbey's early leadership strove to establish a unified, instantly recognizable Cluniac observance across institutional and regional boundaries [IOGNA-PRAT 2002]. Similar observations have also been made for reform 'movements' in Lotharingia [WAGNER 1996] and Flanders

Limits of integration

[3.3 VANDERPUTTEN], Western Francia and Normandy [BULST 1991, POTTS 1997], Italy [FONSECA 2006], and northern Spain [3.3 REGLERO DE LA FUENTE]. Even England's *Regularis Concordia* and its call for unity in liturgical observance should not fool us into thinking that reformist lawmakers considered strict uniformity across institutional boundaries achievable or desirable [CUBITT 1997, YORKE 2003]. This is evidenced in the reformers' reliance on a methodology whereby 'reformist' views on governance and observance were transmitted primarily *verbo et exemplo* ("through word and exemplary deed"), a practice that implied that local communities would soon have to rely on their recollections and interpretations of these views to apply them in a local setting [3.3 VANDERPUTTEN].

Former claims about this being a time when monastic life for men and for women had stopped being "shaped by its practitioners" [MCNAMARA 1996] also no longer ring true. On first inspection, the evidence does seem to suggest this. The absence from the source record for the tenth and early eleventh centuries of new rules and other normative texts, the scarcity of commentaries on monastic observance, and the numerous references in contemporary documents to the *Rule of St Benedict* and (more implicitly) the two *Institutiones* for canons and canonesses, seem to corroborate the notion of passive practitioners. It is as if monastics, once they were reformed, stopped thinking for themselves and strictly observed the precepts enclosed in the normative texts, along with the various additions and emendations provided by representatives of a given 'reform centre'. But as recent studies have shown, the libraries of cloistered men and women across the Latin West held multiple rules and other normative commentaries, which, along with a number of patristic texts, conciliar and canon lawbooks, and various penitentials, formed a comprehensive basis for continued reflection and debate on the nature and purpose of monastic life [BODARWÉ 2004, RABIN 2015]. And contrary to what some have argued, a substantive part of that reflection has been preserved in written form, albeit not in the genres and typologies scholars traditionally used to focus on.

For instance, it is only recently that Odo of Cluny's *Occupatio* has been recognized as a landmark achievement in monastic literature [JONES 2007]: along with his *Collationes* [ROSÉ 2010] it forms but a small part of a considerable body of commentaries that describe 'best (monastic) practice' [COCHELIN 2005, COCHELIN 2014]. For other contexts and regions (including England, Lotharingia, France,

Shaping local observance

Written testimonies

the Empire, and the Italian Peninsula), we have an extensive, miscellaneous corpus of commentaries that are embedded in early customaries, hagiographies, biographies, chronicles, treatises, letters, sermons, and other text typologies, and that merit in-depth study [BARROW 2009, VANDERPUTTEN 2020]. A notable feature of many of these texts is that they unapologetically refer to local interpretations of normative and literary traditions. This is strikingly revealed in Cluniac biographies and customaries, where authors working at different institutions project distinct views of monastic spirituality and practice [3.3 IOGNA-PRAT, BOYNTON 2006]. But they can be found in other contexts too, including those inhabited by women religious [3.1 VANDERPUTTEN]. As far as the diverse reception and interpretation of monastic literary tradition in the tenth and eleventh centuries is concerned, the variations as we find them attested

Reception of rules in these original works are but the tip of the iceberg. Whereas scholarship used to simply assume that communities involved in reform adopted the customs of major reform centres, the trend is now to consider more carefully the transmission, reception, and redaction in local settings of late antique and early medieval rules and other normative commentaries.

Among the more spectacular examples is that of how the *Rule of St Benedict* was reworked for use by women. Close scrutiny of the surviving manuscript copies has revealed notable variations and redactions, all of which were ostensibly created to meet the requirements and expectations of one, or at most a handful of communities and (we can assume) their patrons [3.1 BODARWÉ, 3.1 VANDERPUTTEN]. Similar observations have been made regarding the transmission and reception of texts destined for use by male monastics. Although the documentation from some male monasteries in Spain emphatically refers to the *Rule of St Benedict* as the monks' guiding tradition, in their reading culture, experiences and self-understanding there were still prominent elements of Visigothic monasticism (as represented in Valerius of Bierzo's *Liber regularum* and the work of Isidore of Seville) and of other influences (such as the work of John Cassian and Gregory the Great) [3.3 REGLERO DE LA FUENTE]. As a result, we even see regional models of monastic organization resurfacing as they had existed prior to the fall of the Visigothic dynasty [MARTÍNEZ TEJERA 2006]. From England, there are a number of vernacular versions of the *Rule of St Benedict*, all of which have been studied primarily from a linguistic perspective and deserve further attention by historians [LANGEFELD 2003, RIYEFF 2017]. These and other local traditions and adaptations await full (comparative) investigation.

These theoretical variations are mirrored in the evidence concerning the real life experiences of cloistered monastics [WOLLASCH 1996, 3.3 VANDERPUTTEN]. Liturgical, archival, material, and other sources attest to the existence of countless minor and more substantial localized variations in how the Benedictine model was observed across various parts of the Latin West. Such variations often entailed far more than a series of tweaks to reflect the preferences and fancies of groups of monastics and their patrons. In post-reform England, moral and functional distinctions between monks and clerics remained vague [TINTI 2015], and recently it was argued that even a major proponent of Benedictine reform like Æthelwold of Winchester accepted that some monks would continue to preach to the laity [REIDEL 2015]. Groups of male monastics across the Latin West were also involved in caring for the poor: how they organized this was subject to many local variations [WOLLASCH 1988]. Not enough at present is known about how communities of canons were organized or reorganized, but case studies suggest that local circumstances and expectations in large measure shaped the life experiences of the members [BARROW 1994, LANGEFELD 2003, BARROW 2009]. And for cloistered women, too, the range of variations in their lifestyle, financial status, daily routines, and self-understanding was very broad, much broader than we suspect in fact [3.1 VANDERPUTTEN]. Scattered references in tenth-century sources from Rome, Lotharingia, present-day Switzerland and England attest to the involvement of cloistered women and anchoresses in sacramental tasks, and possibly also in preaching [SCHAEFER 2013, 3.1 VANDERPUTTEN, BUGYIS 2019]. From Lotharingia and northern Italy, we have references to women religious finding ways to remain involved in the running of urban hospices and hospitals [BALZARETTI 2011, 3.1 VANDERPUTTEN].

Lest we forget, there were still very substantial numbers of 'unreformed' communities, left alone because there was no political, symbolic, or other interest in an intervention. Another reason could be that local societies depended on their services, or simply that they were widely respected for their practice of the monastic ideal. Post-Reform, Benedictine houses in England were still vastly outnumbered by secular minsters, although many of the

Real life experiences

latter would gradually be replaced with parish churches staffed by a single cleric [2.5 BLAIR]. For other regions too, situating all the non-reformed communities in the monastic landscape would help a great deal towards nuancing the idea of a 'triumph' of Benedictinism. This has been done, in part at least, by a number of scholars who have looked at 'unreformed' women religious [3.1 VANDER-PUTTEN] and especially also canons [3.2 TRUMBORE JONES]: their work has revealed that a number of communities in both of these cohorts positively thrived under the protection and patronage of local lords.

Intercultural influences

Diversity in monastic practice was not a phenomenon deriving from local circumstances only: it was imported too. A 'wave' of Insular recruits in monastic contexts may have had comparatively little impact on monastic spirituality and practices in mid-tenth-century Lotharingia [3.1 VANDERPUTTEN], however, east of the Rhine the 970s marked the start of an Insular presence that for centuries to come would remain distinct (for example, in terms of ritual and language) from communities that recruited locally [WEBER 2010]. Long dismissed as irrelevant (based on the assumption that they had drifted too far apart), interactions between Greek and Latin monasticism likewise emerge as prominent transcultural exchanges in this period. Notable examples are the numerous southern Italian communities that featured what some have described as a 'mixed' Latin–Greek observance [RAMSEYER 2006]. Significant, too, are the testimonies regarding Greek monks, wandering ascetics, and hermits travelling across the Latin West and settling there [MARTIN 2003].

A similar potential for further exploration of inter- or transcultural exchanges and influence lies in the study of monasticism on the Iberian Peninsula. These include testimonies pertaining to individual monastics who travelled to the East for inspiration; Mozarabic and Carolingian influences in monastic architecture and art [3.3 LORÉS]; and fascinating hybrids of Visigothic script, customs, and liturgies, mixed with Roman and Carolingian influences [HERRERO DE LA FUENTE/FERNÁNDEZ FLÓREZ 2012]. Although some of the Mozarabic monks who travelled to Christian territories met with indifference or even hostility, the commonalities in the ideals and experiences of monastic life in different cultural and ethnic contexts were still far greater than we might think [GALLON 2016]. Similar perspectives may emerge from the future study of interactions between Christian monastics and Jewish faith communities [HOROWITZ 1992].

3.5 The Conversion of the World

Much ink has been spilled over the historical relevance of a 'crisis' of lay masculinity in the decades around 900 and the role played by monastics in fanning it [STONE 2011]. Beginning in the 1990s, a number of historians argued that prior to the eleventh century, a clear distinction between lay and monastic or clerical moralities did not exist. In their interpretation, Odo of Cluny's biography of Gerald of Aurillac reflects the way in which ecclesiastical moralists were facing elite laymen with an impossible task. If they wished to pursue a virile ideal of Christian life they had both to fulfil their divinely assigned role in the world whilst also observing typically 'monastic' virtues, such as humility, poverty, and sexual restraint or even total abstinence [AIRLIE 1992, NELSON 1999]. Presumably, only the Gregorian reformers of the eleventh century solved this problem, by subordinating a disorderly, aggressive lay masculinity to its chaste, protective, and therefore also morally superior clerical counterpart and establishing the servants of the Church as a "Third Sex" [MCNAMARA 1994].

'Crisis of (lay) masculinity'

Against this interpretation, and counter the view that monastic agents in particular had taken things a step too far when pushing for a 'monastization' of lay morals, specialists of the Carolingian period argued that the reforms of the early ninth century had already been marked by "a singularly powerful ideal of differentiation which defined the separateness of those who mediated between God and mankind" [DE JONG 2005]. A number of studies also suggested that Odo's primary goal with the *Life of Gerald* was not to present a template of ideal Christian conduct to a male aristocratic audience (as former scholars had said), but to sanctify Gerald's memory. While specialists have admitted that the *Life* does somewhat uncomfortably insert its lay subject into monastic categories of virtue [SAVIGNI 2002, IOGNA-PRAT 2002b], Odo's other writings hardly show him to be a radical pursuing the 'monastization' of lay morality [ROMIG 2017]. His long-ignored *Occupatio* in particular was recently revealed as a major statement on how monasticism's morality and codes of conduct had been designed to

Existing distinctions

make the Christianity of its practitioners distinct from the rest of the world [3.4 JONES]. These ideas are matched in a revised edition of the *Life of Gerald* from later in the tenth century, which suppresses the critiques of monastic morality found in the former version, and turns Gerald into the (lay) exception that proves the principle that only monks could reach the highest degree of moral achievement [BULTOT-VERLEYSEN 1995].

Extending these arguments to include the clergy, numerous other tenth- and early eleventh-century commentators likewise insisted on the need for distinctions – morally, visually, and behaviourally – between a 'pure' ecclesiastical cohort and its 'secular' or 'impure' lay counterpart [BALZARETTI 1999, ROSÉ 2008, 3.4 BARROW 2009, STEPHENSON 2015, VANDERPUTTEN 2020]. At present, the majority opinion among specialists is that monastic propagandists were not looking to substitute monastic morals for secular ones. Rather, they contributed to the shaping of new ethical and behavioural standards for the laity by replacing "statutory morals" – moral principles linked to one's status – with "absolute" ones [IOGNA-PRAT 2002a]. Certainly there is a great deal of emphasis in sources of the tenth and early eleventh centuries on monastics impressing their secular audiences with particular moral notions, such as personal accountability; the need for the individual to actively pursue redemption of previous sins; and the universal validity of certain monastic virtues such as humility, charity, restraint, and more generally the quest for union with God [TRÂN-DUC 2015].

Several reasons have been identified for the prominence of these arguments in monastic discourse. Many regular leaders reconciled their seigniorial duties and obligations towards patrons and lords with their ascetic identity by adopting a public persona as an 'active extraworldly ascetic'. As part of this they extended their role as spiritual teachers in the cloister to include the secular world [OTTONE 2003, CUBITT 2008, VANDERPUTTEN 2015]. We also know that there existed multiple strands in monastic life, institutionalized and otherwise, where ordinary monastics carried out various pastoral and charitable duties [CONSTABLE 1982; also above, Chapter 3.2]. And finally, there was the positioning of cloistered communities as professional intermediaries with the divine, offering things like intercessory prayers, commemorative services, and a burial place in the local cemetery, in return for material gifts from the laity [3.3 ROSENWEIN, RAPPMANN/ZETTLER 1998, 3.3

Promotion of monastic morals

Reasons

MAZEL 2011]. In order to boost the exchange value of these spiritual services and protect their interests, members of these communities and their associates had to continuously argue in support of their necessity and effectiveness. An essential part of these efforts consisted of encouraging laymen and -women to reflect on how they might positively influence their personal fate after death: hence the continuous references in contemporary sources to redemptive action and conversion. Undoubtedly, millenarian sentiments around the year 1000 helped intensify the perceived urgency of this discourse [VANDERPUTTEN 2015], as did its frequent use in the context of property disputes and other conflicts between monastics and their lay neighbours (below, Chapter 4.1).

For cloistered monastics and their leadership, there was nothing objectionable or surprising about the embedded nature of this discourse in their own interests and in those of their lay and clerical lordship. And as studies from the last three decades have shown, members of the laity responded just as pragmatically to the monastics' appeal for conversion. The decision to patronize a specific community; donate land to establish a new one; have their relatives buried at a certain monastic site; send their relatives there to become a monk, cleric, or woman religious; or actually become a member of a community themselves: all these things were based on an estimation of how to maximize the return on one's 'investment'. For instance, we can often see members of the lower and middle groups of the lay elites donating to a particular institution to enter or remain in the orbit of that community's lordship. Such gifts also helped the donor claim a prominent position in a community that had lost its former patron, or establish a foothold in a site of political or economic significance [MAZEL 2002].

Studies have also established that various redemptive donations by lay patrons to monastic beneficiaries were the subject of extensive prior negotiation and were nearly always intended to either establish or maintain an *amicitia* between these parties. In instances where the documentation allows us to discern the mechanics behind specific property transfers, this reciprocal aspect is obvious [BIJSTERVELD 2007]. We can see that many redemptory donations were part-trade, part-sale and part-gift, or were *precaria*, return gifts by the Church to patronizing members of the laity. Some were even loans [MORELLE 1999, BOUGARD 2010, ROSÉ 2010, DAVIDE 2016]. In other cases, ambitious laymen contested

Lay motivations

Gift-giving relationships

Nature of transactions

redemptory gifts by their deceased ancestors in order to trade those same gifts for an advantageous *amicitia* with the original recipients, and sometimes even get part of an original gift back as compensation for their alleged loss [3.3 ROSENWEIN, VANDERPUTTEN 2010]. While these findings might tempt some observers to take a cynical view of these and other transactions, in reality they did not negate any sincere spiritual intentions on the part of lay donors [WILKIN 2011]. But contrary to what used to be suggested in older studies, no single lay individual would have been tempted to give to a specific group of monastics strictly because of the recent 'restoration' or 'reform' of their institution and observance, or simply out of piety. Indeed, in some regions merely being a reformed house was not a pulling factor at all, as can be witnessed in the dwindling lay support for monks and women religious in the Empire and England in the decades following the year 1000 [LEYSER 1979, 2.5 BLAIR]. The monastics themselves needed something to offer in return, and for that reason had to invest heavily in building a prestigious patronage network, developing a range of spiritual and material return services, and launching a propaganda effort that mobilized members of the laity. Institutional rivalries arising from these strategies remain an ill-explored aspect of monasticism in this period.

Social diversity of communities   Traditional assumptions regarding entrance to the monastic life have likewise been subject to revision. The sheer number of small institutions in this period and the density of the monastic landscape in certain regions (for instance, Lotharingia and Saxony) means that at least some communities had to recruit among the middle or lower strata of the population. A host of relevant observations for specific institutions and regions [WOLLASCH 1982, LEYSER 1979, BOUCHARD 1987, GAZEAU 2007, and specifically for women's communities, FELTEN 2005] are currently waiting to be assembled

Adult conversion   into a synthetic argument. Also unresolved is the question of how exactly the oblation of children and the conversion of adult individuals responded to changing aristocratic family dynamics, ecclesiastical recruitment patterns, and other developments (particularly the emergence of urban societies and mercantile elites) from the later tenth century onwards. Regarding adult converts specifically,

Motivations   we know that some regular leaders of the period were particularly inclined to accept as new converts adult individuals with specific leadership skills and expertise [VANDERPUTTEN 2015]. Conceivably, the individuals entered the monastic life not simply to secure their salvation and strive for spiritual perfection, but also with an eye to gaining a position of prominence in cloistered contexts [MAZEL 2011]. Some local hagiographies were actually tailored to insist on the fact that adult converts could continue to put their former experiences as clerics or lay aristocrats to use after having entered the monastery: according to the eleventh-century *Life* of nobleman-turned-monk William of Gellone (d. 812/814), following his conversion he was called on at least two occasions to go and fight against the infidels [DUHAMEL-AMADO 2002]. Our understanding of the precise scope of this literary source record, its discourse and targeted audience, and its institutional embedding would benefit from further study (also below, Chapter 3.7). Besides a need for more prosopographical research into abbots and other leading figures of the time [GAZEAU 2007], much can also be expected from the anthropological study of skeletal remains.

Representations

3.6 Cluniac and Other Nebulas

Ever since Cluniac monasticism first became a subject of academic enquiry, specialists have been looking for ways to explain how William of Aquitaine's modest foundation transformed into the mighty *ecclesia Cluniacensis*, with its vast network of monasteries, priories, and subpriories. The eleventh century consistently occupies a central place in these discussions, although opinions have differed over what exactly was achieved. Pre-1970, historians believed that Odilo's abbacy (or that of his successor Hugo) witnessed the emergence of a 'Cluniac order', or at the very least a consolidated congregational structure that was centred, legally and in terms of its customs, on Cluny [LEMARIGNIER 1950].

Emergence of the
ecclesia Cluniacensis

Post-1970, the term 'order' was quietly dropped, as scholars realized that the eleventh-century Cluniac federation had none of the characteristics of monastic orders from later centuries, such as a clearly established legal identity, centralized institutions for legislation and supervision, and written statutes [DE VALOUS 1970]. Increasingly, it became apparent that when monks of Cluny disseminated their abbey's distinctive features (such as the absence of lay advocates, exemptions from episcopal oversight, and various aspects of liturgy and practice) to other communities, these institutions did not automatically become a member of a *Klosterverband* (federation of monasteries) with the Burgundian abbey at its centre [POECK 1998]. Studies also definitively toppled the classic view of late tenth- and early eleventh-century Cluniac customaries as instruments of institutional integration, and that of necrologies as reliable indicators of congregation-building [3.4 WOLLASCH 1973].

Since then, the focus in scholarship has been on exploring the nature and outer boundaries of the *ecclesia Cluniacensis*. Those who have studied the abbey's rich charter collection (including, crucially, the various papal privileges) have argued that up until the third quarter of the eleventh century, the *ecclesia* consisted strictly of the monasteries, priories, chapels, and other properties that belonged to the abbots' lordship and in some cases also shared in Cluny's exempt status. The gradual emergence of the *ecclesia* as a federation was primarily due to successive changes in the status of Cluny's abbatial lordship [3.3 ROSENWEIN, 3.3 MÉHU]. In particular, the phasing out of multi-abbatial acquisitions around the middle of the eleventh century and its gradual replacement with a system whereby Cluny's abbot obtained the investiture of the abbots of other institutions was a catalyst for change. One prominent scholar estimated that the Cluniac leadership played a decisive, steering role in this process, justifying claims regarding a "forward-looking reform" of the federation in the eleventh century [CONSTABLE 2010a]. Against these observations, another specialist pointed out that Cluniac federalism was a complex process of integration that even contemporaries must have found difficult to oversee. Around a relatively small group of institutions that were legally subjected to the abbot's lordship also existed monasteries that were likewise subject but did not enjoy the same privileges and exemptions. And around that group, there was an even larger cohort of institutions that were connected to Cluny because of an invitation to the abbot or his monks to introduce Cluny's customs. The expression 'Cluniac nebula' was coined specifically to capture the diffuse nature of the (con)federation in the later tenth to early twelfth centuries [3.4 IOGNA-PRAT].

How the Cluniacs tried to establish a sense of shared identity in this 'nebulous' environment has been a major focus of interest for over three decades. For this purpose, specialists have at their disposal an extraordinary body of evidence – biographies, hagiographical accounts, poems, epitaphs, and even preambles to cartularies – commemorating and celebrating the respective

Margin notes:

Decline of multi-abbacy

Federalism

Cluniac nebula

Shaping a corporate identity

legacies of Abbots Odo, Aymard, Maiolus, Odilo, and Hugo [IOGNA-PRAT 2000]. Written between the middle of the tenth century and the 1120s/1130s, these texts not only celebrated the charisma and governance qualities of the abbey's leadership, but also provided readers with an evolving commentary on Cluny's spectacular ascendance and the emergence, over the course of the eleventh century, of the *ecclesia Cluniacensis* [IOGNA-PRAT 1988, 3.3 IOGNA-PRAT]. As a range of publications has pointed out, these sources all built on the notion of a 'charismatic genealogy' of abbots, providing the basis for the movement's unity and unicity [IOGNA-PRAT 1993, ROSENWEIN 1998, ATSMA/VEZIN 2000, BARRET 2004, 3.3 NEISKE].

The Cluniacs' concurrent self-promotion as purveyors of intercessory prayers and commemorative services for the dead must also be understood within their attempts to establish a distinct social, ideological, and corporate identity [WOLLASCH 1990, LONGO 2000/2001]. This, in turn, paved the way for commentators who were looking to revise the account of Cluny's foundation as not being that of an ordinary monastery, but a place of distinction [HARRIS 2005]. In particular, the notion in contemporary hagiographies and related documents of the abbey as an "asylum of piety" has been linked both to Pope John XIX's 1024 privilege and to the promotion of various forms of lay conversion [3.3 IOGNA-PRAT, CONSTABLE 2010a]. Architectural historians and archaeologists also pointed out that in its architecture and decoration, the massive abbatial church known as Cluny III reveals Abbot Hugo's determination to present Cluny as a spiritual asylum [BAUD 2006; compare with Saint-Bénigne of Dijon around the year 1000, MALONE 2009; and Hirsau in the late eleventh century, SCHREINER 1999]. It is not a coincidence, so various specialists have noted, that these discursive and architectural projects coincided with the creation of Cluny's sacred *ban*, a concentric area of non-interference around the abbey [ROSENWEIN 1999, 3.3 MÉHU].

Much progress has been made, also, in nuacing former views on Cluny's role in the ecclesiastical reform movement of the eleventh century. Case studies have made it obvious that Odilo and especially Hugo were particularly reluctant to alienate local rulers and patronage: both their negotiating skills and their willingness to accommodate the expectations of local patrons are made very evident in the charter material [RACINET 1990, HARRIS 2005, CONSTABLE 2010b]. Notable case studies include the

Involvement in Church reform

foundation of the nunnery of Marcigny [WISCHERMANN 1986] and the eleventh-century 'wave' of Cluniac foundations in England and northern Iberia [BURTON 1994, COWDREY 1999, PICK 2013, REGLERO DE LA FUENTE 2013]. A similar approach can be detected for the leading agents in other 'nebulas' of the early to mid-eleventh century, such as those of Gorze, Saint-Vanne, and Farfa (on these, see above Chapter 3.4). On the other hand, we already saw how Cluny promoted transferral of lay investiture of abbacies to its own abbot from the mid-eleventh century onwards.

Responses   Some rulers, particularly in southern France, responded positively to this trend: but in other places they and the local episcopate subsequently kept Cluny out of their territories [for the Low Countries, VANDERPUTTEN 2007], and in some cases even assisted in creating separate 'nebulas' centred on regional 'reform centres' [WOLLASCH 1992]. Much work in this respect has been done for the Empire, where local agents from the lay and clerical elites relied for this purpose on the monasteries of Siegburg, Sankt Blasien, and Hirsau, among other things to gain control (direct or indirect, depending on the circumstances) over the religious institutional landscape in a particular area [JAKOBS 1968, SEMMLER 1969, and the references to Hirsau scholarship below, Chapter 4.1]. Still, our understanding of what these and other 'nebulas' looked like, how diversified they were, and how they were managed from various 'centres' would benefit from new case studies to replace often outdated or very partial scholarship. But most importantly, our knowledge would be advanced by a major comparative study, aided by

Perceptions   modern digital mapping techniques and network analysis. Also lacking at present is a satisfying answer to how contemporaries and later observers perceived such 'nebulas', and how their members built – if they did – a shared sense of purpose [VANDER-PUTTEN 2015].

3.7 The 'Quest for the Primitive'

One of the reasons why discussions of monasticism in the early and in the later Middle Ages rarely intersect is that the eleventh century was long viewed as an era of revolutionary change in governance, spirituality, and daily practice. According to the traditional view, charismatic reformers stood up against the aristocratic lifestyle and the tightly choreographed but spiritually undemanding prayer service of Carolingian monasticism, and established a new, improved tradition. This New Monasticism, as scholars called it, was inspired by various eremitical and apostolic trends that had emerged around the year 1000. Its focus lay on the spiritual journey of the individual and a return to a more authentic experience of the Benedictine ideal, and on attaining these within experimental forms of community life. The reputation of the founders of these settlements as heroic pioneers of the New Monasticism was established by twelfth- and thirteenth-century commentators: these views were subsequently rehearsed and further adapted by later medieval and early modern historiographers of various congregations and orders, who saw in these experiments the ideological and institutional foundations of their respective movements. In the nineteenth and twentieth centuries, the paradigm was adopted in turn by influential historians, who saw the beginnings of a trend towards authenticity and a more private experience of Christian belief in the later Middle Ages [GRUNDMANN 1935, LEYSER 1984]. Some scholars additionally argued that being out of touch with developments in spirituality and ascetic practice, 'old monastic' communities lost much of their attraction for benefactors and potential recruits. What followed was, as these specialists put it, a "crisis of cenobitism" [CANTOR 1960/1961].

Old vs New Monasticism

Since the 1990s, the trend in scholarship has been to view as problematic this notion of a deep chasm – whether in terms of organization, ideology, or practice – between an 'old' and a 'new' monasticism [Zucchini 2006, d'Acunto 2018]. To begin with, specialists noted that old style institutions were not mere prayer factories where there was no possibility for private contemplation or self-abnegation. Cluny, Gorze, Farfa, and many other male and female houses across the Latin West featured a vibrant intellectual and spiritual culture, where there was room for reflection on the nature and purpose of monastic life [3.4 JONES, O'BRIEN O'KEEFFE 2012, 3.1 VANDERPUTTEN], for personal expressions of private devotion [MANCIA 2019], and finally also for various forms of moderate self-abnegation [CONSTABLE 1996]. Cluny, supposedly the main culprit in perpetuating the Carolingian ideal of monks and women religious performing mindless prayer routines, celebrated the eremitical and apostolic achievements of its abbots, and even owned several hermitages in the Jura and Pyrenees regions.

Nuancing views

On Old Monasticism

Many other institutions had in-house cells where their members could withdraw [CABY 2003]; still others existed in a state of functional and ideological symbiosis with anchorites and anchoresses [SIGNORI 2010]. Some hosted wandering hermits, and even produced a number of leading agents who experimented with eremitism and went out in the world to preach [3.6 VANDERPUTTEN 2015; and above, Chapter 3.5]. And while there are some indications that changing patronage patterns and competition between communities did jeopardize the sustainability of certain 'traditional' monasteries in the eleventh and early twelfth centuries [VANDERPUTTEN 2012], the classic notion of a crisis of cenobitism has been shown to derive from a mixture of anachronistic projections, sweeping generalizations, and overly credulous reading of polemical commentaries [VAN ENGEN 1986]. Similarly, the various reports by eleventh- and early twelfth-century commentators regarding the lax, spiritually disengaged attitudes of such groups, and particularly the dissolute conduct of groups of canonesses, must be treated with caution [ANDERMANN 1996]. And as a number of scholars have recently pointed out, the survival of specific forms of governance and lay involvement in 'traditional' monastic institutions must not *a priori* be taken as indicative of a crisis. One example out of many that could be cited here is the survival of the lay advocacy in the Empire into the twelfth century, the causes of which have recently been the subject of heated debate [LYON 2015, WEST 2017].

On New Monasticism   Critical re-evaluations of the early source record from various foundations additionally revealed the ordinariness of life in many of these houses once they were turned into consolidated institutions [D'ACUNTO 2008, THOMPSON 2014, 3.7 D'ACUNTO 2014]. A number of recent studies showed that leading individuals who later gained a reputation as pioneers of the New Monasticism often fell back on the practices and routines of monastic organization and governance they were familiar with [CABY 2004]. Perhaps the best-known case is that of Peter Damian [D'ACUNTO 2007], although his conduct and attitudes to monastic governance were common among the leaders of the New Monasticism. Like many 'traditional' abbots, Peter actively worked to stabilize Fonte Avellana via the systematic acquisition of concentrated plots of land around the monastery. He also set up various legal ramparts against lay interference, much in line with the abbots of Cluny and various other 'old style' leaders [D'ACUNTO 2007].

While the attraction for patrons and potential recruits of the new communities and their leaders is beyond doubt, the novelty of these institutional experiments was much less obvious to contemporaries than historians used to suspect. For instance, nearly a century after Peter and Odilo, charismatic founder and supposed revolutionary Abbot Norbert essentially owned the abbey of Prémontré as a proprietary institution, and like many of his tenth- and eleventh-century predecessors acted as a consummate networker in promoting his own house and those of the affiliated leaders [FELTEN 2005]. It was knowing what this and other foundations developed into, and particularly the celebration of this by twelfth- and thirteenth-century commentators, that on hindsight turned them into major, paradigm-shifting phenomena.

These findings have brought to prominence three major areas of interest, all of which are in need of further investigation. Firstly, our understanding of the circumstances and social, economic, and legal status of early foundations associated with the New Monasticism still leaves much to be desired. The situation at these places also invites more precise comparison with what was happening in supposedly 'old style' foundations of the period. Especially for all questions concerning the economic consolidation of these communities and their embedding in the geophysical and social environment [BONDE/MAINES 2003, LAUWERS 2013], much promise lies in the use of GIS-mapping and other digital applications [SCHNEIDER 2013]. Scholars have also pointed to the need to take into account the evolving nature of governance practices and models in these newly founded communities. For instance, the role of many second-generation reformers (as opposed to the original founders themselves) was crucial in driving forward processes of change [MELVILLE 2014, TOCK 2015; for a discussion of the 'normalization' of charismatic leadership in 'old' and 'new' monastic contexts, below Chapter 4.1].

Perspectives for research

The second broad area that calls for more investigation concerns the continuity and gradual transformation of concepts between the Old Monasticism and the New. Thus we need to address the various calls for authenticity, sobriety, apostolic agency, separation from secular influences, and private devotion as we encounter them in sources that originated in 'old monastic' contexts of the tenth and eleventh centuries and those we find in evidence that is traditionally linked to the New Monasticism [JESTICE 1997]. Although more

Global transformation of forms and experiences

research is in order to precisely map how certain views and arguments were expressed and how they evolved between c. 900 and 1100, it is quite clear now that the basic tenets of 'new monastic' ideology as they were formulated in the eleventh century were not as revolutionary or, for instance, as closely linked to papal reform as historians previously suspected [3.3 D'ACUNTO].

In a similar fashion, in recent years a new narrative has appeared of continuities in eremitical ideals and practices, and of transformation in response to changes in the social environment. This has replaced an older story in which ascetic practitioners like hermits and anchorites moved from being marginal and obscure, to becoming – spiritually and socially – highly prominent. At present, we are beginning to see the contours – running across many different 'old' and 'new' contexts and settings – of a continuous reflection on the nature and purpose of monastic life and its relationship with a rapidly changing secular environment [ZUCCHINI 2006]. These reflections led to a wide range of responses and experiments occurring in an equally wide range of institutional and non-institutional settings, to which a rigid classification of 'old' and 'new' monasticisms does not apply [JESTICE 1997, SANSTERRE 2003, SIGNORI 2010, MCAVOY 2010, LICENCE 2011].

Later medieval perceptions and narratives: Finally, there is still much potential in the study of twelfth- and thirteenth-century accounts of the New Monasticism. Particularly we can mine these for insight into how various communities and congregations tried to come to terms with the 'routinization' of charismatic leadership and rapid institutional transformations (on this, below Chapter 4.1). They can also illuminate how then-current realities and expectations were projected onto the lives of founders and the communities they established. For instance, in the context of tense relations with Normandy's clerical authorities, the Le Bec monks in the late eleventh and early twelfth century spent nearly six decades revising their institution's origins, arguing the unique nature of its home-grown observance and contrasting its legal status with other monasteries in Normandy and beyond [VANDERPUTTEN 2017]. And at Tiron, throughout the twelfth and early thirteenth centuries members of the community kept revising their narrative of origins, with striking results. Various twelfth-century versions skip over the abbey's eremitical origins and postulate its identity at a very early stage as a conventional Benedictine community. In the thirteenth century, however, a local author drastically shifted the argument to focus on the founder Bernard's life as a wandering preacher and on his contacts with fellow peripatetic preacher, and monastic founder, Robert of Arbrissel. This author also foregrounded elements of (what he presented as) the community's original observance – such as poverty, manual labour, relief for the poor, inclusiveness for both men and women of all backgrounds – and a fictional rivalry with Cluny [THOMPSON 2014].

Numerous other such case studies, including the various accounts of the Cistercians' earliest beginnings [BERMAN 2000; also below, Chapter 4.1], are in need of further investigation. Undertaking this will help us to identify and deconstruct inaccurate narratives of institutional origins, and understand what it was exactly that drove later generations to drastically revise the memories and achievements of their predecessors. Finally, it will allow us to also chart the impact of these later narratives on modern understandings of eleventh-century monastic realities. More such studies are being published [2.6 ANDENNA, SYKES 2011], and more historians are acknowledging the need to look beyond normative and other biased accounts and include, for instance, archaeological findings in their analysis [GILCHRIST 1995, MENESTÒ 2015]. With this, it is becoming increasingly clear that the tenth to early thirteenth centuries were a time when society – and also monastic practices and identities – were evolving at such a fast rate that communal memories required almost continuous updating and revision, with dramatic results.

Impact on modern perceptions

Looking at monasticism's situation against the broader background of the eleventh-century Church reform, there remains a need to clarify the link between the liberties awarded to specific monasteries by late eleventh- and early twelfth-century reform popes, and the subsequent role of these institutions in disseminating ideals of papal reform [LUNGO 2016]. The current view on how the papacy built a vast network of 'reform relays' across the Latin West – which tellingly included institutions from the 'old' and the 'new' monasticism – needs fleshing out via a systematic study of papal privileges and letters, and also of charters and letters by reformist bishops.

Church reform

Closely linked to this research agenda is the need for further investigation of the papacy's promotion of canons regular, whose status in life made them eminently suited to promote the ideals of the reform. By means of a carefully coordinated policy of synodal legislation and the award of privileges to specific institutions, the papacy managed to obtain a controlling stake in their early devel-

Canons regular opment as an ecclesiastical cohort. Concurrently, it also arranged for canonical institutions to directly represent the interests of the so-called Gregorian reformers in various territories of Latin Christianity [PARISSE 2009, MEIJNS 2010]. However, such legal and ideological integration did not lead to the quasi-instant emergence of a cohesive, more or less homogeneous observance for canons regular: indeed, the transition to a 'regularized' observance was compromised – for want of better word – by the embedding of communities in local societies, the various roles these had previously fulfilled, the positioning in the religious landscape, and the expectations of patrons and community members [MEIJNS 2002, 3.2 TRUMBORE JONES]. Study of manuscripts attesting to the ritual and other practices of individual communities has revealed that the *Rule of St Augustine* did not become the standard rulebook until well into the twelfth century [VEYRENCHE 2016; for case studies in England, BURTON/STÖBER 2011].

Categorizing forms Some historians have been trying to retrospectively establish a clear distinction between monks and canons by integrating contemporary arguments over legal, administrative, and ritual matters. However, these attempts risk projecting anachronistic classifications of religious life onto a complex, shifting, and above all not rigidly defined eleventh- and early twelfth-century reality. Similar remarks can be made for the fruitless attempts in past studies to establish clear criteria for distinguishing Benedictine women religious (increasingly referred to as *nonnae*, "nuns") from canonesses, a problematic exercise until well into the early thirteenth century.

Military movements Quite distinct from all the above research is the study of the military movements. Part of the explanation for this is that much of the relevant evidence for their presence in the Western monastic landscape dates from a later period, and that their twelfth- and early thirteenth-century action often focused on specific parts of the Mediterranean and the Near East. But in part it is also because former narratives of the origins and early development of military movements are an awkward fit with scholars' approach to the New Monasticism. Be that as it may, just as we have seen for these other eremitical and apostolic settlements we find that the military ones went through processes over the course of the twelfth and thirteenth centuries that utterly changed their identity, societal embedding and role(s), and even their geographical focus.

Various efforts to assess the state of research allow us to get
a sense of the sheer scope of these transformations, the diversity
of forms and expressions within this military strand, the relation
to papal reform throughout the later eleventh to early thirteenth
centuries, and the challenges facing future researchers of this
complex phenomenon [BÉRIOU/JOSSERAND 2009, FERREIRA 2012].
For instance, in recent decades, important work has been done on
the incorporation of some into the conquest strategies of secular
rulers [Jaspert 2001] and papal policies [FONSECA 2000, POWELL
2000]. How these communities became settled and how they functioned in their social environment have likewise been a focus of
intensive study [MARCOMBE 2003, SARNOWSKY 2007, SARNOWSKY
2011], as has the emergence and nature of the female branches of
various military orders [LUTTREL/NICHOLSON 2006]. Much promise
also lies in study of evidence relating to the self-understanding and
self-representation of these orders, movements, and the various
male and female branches, and – perhaps most important of all –
their perception by outsiders [CARRAZ/DEHOUX 2016].

Transformations

Embedding

4 Later Medieval Monasticisms

4.1 Transformations in Monastic Governance

The origins and early development of new forms of monastic governance in the later eleventh and early twelfth century have long
been obscured by a thick fog of biased commentaries and questionable interpretations [DEFLOU-LECA 2013]. Beginning in the late
twelfth century and continuing well into the twentieth, historians
of various orders and congregations typically projected onto an
earlier past institutional realities that became consolidated only at
a later stage in the development of these movements [CONSTABLE
2010a]. In doing so, they overstated the programmatic nature of
various trends in network formation and institutional collaboration
c. 1100, with the result that it seemed as if these trends had signified
a deliberate and abrupt break with early and high medieval modes
of monastic governance. At the same time, this earlier scholarship
underplayed the experimental nature of various procedures and
instruments (for example, General Chapters, statutes, and visitations) that emerged from these trends. Although not all specialists

Narratives of origins

Questioning
programmatic trends

had been convinced that the classic narrative of radical transformation would hold up to closer scrutiny, it was only in the 1990s and early 2000s that scholars explicitly started to call it into question. The field quickly acknowledged the significance of their criticisms and in a number of cases also fiercely debated them.

Origins of the
Cistercian order

The most notorious of such debates concerned the origins and early development of the Cistercians. The principal discussions revolved around the circumstances in which the movement's earliest written legacy originated (foundational narratives, in particular the *Carta Caritatis*, but also statutes, customs, and other normative documents), and as a consequence also the relevance of this documentation to reconstructing the emergence of its institutions. While one major specialist declared these documents completely authentic and relevant to the specific time period from which they claim to originate [WADDELL 2000], another argued that nearly the entire corpus consists of forgeries or revised redactions dating from the 1170s or later [3.7 BERMAN]. Even if the latter interpretation presumably went a step too far in its revisionist outlook on early Cistercian origins – claiming that our understanding of the movement's structure and functioning is fundamentally compromised by these later interventions – it nevertheless drew attention to the problems inherent in the traditional view of the Cistercians' dramatic transformation into an order-like organization.

Today, few commentators would still be tempted to subscribe to twelfth-century Cistercian development as a radically innovative programme for reform of monastic spirituality and (especially) governance, originally described in the 1119 *Carta Caritatis* and subsequently implemented, with some modifications, over the course of the following decades. Historians have also abandoned an alternative view that postulates Bernard of Clairvaux's leadership of the movement as marking a drastic rupture with early Cistercian origins, by which restrictions were imposed on members' economic activities and a rigid behavioural framework created through its General Chapter. These former accounts have been replaced by one that emphasizes the movement and its institutions as being highly responsive to internal dynamics. It likewise pays due attention to the growth patterns of the Cistercian membership; the expectations of founders, patrons, and lay and clerical rulers; and finally also societal impulses in various regions where the movement was represented [BAUDIN/GRÉLOIS 2016].

To an extent, this new interpretation can be corroborated by comparing the Cistercians' continuously evolving situation with that of other movements, such as the Premonstratensians and Carthusians. However, correctly dating and interpreting the twelfth-century evidence [in particular the statutes issued by the different General Chapters, MELVILLE 2005; for the Premonstratensians, KRINGS 2000, WEINFURTER 2005] remains a challenge. Given these issues and also given the experimental nature of various institutions pre-1170/1180 and even beyond, it is understandable that the single major comparative study of General Chapters in the Middle Ages awards relatively few pages to the period before the very end of the twelfth century [CYGLER 2001]. Part of the solution to these issues is to include in the analysis forms of institutional collaboration as they existed prior to and alongside those of the emerging orders. Obvious case studies for this comparative approach are the *ecclesia Cluniacensis* (above, Chapter 3.6), Hirsau's congregation [3.6 Schreiner], and that of Camaldoli [3.7 D'ACUNTO 2014]. All of these featured procedures for collaboration, exchange of social and cultural capital and resources, and even shared governance – things that we can also recognize in the emerging Cistercian and Premonstratensian movements.

Beyond that, there is also great potential in studying how various confraternity networks of the late eleventh and early twelfth centuries – including several that ultimately did not evolve into congregations or orders – were redesigned with the purpose of facilitating collaboration and mutual aid [PATZOLD 2006, MIEGEL 2014, 3.3 REGLERO DE LA FUENTE]. Increasingly it is becoming clear to us that late eleventh- and early twelfth-century agents viewed confraternities as an essential tool for institutional collaboration and integration: it is not a coincidence that the earliest known documents issued by several General Chapters actually establish such a confraternity [VANDERPUTTEN 2015]. Yet, under what circumstances the transformation of confraternities took place and how these redesigned agreements functioned in practice remains in part unknown, due to the fragmentary state of the primary evidence and the lack of dedicated research. A number of recent studies have nonetheless made a strong case for pursuing this line of enquiry [LECOUTEUX 2015, BELAEN 2018]. How and in what circumstances some confraternities ended up experimenting with holding chapter meetings and issuing statutes is an additional, promising line of enquiry [VANDERPUTTEN/BELAEN 2016].

Other orders

Precedents and parrallels

Confraternal networks

Written instruments
of governance

We need also to improve our understanding of the changing purpose and use of various written instruments of monastic governance, and their role in facilitating institutional collaboration or even integration. The relevant scholarship considers such wide-ranging topics as the drastically evolving nature and use of customaries [SCHREINER 1992, TUTSCH 1998]; the creation of ritual scripts that bound monastics to each other and to their clerical superiors (see the above discussion of confraternity agreements); and finally also the management of archival memories (particularly the creation of cartularies), the acquisition of new legal documentation, and the abundant production of forgeries of immunity and exemption privileges [BERKHOFER 2004, POHL/VANDERPUTTEN 2016, POHL forthcoming, ROACH forthcoming; also above, Chapter 3.5]. Along with chronicles, foundation narratives, and biographical treatments of 'congregational founders', these practices of the written word allowed communities that were in the process of adopting new governance procedures to ground their present situation in a legit-

Shift to
Amtscharisma

imizing past [ECRIRE 2006; also above, Chapters 3.6 and 3.7]. More specifically, such writing practices assisted in the transition in the monastic leadership model, from a focus on authority that derived from an individual's personal qualities and charisma, to authority based on *Amtscharisma* [3.3 NEISKE, MELVILLE 2008].

Implications

In a number of cases such developments must also be framed in the context of attempts to reduce the direct involvement of lay and clerical stakeholders in governance and estate management. Particularly in France and the Low Countries, relations between monastic communities and their secular neighbours became increasingly fractious, disrupting long-standing *amicitiae* [3.3 MAZEL 2005]. These transformations may have rendered the perceived need for collaboration between communities more obvious towards the end of the eleventh century, and along with the changing nature of governance may have paved the way for greater integration. Much remains to be clarified regarding the precise degree to which these trends inspired monastic leaders to engage in collaborative agreements with other institutions, and whether they were also present in female monasticism [3.7 BERMAN, FELTEN 2009].

Diverse stakeholders

Finally, we also need to consider more closely the numerous elements that point to a complex stakeholdership in the emergence of confraternal, congregational, and other networks. So it has been noted that exemption privileges bear witness not to how monastic agents became completely emancipated from outside interference, but to how different monastic and non-monastic agents cooperated to create a new status for monasteries and their affiliated institutions [ROSENWEIN/HEAD/FARMER 1991, JÉGOU 2015, VANDERPUTTEN forthcoming]. Certainly from the later eleventh century onwards, the papacy actively worked to establish a vast network of institutions from which the reform of the Church could be propagated and supported, and which also created direct legal and fiscal links between these institutions and the Roman curia [DEFLOU-LECA 2013; also above, Chapter 3.7]. At the same time, it also attempted to bring a hierarchical structure, or at least some form of systematic organization, to a number of confederations as they had emerged over the course of the previous century, among other things by experimenting with a system where individual abbots would fall under the authority of an 'arch-abbot' [CARIBONI 2013].

Such interventions fostered integration, in several respects. One example is the Iberian Peninsula, where various studies have established that the *Rule of St Benedict* and Roman rites became the standards in monastic practices only with the papacy-driven reorganization of the regional Church in the late eleventh century [REGLERO DE LA FUENTE 2014]. The surge of papal exemptions from the late eleventh century onwards also led a number of bishops in northern France and England to adapt the (liturgical and other) mechanisms through which they tied monastic institutions and leadership to their own, episcopal authority, with the result that abbots and abbesses became more visible as a cohort in diocesan ecclesiastical structures [VANDERPUTTEN 2012a, JÉGOU 2015]. In the Empire specifically, the emergence and expansion of monastic federations and congregational movements was primarily driven by local and regional rulers, who took advantage of the special status of exempted institutions (particularly Sankt Blasien and Hirsau) to intervene at other monasteries and include these in their own influence sphere (see the discussion above, Chapter 3.6). Such interventions often took place against the better judgement of the leaders and membership of 'reform centres', who keenly felt the strain these put on their institutional resources [SCHREINER 1999] and the risk posed to *amicitiae* and other connections they held with the lay rivals of their reformist lordship [BEACH 2017]. More benign but no less significant are indications that in the mid- to late eleventh century, secular patrons were instrumental in transferring to the regular heads of major institutions the lay investiture of abbots. Much later they were similarly involved with the absorption into the Cistercian congregation of the Savigniac and Obazine movements [HOLDSWORTH 2004].

'Inter-congregational transfers'

Beyond these interests, there are others still that deserve closer consideration by scholars. One major issue is that of 'inter-congregational transfers', or the extent to which the development of congregational and other movements influenced that of others, particularly in areas and in contexts where we know of significant interactions between prominent representatives and sponsors of each. One example is that of 1120s/1130s north-eastern France and the Low Countries, where there was a great deal of mutual influence between Premonstratensian, Cistercian, and even some Cluniac-influenced Benedictine groups. Prominent reform agents (including various lay and clerical rulers) were here actively encouraging individuals and communities from different movements to exchange ideas, texts, and expertise, and to support each other's initiatives to establish General Chapters, issue statutes, and develop other new instruments and procedures for shared governance [VANDERPUTTEN 2015]. For the period beginning in the 1140s, there also remains a great deal to be understood about the circumstances and purpose of confraternity agreements that were concluded between major movements (for example, Cluniacs, Premonstratensians, and Cistercians), and subsequently also between each of these movements and individual, 'non-affiliated' communities from the mid-twelfth century onwards [WADDELL 2000, CONSTABLE 2010b]. None of these agreements has so far received serious attention, or a detailed reconstruction of its chronology, content, or implications.

Semantic shifts

A final area in which there is still considerable room to improve our understanding of twelfth-century perceptions and realities is that of the semantic shift in the use of the terms *congregatio* and *ordo*. These travelled from, respectively, "community or gathering of monastics" and "mode of observance", to the rather more specific "congregation" and "order". Although there have been several major studies that have looked at general trends [3.7 BERMAN, MELVILLE 2003, WEINFURTER 2005], case studies that document the precise chronology and implications of this shift in concrete settings and specific genres remain a major desideratum.

4.2 Monastic Experiences in the Long Twelfth Century

The 'long twelfth century' and its reputation as an age of revolutionary change are the subject of a long-standing debate. We have already seen that up until the later 1980s, the prevailing trend in historical discussions was to postulate two key phenomena. The first was the decline of 'traditional' cenobitism. This decline was manifested, so commentators used to argue, in its inability both to keep up with institutional developments taking place in other movements, and also to meet lay expectations of its social and spiritual role. The second postulated phenomenon was the rapid rise to dominance of new movements that radically broke with the Carolingian tradition of monasteries as 'prayer factories' and with the aristocratic lifestyle of such communities; developed radically new forms of governance; and established their relationship with secular society on a completely different basis. Since the 1980s, this double notion of a 'crisis of cenobitism' and of the paradigm-shifting nature of the New Monasticism has been subject to considerable nuancing (above, Chapters 3.7 and 4.1). Sweeping statements in the older scholarship regarding fundamental differences between life in communities belonging to the 'old' and 'new' forms are now understood to be based on an inadequate understanding of both the diversity of monasticism pre-1050, and the continuing role of local variables in shaping experiences inside and around monastic houses. Also seen in older historiography was a tendency to work with overly rigid assumptions about the boundaries that supposedly existed between different forms and experiences: these too have now been largely abandoned.

Besides observing that there are significant problems with a narrative that postulates the long twelfth century as an era of fundamental ruptures and dramatic new beginnings, historians also began looking for the origins of this narrative. To an extent, we can find it in various polemical writings by prominent critics of 'traditional' monasticism and in the various foundation narratives of monastic orders (discussed above, Chapters 3.7 and 4.1). But a number of studies have also drawn our attention to the rising prominence in monastic commentaries of the term *reformatio*, rarely encountered in sources dating from an earlier period [NEWMAN 1996, 3.1 BARROW]. According to several specialists, this phenomenon reflects shifting attitudes to deliberate change

Traditional approaches

Criticism

Origins of the former view

Shifting notions of reform

in spirituality and institutionalism: it refers to the notion of re-creating or re-forming the 'authentic' spirit of monastic life without necessarily looking for precedents in normative or practice-based tradition [CONSTABLE 1982]. Related to this semantic shift in reform vocabulary, it became progressively more acceptable to publicize the newly created nature of certain rites, modes of conduct, and forms of governance, as long as they were considered effective in the quest for authenticity [CONSTABLE 1996].

Shifting notions of identity

Contemporary commentators felt fewer inhibitions than before in promoting certain forms of monastic life as entirely new, and in emphasizing that different forms of monastic life were not just variants on a shared legacy built up over many centuries, but were actually rooted in fundamentally different interpretations of the original monastic ideal. For the first time, if they no longer matched real-life experiences, then the traditional categories encountered in late antique and early medieval commentaries were abandoned. For instance, the anonymous author of the "Booklet on the diversity of orders and professions that exist in the Church" (discussed in Part 1, Chapter 4.2) described five categories of legitimate monastics instead of the traditional two (hermits and monastics living in a community). In doing so, he, and others, helped shape the influential but inaccurate view that a previously homogeneous monastic experience had now fractured into many different (albeit internally homogeneous) strands.

Responsiveness to context

Every time a case study is published that takes a bottom-up view on monastic development in this period, our understanding of diversity and permeable boundaries gains detail and nuance. A continuously growing number of such publications reveal to us that individual monasteries remained highly responsive – structurally, functionally, and even morphologically – to local circumstances and traditions, the profiles of their membership, their embedding within an existing religious landscape, and especially also the needs and expectations of their social environment. This is certainly the case for women's communities, research into which has yielded an image of a highly diverse cohort. Part of this cohort consisted of contemplative religious practising strict enclosure and focussing on intercessory prayer and commemorative service. But there were also many communities whose profile was more diversified, and who, in addition, also helped the elderly, sick, or indigent, and provided education and pastoral care even, all in different degrees and in different ways depending on local circumstances [LESTER 2011, BERMAN 2018].

Study of individual communities and their observance, functioning, and membership has also revealed that many continued to elude the strict categorization of being either nuns or canonesses, even though supervision by men was more strictly enforced than in earlier times [LUTTER 2005b, SCHLOTHEUBER 2018]. For male communities too, study of the situation 'on the ground' has revealed substantial variety in how members experienced and fulfilled their ascetic purpose in life, even between those that belonged to the same movement or order [for example, for the various pastoral, charitable, and other roles of canons regular, 3.7 PARISSE, 2.6 ANDENNA]. Put differently, it is now clearly established that the roles and identities of male and female monasteries can no longer be defined strictly by looking at their institutional or congregational affiliation.

Likewise evident is the fact that we can no longer rely on normative or other prescriptive texts to reconstruct with any degree of precision what life in various monastic communities must have looked like – how the full range of activities were organized, how both insiders and outsiders understood their purpose in life, how the service to surrounding society was enacted, and how success was experienced in achieving unity with the divine. Traces of this open-ended identity are found all over the primary evidence, including charters and other documents relating to the management of monastic wealth and institutions, but also in liturgical sources, chapter books, and various other documents deriving from, or conceived in support of, monastic practice. One of several ways in which historians of the last few decades have added a much-needed material dimension to these discussions is by looking at the use and perceived significance of space in shaping communal identities, roles, and perceptions [on 'gendered' spaces, GILCHRIST 1994; on opportunities for digital mapping and spatial modelling also above, Chapter 3.7]. In a similar fashion, recent discussions of Cistercian architecture and art have provided us with indications of highly situated expressions of practical, relational, and spiritual concerns [COOMANS 2013, REILLY 2013, REILLY 2018]. These and many other studies help us to better assess the true impact of various directives issued by the General Chapters from the second quarter of the twelfth century onwards. In short,

Open-ended identities

they enable us to put into perspective the canonists' insistence on the creation of strict, impermeable boundaries between different orders and movements [DANNENBERG 2008].

Negotiated forms and experiences

We must certainly not discount the role of community members in shaping the diverse experiences of monasticism; nor should we be oblivious to the influences and pressures that came with a given community's involvement with a particular movement or order. Nevertheless, recent publications have insisted that experiences and other realities of monastic community life remained subject to continuous processes of negotiation between various local stakeholders, just as they had been in earlier centuries [CARIBO-NI/D'ACUNTO 2017]. Cistercian communities in particular were apt at manipulating those processes to their advantage. However, they were never able to extract themselves from such negotiations, nor did they intend to [BERMAN 2002, JAMROZIAK 2005, SALZER 2017] – including in regions they supposedly helped 'colonize' [JAMROZIAK 2011]. Generally speaking, the involvement of secular and clerical patrons – lay founders, bishops, and increasingly also rural and urban communes and other interest groups [CARIBONI 2012, SEALE 2017] – remained very significant in shaping a monastery's economic affairs, governance model, membership profile, service to society, and even observance. One of many examples that could be cited here is that of a number of female Cistercian houses in late twelfth- and early thirteenth-century France and the Low Countries. Here, aristocratic founders actively pursued a specific vision of how the religious landscape in their region should look, and on the basis of that vision precisely determined the women's roles and activities in order to complement those of neighbouring male communities [JORDAN 2012].

'Nebulas'

Research like this has in turn inspired scholars to take a more systematic interest in those institutions that became part of the 'nebula' of a congregation or order. Many male and female communities of the period adopted, or were told to adopt, Cluniac, Cistercian, or other practices and even identities, even though they had not actually joined the corresponding movement. For instance, numerous foundation and reform charters of female houses of the early to mid-twelfth century refer to groups following the customs of the Cluniac nunnery of Marcigny, without becoming affiliated to the *ecclesia Cluniacensis*. And while Cistercian and Premonstratensian commentators of the twelfth century often underplayed – or in some cases outright rejected – all female participation in their respective movements, interactions between a substantial number of women's communities and institutions formally associated to a particular movement were so intense and so instrumental in shaping local identities and practices, that the question of formal membership almost becomes moot [FELTEN 2011].

For lay or clerical founders and various other stakeholders in these institutions, such 'quasi-transitions' and 'quasi-affiliations' had multiple advantages. Besides allowing local agents to retain a measure of control, they also created opportunities for a flexible approach to estate management, collection and distribution of revenues, and various other aspects of internal governance. Equally, they determined flexibility in establishing the financial status of members, their service, and their daily routines. At the same time, these 'quasi-transitions' and 'quasi-affiliations' had the potential to bestow on communities a certain degree of prestige or even legal protection. Such is likely to have been the reasoning behind a number of female monasteries in France, Germany, and the British Isles, in seeking recognition of their self-assumed Cistercian identity. They did this not in an attempt to join the order but to claim its various exemptions, including from the payment of tithes [on tithes generally, CABY 2012]. Along with those communities (particularly of women) that were ousted from various movements but renewed their links with member groups once they had resettled, this substantial cohort of monastic communities deserves much greater attention than it has so far received. Situating these and other institutions more explicitly than before in the monastic landscape would also help resolve a number of questions about the seemingly unequal distribution of male and female houses, and of those belonging to different movements, across the Latin West.

The trend to abandon a strict categorization of institutional and ideological identities and to pay closer attention to local circumstances is also noticeable in the ways in which specialists currently address the phenomenon of the so-called 'double monasteries'. In the traditional understanding, these belonged to a distinct cohort of institutions that comprised strictly separate groups of male and female monastics but that practised a similar observance and relied on the same estate. Such arrangements, so historians argued, emerged as a result of reform interventions from the later eleventh century onwards, and derived from the

'Quasi-affiliations'

Double monasteries

tendency of the 'new monasticism' to include female groups in its male-dominated movements. However, beginning in the 1980s various scholars suggested that this definition obscures the functional background of the settings in which male and female monastics cohabited, and imposes far too systematic a perspective on the circumstances in which such cohabitations originated. They also pointed to the strong continuity with earlier settings (discussed in earlier chapters of this book), where groups of female monastics (cloistered women, but also anchoresses) co-existed in a state of functional and spiritual symbiosis with monks, clerics, and other male monastics [ELM/PARISSE 1992].

Reciprocal relationships Since then, the trend has been to focus less on the various institutional and legal implications of these co-existing male and female communities, and more on the ways in which members interacted and established reciprocal relationships across the gender divide [GRIFFITHS/HOTCHIN 2014]. Under the influence of developments in gender studies, other themes have also risen to prominence, such as the role of aristocratic founders in shaping cohabitations of male and female monastics [BERMAN 2018], and the exercise of female authority over male monastics (for example, abbesses ruling over double communities, such as at Fontevraud, but also women religious acting as spiritual advisers). Also coming into focus are the intense exchanges between men and women that occurred in the course of teaching and learning, the production and transmission of new manuscripts, and a range of related subjects [BEACH 2003, LUTTER 2005a]. Most important of all of these scholarly trends is the reconsideration of claims by various commentators of the period that male monastics saw their involvement in female monasticism as a necessary but unwanted burden, and as a potential risk to their own purity and spiritual integrity. Renewed investigation of the testimonies of the clerics and monastics who carried out various services for cloistered women, anchoresses, and household ascetics, reveals that many of these men saw their work as integral to their spiritual identity and as a valid form of devotional practice [GRIFFITHS 2018]. The reciprocal element in the spiritual relationship of male and female monastics is a topic that has stirred a great deal of interest in recent years [HOTCHIN 2001, MEWS 2007]. It deserves to be further explored, including in the broader setting of the contribution of women to Church reform in the eleventh and twelfth centuries.

Women in Church Reform

Further, scholars have been inspired to reconsider former views on distinctions within monastic communities. In the study of lay converses, approaches that focused on defining and describing the phenomenon in a purely institutional or juridical sense have been gradually replaced. These days historians are more interested in looking at class distinctions as they determined access to either this cohort or that of cloistered monastics, but also as they played out in the division of roles and tasks, in the living conditions of individual members, their access to various material and immaterial resources, and even in the way they used monastic space [FRANCE 2012, NOELL 2006]. These approaches have opened the way for a broader, more inclusive view of the people living in and around monastic settlements, with one consequence being that study of converses in (for instance) Cistercian and Gilbertine contexts, is no longer regarded as fundamentally different from that of laypeople working on or around 'traditional' institutions and their estates. Lay converses

Likewise, a second research strand that focuses on cloistered and other vowed monastics has recently started to think in terms that allow for fewer drastic ruptures with the past. Until the early 2000s, the common view was that after many centuries dominated by practices of child oblation, there was a dramatic re-emergence of adult conversion. This was reflected in the post-1050 development of a "theology of conversion" [DE MIRAMON 1999]. But as we saw earlier, there are indications that adult conversions were far more common in the tenth and eleventh centuries than scholars formerly suspected, and that shifts in recruitment patterns may have been occurring as early as the decades around the year 1000 (above, Chapter 3.4). In 'traditional' contexts of the early to mid-eleventh century, such as at Cluny and St Gall the ratio of adult converts to oblates already appears to have been far more even than previously thought [BREITENSTEIN 2008]. Although it is now clear that the transformation in the recruitment of institutionalized monastics was far more gradual than previously thought, precisely how it ran its course over several decades and across different institutional contexts, and precisely what social, religious, and institutional dynamics drove it forward, are all things that remain ill-understood. Case studies will undoubtedly yield new answers to these questions, provided that they take into account such variables as the social context [in particular, local modes of managing transferrals of aristocratic power and wealth, 3.5 BOUCHARD]; Conversion the size and ability of specific institutions to provide the adequate training to adult novices [BREITENSTEIN 2008]; a monastery's functional identity; and the proximity of, and competition from, other communities. Comparison of these case studies with early medieval instances of self-donation by lay individuals [e.g. PETERSON 2019] will also help us get a better sense of the extent to which contextual factors (particularly political and economic circumstances) drew members of the laity to engage in such an intimate bond with monastic institutions.

Private practitioners   Yet another major factor to consider is the presence, near monastic institutions and all over the rural and urban landscape, of people practising non-institutional forms of ascetic withdrawal. Earlier on in this book it was made clear that members of the laity had continuously participated in monastic life since late antiquity. From the mid-1950s, scholars have charted the growing frequency, from the mid-eleventh century onwards, of reports of rural hermits and recluses (above, Chapter 3.7). They have particularly noted the rising prominence in urban contexts of anchorites and of anchoresses [3.7 GRUNDMANN]. Recent studies have paid particular attention to the latter, many of whom were celebrated by their contemporaries for their high moral reputation, their ascetic achievements, and their role as spiritual counsellors to members of the laity, the clergy, and cloistered monastics [MULDER-BAKKER 2005, BENVENUTI 2011, 3.7 LICENCE, GUNN/MCAVOY 2017]. Further studies have documented the presence, in urban and rural contexts, of married couples, widows, and a range of other people practising ascetic ideals of contemplation, manual labour, preaching, and support for the sick and needy [SIMONS 2009]. Many testimonies survive to show that such individuals intensely interacted with semi-institutionalized and institutionalized groups of male and female monastic practitioners, sometimes even developing spiritually and functionally symbiotic relationships (below, Chapters 4.4 and 4.5).

Renewed literary   Also enjoying renewed attention is a literary tradition, rejuve-
traditions   nated from the mid-eleventh century, of exhortatory literature for anchorites and anchoresses [HUGHES-EDWARDS 2012]. In addition to revisiting and updating late antique and early medieval exemplars [SIGNORI 2005], this literary activity stood at the intersection of (on the one hand) high theological and mystical thought, and (on the other), pastoral discourses destined for lay audiences [GUNN 2008].

It is telling of the close involvement of anchoritic practitioners with institutional monasticism that these texts were intensely read and studied in cloistered contexts throughout this period and the later Middle Ages. More generally speaking, the twelfth century marked an upswing in written genres dedicated to guiding the individual on the path to spiritual perfection [LECLERCQ 1961]. While the phenomenon has been described in ample detail in studies from the second half of the twentieth century, the current trend is to consider the fact that here too, we can see strong and deliberate continuities with prior achievements in monastic culture. Certainly texts from a wide range of genres were produced in far greater numbers than in earlier centuries, including: commentaries on various rules; manuals for novices, anchorites and anchoresses; and *exempla* collections [BYNUM 1982, SONNTAG 2008, SMIRNOVA/POLO DE BEAULIEU/BERLIOZ 2015].

Spiritual trends

But in terms of their content and the reading culture in which they were embedded, the break with the preceding period might not have been as significant as has often been claimed. For instance, study of twelfth-century manuscripts of ascetic florilegia has shown that the Cistercians in particular copied large numbers of such collections dating from late antiquity and the early Middle Ages as they thought suitable for their membership [FALMAGNE 1997]. As was the case with early customaries of the later tenth to early twelfth centuries [COCHELIN 2016], many of these older florilegia had originated as topical, localized commentaries on current issues and presumably had not been intended for wide circulation. Exactly in what circumstances they were rediscovered and subsequently circulated remains to be understood, particularly the terms in which they were still considered relevant for contemporary audiences. Regarding the production of new texts, it remains to be verified if these referred to profound transformations of monastic views and attitudes, or (more likely) a shift towards more intensive use of the written word in monastic education, and a greater focus on individual reading. Regardless of the answer to this question, real life education and formation of monastics was still very much grounded in a culture of face-to-face interactions. Looking specifically at lifelong learning processes in monastic contexts, 'horizontal' practices of education – teacher–disciple relations in which the process of learning went both ways – constitute a very promising line of enquiry [LONG 2017].

Reading culture

Educational practices

4.3 Law, Custom, and the Early Thirteenth-Century Papal Reforms

Former studies of papal reform in the later twelfth to mid-thirteenth century emphasized the supposedly objective need to insert unaffiliated monastic groups into recently developed paradigms of monastic governance, in order to save them from financial ruin, institutional decline, and spiritual redundancy. But more recent work has nuanced these assumptions, particularly the supposed contrast between the effervescence of communities belonging to the Cistercian, Premonstratensian, and Carthusian orders and the perilous situation of many non-affiliated, 'Benedictine' houses. In one strand of research that is focused on socio-economic issues, specialists have pointed out that there existed no single, uniform Benedictine or Cistercian model of estate management in the twelfth century [4.1 BAUDIN/GRÉLOIS], and that many of those in the former cohort were quite successful at adapting to changing economic circumstances [JORDAN 2005, 3.3 ANDENNA]. Likewise, many were skilled at retaining, reinvigorating, and creating new patronage connections [VANDERPUTTEN 2012]. Regional and local case studies reveal an extremely variegated picture, including a substantial number of foundations that boasted healthy economies and institutions well into the fourteenth or even fifteenth centuries [RACINET 1990]. Scholars have also pointed out that the accounts of Cistercian, Premonstratensian, and other successes should not fool us into thinking that all communities in these movements thrived [BOUCHARD 1991, 4.2 JAMROZIAK].

Diverse state of organized monasticism

In a second strand of research, studies have indicated that the notion of a complete lack of supra-institutional coordination in 'traditional' monastic contexts is a myth. Earlier we already saw how confraternity links were redesigned from the mid-eleventh century onwards with a view to facilitating collaboration and mutual support between individual communities (above, Chapter 4.2). And for the period beginning in the 1130s and ending just before the Fourth Lateran Council, we have numerous references to experiments with regional chapters of Benedictine abbots in Reims, Brittany, Saxony, England, and northern Italy [SCHMIDT 2013]. In other contexts too, efforts at setting up congregational structures continued until well into the early thirteenth century [EXCOFFON 1997, ADAMO 2014].

Earlier experiments at integration

Thanks to a number of publications from the last two decades, we now have a fairly detailed understanding of the nature and

Nature of the reforms

content of papal reform measures, and about their background in late twelfth-century developments in canon law and ecclesiastical governance [MACCARRONE 1995, BALDWIN 1997, FALKENSTEIN 1997, BOUREAU 2001, FELTEN 2003], papal finances [on Honorius III's use of the military orders to organize the financing of the fifth crusade, SMITH 2017], and finally also shifts in attitudes towards monastic governance and abbatial lordship [MELVILLE 1994].
However, there is still a distressing lack of scholarship that takes a bottom-up look at the reforms and their implementation. Much additional work is still needed to chart, on a region-by-region and a monastery-by-monastery basis, how instructions by the papacy and the Lateran council of 1215 were communicated to local communities in various parts of the Latin West and beyond, and how they were received in these places [on the lack of proper institutional channels for communication and the problems with relying on individual members of various orders, SCHMIDT 2013; for a somewhat different view, JOHRENDT/MÜLLER 2012, CAPPUCCIO 2017].

Lack of bottom-up perspectives

Increasingly, papal reform as applied in these local settings emerges from scholarship as a balancing act in which the interests of various stakeholders had to be taken into consideration. Evidence indicating that Popes Innocent and Honorius tried to avoid overruling episcopal visitation rights [BALDWIN 1997] invites careful investigation – of the clerical leaders who enforced papal reform measures, the supervision of the earliest General Chapters post-1215, and of the interactions of these institutions with the local episcopate [DAVIS 2006]. Also lacking at present is detailed information about the scope of a phenomenon, in the later twelfth and very early thirteenth centuries, where abbots and abbesses petitioned the papacy to support local reforms of governance and observance [for the example of Cluny, MELVILLE 1994; on implementation, e.g. REGLERO DE LA FUENTE 2008] and how these case studies might have influenced reform policies as they were developed at the curia and during sessions of the Fourth Lateran council.

Responses and experiences

There is considerable potential, also, in a systematic review of the nature, membership, content, and outcomes (be they written statutes or governance measures) of the earliest provincial chapters of Benedictine abbots post-1215. Most of the relevant scholarship dates back to the late nineteenth and early decades of the twentieth century [BERLIÈRE 1891, PANTIN 1927]. Some of the findings have been corrected in more recent studies, and scholars have also

Benedictine Chapters

warned against using overly rigid definitions for determining what constituted a chapter [3.7 VANDERPUTTEN 2017]. Yet, how these institutions actually functioned and especially also how they interacted with the local (arch)episcopate, papal legates, and with the papacy itself, remains to a large extent unclear to us [BELAEN 2017].

Gregory IX's reforms   Similarly, scholars' understanding of responses to Pope Gregory IX's reform efforts remains woefully incomplete, a problem that could be solved partially by looking in a more detailed manner at the surviving protocols of chapter meetings, petitions to the Roman Curia, and sermons held at regional chapter meetings. We now know a great deal about Gregory's interest in promoting (archi) episcopal oversight of male and female communities, and also his efforts to roll out that policy in collaboration with mendicant and Cistercian agents [FELTEN 2011a]. However, the precise nature of his monastic legislation – particularly how the 1235 and 1237 versions of his statutes relate to each other – and the degree to which it might have been drafted and re-drafted in response to local impulses and initiatives, are both topics that remain in need of further scrutiny [NEISKE 1988, MALECZEK 2011].

Responses   Another issue that currently remains ill-understood is the response by the General Chapters [KRINGS 2007, VANDERPUTTEN 2017] and particularly also by various (associations of) local communities, some of which are known to have petitioned for exemptions, revised the statutes to match their own preferences, or issued their own, completely distinct sets of statutes [BOUREAU 2001, FELTEN 2011b]. The records of episcopal visitations, which have been studied both as an institution [OBERSTE 1996] and in their concrete implementation [CHENEY 1931, DAVIS 2006], to some extent help fill this gap. However, investigation of this transitional phase in the development of institutional monasticism would also benefit from a systematic effort to identify and (re-)edit key sources deriving from the activities of various regional and general chapters.

4.4 Emergence and Integration of the Mendicants

Early narratives of identity   Within a few decades after their initial rise to prominence, several mendicant movements set out to establish operational, legitimizing narratives of their ascetic identity and mission. A wealth of surviving material – hagiographies, biographies, chronicles, rules, statutes, iconography in manuscripts, frescoes, and even architectural arrangements – offers us detailed insight into how these movements defined their place in the monastic landscape, in the Church, and more generally also in Christian society. The evidence also speaks to the sheer pace at which changing circumstances compelled adaptation of these definitions [WESJOHANN 2012].

By far the most complex of these definitions (and therefore also that which has received by far the most interest from scholars) concerns the male and female branches of the Franciscans. For the male branch, the source record reveals a bewildering succession of attempts, beginning as early as 1209 and continuing until at least the 1260s, to establish the nature and observance of the movement, its structure and role in the contemporary Church, and its mission in society. Ongoing debates over the dating, authorship, argument, audience, and intended purpose of these sources have contributed to revisionist treatments of early Franciscan identity and institutional development [MAPELLI, 2003, BROOKE 2004, DALARUN 2010, ROBSON/RÖHRKASTEN 2010]. They also highlight the uneasy relationship of the movement with Francis's legacy, the earliest indications of which can be traced back as far as the man's own twilight years [VAUCHEZ 2009, ROBSON 2012, FIELD 2016]. Reconstruction of this painful, highly disputed quest for an identity that was simultaneously true to Francis's ideals and the needs and expectations of both insiders and outsiders, has also been extended to the period beyond c. 1260. Studies of this later period look at the long-drawn disputes over Franciscan poverty that divided the Spirituals and Conventuals [NOLD 2003; also below, Chapter 4.6]. They highlight how unresolved tensions in Franciscan spirituality and ascetic practice had an impact on its internal dymanics as an order, and on its status in the Church and in society throughout the later Middle Ages.

Recent scholarship on the female Franciscans has likewise yielded new insights into the life and legacy of Clare of Assisi, especially in the emergence of her Order of Poor Clares. From these publications emerges clear evidence of a continuous dialectic, some might argue struggle, between (on the one side) the ecclesiastical hierarchy, and (on the other) Clare and her various supporters. This ongoing debate concerned the status of her movement, its organization, and the role of the clergy and male monastics in shaping

Franciscans

Disputes

Clarisse identities

the observance and life experience of its members [MOONEY 2016].

Clarisse 'nebula' Even after the definitive version of the movement's rule was published in the mid-thirteenth century, many communities previously thought to have been full members of the order actually belonged to a 'Clarisse nebula' and on that basis were presumably more free to adapt their mode of life to local expectations [KNOX 2008; on other 'nebulas', above Chapter 4.3]. Although a comprehensive re-evaluation of Clarisse history in the later Middle Ages was published recently [ROEST 2013], further exploration of this 'nebula' in the form of case studies will likely yield important new insights into how far that freedom extended.

Dominican narratives Less spectacular but no less relevant are the identity narratives of other mendicant movements. For the early Dominicans, the accounts of the life and legacies of founder Dominic has mostly been discussed in case studies, many of which are in need of updating [WESJOHANN 2005]. But the greatest interest perhaps lies in the normative and executive documentation that was drafted in support of the emerging order's revolutionary governance model. In recent decades, these sources (which arguably constitute an evolving narrative of legal and organizational identity in their own right) have been used extensively to rewrite the history of this movement

Other movements in its early stages [CYGLER 2001, MELVILLE 2010]. In contrast, the Augustinian (or Austin) Friars and Carmelites had no tales about a charismatic founder or a revolutionary governance model around which to build a legitimizing narrative of origins. Instead, they went looking much further back in the past – in the former case by linking their observance directly to St Augustine, and in the latter by tracing their mode of life to Eliah and Paul of Thebes [RANO 1994, JOTISCHKY 2005]. While Franciscan and Dominican accounts were widely reproduced in late medieval culture, those of the Carmelites and Augustinian Friars were designed in the first place for internal use. To an extent, this is reflected in the comparatively restricted outlook and scope of much of the scholarship on these movements, and also of that on a range of short-lived mendicant movements of the thirteenth century [see however ANDREWS 2006]. Generally speaking, much also remains to be understood about secular perceptions of early mendicant life and of its societal impact generally [for the pre-1300 period, SICKERT 2006].

Societal embedding Before we can claim to better understand how mendicant communities became settled and how they functioned in their social environment, a great deal of comparative research will be necessary. Much promise lies in the systematic harvesting and synthesizing of the immense amount of data that is currently available in case studies. These publications cover such diverse thematic interests as governance structures and supervision mechanisms of individual groups [MELVILLE/OBERSTE 1999, LINDE 2018]; principles of mendicant organization and social interaction and how these were realized in concrete, localized settings [HOLDER 2017, GARCIA-SERRANO 2018]; economic practices [BÉRIOU/CHIFFOLEAU 2009, DE CEVINS/VIALLET 2018]; the mendicants' role in shaping monastic and public space and in managing religious and political networks [BRUZELIUS 2014, ROMHÁNYI 2016]; their educational practices and intellectual activities [ROEST 2000, ŞENOCAK 2012]; and finally also their preaching [CONTI 2015]. To these interests, we must add the mendicants' cross-cultural and cross-ethnic contacts. These were particularly active with the Muslim and Far Eastern worlds [MÜLLER 2002, VOSE 2009], the inhabitants of various 'border regions' of the Latin West [for Ireland, LAFAYE 2018], and with settlers and occupiers in newly conquered regions [for the Byzantine Empire in the early thirteenth century, TSOUGARAKIS 2012].

A common feature of discussions across institutional, regional, and even methodological boundaries is that studies of male and of female strands rarely intersect. Concerning female Dominican and Franciscan communities, the trend has traditionally been to focus on how the women in these institutions negotiated the various gender-specific strictures imposed on them. Much work has been done on such issues as education and spirituality [EHRENSCHWENDTNER 2004, NEIDHARDT 2017]. The organization of monastic space in these convents has also been interrogated for how it shaped the members' experience, their spirituality, and finally also their relationship with the surrounding world [JÄGGI 2006]. But more recently, the focus has somewhat shifted to looking at how women in these houses and those involved in various mendicant 'nebulas' participated in pastoral care [ROEST/UPHOFF 2016; also further, Chapter 4.5]; how these groups interacted with non- or semi-institutionalized monastics practitioners, such as recluses, anchoresses, and Beguines [BENVENUTI PAPI 1990]; and finally also how the relationship with their male counterparts and with patrons played out. A number of collective publications have made a strong case for comparative study of these issues across different

Female forms and experiences

regions, societal contexts (for instance, urban versus rural), and filiations or 'nebulas' [COLESANTI/GARÍ/JORNET-BENITO 2017]. These pioneering works have made it obvious that there are unexplored opportunities for an integrated analysis of female monastic community life. These communities include (among others) mendicant houses and 'Third Order' groups, and also those that belonged to the Cistercian and Premonstratensian orders and their respective 'nebulas' (above, Chapter 4.3).

4.5 'Semi-religious' Movements in the Later Middle Ages

'Semi-religious' categories

In discussions of lay monasticism in the later Middle Ages, historians often use such terms as 'semi-religious', 'quasi-religious', or 'marginal' [ELM 1998]. All might be taken to imply that these scholars are of the opinion that practitioners were not fully committed to the monastic life (*vita religiosa*) or that their lifestyle did not objectively match the criteria that allow us to label them as 'monastics' [MORE 2018]. In reality, these terms reflect the viewpoint of ecclesiastical administrators of the late twelfth century and beyond, many of whom were determined to turn a highly diverse landscape of ascetic community life into one consisting of fully incorporated, clearly defined, and tightly supervised cohorts of vowed monastics. On the one hand, these 'marginal' labels reflect a dismissive discourse that was propagated whenever administrators were looking to ridicule, suppress, or incorporate specific lay practices and experiences. On the other, they also echo the ambivalent position of these churchmen and canon law specialists with regard to various lay movements that had to a greater or lesser extent been incorporated within ecclesiastical structures but were still not thought of as central to the Church's organization and mission [MAKOWSKI 2005, BÖHRINGER/KOLPACOFF DEANE/VAN ENGEN 2014].

Criticisms

Responses

Significantly, twelfth-century and later authors expressed comparatively few concerns, and even a great deal of admiration, regarding the existence of hermits, anchorites and recluses, and even of small, 'private' settlements housing multiple ascetic individuals (above, Chapter 4.2). Major concerns arose only when lay monastics began to organize themselves, gained prominence as a social phenomenon within urban societies especially, and started claiming forms of ascetic agency that were considered potentially subversive by the ecclesiastical authorities [on the conservative attitudes of the papacy with regard to groups of lay ascetics, WEHRLI-JOHNS 1996]. Exactly how challenges were voiced and how the clerical hierarchy responded remains difficult to reconstruct: our understanding of late twelfth-century interactions between, on the one hand, lay movements like that of the *Humiliati* and the Waldensians, and, on the other, the papacy and the members of the episcopal elite, is complicated by the biased reporting of thirteenth-century commentators [ALBERZONI 1999].

What is becoming increasingly clear, though, is that negotiations and confrontations between parties were about much more than the mere existence and preaching ambitions of specific groups, and must be understood in the context of broader tensions. These tensions include drastically changed social circumstances (for example, the rise of urban societies, communes, and educated middle classes), the changing nature of lay spirituality, and the changing expectations of the laity as regards its involvement in moral and dogmatic instruction [ANDREWS 1999]. Also unquestionably significant were intense theoretical and legal reflections on the role of the laity in a changing Church, the details of which remain elusive to scholars. More insight into these matters would allow us to get a better understanding of (among other things) the developments leading up to Pope Innocent's revolutionary proclamation that, along with the contemplative monastics and those dedicated to pastoral tasks, there was room in the Church for a 'Third Order' [4.2 SIMONS].

Settings

Processes of (semi-)incorporation of various forms and movements in the early to mid-thirteenth century remain likewise difficult to distinguish in their finer details. For instance, study of the Penitents as a global phenomenon is complicated by deep embedding of individual groups in local contexts, and by their lack of internal drive towards a shared 'corporate' culture [BENVENUTI PAPI 1990, CASAGRANDE 1998]. Although the 'movement' was recognized by the papacy and although communities became implicated in Dominican [CARIBONI 1999, LEHMIJOKI-GARDNER 2005] and Franciscan [ANDREOZZI 1993–1995] 'nebulas', attempts to institutionalize specific Third Order strands and establish order-like procedures and structures for these never entirely succeeded [MORE 2014]. However, these observations are less an obstacle to the study of their experiences and perceptions, than an invitation to scrutinize them from a local perspective.

Incorporation processes

Local perspectives   Specifically, the late medieval source record contains extensive evidence of attempts to regulate individual communities and local or regional clusters, and of the response to these attempts by the monastics and their direct supervisors [LEHMIJOKI-GARDNER 2004, MORE 2018]. Similar remarks have been made about the documentation concerning attempts in the final centuries of the Middle Ages to merge some of these groups with Beguine communities [VAN ENGEN 2006]. Along with sources that provide an insight into the daily practice and spiritual culture of these places, these records help the researcher to gain a situated understanding of the phe-

Unregulated forms   nomenon. Often overlooked in these discussions are the many informal communities of lay monastics in towns, and here lies a major but challenging field of enquiry [VAN ENGEN 2004]. Lay confraternities and miscellaneous other groups that existed in the orbit of monastic institutions also deserve more systematic enquiry [TERPSTRA 1995, MOUVANCES 1996], if only to integrate the specific case studies that have already been undertaken into a comparative analysis across regional and other boundaries.

Beguine forms and   Any attempts to describe the Beguine phenomenon as a move-
experiences   ment with a universally shared narrative of self and a likewise universal social, functional, and spiritual profile are bound to fail. But here too, a wealth of regional and local case studies allows us to chart its highly diverse expressions in significant detail [REICHSTEIN 2001, SIMONS 2001, VOIGT 2012, BÖHRINGER/KOLPACOFF DEANE/ VAN ENGEN 2014]. One of the key insights deriving from recent work is that the earliest communities were highly informal and hard to distinguish from other forms of lay monasticism [WEHRLI-JOHNS 1998]. Early testimonies about the phenomenon's rise as a distinct strand of lay monasticism are heavily biased, and should definitely not be taken to reflect views and experiences by the practitioners. The earliest commentaries to identify the Beguines as a separate phenomenon were written by critical observers who had little interest in describing the women's mode of life, and merely sought to indicate how lay monastic groups, particularly female, had become a prominent social phenomenon. Later on, biographers and hagiographers of particularly admired Beguines would present their readership with a cohesive vision of life in these communities, erasing any memories of a far 'messier' reality [on these texts, SIMONS 2015]. That reality does emerge if we shift our attention to those points in time when individual communities were compelled,

either by their particular situation or from above, to negotiate a specific institutional and normative identity. The evidence deriving from these negotiations with ecclesiastical superiors and interested stakeholders allows us to discern that Beguine community life was highly responsive to local circumstances and expectations [BÖHRINGER 2014], and highly situated chronologically and contextually [MAKOWSKI 2005, DE VRIES 2016]. Negotiations and interventions

It was this variety in local arrangements and the lack of clear structures and procedures for supervision that triggered a backlash by the higher ecclesiastical hierarchy in the later thirteenth century. Under the influence of various debates on the place of women's monastic life in the Church [SCHMIDT 2015], a series of top-down measures were taken that brought the experience of life in many Beguine and Third Order communities considerably closer to that of cloistered groups [ANDREOZZI 1993–1995]. What seems to have irked Church leaders was not so much the fact that women religious explored their ascetic spirituality, but that they did so outside of conventional institutional settings. A recent study for Languedoc noted that Clarisse communities – some of which participated, along with Beguines, in an ideology marked by Spiritualist pauperism and millenarianism – are notably omitted from inquisitors' reports, as if contemporary churchmen were more concerned with attacking the Beguines as a form of lay monasticism than with rooting out unorthodox ideas per se [NIETO-ISABEL 2017].

For those parts of Europe where Beguine communities and similar forms of monastic life for laywomen were not wiped out or incorporated, there is substantial evidence of a continuing, indeed increasing, impact of these women on education, socio-economic life, popular devotion, and spiritual reflection and debate. All of this necessitated that their communities be flexible in adapting to a secular environment that was prone to rapid, sometimes drastic change [STABLER MILLER 2014, SIMONS 2009, BRAGUIER 2019]. The relationship in the later Middle Ages with various mendicant agents who had been appointed to oversee their ideas and conduct has surfaced from recent studies as less straightforwardly negative than was formerly assumed [VON HEUSINGER 2000]. Together with these men, Beguines from the Low Countries often became involved in intense spiritual reflection and debate, as some would do later on with prominent individuals of the Modern Devotion movement [VAN LUIJK 2004, VAN ENGEN 2006, GOUDRIAAN 2016]. Interactions with other monastics

Similar observations have been made for Italian lay monastics and their mendicant confessors [BARTOLOMEI ROMAGNOLI/PAOLI/PIATTI 2016].

Modern Devotion

In itself, the Modern Devotion movement is also a major case study for the complex interaction between, and mutual influence of, various interpretations and experiences of the monastic life. Study of its spirituality, organization, and influence has yielded a considerable bibliography covering a vast range of subjects. Now that the origins, embedding in contemporary culture and spirituality, and subsequent institutionalization of the movement are well understood [STAUBACH 2005, VAN ENGEN 2008], the focus of recent studies has shifted. Scholars are investigating the active contribution of women in the early movement [VAN DIJK/HOFMAN/VAN DEN BERG 2015]; cultural transfers and interactions with other monastics and with lay society [DE BOER/KWIATOWSKI 2013]; the movement's involvement in the dissemination of spiritual texts and promoting new media, including the printed book [GOUDRIAAN 2016]; and the social and even cognitive implications of the members' insistence on using the vernacular in their written output and oral communication [JOLDERSMA 2008].

4.6 Late Medieval Challenges and Experiences

The study of monasticism between c. 1250 and the beginning of the sixteenth century is marked by a great disparity of research interests. This is understandable, as even the most seasoned observers have found it difficult to distil a cohesive narrative out of a massive source record detailing an almost incomprehensible range of top-down reform attempts, 'bottom-up' movements for spiritual or institutional renewal, and regional and local trends and developments.

Biased accounts

Finding answers to the question of how to characterize monasticism's status in this period is further complicated by a stratigraphy of biased commentaries dating from the sixteenth century until the near-present, the goal of which was to argue (among other things) the 'triumph' of the great monastic orders in the 1100s–1200s and their subsequent decline. This narrative also pitched various developments and debates as laying the groundwork for the Protestant Reformation and the dissolution of monastic houses in various parts of Europe [VAN ENGEN 2008].

The few successful attempts to test these narratives against the Recent nuancing primary evidence have all indicated that previous notions about the later Middle Ages as an age of contraction and decline, or (alternatively) of reform, tend to ignore the sheer diversity of monastic lifestyles and experiences in this period, as well as the immense variety of political, socio-economic, and cultural contexts in which these individuals and communities lived. More generally, such recent scholarship has also observed that former narratives tend to rely on questionable assumptions about cyclical patterns of decline and renewal in monastic history and on overly vague semantics, particularly when they use the term 'reform' [ELM 2016, VAN ENGEN 2008]. And while older scholarship relied on anti-monastic and anti-fraternal satire in literary texts of the period to argue that laypeople became disenchanted with the morality and service of institutionalized monasticism, recent publications have questioned the relevance of these sources as a mirror of public opinion [STECKEL 2020]. A wealth of studies addressing lay expec- Lay expectations tations and perceptions of contemplative, mendicant, and other and responses strands of organized monastic life (as documented, for example in charters, letters, ego-documents, and commissioned works of art and architecture) provide ample support to the notion that institutional monasticism as a whole was definitely not struggling to gain and retain the favours of the laity. Much depended, so it seems, on the ability of specific strands and also of individual communities to sustain their perceived relevance to their secular environment, by engaging with it in a range of mutually beneficial interactions.

It is no wonder, then, that scholars over the last few decades have preferred specific topics within specific geographical, institutional, ideological, and even personal settings. Likewise, they have tended to look at the situation of specific institutions and communities on a case-by-case basis. The present trend to move Situated away from categorical views on the state of monastic life globally is perspectives revealed, among other things, in the way historians currently look at the relationship between monastics and their social environment. Regional and local case studies make clear that, on a local level too, former claims about the rampant success of monasteries belonging to 'progressive' movements and the pitiful state of those in 'traditional' ones are no longer tenable [3.6 BURTON, RACINET 1997, SPEAR 2005, PEREZ RODRIGUEZ 2009, KING 2013, HEALE 2016]. While the traditional view postulated that lay and clerical observers were becoming increasingly uninterested in investing their energies and resources in 'traditional' strands, the picture that is currently emerging largely dispenses with preconceived notions about the outdated spirituality, patronage models, and social engagement of these communities. 'Traditional' institutions (including those that deliberately remained outside the influence of Observant Reform) continued to provide vital services to local society right until the end of the medieval period, including in remote parts of the West [KERR 2007, KRISTJÁNSDÓTTIR/LARSSON/ASEN 2014]: they were also able to maintain mutually beneficial relations with their aristocratic patrons [STÖBER 2007]. In various parts of Germany and Scandinavia, agents of the Reformation immediately set out to reinvest confiscated monastic resources into hospitals, centres of education, and various other public institutions, which indicates that there was a need to replace services that had previously been provided by these institutions [GRELL 1995, CAHILL 1996]. Recent investigations of Humanist scholarship in Benedictine contexts has also revealed a high degree of engagement with trends in intellectual and spiritual life [KAARTINEN 2002, SCHLECHTER/PELGEN 2016]. The picture becomes even fuller if we consider the ambitions and expectations of the monastics themselves. Studies of the workings and recruitment of regular colleges in university towns of the fifteenth and sixteenth centuries offer one of many perspectives on this question [SOHN/VERGER 2012], as do those concerning apostate monks [LOGAN 1996] and nuns.

Enduring societal relevance

However, other groups and movements did experience difficulties in developing an identity that was sufficiently distinct from that of the other ecclesiastical and secular cohorts. A number of publications have investigated the precise mechanisms behind their decline. One such case study is that of the twelfth-century Chalaisian movement (after the name of its founding house Chalais), which revealed that prior to its dissolution in the early fourteenth century, outside observers had found it difficult to distinguish its quasi-eremitical identity from the far more prominent Carthusians [EXCOFFON 2001]. In contrast, the Carthusians had been far more successful at developing a distinct identity and at nurturing a perception of relevance and impact, for instance through their production of books for other communities and for the open market. They also profiled their monasteries as centres of spiritual learning [SÖNKE 2002, PANSTERS 2014]; took an active role as visitators of

Challenges

Adaptations

communities belonging to other movements; and were involved as 'influencers' in a range of known reform endeavours [RÜTHING 1989]. Another eremitical movement, that of the Camaldolenses, had successfully shifted its action from primarily rural settings to urban ones [CABY 1999]. Questions about a community's ability to develop a distinct spiritual and functional identity and promote it effectively to its secular environment also apply to more recently emerged movements. Such is the case for the Celestines [thirteenth century onwards, SHAW 2018] and the Brigittines [in the late fourteenth and early fifteenth century, STUDIES 1993], in particular as concerns their ability to fulfil specific needs in their local environment. Such enquiries would take the study of these movements beyond the question of how they attempted to realize an ideal vision of the primitive Church.

The push to do away with preconceived notions and sweeping generalizations has also affected current views on reform and its implications in local settings, and on resistance against reform. So it has been argued that the involvement of individual communities in the Observant Reform was definitely not a recipe for improved perceptions and relationships. A key study for France has suggested that Observant Reform in the fifteenth and early sixteenth centuries was actually one of the primary factors driving anti-monastic sentiments in broad layers of secular society. Many reformed communities set out to enforce their rights and privileges, reclaim direct exploitation of their estates, adjust rents and other incomes to the market, and systematically collect tithes. In ruthlessly pursuing this agenda of institutional and economic recovery, they often ended up alienating their aristocratic neighbours and patrons, as well as their tenants and other members of the rural population [LE GALL 2001]. *Reconceptualizing reform*

Fears of disrupting a delicate balance of interests and expectations with a range of social partners is what appears to have brought a substantial number of communities to resist top-down reform attempts, including various ones by the thirteenth- and fourteenth-century papacy [FELTEN 1992]. Striking examples of this are provided in case studies that consider the implementation of the papal decretal *Periculoso*. They have yielded a substantial dossier in support of the negotiated and locally embedded nature of real-life experiences in female convents of the later Middle Ages [MAKOWSKI 1997]. Other studies have considered the disputes *Responses*

Schisms and disputes

between Conventualist and Spiritualist Franciscans, pointing to the disruptive impact on their social status and reputation, and noting also the frequent verbal and physical attacks members of this divided strand of mendicant monasticism suffered [GELTNER 2012].

Recent scholarship has also emphasized that the term Observant Reform refers to diverse initiatives, many of which were highly embedded locally or regionally [ELM 1989, BISCHOF/THURNER 2013, MIXSON/ROEST 2015]. A number of studies have addressed the question of how various orders and ecclesiastical rulers tried to maintain unity in this diversity – in other words, how they determined the limits of legitimate experimentation [ZERMATTEN 2016]. Others have framed reform specifically in the context of ideological and practical tensions within certain movements, for instance over the principle of poverty and its implications for the experience and organization of monastic groups [MIXSON 2009, VIALLET 2014]. A similar struggle has been witnessed over the involvement of members in pastoral action [ROEST/UPHOFF 2016, CLARK/BUSH 2020]. In yet another strand of research, specialists have adopted a more 'political' approach, looking among other things at how sovereigns integrated monastic cohorts in the exercise of secular rule [LE GALL 2001].

'Reform transfers' Building on observations about the locally and contextually situated nature of late medieval reform, scholars have also become more interested in how reform ideals and procedures were transmitted between institutions, movements, regions, and even cultures [ISRAEL 2006]. Sources deriving from, or relating to, daily practice – visitation records, local charter collections and cartularies, historiographical projects [REY 2010], financial records [DEWEZ 2012], ledgers, documents relating to archival management, chronicles, biographies, ego-documents, and letters – provide the evidence for the type of comparative analysis that is needed to reconstruct these transfers and their implications. Major case studies have considered an immense array of subjects. They range from reading practices and networks [HOTCHIN 2011, BÉRIOU/MORARD/NEBBIAI-DELLA GUARDA 2014], over the composition, performance, and transmission of music [KENDRICK 2002, JONES 2018], to the correction and incarceration of delinquent monastics [LUSSET 2017], and even food preparation and consumption [FRITSCH 2008]. Thanks to an impressive number of architectural and art historical studies, our understanding has also improved of the social positioning of communities in reform settings, as also their self-identity. These publications provide irrefutable evidence that the architectural and iconographic models that were transmitted through reform networks were subject to adaptations to local circumstances and expectations. In the process, these adaptations often changed both the intended message and its impact [HAMBURGER 1997, HAMBURGER/SUCKALE 2005, MERSCH 2012, CARRAZ/DEHOUX 2016].

III Bibliography

1 Introductory Comments, General References, and Sources

This bibliography does not pretend to chart the full scope of the literature. Because of space constraints and because its main objective is to provide references for the titles cited in Part 2, it prioritizes publications that give users an impression of the current state of the art as well as indications of what might be achieved in the near and more distant future. It is for the same two reasons that this bibliography contains no references to dictionaries, encyclopaedia, handbooks, monastica, atlases, or major editions and translations of primary sources. Most major reference works and text editions published before 2003 are listed and discussed in the handbooks cited in Section 1.1 below, and in far greater detail than would be possible here. In contrast, more recent such resources (including, crucially, many digital editions and repertories) urgently await full coverage, preferably in the form of a multi-authored, periodically updated online resource.

Finally, readers should also take note that this bibliography is subjective, in that it reflects the attempt by a single scholar to provide an introductory view of a field that may appear fairly unified and slow moving on the surface, but in reality consists of many distinct, constantly evolving research interests. In nearly all of these, the last three decades have seen standard narratives of the monastic past being challenged and major steps being taken in identifying and exploring new methodologies and thematic interests, not all of which can be given more than a passing mention in these pages.

Note: Titles that are referenced in multiple chapters of Part 2 are listed here only for the first chapter in which they appear. Part 2 uses cross-references to the relevant section of this bibliography for further appearances.

1.1 Reference Works

G. CONSTABLE, Medieval Monasticism: A Select Bibliography. Toronto 1976.

https://doi.org/10.1515/9783110543780-003

W.M. JOHNSTON (ed.), The Encyclopedia of Monasticism, 2 vols. Chicago, IL 1998–2000.

A. VAUCHEZ/C. CABY, L'histoire des moines, chanoines et religieux au Moyen Age. Guide de recherche et documents. Turnhout 2003.

Note: For scholarship published in the last two decades, readers are advised to refer to general bibliographies such as the International Medieval Bibliography (http://www.brepolis.net) and Regesta Imperii Opac (http://opac.regesta-imperii.de/lang_en/). Also recommended are annual bibliographies and surveys of ongoing research in specialized journals such as *The Journal of Medieval Monastic Studies* and many others cited in VAUCHEZ/CABY. Book reviews in journals and on dedicated websites (for instance The Medieval Review, http://scholarworks.iu.edu/journals/index.php/tmr) are helpful sources of information, as of course are the bibliographies that are included in the scholarly publications cited below. Keeping track of the stream of newly published research remains a challenging task: researchers will find it helpful to subscribe to the websites and social media accounts of selected publishers, research groups, and individual scholars.

1.2 Recent Monographic Surveys

C. BROOKE, The Age of the Cloister. The Story of Monastic Life in the Middle Ages. New York, NY 2001.

C.H. LAWRENCE, Medieval Monasticism: Forms of Religious Life in Western Europe in the Middle Ages. Harlow 2001 (third edition).

G. MELVILLE, Die Welt der mittelalterlichen Klöster. Munich 2012 (translated into English as The World of Medieval Monasticism. Collegeville, MN 2016).

1.3 Major Discussions of the State of the Art

G. ANDENNA (ed.), Dove va la storiografia monastica in Europa? Temi e metodi di ricerca per lo studio della vita monastica e regolare in età medievale alle soglie del terzo millennio. Milan 2001.

A. BEACH/I. COCHELIN (ed.), The Cambridge History of Medieval Monasticism in the Latin West, 2 vols. Cambridge 2020.

G. MELVILLE/A. MÜLLER (ed.), Mittelalterliche Orden und Klöster im Vergleich. Methodische Ansätze und Perspektiven. Berlin 2007.

Monachesimi d'oriente e d'occidente nell'alto medioevo, 2 vols. Spoleto 2017.

S. VANDERPUTTEN/B. MEIJNS (ed.), Ecclesia in medio nationis. Reflections on the Study of monasticism in the Central Middle Ages/Réflexions sur l'étude du monachisme au Moyen Age Central. Leuven 2011.

1.4 A Selection of Written Primary Sources

The corpus of written primary texts for the study of monastic forms and experiences in late antiquity and the Middle Ages is immense. Because of space constraints, it is impossible to give even a cursory overview in these pages. For a systematic introduction to the typology of these sources as well as an overview of the principal text editions and series, refer to 1.1 Vauchez/Caby. The sole purpose of the list below is to support the argument in Part 1 with a selection of key documents and to give the novice reader a first taste of what lies in store for them. Each of the sources cited here contains a descriptor of the typology and is referenced in Part 1 by the name of the author or the abbreviated title, preceded by an **S**. When selecting the relevant sources, priority was given to narrative and normative texts, and to those for which a translation in English, German, or French is available.

Key to the typologies: *A (autobiography), B (biography), Arch (archival document), Conf (confraternity agreement), Cons (constitutions), Cust (customary), D (drama), Ex (exempla), F (florilegium), Hag (hagiography), Hist (historiography), Hom (homily), Inst (instructional text), Inq (inquisitor's handbook), L (letters), Mem (memorial handbook), Pi (pilgrim's account), Po (poetry), R (rule), Rit (ritual manual), Sag (saga), Sat (satire), Say (sayings), Ser (sermon) Stat (statutes), T (treatise), Vis (visitation records).*

1.4.1 The Beginnings of Monasticism(s)

(T) Aldhelm, De Laude virginitatis (In praise of virginity), ed. R. Ehwald, Monumenta Germaniae Historica. Auctores antiquissimi 15. Berlin 1919, trans. M. Herren/M. Lapidge, Aldhelm. The Prose Works. Cambridge 1979.

(Say) Apophthegmata patrum (Sayings of the Fathers), partial ed. and trans. J. Wortley, The Anonymous Sayings of the Desert Fathers. Cambridge 2013.

(R) Augustine of Hippo, Rule(s), ed. L. Verheijen, La Règle de Saint Augustin, vol. 1. Paris 1967, trans. G. Lawless, Augustine of Hippo and His Monastic Rule. Oxford 1987 and W. Hümpfner, Augustinus. Klosterregeln. Ordo Monasterii, Praeceptum, St. Ottilien 2012.

(R) Aurelian of Arles, Regula ad virgines (Rule for virgins), ed. H. Mayo, Three Merowingian Rules for Nuns, 2 vols. Unpublished doctoral dissertation, Harvard 1974, vol. 2, p. 4–68, trans. K. Hauschild, Aurelianus von Arles. Mönchsregel, Nonnenregel. St. Ottilien 2012.

(R) Basil of Cesarea, Regula (Rule, translation by Rufinus), ed. K. Zelzer, Corpus scriptorum ecclesiasticorum Latinorum 86. Vienna 1986, trans.

A.M. Sɪʟᴠᴀs, The Rule of St Basil in Latin and English. Collegeville, MN 2013 and K.S. Fʀᴀɴᴋ, Basilius von Caesarea: Mönchsregeln. St. Ottilien 2010.

(Hɪsᴛ) Bᴇᴅᴇ ᴛʜᴇ Vᴇɴᴇʀᴀʙʟᴇ, Historia ecclesiastica gentis Anglorum (Ecclesiastical history of the English people), ed. B. Cᴏʟɢʀᴀᴠᴇ/R.A. Mʏɴᴏʀs, Bede's Ecclesiastical History of the English People. Oxford 1969, trans. D.H. Fᴀʀᴍᴇʀ/L. Sʜᴇʀʟᴇʏ-Pʀɪᴄᴇ/R. Lᴀᴛʜᴀᴍ, Bede. Ecclesiastical History of the English People. London 1991 and G. Sᴘɪᴛᴢʙᴀʀᴛ, Beda der Ehrwürdige. Kirchengeschichte des Englischen Volkes, 2 vols. Darmstadt 1982.

(Hᴀɢ) Bᴇᴅᴇ ᴛʜᴇ Vᴇɴᴇʀᴀʙʟᴇ/Anonymous, Vitae sancti Cuthberti (Two Lives of St Cuthbert), ed. and trans. B. Cᴏʟɢʀᴀᴠᴇ, Two Lives of Saint Cuthbert: A Life by an Anonymous Monk of Lindisfarne and Bede's Prose Life. Cambridge 1940.

(R/T) Jᴏʜɴ Cᴀssɪᴀɴ, Collationes (Conferences), ed. and trans. E. Pɪᴄʜᴇʀʏ, 3 vols. Paris 1955/1958/1959 and trans. B. Rᴀᴍsᴇʏ, John Cassian: The Conferences. New York, NY 1997.

(R) Cᴇsᴀʀɪᴜs ᴏꜰ Aʀʟᴇs, Regula ad virgines (Rule for virgins), ed. and trans. A. Dᴇ Vᴏɢüé/J. Cᴏᴜʀʀᴇᴀᴜ, Césaire d'Arles. Oeuvres monastiques, vol. 1. Paris 1988, p. 170–272, also trans. I. Aᴜꜰ ᴅᴇʀ Mᴀᴜʀ, Caesarius von Arles, Klosterregeln für Nonnen und Mönche. St. Ottilien 2008.

(R) Cᴏʟᴜᴍʙᴀɴᴜs, Regula monachorum (Rule for monks), ed. and trans. G.S.M. Walker, Columbani Opera. Dublin 1956, p. 124–142, also trans. I. Aᴜꜰ ᴅᴇʀ Mᴀᴜʀ, Columban von Luxeuil. Mönchsregeln, St. Ottilien 2007.

(F) Dᴇꜰᴇɴsᴏʀ ᴏꜰ Lɪɢᴜɢé, Liber Scintillarum (The Book of Sparks), ed. and trans. H.-M. Rᴏᴄʜᴀɪs, Le livre des étincelles, 2 vols. Paris 1976.

(Pɪʟ) Eɢᴇʀɪᴀ, Peregrinatio (Pilgrim's journey to the Holy Land), ed. and trans. P. Mᴀʀᴀᴠᴀʟ, Egerie, Journal de Voyage. Paris 1982, also trans. J. Wɪʟᴋɪɴsᴏɴ, Egeria's Travels. London 1971 and K. Bʀᴏᴅᴇʀsᴇɴ, Aetheria/Egeria, Reise ins Heilige Land. Berlin 2016.

(R) Fʀᴜᴄᴛᴜᴏsᴜs ᴏꜰ Bʀᴀɢᴀ, Regula monachorum (Rule for monks), ed. J. Cᴀᴍᴘᴏs Rᴜɪᴢ, San Leandro, San Isidoro, San Fructuoso. Reglas monásticas de la España visigoda. Madrid 1971, p. 129–162 and trans. C.W. Bᴀʀʟᴏᴡ, Iberian Fathers, 2 vols. Washington, DC 1969, vol. 2, p. 155–175. Also his Pactum, ed. Cᴀᴍᴘᴏs Rᴜɪᴢ, p. 208–211 and trans. Bᴀʀʟᴏᴡ, p. 207–209.

(T/H) Gʀᴇɢᴏʀʏ ᴛʜᴇ Gʀᴇᴀᴛ, Dialogi (Dialogues), ed. and trans. A. Dᴇ Vᴏɢüé/P. Aɴᴛɪɴ, 3 vols. Paris 1978–1980, also trans. E.G. Gᴀʀᴅɴᴇʀ, The Dialogues of Saint Gregory the Great. London 1911 and J. Fᴜɴᴋ, Des heiligen Papstes und Kirchenlehrers Gregor des Grossen vier Bücher Dialoge. Munich 1933.

(R) Isɪᴅᴏʀᴇ ᴏꜰ Sᴇᴠɪʟʟᴇ, Regula (Rule), ed. J. Cᴀᴍᴘᴏs Rᴜɪᴢ, San Leandro, San Isidoro, San Fructuoso. Reglas monásticas de la España visigoda, Madrid 1971, p. 79–125, trans. K.S. Fʀᴀɴᴋ, Hispanische Klosterregeln. Leander von Sevilla: Brief und Regel für Florentina, Isidor von Sevilla: Mönchsregel, St. Ottilien 2011.

(R) Jᴏɴᴀs ᴏꜰ Bᴏʙʙɪᴏ (?), Regula cuiusdam ad virgines (Rule for virgins), ed. L. Hᴏʟsᴛᴇɴɪᴜs/M. Bʀᴏᴄᴋɪᴇ, Codex regularum monasticarum et canonicarum, vol. 1. Augsburg 1759, p. 393–404, trans. A. Dɪᴇᴍ, Das

Ende des monastischen Experiments. Liebe, Beichte und Schweigen in der Regula cuiusdam ad virgines, in G. MELVILLE/A. MÜLLER (ed.), Female vita religiosa Between Late Antiquity and the High Middle Ages. Structures, Developments and Spatial Contexts. Münster 2011, p. 81–136.

(HAG) JONAS OF BOBBIO, Vita Columbani (Life of Columbanus), ed. B. KRUSCH, Monumenta Germaniae Historica, Scriptores Rerum Germanicarum in usum scholarum 37. Hannover 1905, p. 148–224, trans. A. O'HARA/I. WOOD, Jonas of Bobbio: Life of Columbanus, Life of John of Réomé, and Life of Vedast, Liverpool 2017.

(R) PACHOMIUS, Regula (Rule, Latin version), ed. A. BOON, Pachomiana Latina. Louvain 1932, p. 1–74 and trans. A. VEILLEUX, Pachomian Koinonia, vol. 2, Kalamazoo, MI 1981, p. 141–183 and H. BACHET, Pachomius. Mönchsregelen. St. Ottilien 2010.

(L) PAULINUS OF NOLA, Letters, ed. and trans. G. SANTANIELLO, Paolino di Nola: Le Lettere, 2 vols. Marigliano 1992, also trans. P.G. Walsch, Letters of St Paulinus of Nola, 2 vols. Westminster, Md 1966–1967.

(R) Regula Benedicti (Rule of St Benedict), ed. R. HANSLIK. Vienna 1972, trans. B.L. VENARDE, The Rule of Saint Benedict. Cambridge, Mass 2011 and U. FAUST, Die Benediktsregel. Stuttgart 2009.

(R) Regula quattuor patrum (Rule of the Four Fathers), ed. and trans. A. DE VOGÜÉ, Pères de Lérins. Règle des Quatre Pères/Règle des Pères/ Règle de Macaire. Paris 1982, p. 180–204, also trans. C. FRANKLIN/I. HAVENER/J.A. FRANCIS, Early Monastic Rules. Collegeville, MN 1982 and M. PUZICHA, Mönchsregeln von Lérins. Regel der Vier Väter, Zweite Regel der Väter, Dritte Regel der Väter. St. Ottilien 2010.

(HAG) RODULPH OF FULDA, Vita Leobae (Life of Leoba), ed. G. WAITZ, Monumenta Germaniae Historica. Scriptores 15. Hannover 1887, p. 127–131, trans. D. WHITELOCK, English Historical Documents, 1: c. 500–1042. London 1955 (second edition), p. 719–722.

(HAG) SULPICIUS SEVERUS, Vita sancti Martini (Life of St Martin), ed. and trans. J. FONTAINE, 2 vols. Paris 2011, also trans. C. WHITE, Early Christian Lives. London 1998, p. 129–159 and J. DRUMM, Martin von Tours. Der Lebensbericht von Sulpicius Severus. Ostfildern 1997.

(T/A) VALERIUS OF BIERZO, "Autobiography", ed. and trans. C.M. AHERNE, Valerio of Bierzo, An Ascetic of the Late Visigothic Period. Washington, DC 1979, p. 69–159.

(HAG) VENANTIUS FORTUNATUS, Vita sanctae Radegundis (Life of St Radegonde), ed. B. KRUSCH, Monumenta Germaniae Historica. Scriptores rerum Merovingicarum 2. Hannover 1888, p. 364–395, trans. J.A. McNAMARA/J. HALBORG, The Life of the Holy Radegund, Sainted Women of the Dark Ages. Durham, NC 1996, p. 60–106 and G. HUBER-REBENICH, Vita sanctae Radegundis/Das Leben der heiligen Radegunde. Stuttgart 2008.

(HAG) Vita abbatum Acaunensium, ed. and trans. E. CHEVALLEY/C. RODUIT, La mémoire hagiographique de l'abbaye de Saint-Maurice d'Agaune. Lausanne 2014.

(Hag) Vita sanctae Geretrudis (Life of St Gertrudis of Nivelles), ed. B. Krusch, Monumenta Germaniae Historica. Scriptores rerum Merovingicarum 2. Hannover 1889, p. 447–474, trans. J.A. McNamara/J.E. Halborg, Sainted Women of the Dark Ages. Durham, NC 1996, p. 220–234.

1.4.2 Early and High Medieval Monasticisms

(T) Ælfric, Letter to the Monks of Eynsham, ed. and trans. C.A. Jones. Cambridge 1998.

(R) Æthelwold of Winchester, Old English Rule of Saint Benedict, ed. A. Schroër, Die angelsächsischen Prosabearbeitungen der Benediktinerregel (updated edition by H. Gneuss). Darmstadt 1964, trans. J. Riyeff. Collegeville, MN 2017.

(Hag/B) Andreas of Fleury, Vita Gauzlini abbatis Floriacensis monasterii (Life of Abbot Gozelin of Fleury), ed. and trans. R.-H. Bautier/G. Labory. André de Fleury, Vie de Gauzlin, abbé de Fleury. Paris 1969.

(B/Hag) Ardo, Vita sancti Benedicti abbatis Anianensis (Life of St Abbot Benedict of Aniane), ed. G. Waitz, Monumenta Germaniae Historica. Scriptores 15/1. Hannover 1887, p. 198–220, trans. A. Cabaniss, Benedict of Aniane, The Emperor's Monk. Ardo's Life, Kalamazoo, MI 2008 and P. Bonnerue/Baumes/A. de Vogüé, in Vie monastique. Série monachisme ancien 39. Abbaye de Bellefontaine 2001.

(B) Baudri of Bourgueil/Andreas, Vitae Roberti (Two Lives of Robert of Arbrissel), ed. and trans. J. Dalarun/G. Giordanengo/A. Le Huërou/J. Longère/D. Poirel/B.L. Venarde. Les deux vies de Robert d'Arbrissel fondateur de Fontevraud/The Two Lives of Robert of Arbrissel Founder of Fontevraud. Turnhout 2006.

(C) Benedict of Aniane, Concordia regularum (Concordance of monastic rules with the Rule of St Benedict), ed. P. Bonnerue. Turnhout 1999.

(Hag) Bernard of Angers, Liber miraculorum sanctae Fides (Book of Miracles of St Foy), ed. and trans. L. Robertini, Liber miraculorum sancte Fidis, Spoleto 1994, also trans. A. Bouillet/L. Servières, Sainte Foy vierge et martyre. Rodez 1900, p. 423–627.

(T) Byrhtferth of Ramsey, Enchiridion, ed. P.S. Baker/M. Lapidge. Oxford 2009.

(Arch) Cartulary of the female Cluniac priory of Marcigny, ed. J. Richard, Le cartulaire de Marcigny-sur-Loire 1045–1144. Essai de reconstitution d'un manuscrit disparu. Dijon 1957.

(R) Chrodegang of Metz, Old English version of his rule for canons, ed. B. Langefeld, The Old English Version of the Enlarged Rule of Chrodegang. Frankfurt am Main 2003.

(Hist) Chronicon Mosomense (Chronicle of Mouzon), ed. and trans. M. Bur, Chronique ou livre de fondation du monastère de Mouzon. Paris 1989.

(Inst) The *Disputatio puerorum*. A Ninth-Century Monastic Instructional Text, ed. A. Rabin/L. Felsen, Toronto 2017.

(Rit) The Death Ritual at Cluny in the Central Middle Ages, ed. F.S. Paxton/I. Cochelin. Turnhout 2013.

(B/H) Ekkehart of Sankt Gall, Vita Wiboradae (Life of Wiborada), ed. and trans. W. Berschin, Vita Sanctae Wiboradae. Die älteste Lebensbeschreibung der heiligen Wiborada. St Gall 1983.

(Inst) Goscelin of Saint-Bertin, Liber confortatorius (Book of consolation), ed. C.H. Talbot, Analecta monastica, textes et études sur la vie des moines au moyen âge. Rome 1955, p. 1–117, trans. M. Otter, Goscelin of St Bertin. Book of Encouragement and Consolation (Liber Confortatorius). Cambridge 2004.

(Inst) Grimlaicus, Regula solitariorum (Rule for solitaries), ed. L. d'Achéry, Regula solitariorum. Paris 1653, trans. A. Thornton, Grimlaicus. Rule for Solitaries. Collegeville, MN 2011.

(T/S) Hildebrand, Invective against canons and canonesses at the 1059 synod of Rome, ed. D. Jasper, Die Konzilien Deutschlands und Reichsitaliens 1023–1059. Hannover 2010, p. 396–398, partial trans. S. Vanderputten, Dark Age Nunneries. The Ambiguous Identity of Female Monasticism, 800–1050. Ithaca, NY 2018, p. 188–191.

(Inst) Hildemar of Civate/Corbie, Expositio Regulae (Commentary on the Rule of St Benedict), ed. R. Mittermüller, Expositio Regulae ab Hildemaro tradita. Regensburg 1880, trans. The Hildemar Project (http://hildemar. org, accessed 12 May 2019) and M.-M. Caillard, Hildemar de Corbie. Commentaire de la Règle de Saint-Benoît. Le Coudray-Macouard 2015.

(D) Hrotsvit of Gandersheim, Plays, ed. W. Berschin, Hrotsvit. Opera omnia, Munich 2001, trans. M. Goullet, Les drames de Hrotsvit de Gandersheim. Metz 1993.

(Hag/B) Hystoria de vita sancti Bonfilii episcopi et confessoris (Life of St Bonfilius), ed. and trans. M. Bassetti/N. D'Acunto, Storia di Bonfilio, un monaco-vescovo alla prima crociata. Spoleto 2017, p. 238–281.

(Hist) Hugo of Flavigny, Chronicon, ed. G.H. Pertz, Monumenta Germaniae Historica. Scriptores 8. Hannover 1848, p. 288–502.

(R/Inst) Institutio Sanctimonialium (Instructions for non-Benedictine women), ed. A. Werminghoff, Monumenta Germaniae Historica. Concilia 2.1. Hannover/Leipzig 1906, p. 421–456.

(Arch) Irmino, Polyptychon, ed. K. Elmshäuser/A. Hedwig, Das Polyptychon von Saint-Germain-des-Près. Cologne 1993.

(T) John of Fécamp, Confessio Theologica (Theological confession), ed. J. Leclercq/J.-P. Bonnes, Un maitre de la vie spirituelle au XIe siecle: Jean de Fecamp. Paris 1946, p. 109–183, trans. P. de Vial, Jean de Fécamp: La confession théologique. Paris 1992.

(B/Hag) John of Saint-Arnoul, Life of John of Gorze, ed. and trans. P.C. Jacobsen, Die Geschichte vom Leben des Johannes von Gorze. Wiesbaden 2016, also trans. M. Parisse, La vie de Jean, abbé de Gorze. Paris 1999.

(B/Hag) Jotsald of Saint-Claude, Vita Odilonis (Life of Abbot Odilo of Cluny), ed. and trans. J. Staub, Iotsald von Saint-Claude, Vita des Abtes Odilo von Cluny. Hannover 1999.

(Cust) Lanfranc, Constitutiones, ed. and trans. D. Knowles/C.N.L. Brooke, The Monastic Constitutions of Lanfranc. Oxford 2002.

(Mem) Liber memorialis of San Salvatore and Santa Giulia in Brescia, ed. D. Geuenich/U. Ludwig, Der Memorial- und Liturgiecodex von San Salvatore/ Santa Giulia in Brescia. Hannover 2000.

(Rit) Monastic Maledictions, ed. L.K. Little, Liturgical Cursing in Romanesque France. Ithaca, NY 1994, p. 254–267.

(B/Hag) Odo of Cluny, Vita sancti Geraldi Aurillacensis (Life of Count Gerald of Aurillac), ed. A.-M. Bultot-Verleysen, Vita sancti Geraldi Auriliacensis/ Vita prolixior prima. Brussels 1989, trans. G. Sitwell, Odo of Cluny, The Life of Saint Gerald of Aurillac, in T.F.X. Noble/T. Head, Soldiers of Christ. Saints and Saints' Lives from Late Antiquity and the Early Middle Ages. University Park, PA 1995, p. 293–362.

(Inst/L/R) Peter Damian, Letter 18 with a rule for the hermits of Fonte Avellana, ed. K. Reindel, Die Brief des Petrus Damiani 1: nr. 1–40. Munich 1983, p. 168–179, trans. O.J. Blum, The Letters of Peter Damian, 1–30. Washington, DC 1989, p. 159–170.

(T) Peter Damian, Liber Gomorrhianus, ed. J.P. Migne, Patrologia Latina 145, c. 159–190, trans. P.J. Payer, Book of Gomorrah: An Eleventh-Century Treatise against Clerical Homosexual Practices. Waterloo, ONT 1982.

(B/Hag) Peter Damian, Vita beati Romualdi (Life of the blessed Romuald), ed. G. Tabacco. Rome 1957, trans. C.R. Phipps, Saint Peter Damian's 'Vita beati Romualdi': Introduction, Translation and Analysis. Unpublished Doctoral Dissertation, London 1988 and partial trans. H. Leyser, in T. Head, Medieval Hagiography: An Anthology. New York, NY 2000, p. 295–316.

(Hist/B) Radulph Glaber, Historiarum libri quinque (Five books of histories), ed. and trans. J. France, Rodulfi Glabri Historiarum libri quinque/The Five Books of the Histories. Oxford 1989. Also, for the section with the *Life* of William of Volpiano, trans. V. Gazeau/M. Goullet, Guillaume de Volpiano, un réformateur en son temps (962–1031). Caen 2008.

(Hist) Ratpert of Saint Gall, Casus Sancti Galli (Fall of St Gall), ed. and trans. H. Steiner, Monumenta Germaniae Historica. Scriptores 75. Hannover 2002, p. 136–238.

(Hist) Regino of Prüm, Chronica, ed. F. Kurze, Monumenta Germaniae Historica. Scriptores rerum Germanicarum 50. Hannover 1890, trans. S. MacLean, History and Politics in Late Carolingian and Ottonian Europe. The Chronicle of Regino of Prüm and Adalbert of Magdeburg. Manchester 2009 and R. Rau, Quellen zur karolingischen Reichsgeschichte, III, in Ausgewählte Quellen 7 (1960), p. 181–318.

(R/Cust/T) Regularis concordia, ed. and trans. T. Symons, The Monastic Agreement of the Monks and Nuns of the English Nation, London 1953.

(L) Richard of Saint-Vanne, Letter "to all the sons of the Church", in Hugo of Flavigny, Chronicon, ed. G.H. Pertz, Monumenta Germaniae Historica. Scriptores 8. Hannover 1848, p. 381–391, trans. C. Carozzi, Le voyage de l'âme dans l'au-delà d'après la littérature latine (Ve-XIIIe siècle). Rome 1994, p. 392–416.

(Hist) Richer of Saint-Remi, Historiarum libri IV (Four books of Histories), ed. H. Hoffmann, Monumenta Germaniae Historica. Scriptores 38. Hannover

2000, trans. J. Lake, Richer of Saint-Rémi. Histories, 2 vols. Cambridge, Mass 2011.

(Hist) Rodulph of Saint-Trond, Gesta abbatum Trudonensium (Deeds of the abbots of Saint-Trond), ed. P. Tombeur. Turnhout 2013, trans. E. Lavigne, Kroniek van de abdij van Sint-Truiden, 2 vols. Assen 1986.

(R/T) Salvus of Albelda, Libellus a regula Sancti Benedicti substractus (Booklet excerpted from the Rule of St Benedict), ed. A. Linage Conde, Una regla monastica riojana femenina del siglo X: El "Libellus a regula sancti Benedicti substractus". Salamanca 1973.

(Inst) Smaragdus of Saint-Mihiel, Diadema Monachorum (The Diadem of Monks), ed. J. Le Louchier, Diadema monachorum R. P. Smaragdi, Paris 1640, trans. D. Barry, The Crown of Monks, Collegeville, MN 2013, and C. Schütz, Diadem der Mönche. St. Ottilien 2009.

(L) Thiathildis of Remiremont, Letters, ed. and trans. M. Parisse, La correspondance d'un évêque carolingien: Frothaire de Toul (ca 813–847) avec les lettres de Theuthilde, abbesse de Remiremont. Paris 1998, p. 151–163.

(Hist) Ugo of Farfa, Destructio monasterii Farfensis (Destruction of the monastery of Farfa), ed. U. Balzani, Fonti per la storia dell'Italia 33 (1903), p. 27–51.

(Cust) Ulrich of Zell, Consuetudines Cluniacenses (Customary of Cluny), ed. L. d'Achéry, Spicilegium sive collectio veterum aliquot scriptorum qui in Galliae bibliothecis maxime Benedictinorum delituerant, vol. 1. Paris 1723 (revised edition), c. 641–703.

(Hag) Vita Caddroe abbatis Walciodorensis (Life of Abbot Caddroë of Waulsort), ed. J. Colgan, Acta Sanctorum veteris et maioris Scotiae seu Hiberniae sanctorum Insulae, vol. 1. Louvain 1645, p. 494–507.

(Cust) William of Hirsau, Constitutiones Hirsaugienses (Constitutions of Hirsau), ed. P. Engelbert, Corpus Consuetudinum Monasticarum 15, 2 vols. Siegburg 2010.

1.4.3 Later Medieval Monasticisms

(L) Adam of Perseigne, Letters, ed. and trans. Anonymous/J. Bouvet/P. Deseille, 3 vols. Paris 1960/2015/2015, also partial trans. G. Perigo, The Letters of Adam of Perseigne, vol. 1. Kalamazoo, MI 1976.

(Inst) Ancrene wisse, ed. E.J. Dobson/R. Dance, A Corrected Edition of the Text in Cambridge, Corpus Christi College, MS 402, with variants from other manuscripts, 2 vols. Oxford 2005–2006, trans. B. Millett, Ancrene Wisse: A Translation. Exeter 2009.

(L/T) Bernard of Clairvaux, Apologia (Apology) ed. J. Leclercq/H. Rochais, S. Bernardi Opera omnia, vol. 3. Rome 1963, p. 81–108, trans. B.S. James, The letters of St. Bernard of Clairvaux, Kalamazoo, MI 1998, p. 95–99.

(Sat) Bernard of Morval (?), De contemptu mundi (On scorn for the world),
ed. and trans. R.E. Pepin, Scorn for the World: Bernard of Cluny's De
contemptu mundi. East Lansing, MI 1991.

(Inq) Bernard Gui, Practica officii inquisitionis (Handbook of the inquisitor),
ed. and trans. G. Mollat, Manuel de l'inquisiteur. Paris 1964, p. 1–19.

(T/Hist) Bernardino of Fossa, Chronica Fratrum Minorum Observantiae
(Chronicle of the Franciscans of the Minor Observance), ed. L. Lemmens.
Rome 1902.

(Arch) Cartulary of the priory of Saint-Georges in Hesdin, ed. R. Fossier,
Cartulaire-chronique du prieuré Saint-Georges d'Hesdin. Paris 1988.

(Ex/Inst) Cesarius of Heisterbach, Dialogus miraculorum (Dialogue on
Miracles), ed. J. Strange, Caesarii Heisterbacensis monachi ordinis
Cisterciensis Dialogus miraculorum, 2 vols. Cologne 1851/Index.
Cologne 1922 (second edition), trans. E. Scott/C.S. Bland, Caesarius
of Heisterbach, The Dialogue on Miracles, 2 vols. London 1929 and
N. Nösges/H. Schneider, Caesarius von Heisterbach. Dialogus
miracolorum/Dialog über die Wunder, 5 vols. Turnhout 2009.

(Arch) Charters of (the order of) Chalais, ed. J.-C. Roman, Les chartes de
l'ordre de Chalais, 1101–1400, 3 vols. Ligugé 1923.

(Cust/Inst) Cistercian Lay Brothers: Twelfth-Century Usages with Related
Texts, ed. and trans. C. Waddell. Brecht 2000.

(T/R) Clara of Assisi, Writings, ed. and trans. M.-F. Becker, Claire d'Assise.
Ecrits. Paris 1985.

(Sat) Concilium in Monte Romarici (Council of Remiremont), ed. and trans.
A. Schulz, Das Konzil der fröhlichen Fräulein von Remiremont/Concilium
in monte Romarici. Butjadingen-Burhave 2013, also trans. M. Parisse,
Le concile de Remiremont, poème satirique du XIIe siècle, Le Pays de
Remiremont 4 (1981), p. 10–15.

(Conf) Confraternity agreement between the Cluniacs and the Carthusians,
ed. B. Bligny, Recueil des plus anciens actes de la Grande-Chartreuse,
1086–1196. Grenoble 1958, p. 64–69.

(Cons) Constitutiones canonicorum Windeshemensium (Constitutions of the
canons of Windesheim), ed. and trans. M. Haverals/F.J. Legrand, Aux
origines de la Devotio Moderna. Les constitutions des chanoines réguliers
de Windesheim. Turnhout 2014.

(Cust) Consuetudines canonicorum regularium Springirsbacenses-
Rodenses (Customary of the regular canons of Klosterrath), ed.
S. Weinfurter. Turnhout 1997, trans. S. Weinfurter/
H. Deutz. Freiburg im Breisgau 1993.

(Cust/Rit) Ecclesiastica officia ('Customary' of the Cistercians), ed. and trans.
D. Choisselet/P. Vernet. Reiningue 1989 and H.M. Herzog/J. Müller.
Langwaden 2003.

(Vis) Eudes Rigaud, Registrum, ed. T. Bonnin, Regestrum visitationum
archiepiscopi Rothomagensis. Rouen 1852, trans. S.M. Brown, The
Register of Eudes of Rouen. New York, NY 1964.

(T/L) Geoffrey of Vendôme, Letters, polemical texts, and spiritual treatises, ed.
and trans. G. Giordanengo, Geoffroy de Vendôme. Oeuvres. Turnhout 1996.

(HAG) GEOFFREY GROSSUS, Vita Bernardi Tironiensi (Life of Bernard of Tiron), ed. and trans. B. BECK, Saint Bernard de Tiron, l'ermite, le moine et le monde, Caen 1998, p. 303–461, also trans. R. HARWOOD CLINE, The Life of Blessed Bernard of Tiron. Washington, DC 2010.

(STAT) POPE GREGORY IX, Statutes for the Benedictine order, ed. T. BONNIN, Regestrum visitationum archiepiscopi Rothomagensis. Rouen 1852, p. 643–648, trans. S.M. BROWN, The Register of Eudes of Rouen. New York, NY 1964, p. 737–746.

(AUTO) GUIBERT OF NOGENT, De vita sua (On his life), ed. and trans. E. WILHELM/W. BERSCHIN, Guibert von Nogent, Die Autobiographie, Stuttgart 2012, also trans. J.F. BENTON, Self and Society in Medieval France. The Memoirs of Abbot Guibert of Nogent. New York, NY 1970.

(CUST) GUIGO THE CARTHUSIAN, Carthusian customs, ed. and trans. M. LAPORTE, Coutumes des Chartreuses. Paris 1984.

(HOM) HILDEGARD OF BINGEN, Expositiones evangeliorum (Homilies on the Gospels), ed. B.M. KIENZLE/C. MUESSIG. Turnhout 2007, trans. B.M. KIENZLE, Hildegard of Bingen, Homilies on the Gospels. Trappist, KY 2011.

(SER) HUGO OF SAINT-CHER, Sermon on marriage, ed. and trans. D.L. D'AVRAY, Medieval Marriage Sermons: Mass Communication in a Culture Without Print. Oxford 2001, p. 151–165.

(T/INST) HUGO OF SAINT-VICTOR, De institutione novitiorum/De virtute orandi (On the education of novices/On the virtue of praying), ed. and trans. H.B. FEISS/D. POIREL/H. ROCHAIS/P. SICARD, L'oeuvre de Hugues de Saint-Victor, vol. 1. Turnhout 1997.

(T) IDUNG OF PRÜFENING, Dialogus duorum monachorum, ed. R.B.C. HUYGENS, Le moine Idung et ses deux ouvrages: 'Argumentum super quatuor questionibus' et 'Dialogus duorum monachorum', in Biblioteca degli Studi medievali 11. Spoleto 1980, p. 91–186, trans. J.F. O' SULLIVAN/J. LEAHEY, Cistercians and Cluniacs. The Case for Cîteaux. A Dialogue between two Monks. An Argument on Four Questions. Kalamazoo, MI 1977, p. 19–141.

(HIST/B) JORDANUS OF SAXONY, Libellus de initiis Ordinis Praedicatorum (Booklet on the beginnings of the Dominican Order), ed. and trans. H.C. SCHEEBEN, Monumenta Ordinis Praedicatorum historica 16 (1935), p. 25–88, also trans. W. HOYER, Jordan von Sachsen: Ordensmeister, Geschichtsschreiber, Beter. Eine Textsammlung. Leipzig 2002, p. 27–94 and M.H. VICAIRE, S. Dominique et ses frères. Paris 1967, p. 47–144.

(T) Libellus de diversis ordinibus et professionibus qui sunt in aecclesiae (Booklet on the diverse orders and professions that exist in the Church), ed. and trans. G. CONSTABLE/B. SMITH. Oxford 1972.

(HIST) Liber Eliensis (History of the Isle of Ely), ed. E.O. BLAKE. London 1962, trans. J. FAIRWEATHER. Woodbridge 2005.

(HAG) Life of Christina of Markyate, ed. and trans. C.H. TALBOT. Oxford 1987.

(HIST) MATTHEW PARIS, Chronicon (Chronicle), ed. and trans. R. VAUGHAN, Chronicles of Matthew Paris. Monastic Life in the Thirteenth Century. Gloucester 1984.

(PO) MECHTILD OF MAGDEBURG, Mystical revelations, ed. H. NEUMANN/G. VOLLMANN-PROFE, Mechthild von Magdeburg. Das fließende

Licht der Gottheit, 2 vols. Munich 1990–1993, trans. F. TOBIN, Mechthild of Magdeburg. The Flowing Light of the Godhead, New York, NY 1998 and G. VOLLMAN-PROFE, Das fließende Licht der Gottheit, Berlin 2010.

(HIST/R/CUST/INST) Narrative and Legislative Texts From Early Cîteaux, ed. and trans. C. WADDELL. Cîteaux 1999.

(HIST) ORDERIC VITALIS, Historia ecclesiastica (Ecclesiastical history), ed. and trans. M. CHIBNALL, The Ecclesiastical History of Orderic Vitalis, 6 vols. Oxford 1968–1980.

(L) PETER THE VENERABLE, Letters, ed. G. CONSTABLE, 2 vols. Cambridge, Mass 1967.

(HAG) PHILIP OF CLAIRVAUX, Vita Elisabethis monialis in Erkenrode (Life of Elisabeth of Spalbeek), ed. Catalogus codicum hagiographicorum bibliothecae Regiae Bruxellensis, vol. 1. Brussels 1886, p. 362–378, partial trans. E. SPEARING, Medieval Writings on Female Spirituality. New York, NY 2002, p. 107–119.

(PO/T) Relatio metrica de duobus ducibus. A Twelfth-Century Cluniac Poem on Prayer for the Dead, ed. and trans. C.A. JONES/S.G. BRUCE, Turnhout 2016.

(R) Rule of the Knights Templar, ed. G. SCHNÜRER, Die ursprüngliche Templerregel. Freiburg im Breisgau 1908, trans. L. DAILLIEZ/J.-P. LOMBARD, Règle et statuts de l'Ordre du Temple. Paris 1996.

(R) Rule of the Spanish Military Order of St. James, ed. E. GALLEGO BLANCO. Leiden 1971.

(T/HIST) RUPERT OF DEUTZ, De incendio Tuitiensi (On the fire at Deutz), ed. H. GRUNDMANN, Der Brand von Deutz 1128 in der Darstellung Abt Ruperts von Deutz. Interpretation und Text-Ausgabe, Deutsches Archiv für Erforschung des Mittelalters 22 (1966), p. 441–471, partial trans. W. BECKER, Der Brand von Deutz im Jahre 1128. Auszüge aus dem Buch De Incendio des Abtes Rupert von Deutz, Rechtsrheinisches Kölner Jahrbuch für Geschichte und Landeskunde 6 (1980), p. 121–139.

(SAG) La saga islandese di San Benedetto, ed. M. CAMIZ. Rome 2017.

(MEM) Mortuary rolls for Abbot Bruno of Cologne (d. 1100), Abbess Mathilda of Sainte-Trinité in Caen (d. 1113), and Abbot Vitalis of Savigny (d. 1122), ed. J. DUFOUR, Recueil des rouleaux des morts. (viiie siècle- 1536). 1: VIIIe siècle-1180. Paris 2005.

(T) SUGER OF SAINT-DENIS, Libellus de consecratione ecclesiae S. Dionysii (Booklet on the consecration of the church of Saint-Denis), ed. and trans. E. PANOFSKY/G. PANOFSKY-SOERGEL, Abbot Suger on the Abbey Church of St.-Denis and its Art Treasures. Princeton, NJ 1979 (revised edition).

(RIT) The Monastic Ritual of Fleury, ed. A. DAVRIL. London 1990.

(HAG/B) THOMAS OF CELANO, Three Early Lives of St Francis, ed. and trans. D. POIREL/J. DALARUN, Les vies de saint François d'Assise. Paris 2009 and J. DALARUN, La vie retrouvée de François d'Assise, Paris 2015, also trans. E. GRAU, Leben und Wunder des heiligen Franziskus von Assisi. Werl 1994 and J. DALARUN/J. SCHNEIDER, Das neuentdeckte Franziskusleben des Thomas von Celano. St. Ottilien 2017.

(T) Three Treatises from Bec on the Nature of Monastic Life, ed. and trans. G. CONSTABLE/B.S. SMITH. Toronto 2008.

(STAT) Statutes of the 1130s–1140s General Chapters of Benedictine Abbots of Reims, ed. S. VANDERPUTTEN, The Statutes of the Earliest General Chapters of Benedictine Abbots (1131–c. 1135/40), The Journal of Medieval Monastic History 5 (2016), p. 61–91.
(STAT) Statutes of the General Chapter of the Bursfeld Congregation, ed. P. VOLK, Die Generalkapitels-Rezesse der Bursfelder Kongregation, 4 vols. Siegburg 1955–1972.
(STAT) Statutes of the General Chapter of the Dominicans, ed. B. REICHERT, Acta Capitulorum Generalium Ordinis Praedicatorum. Rome 1898–1905 and G.M. LÖHR, Supplementum ad Acta Capitulorum Generalium editionis B. Reichert, Archivum Fratrum Praedicatorum 5 (1935), p. 289–310.
(STAT/ARCH/HIST) Documents on the origins and early development of the Franciscan Third Order, ed. and trans. Testi e documenti sul Terzo Ordine Francescano (sec. XIII–XV). Rome 1991.
(HIST) JOHN TRITHEMIUS, Annales Hirsaugienses, ed. J.G. SCHLEGEL, 2 vols. St Gall 1690.
(STAT) Twelfth-Century Statutes from the Cistercian General Chapter, ed. and trans. C. WADDELL. Cîteaux 2002.
(HAG) Vita Stephani Obazinensis (Life of Stephen of Obazine), ed. and trans. M. AUBRUN, Vie de Saint Etienne d'Obazine. Clermont-Ferrand 1970, also trans. H. FEISS/M. O'BRIEN/R. PEPIN, Robert of La Chaise-Dieu and Stephen of Obazine. Collegeville, MN 2010.

2 The Beginnings of Monasticism(s)

2.1 Earliest Monasticisms

K. BOWES, Private Worship, Public Value, and Religious Change in Late Antiquity. Cambridge 2008.
D.L. BROOKS HEDSTROM, The Monastic Landscape of Late Antique Egypt. An Archaeological Reconstruction. Cambridge 2017.
D.F. CANER, Wandering, Begging Monks. Spiritual Authority and the Promotion of Monasticism in Late Antiquity. Berkeley, CA 2002.
K. COOPER. The Virgin and the Bride. Idealized Womanhood in Late Antiquity. Cambridge, Mass 1996.
H.W. DEY, Diaconiae, xenodochia, hospitalia and Monasteries: 'Social Security' and the Meaning of Monasticism in Early Medieval Rome, Early Medieval Europe 16 (2008), p. 398–422.
A. DIEM/P. ROUSSEAU, Monastic Rules (4th–9th Centuries), in A. BEACH/ I. COCHELIN (ed.), The Cambridge History of Medieval Monasticism in the Latin West, 2 vols. Cambridge 2020, p. 162–194.
L. DOSSEY, The Social Space of North African Asceticism, in H.W. DEY/E. FENTRESS (ed.), Western Monasticism ante litteram. The

Space of Monastic Observance in Late Antiquity and the Early Middle Ages. Turnhout 2011, p. 137–157.

S. Elm, Virgins of God. The Making of Asceticism in Late Antiquity. Oxford 1994.

G. Frank, The Memory of the Eyes. Pilgrims to Living Saints in Christian Late Antiquity. Berkeley, CA 2000.

W. Harmless, Desert Christians. An Introduction to the Literature of Early Monasticism. Oxford 2004.

A.-M. Helvétius, Normes et pratiques de la vie monastique en Gaule avant 1050: Présentation des sources écrites, in O. Delouis/M. Mossakowska Gaubert (ed.), La vie quotidienne des moines en Orient et en Occident (IVe-Xe siècle). 1: L'état des sources. Cairo 2015, p. 371–386.

A.-M. Helvétius, Le monachisme féminin en Occident de l'Antiquité tardive au haut Moyen Age, in Monachesimi d'oriente e d'occidente nell'alto medioevo, 2 vols. Spoleto 2017, vol. 1, p. 193–230.

P. Laurence, Le monachisme féminin antique: Idéal hiéronymien et réalité historique. Louvain 2010.

C. Leyser, Authority and Asceticism from Augustine to Gregory the Great. Oxford 2000.

E. Magnani, Female House Ascetics, From the Fourth to the Twelfth Centuries, in A. Beach/I. Cochelin (ed.), The Cambridge History of Medieval Monasticism in the Latin West, 2 vols. Cambridge 2020, p. 213–231.

C. Rapp, The Social Organization of Early Monasticism in the East: Challenging Old Paradigms, in Monachesimi d'oriente e d'occidente nell'alto medioevo, 2 vols. Spoleto 2017, vol. 1, p. 33–52.

L. Ripart, De Lérins à Agaune: Le monachisme rhodanien reconsidéré, in Monachesimi d'oriente e d'occidente nell'alto medioevo, 2 vols. Spoleto 2017, vol. 1, p. 123–186.

B.H. Rosenwein, One Site, Many Meanings: Saint-Maurice d'Agaune as a Place of Power in the Early Middle Ages, in M. De Jong/F. Theuws (ed.), Topographies of Power in the Early Middle Ages. Leiden 2001, p. 271–290.

S. Rubenson, Christian Asceticism and the Emergence of the Monastic Tradition, in V.L. Wimbusch/R. Valantasis (ed.), Asceticism. New York, NY 1998, p. 49–57.

E. Wipzycka, Moines et communautés monastiques en Egypte (IVe–VIIIe siècles). Warsaw 2009.

2.2 The 'Rise of Cenobitism'

D.L. Brooks Hedstrom, The Geography of the Monastic Cell in Early Egyptian Monastic Literature, Church History 78 (2009), p. 756–791.

G. Clark, Women and Asceticism in Late Antiquity: The Refusal of Status and Gender, in V.L. Wimbush/R. Valantasis (ed.), Asceticism. New York, NY 1998, p. 33–48.

H. Dey, Building Worlds Apart: Walls and the Construction of Communal
Monasticism from Augustine Through Benedict, Antiquité tardive 12
(2004), p. 357–371.
L. Dossey, The Social Space of North African Asceticism, in H. Dey/E. Fentress
(ed.), Western Monasticism ante litteram. The Spaces of Monastic Observance
in Late Antiquity and the Early Middle Ages. Turnhout 2011, p. 137–157.
R. Finn, Asceticism in the Graeco-Roman World. Cambridge 2009.
D. Istria/P. Pergola, Moines et monastères dans les îles des mers Ligure et
Tyrrhénienne (Corse, Sardaigne, archipel toscan et archipel ligure), Hortus
Artium Medievalium 19 (2013), p. 73–78.
G. Jenal, Italia ascetica atque monastica. Das Asketen- und Mönchtum in
Italien von den Anfängen bis zur Zeit der Langobarden (ca. 150/250–604),
2 vols. Stuttgart 1995.
J. Patrich, Sabas, Leader of Palestinian Monasticism: A Comparative Study in
Eastern Monasticism, Fourth to Seventh Centuries. Washington, DC 1995.
P. Rousseau, Pachomius: The Making of a Community in Fourth-Century Egypt.
Berkeley, CA 1985.
S.J.-G. Sanchez, Priscillien, un chrétien non-conformiste: Doctrine et pratique
du priscillianisme du IVe au VIe siècle. Paris 2009.

2.3 Early Cenobitisms in Southern Gaul

R. Alciati, Monaci, vescovi et scuola nella Gallia tardoantica. Rome 2009.
R. Alciati, And the Villa Became a Monastery: Sulpicius Severus' Community
of Primuliacium, in H. Dey/E. Fentress (ed.), Western Monasticism ante
litteram. The Spaces of Monastic Observance in Late Antiquity and the
Early Middle Ages. Turnhout 2011, p. 85–98.
Y. Codou/M. Lauwers (ed.), Lérins, une île sainte de l'antiquité au Moyen Age.
Turnhout 2009.
A. Diem, Das monastische Experiment: Die Rolle der Keuschheit bei der
Entstehung des westlichen Klosterwesens. Münster 2005.
A. Diem, Inventing the Holy Rule: Some Observations on the History of
Monastic Normative Observance in the Early Medieval West, in H.
Dey/E. Fentress (ed.), Western Monasticism ante litteram. The Spaces
of Monastic Observance in Late Antiquity and the Early Middle Ages.
Turnhout 2011, p. 53–84.
A. Diem, ...ut si professus fuerit se omnia impleturum, tunc excipiatur.
Observations on the Rules for Monks and Nuns of Caesarius and
Aurelianus of Arles, in V. Zimmerl-Panagl (ed.), Edition und Erforschung
lateinischer patristischer Texte: 150 Jahre CSEL. Festschrift für Kurt
Smolak zum 70. Geburtstag. Berlin 2014, p. 191–224.
M. Fixot/J.-P. Pelletier (ed.), Saint Victor de Marseille: Etudes archéologiques
et historiques. Turnhout 2009.
R.J. Goodrich, Contextualizing Cassian: Aristocrats, Asceticism, and
Reformation in Fifth-century Gaul. Oxford 2007.

A.-M. Helvétius, L'abbaye de Saint-Maurice d'Agaune dans le haut Moyen Age, in N. Brocard/F. Vannotti/A. Wagner (ed.), Autour de Saint-Maurice. Actes du colloque Politique, Société et construction identitaire. Saint-Maurice 2012, p. 113–130.

M.-C. Isaia/T. Granier (ed.), Normes et hagiographie dans l'Occident latin (VIe–XVIe siècle). Turnhout 2014.

C.M. Kasper, Theologie und Askese: Die Spiritualität des Inselmönchtums von Lérins im 5. Jahrhundert. Münster 1991.

M. Lauwers, Interiora et exteriora, ou la construction monastique d'un espace social en Occident entre le Ve et le XIIe siècle, in M. Botazzi/P. Buffo/C. Ciccopiedi et al. (ed.), La società monastica nei secoli VI–XII: Sentieri di ricerca. Trieste 2016, p. 59–88.

F. Prinz, Frühes Mönchtum im Frankenreich. Kultur und Gesellschaft in Gallien, den Rheinlanden und Bayern am Beispiel der monastischen Entwicklung (4. bis 8. Jahrhundert). Darmstadt 1988 (second edition).

L. Rudge, Dedicated Women and Dedicated Spaces: Caesarius of Arles and the Foundation of St John, in H.W. Dey/E. Fentress (ed.), Western Monasticism ante litteram. The Space of Monastic Observance in Late Antiquity and the Early Middle Ages. Turnhout 2011, p. 99–116.

C. Scherliess, Literatur und conversio: Literarische Formen im monastischen Umkreis des Klosters von Lérins. Frankfurt am Main 2000.

2.4 Experiments on the Italian and Iberian Peninsulas

S. Bully/E. Destefanis, The Archaeology of the Earliest Monasteries in Italy and France (Second Half of the Fourth Century to the Eighth Century) in A. Beach/I. Cochelin (ed.), The Cambridge History of Medieval Monasticism in the Latin West, 2 vols. Cambridge 2020, p. 232–257.

F. Clark, The 'Gregorian' "Dialogues" and the Origins of Benedictine Monasticism. Leiden 2003.

A. De Vogüé, The Master and St Benedict: A Reply to Marilyn Dunn, The English Historical Review 112 (1992), p. 95–103.

P.C. Díaz, Monasticism and Liturgy in Visigothic Spain, in A. Ferreiro (ed.), The Visigoths. Studies in Culture and Society. Leiden 1999, p. 169–199.

P.C. Díaz, Regula Communis. Monastic Space and Social Context, in H.W. Dey/E. Fentress (ed.), Western Monasticism ante litteram. The Space of Monastic Observance in Late Antiquity and the Early Middle Ages. Turnhout 2011, p. 117–135.

P.C. Díaz, Visigothic Monasticism. Written Sources and Everyday Life, in O. Delouis/M. Mossakowska Gaubert (ed.), La vie quotidienne des moines en Orient et en Occident (IVe–Xe siècle). 1: L'état des sources. Cairo 2015, p. 339–351.

A. Diem/C. Rapp, The Monastic Laboratory: Perspectives of Research in Late Antique and Early Medieval Monasticism, in A. Beach/I. Cochelin (ed.),

The Cambridge History of Medieval Monasticism in the Latin West, 2 vols. Cambridge 2020, p. 19–39.

M. Dunn, The Emergence of Monasticism. From the Desert Fathers to the Early Middle Ages. Oxford 2000.

J.A. García de Cortázar y Ruiz de Aguirre (ed.), El monacato espontáneo: Eremitas y eremitorios en el mundo medieval. Aguilar de Campóo 2011.

J. Fried, Der Schleier der Erinnerung. Grundzüge einer historischen Memorik. Munich 2004.

L.A. García Moreno, Los monjes y monasterios en las ciudades de las Españas tardoromanos y visigodas, Habis 24 (1993), p. 179–192.

C. Leyser, Charisma in the Archive: Roman Monasteries and the Memory of Gregory the Great, c. 870–c. 940, in F. De Rubeis/W. Pohl (ed.), Le scritture dei monasteri. Rome 2003, p. 207–226.

J. López Quiroga/A.M. Martínez Tejera/J. Morín de Pablos (ed.), Monasteria et territoria: Elites, edilicia y territorio en el Mediterráneo medieval (siglos V–XI). Oxford 2007.

J. López Quiroga, Monasterios altomedievales hispanos: Lugares de emplazamiento y ordenación de sus espacios, XXIX Seminario sobre Historia del Monacato (2016), p. 66–99.

B. Müller, Gregory the Great and Monasticism, in N. Bronwen/M.J. Dal Santo (ed.), A Companion to Gregory the Great. Leiden 2013, p. 83–108.

K. Rennie, Freedom and Protection. Monastic Exemption in France, c. 590–c. 1100. Manchester 2018.

J. Salgado Raffaeli, Conflito e legitimario: O eremitismo na auto-hagiografía de Valerio do Bierro (século VII), in L. Rodrigues da Silva/P. Duarte Silva/R. Ballesteiro Pereira Tomaz/B. Borgonino (ed.), A igreja em construção. Poder e discurso cristão na Alta Idade Média (séculos IV–VIII). Rio de Janeiro 2013, p. 167–189.

F.R. Stassola, Il monachesimo in Italia dalle origini a Gregorio Magno: Modalità insediative, architetture, organizzazione topografica e spaziale, in Monachesimi d'oriente e d'occidente nell'alto medioevo, 2 vols. Spoleto 2017, vol. 1, p. 321–353.

D. von der Nahmer, Martin von Tours. Sein Mönchtum, seine Wirkung, Francia 15 (1987), p. 1–42.

J. Wollasch, Benedikt von Nursia. Person der Geschichte oder fiktive Idealgestalt?, Studien und Mitteilungen zur Geschichte des Benediktinerordens und seiner Zweige 118 (2007), p. 7–30.

J. Wood, The Politics of Identity in Visigothic Spain Religion and Power in the Histories of Isidore of Seville. Leiden 2012.

2.5 Irish and 'Iro-Frankisch' Monasticisms

J. Blair, The Church in Anglo-Saxon Society. Oxford 2005.

S. Bully/A. Dubreucq/A. Bully (ed.), Columban et son influence. Moines et monastères du Haut Moyen Âge en Europe/Columbanus and his influence. Monks and monasteries in early medieval Europe/Colombano e la sua influenza. Monaci et monasteri nell'alto medioevo in Europa. Rennes 2018.

T. COLLINS, An Archaeological Perspective on Female Monasticism in the Middle Ages, in J. BURTON/K. STÖBER (ed.), Women in the Medieval Monastic World. Turnhout 2015, p. 229–252.

E. DAWSON, The Vita Patricii by Tírechán and the Creation of St Patrick's Nationwide Status in Seventh-Century Ireland, in T.F. HEAD/G. KLANICZAY et al. (ed.), Cuius Patrocinio Tota Gaudet Regio. Saints' Cults and the Dynamics of Regional Cohesion, Zagreb 2014, p. 1–20.

A. DIEM, Columbanian Monastic Rules: Dissent and Experiment, in R. FLECHNER/S.M. MEEDER (ed.), The Irish in Early Medieval Europe: Identity, Culture and Religion. London 2016, p. 68–85 and 248–249.

C. ETCHINGHAM, Bishops and Abbots in the Early Irish Church, with some Observations on the Irish Perception of Rome, in Chiese locali e chiese regionali nell'alto medioevo, 2 vols. Spoleto 2014, vol. 2, p. 1073–1094.

Y. FOX, Power and Religion in Merovingian Gaul: Columbanian Monasticism and the Frankish Elites. Cambridge 2014.

Y. FOX, The Political Context of Irish Monasticism in Seventh-Century Francia: Another Look at the Sources, in R. FLECHNER/S.M. MEEDER (ed.), The Irish in Early Medieval Europe: Identity, Culture and Religion. London 2016, p. 53–67.

M. GAILLARD, Les fondations d'abbayes féminines dans le Nord et l'Est de la Gaule à la fin du VIe siècle, Revue d'histoire de l'église de France 76 (1990), p. 6–20.

S. HAARLÄNDER, Innumerabiles populi de utroque sexu confluentes (...). Klöster für Männer und Frauen im frühmittelalterlichen Irland, in G. MELVILLE/A. MÜLLER (ed.), Female vita religiosa between Late Antiquity and the High Middle Ages. Structures, Developments and Spatial Contexts. Münster 2011, p. 137–150.

M. HERITY, Studies in the Layout, Buildings and Art in Stone of Early Irish Monasteries. London 1995.

A. KEHNEL, Clonmacnois. The Church and Lands of St. Ciarán. Change and Continuity in an Irish Monastic Foundation (6th to 16th Century). Münster 1997.

E. MARRON, In his silvis silere. The Monastic Site of Annegray: Studies in a Columbanian Landscape. Unpublished doctoral dissertation, National University of Ireland 2012 (https://aran.library.nuigalway.ie/handle/ 10379/3361?show=full, accessed 27 June 2018).

M. RICHTER, Bobbio in the Early Middle Ages. Dublin 2008.

G. THOMAS/A. KNOX (ed.), Early Medieval Monasticism in the North Sea Zone. Oxford 2017, p. 17–24.

I. WOOD, Columbanian Monasticism: A Contested Concept, in R. FLECHNER/S.M. MEEDER (ed.), The Irish in Early Medieval Europe: Identity, Culture and Religion. London 2016, p. 86–115.

I. WOOD, Merovingian Monasticism and England, in G. THOMAS/A. KNOX (ed.), Early Medieval Monasticism in the North Sea Zone. Oxford 2017, p. 17–24.

B. Yorke, Queen Bathildis' Monastic Policy and the Origins of Female
Religious Houses in Southern England, in G. Thomas/A. Knox (ed.), Early
Medieval Monasticism in the North Sea Zone. Oxford 2017, p. 7–16.

2.6 Monastic Experiences at the Dawn of the Eighth Century

G. Andenna, San Salvatore di Brescia e la scelta religiosa delle donne
aristocratiche tra eta langobarda ed eta franca (VIII–IX secolo), in
G. Melville/A. Müller (ed.), Female vita religiosa between Late Antiquity
and the High Middle Ages. Structures, Developments and Spatial
Contexts. Münster 2011, p. 209–233.
A. De Vogüé, Histoire littéraire du mouvement monastique dans l'antiquité.
Première partie: Le monachisme latin, 11 vols. Paris 1991–2007.
H.W. Dey, Public Service or Private Devotion? The Diverse Faces of Monasticism
in Late Antique and Early Medieval Rome, Acta Ad Archaeologiam et
Artium Historiam Pertinentia 33 (2011), p. 209–228.
F. Felten, Frauenklöster im Frankenreich. Entwicklungen und Probleme von
den Anfängen bis zum frühen 9. Jahrhundert, in S. Lorenz/T. Zotz (ed.),
Frühformen von Stiftskirchen in Europa: Funktion und Wandel religiöser
Gemeinschaften vom 6. bis zum Ende des 11. Jahrhunderts. Leinfelden-
Echterdingen 2005, p. 31–95.
R. Flechner, Identifying Monks in Early Medieval Britain and Ireland:
A Reflection on Legal and Economic Aspects, in Monachesimi d'oriente
e d'occidente nell'alto medioevo, 2 vols. Spoleto 2017, vol. 2,
p. 805–844.
R. Flechner/S.M. Meeder (ed.), The Irish in Early Medieval Europe: Identity,
Culture and Religion. London 2016.
L'origine des sites monastiques: Confrontation entre la terminologie des
sources textuelles et les données archéologiques. Auxerre 2016 (http://
journals.openedition.org/cem/14481, accessed 14 March 2018).
E. Louis, Espaces monastiques sacrés et profanes à Hamage (Nord), VIIe–IXe
siècles, in M. Lauwers (ed.), Monastères et espace social. Génèse et
transformation d'un système de lieux dans l'occident médiéval. Turnhout
2014, p. 435–471.
R. McKitterick, Nun's Scriptoria in England and Francia in the Eighth Century,
Francia 19 (1992), p. 1–35.
M. Richter, Bobbio in the Early Middle Ages. Dublin 2008.
J.-M. Sansterre, Les moines grecs et orientaux à Rome aux époques byzantine
et carolingienne (milieu du VIe s.-fin du IXe s.), 2 vols. Brussels 1993.
V. West-Harting (ed.), Female Monasticism in Italy in the Early Middle Ages:
New Questions, New Debates (special issue of Reti Medievali). Firenze
2019.
I. Wood, Merovingian Monasticism and England, in G. Thomas/A. Knox (ed.),
Early Medieval Monasticism in the North Sea Zone. Oxford 2017, p. 17–24.

3 Early and High Medieval Monasticisms

3.1 Continuities and Transformations in the Long Eighth Century

S. Airlie, The Frankish Aristrocracy as Supporters and Opponents of Boniface, in F.J. Felten/J. Jarnut/L.E. von Padberg (ed.), Bonifatius – Leben und Nachwirken: Die Gestaltung des christlichen Europa im Frühmittelalter. Mainz 2007, p. 255–270.

J.S. Barrow, Ideas and Applications of Reform, in T.F.X. Noble/J.M.H. Smith (ed.), The Cambridge History of Christianity 3: Early Medieval Christianities, c. 600–1100. Cambridge 2008, p. 345–362.

K. Bodarwé, Eine Männerregel für Frauen. Die Adaption der Benediktsregel im 9. und 10. Jahrhundert, in G. Melville/A. Müller (ed.), Female vita religiosa between Late Antiquity and the High Middle Ages. Structures, Developments and Spatial Contexts. Münster 2011, p. 235–274.

C.M. Booker, Iusta murmuratio: The Sound of Scandal in the Early Middle Ages, Revue bénédictine 126 (2016), p. 236–270.

R.S. Choy, Intercessory Prayer and the Monastic Ideal in the Time of the Carolingian Reforms. Oxford 2016.

J. Contreni, Learning for God: Education in the Carolingian Age, The Journal of Medieval Latin 24 (2014), p. 89–129.

F. Cusimano, La biografia di Benedetto di Aniane tra storia e topoi agiografici, in A. Bartolomei Romagnoli/U. Paoli/P. Piatti (ed.), Hagiologica: Studi per Réginald Grégoire, 2 vols. Fabriano 2012, vol. 2, p. 693–726.

M.A. Clausen, The Reform of the Frankish Church: Chrodegang of Metz and the Regula canonicorum in the Eighth Century. Cambridge 2004.

M. De Jong, Carolingian Monasticism: The Power of Prayer, in R. McKitterick (ed.), New Cambridge Medieval History II: c. 700–c. 900. Cambridge 1995, p. 622–653.

P. Engelbert, Benedikt von Aniane und der Codex regularum Clm 28118 der bayerischen Staatsbibliothek München, Studia monastica 57 (2015), p. 69–90.

F. Felten, Auf dem Weg zu Kanonissen und Kanonissenstift. Ordnungskonzepte der weiblichen vita religiosa bis ins 9. Jahrhundert, in I. Crusius (ed.), Vita religiosa sanctimonialium: Norm und Praxis des weiblichen religiösen Lebens vom 6. bis zum 13. Jahrhundert. Korb 2005, p. 71–92.

D. Geuenich, Kritische Anmerkungen zur sogenannten "anianischen Reform", in D.R. Bauer/R. Hiestand/B. Kasten/S. Lorenz (ed.), Mönchtum – Kirche – Herrschaft 750–1000: Josef Semmler zum 65. Geburtstag. Sigmaringen 1998, p. 99–112.

W. Kettemann, Subsidia Anianensia. Überlieferungs- und textgeschichtliche Untersuchungen zur Geschichte Witiza-Benedikts, seines Klosters Aniane und zur sogenannten "anianischen Reform". Unpublished doctoral dissertation, Universität Duisburg 1999.

R. Kottje, Einheit und Vielfalt des kirchlichen Lebens in der Karolingerzeit, Zeitschrift für Kirchengeschichte 76 (1965), p. 323–342.

R. Kramer, Rethinking Authority in the Carolingian Empire. Ideals and Expectations during the Reign of Louis the Pious (813–828). Amsterdam 2019.

S. Meeder, Monte Cassino and Carolingian Politics Around 800, in R. Meens (ed.), Religious Franks: Religion and Power in the Frankish Kingdoms. Studies in Honour of Mayke de Jong. Manchester 2016, p. 279–295.

M. Parisse, Religieux et religieuses en Empire du Xe au XIIe siècle. Paris 2011.

H.-C. Picker, Der St. Galler Klosterplan als Konzept eines weltoffenen Mönchtums: Ist Walahfrid Strabo der Verfasser?, Zeitschrift für Kirchengeschichte 119 (2008), p. 1–29.

M. Ponesse, Smaragdus of St Mihiel and the Carolingian Monastic Reform, Revue bénédictine 116 (2006), p. 367–392.

J. Raaijmakers, The Making of the Monastic Community of Fulda, c. 744–c. 900. Cambridge 2012.

T. Schilp, Norm und Wirklichkeit religiöser Frauengemeinschaften im Frühmittelalter. Göttingen 1998.

L. Schneider, Une fondation multiple, un monastère pluriel. Les contextes topographiques de la genèse du monastère d'Aniane d'après l'archéologie et la vie de saint Benoît (fin VIIIe–IXe siècle), in L'origine des sites monastiques: confrontation entre la terminologie des sources textuelles et les données archéologique. Auxerre 2016 (http://journals.openedition.org/cem/14481, accessed 14 March 2018).

J. Semmler, Benedictus II: una regula – una consuetudo, in W. Lourdaux/D. Verhelst (ed.), Benedictine Culture 750–1050. Leuven 1983, p. 1–49.

J. Semmler, Monachus – clericus – canonicus: Zur Ausdifferenzierung geistlicher Institutionen im Frankenreich bis ca. 900, in S. Lorenz/T. Zotz (ed.), Frühformen von Stiftskirchen in Europa: Funktion und Wandel religiöser Gemeinschaften vom 6. bis zum Ende des 11. Jahrhunderts, Leinfelden-Echterdingen 2005, p. 1–18.

G. Schmitz, Zu den Quellen der Institutio Sanctimonialium Ludwigs des Frommen (a. 816). Die Homiliensammlung des Codex Paris lat. 13440, Deutsches Archiv für Erforschung des Mittelalters 68 (2012), p. 23–52.

S. Vanderputten, Dark Age Nunneries. The Ambiguous Identity of Female Monasticism, 800–1050. Ithaca, NY 2018.

3.2 Ninth-Century Monasticisms

G. Althoff/K. Schmid (ed.), Die Klostergemeinschaft von Fulda im früheren Mittelalter, 3 vols. Munich 1978.

J. Billet, The Divine Office in Anglo-Saxon England, 597–c. 1000. Woodbridge 2019.

G. Boto Varela, Topografía de los monasterios de la Marca de Hispania (ca. 800–ca. 1030), in J.A. García de Cortázar y Ruiz de Aguirre/R. Teja Casuso (ed.), Monjes y monasterios hispanos en la edad media. Aguilar de Campos 2006, p. 147–203.

S. Bully/C. Sapin (ed.), Au seuil du cloître: La présence des laïcs (hôtelleries, bâtiments d'accueil, activités artisanales et de services) entre le Ve et le XIIe siècle. Auxerre 2015 (https://journals.openedition.org/cem/13574?lang=en, accessed 14 March 2018).

E.-M. Butz, Herrschergedenken als Spiegel von Konsens und Kooperation. Zur politischen Einordnung von Herrschereinträgen in den frühmittelalterlichen Libri memorialis, in D. Geuenich/U. Ludwig (ed.), Libri vitae. Gebetsgedenken in der Gesellschaft des Frühen Mittelalters. Cologne 2015, p. 305–328.

G. Calvet-Marcadé, L'abbé spoliateur de biens monastiques (Francie du Nord, IXe siècle), in P. Depreux/F. Bougard/R. Le Jan (ed.), Compétition et sacré au Haut Moyen Age: Entre médiation et exclusion. Turnhout 2015, p. 313–327.

J. Contreni, Learning for God: Education in the Carolingian Age, The Journal of Medieval Latin 24 (2014), p. 89–129.

L.L. Coon, Dark Age Bodies. Gender and Monastic Practice in the Early Medieval West. Philadelphia, PA 2011.

M. De Jong, In Samuel's Image. Child Oblation in the Early Medieval West. Leiden 1996.

M. De Jong, Charlemagne's Church, in J.E. Story (ed.), Charlemagne: Empire and Society, Manchester 2005, p. 103–135.

J.-P. Devroey, Monastic Economics in the Carolingian Age, in A. Beach/I. Cochelin (ed.), The Cambridge History of Medieval Monasticism in the Latin West, 2 vols. Cambridge 2020, p. 466–484.

F. Felten, Äbte und Laienäbte im Frankenreich. Studie zum Verhältnis von Staat und Kirche im früheren Mittelalter. Stuttgart 1980.

K.S. Frank, Grimlaicus, 'Regula solitarium', in F.J. Felten/N. Jaspert (ed.), Vita religiosa im Mittelalter: Festschrift für Kaspar Elm zum 70. Geburtstag. Berlin 1999, p. 21–35.

V.R. Garver, Learned Women? Liutberga and the Instruction of Carolingian Women, in P. Wormald/J.L. Nelson (ed.), Lay Intellectuals in the Carolingian World. Cambridge 2007, p. 121–138.

D. Geuenich/U. Ludwig (ed.), Libri vitae. Gebetsdenken in der Gesellschaft des Frühen Mittelalters. Cologne 2015.

C. Heitz, L'architecture religieuse carolingienne. Les formes et leurs fonctions, Paris 1980.

A.-M. Helvétius, L'abbatiat laïque comme relais du pouvoir royal aux frontières du royaume: Le cas du nord de la Neustrie au IXe siècle, in R. Le Jan (ed.), La royauté et les élites dans l'Europe Carolingienne (du début du IXe aux environs de 920). Villeneuve d'Ascq 1998, p. 285–299.

G. Jordan, "Nichts als Nahrung und Kleidung": Laien und Kleriker als Wohngäste bei den Mönchen von St. Gallen und Redon (8. und 9. Jahrhundert). Berlin 2007.

S. Joye/P. Bertrand, Les "testaments des saints" en Chrétienté occidentale, in M.-C. Isaïa/T. Garnier (ed.), Normes et hagiographie dans l'Occident (VIe–XVIe siècle). Turnhout 2014, p. 293–307.

E. Kurdziel, Chanoines et institutions canoniales dans les villes du royaume d'Italie, du milieu du IXe au milieu du XIe siècle. Unpublished doctoral dissertation, Université de Paris 2015.

M. Lauwers, Circuitus et figura. Exégèse, images et structuration des complexes monastiques dans l'occident médiéval (IXe–XII siècle), in M. Lauwers (ed.), Monastères et espace social. Génèse et transformation d'un système de lieux dans l'occident médiéval. Turnhout 2014, p. 42–109.

S. Lebecq, The Role of Monasteries in the Systems of Production and Exchange of the Frankish World between the Seventh and the Ninth Centuries, in I. Lyse Hansen/C. Wickham (ed.), The Long Eighth Century: Production, Distribution and Demand. Leiden 2000, p. 121–148.

S. Maclean, Queenship, Nunneries and Royal Widowhood in Carolingian Europe, Past and Present 178 (2003), p. 3–38.

F. Marazzi, La règle et le projet. Réflexions sur la topographie du monastère de Saint-Vincent au Volturne à l'époque carolingienne, in M. Lauwers (ed.), Monastères et espace social. Génèse et transformation d'un système de lieux dans l'occident médiéval. Turnhout 2014, p. 227–253.

H.W. Matis, The Seclusion of Eustochium: Paschasius Radbertus and the Nuns of Soissons, Church History 85 (2016), p. 665–689.

O.G. Oexle, Forschungen zu monastischen und geistlichen Gemeinschaften im westfränkischen Bereich, Munich 1978.

M.-L. Pain (ed.), Groupes cathédraux et complexes monastiques. Le phénomène de la pluralité des sanctuaires à l'époque carolingienne. Rennes 2015.

T. Reuter, "Kirchenreform" und "Kirchenpolitik" im Zeitalter Karl Martells: Begriffe und Wirklichkeit, in J. Jarnut (ed.), Karl Martell in seiner Zeit. Sigmaringen 1994, p. 34–59.

J.T. Schulenburg, Strict Active Enclosure and its Effects on the Female Monastic Experience, ca. 500–1100, in J.A. Nichols/L.T. Shank (ed.), Medieval Religious Women, 1: Distant Echoes. Kalamazoo, MI 1984, p. 51–86.

R. Sullivan, What was Carolingian Monasticism? The Plan of St Gall and the History of Monasticism, in A.C. Murray (ed.), After Rome's Fall. Narrators and Sources of Early Medieval History. Toronto 1998, p. 251–287.

A. Trumbore Jones, "The Most Blessed Hilary Held an Estate": Property, Reform, and the Canonical Life in Tenth-Century Aquitaine, Church History 85 (2016), p. 1–39.

S.F. Wemple, Women in Frankish Society. Marriage and the Cloister, 500 to 900. Philadelphia, PA 1981.

J. Wollasch, Das Projekt 'Societas et Fraternitas', in D. Geuenich/O.G. Oexle (ed.), Memoria in der Gesellschaft des Mittelalters. Göttingen 1994, p. 11–31.

3.3 Restorations, Reforms, and The Problem of Monastic Lordship

G. ALTHOFF, Ottonische Frauengemeinschaften im Spannungsfeld von Kloster und Welt, in J. GERCHOW/T. SCHILP (ed.), Essen und die sächsischen Frauenstifte im Frühmittelalter. Essen 2003, p. 22–49.

G. ANDENNA, Cum monasteriis, cellis, ecclesiis, curtibus et mansis: I monasteri autocefali altomedievali e le loro dipendenze, in N. D'ACUNTO (ed.), Dinamiche istituzionali delle reti monastiche e canonicali nell'Italia dei secoli X–XII. Negarine di S. Pietro in Cariano 2007, p. 33–59.

N. BEREND/J. LASZLOVSZKY/B. ZSOLT SZAKÁCS, The Kingdom of Hungary, in N. BEREND (ed.), Christianization and the Rise of Christian Monarchy: Scandinavia, Central Europe and Rus' c. 900–1200. Cambridge 2007, p. 319–368.

J.W. BERNHARDT, Itinerant Kingship and Royal Monasteries in Early Medieval Germany, c. 936–1075. Cambridge 1993.

E. BOSHOF, Kloster und Bischof in Lotharingen, in R. KOTTJE/H. MAURER (ed.), Monastische Reformen im 9. und 10. Jahrhundert. Sigmaringen 1989, p. 197–245.

N. BULST, Untersuchungen zu den Klosterreformen Wilhelms von Dijon (962–1031). Bonn 1973.

G. CONSTABLE, Cluny in the Monastic World of the Tenth Century, in The Abbey of Cluny. A Collection of Essays to Mark the Eleven-Hundredth Anniversary of its Foundation. Münster 2010, p. 43–80.

C. CUBITT, Abbots as a Human Resource in the English Benedictine Reforms, in S. VANDERPUTTEN (ed.), Abbots and Abbesses as a Human Resource in the Ninth- to Twelfth-Century West. Zürich 2018, p. 25–38.

N. D'ACUNTO, Abbots as Human Resources in Tenth- and Eleventh-century Italy, in S. VANDERPUTTEN (ed.), Abbots and Abbesses as a Human Resource in the Ninth- to Twelfth-Century West. Zürich 2018, p. 57–75.

M. DELL'OMO, Montecassino altomedievale e il suo sistema di dipendenze: Genesi e fenomeno di un'irradiazione patrimoniale e giurisdizionale, in N. D'ACUNTO (ed.), Dinamiche istituzionali delle reti monastiche e canonicali nell'Italia dei secoli X–XII. Negarine di S. Pietro in Cariano 2007, p. 101–114.

D. IOGNA-PRAT, La geste des origines dans l'historiographie clunisienne des XIe–XIIe siècles, Revue bénédictine 102 (1992), p. 135–191.

J. JARRETT, Power over Past and Future: Abbess Emma and the Nunnery of Sant Joan de les Abadesses, Early Medieval Europe 12 (2003), p. 229–258.

G. KOZIOL, The Politics of Memory and Identity in Carolingian Royal Diplomas. The West Frankish Kingdom (840–987). Turnhout 2012.

L.K. LITTLE, Benedictine Maledictions. Liturgical Cursing in Romanesque France. Ithaca, NY 1993.

I. LORÉS, Monastères du Xe siècle en Espagne: Nouvelles approches, in D. IOGNA-PRAT/M. LAUWERS/F. MAZEL/I. ROSÉ (ed.), Cluny: Les moines et la société au premier âge féodal. Rennes 2013, p. 561–573.

F. Mazel, Amitié et rupture de l'amitié: Moines et grands laïcs provençaux au temps de la crise grégorienne (milieu XI-milieu XII siècle), Revue historique 307 (2005), p. 53–96.

F. Mazel, Monachisme et aristocratie aux Xe–XIe siècles. Un regard sur l'historiographie récente, in S. Vanderputten/B. Meijns (ed.), Ecclesia in medio nationis. Reflections on the Study of Monasticism in the Central Middle Ages/Réflexions sur l'étude du monachisme au Moyen Age Central. Leuven 2011, p. 47–75.

D. Méhu, Paix et communautés autour de l'abbaye de Cluny, Xe–XVe siècle. Lyon 2010.

D. Müller-Wiegand, Vermitteln – beraten – erinnern: Funktionen und Aufgabenfelder von Frauen in der ottonischen Herrscherfamilie (919–1024). Kassel 2005.

F. Neiske, Charismatischer Abt oder charismatische Gemeinschaft? Die frühen Äbte Clunys, in G. Andenna/M. Breitenstein/G. Melville (ed.), Charisma und religiöse Gemeinschaften im Mittelalter. Münster 2005, p. 55–72.

J. Nightingale, Monasteries and Patrons in the Gorze Reform. Lotharingia c. 850–1000. Oxford 2007.

M. Parisse, Noblesse et monastères en Lotharingie du IXe au XIe siècle, in R. Kottje/H. Maurer (ed.), Monastische Reformen im 9. und 10. Jahrhundert. Sigmaringen 1989, p. 167–196.

M. Parisse/O.G. Oexle (ed.), L'abbaye de Gorze au Xe siècle. Nancy 1993.

C.M. Reglero de la Fuente, Founders and Reformers. Abbots in the Kingdoms of Leon and Navarre, Ninth to Twelfth Centuries, in S. Vanderputten (ed.), Abbots and Abbesses as a Human Resource in the Ninth- to Twelfth-Century West. Zürich 2018, p. 77–95.

I. Rosé, Les origines de Cluny, le Cluny des origines. Réflexions sur la construction d'une domination monastique au premier âge féodal, in D. Iogna-Prat/M. Lauwers/F. Mazel/I. Rosé (ed.), Cluny: Les moines et la société au premier âge féodal. Rennes 2013, p. 35–51.

B.H. Rosenwein, To Be the Neighbor of Saint Peter. The Social Meaning of Cluny's Property, 909–1049. Ithaca, NY 1989.

H. Seibert, Libertas und Reichsabtei. Zur Klosterpolitik der Salischen Herrscher, in S. Weinfurter (ed.), Die Salier und das Reich. 2. Die Reichskirche in der Salierzeit. Sigmaringen 1991, p. 503–569.

J. Semmler, Das Erbe der karolingischen Klosterreform im 10. Jahrhundert, in R. Kottje/H. Maurer (ed.), Monastische Reformen im 9. und 10. Jahrhundert. Sigmaringen 1989, p. 29–77.

S. Steckel, Kulturen des Lehrens im Früh- und Hochmittelalter: Autorität, Wissenkonzepte und Netzwerke von Gelehrten. Cologne 2010.

J. Thibaut, Intermediary Leadership. The Agency of Abbesses in Ottonian Saxony, in S. Vanderputten (ed.), Abbots and Abbesses as a Human Resource in the Ninth- to Twelfth-Century West. Zürich 2018, p. 39–56.

S. Vanderputten, Monastic Reform as Process: Realities and Representations in Medieval Flanders, 900–1100. Ithaca, NY 2013.

T. Vogtherr, Die Reichsabteien der Benediktiner und das Königtum im hohen Mittelalter (900–1125), Stuttgart 2000.

J. WOLLASCH, Monasticism: The First Wave of Reform, in T. REUTER (ed.), The New Cambridge Medieval History 3: c. 900–c. 1024. Cambridge 1999, p. 163–185.

3.4 (Un)Reformed Experiences at the Turn of the First Millennium

R. BALZARETTI, Women, Property and Urban Space in Tenth-Century Milan, Gender & History 23 (2011), p. 547–575.

J. BARROW, English Cathedral Communities and Reform in the Late Tenth and the Eleventh Centuries, in D. ROLLASON/M.M. HARVEY/M.C. PRESTWICH (ed.), Anglo-Norman Durham 1093–1193. Woodbridge 1994, p. 25–39.

J.S. BARROW, The Ideology of the Tenth-Century English Benedictine 'Reform', in P. SKINNER (ed.), Challenging the Boundaries of Medieval History: The Legacy of Timothy Reuter. Turnhout 2009, p. 141–154.

K. BODARWÉ, Sanctimoniales litteratae: Schriftlichkeit und Bildung in den ottonischen Frauenkommunitäten Gandersheim, Essen und Quedlinburg. Münster 2004.

S. BOYNTON, Shaping a Monastic Identity: Liturgy & History at the Imperial Abbey of Farfa, 1000–1125. Ithaca, NY 2006.

K.A.-M. BUGYIS, The Care of Nuns: The Ministries of Benedictine Women in England during the Central Middle Ages. Oxford 2019.

N. BULST, La filiation de St-Bénigne de Dijon au temps de l'abbé Guillaume, in Naissance et fonctionnement des réseaux monastiques et canoniaux. Saint-Etienne 1991, p. 33–41.

I. COCHELIN, Evolution des coutumiers monastiques dessinée à partir de l'étude de Bernard, in S. BOYNTON/I. COCHELIN (ed.), From Dead of Night to End of Day: The Medieval Customs of Cluny/Du cœur de la nuit à la fin du jour: Les coutumes clunisiennes au Moyen Age. Turnhout 2005, p. 29–66.

I. COCHELIN, Customaries as Inspirational Sources, in C.M. MALONE/C. MAINES (ed.), Consuetudines et regulae. Sources for Monastic Life in the Middle Ages and the Early Modern Period. Turnhout 2014, p. 27–72.

C. CUBITT, The Tenth-century Benedictine Reform in England, Early Medieval Europe 6 (1997), p. 77–94.

C.D. FONSECA, Farfa abbazia imperiale, in Farfa abbazia imperiale. Negarine di S. Pietro in Cariano 2006, p. 1–17.

F. GALLON, "Adveniens a cordubensi patria". Les relations entre moines mozarabes et moines de chrétienté dans la péninsule Ibérique du haut Moyen Age (VIIIe–XIIe siècles), in S. EXCOFFON/D.-O. HUREL/A. PETERS-CUSTOT (ed.), Interactions, emprunts, confrontations chez les religieux: Antiquité tardive-fin du XIXe siècle. Saint-Etienne 2016, p. 113–129.

K. HALLINGER, Gorze-Kluny. Studien zu den monastischen Lebensformen und Gegensätzen im Hochmittelalter, 2 vols. Rome 1950–1951.

M. Herrero de la Fuente/J.A. Fernández Flórez, Sobre la escritura
   visigótica en León y Castilla durante su etapa primitiva (siglos VII–X):
   Algunas reflexiones, in J. Alturo Perucho/M. Torras Cortina/C.
   Correa (ed.), La escritura visigótica en la Península Ibérica: Nuevas
   aportaciones. Bellaterra 2012, p. 55–104.

E.S. Horowitz, Towards a Social History of Jewish Popular Religion: Obadiah
   of Bertinoro on the Jews of Palermo, Journal of Religious History 17 (1992),
   p. 138–151.

D. Iogna-Prat, Order & Exclusion. Cluny and Christendom Face Heresy,
   Judaism, and Islam (1000–1150). Ithaca, NY 2002.

C.A. Jones, Monastic Identity and Sodomitic Danger in the Occupatio by Odo of
   Cluny, Speculum 82 (2007), p. 1–53.

D. Knowles, The Monastic Order in England. A History of Its Development
   from the Times of St Dunstan to the Fourth Lateran Council, 940–1216.
   Cambridge 1963.

R. Kottje, Einleitung, in R. Kottje/H. Maurer (ed.), Monastische Reformen im
   9. und 10. Jahrhundert. Sigmaringen 1989, p. 9–13.

B. Langefeld, The Old English Version of the Enlarged Rule of Chrodegang:
   Edited Together with the Latin Text and an English Translation. Frankfurt
   am Main 2003.

J.M. Martin, L'érémitisme grec et latin en Italie méridionale (Xe–XIIIe siècle),
   in A. Vauchez (ed.), Ermites de France et d'Italie (XIe–XVe siècle). Rome
   2003, p. 175–198.

A.M. Martínez Tejera, La realidad material de los monasterios y cenobios
   rupestres hispanos (siglos V–X), in J.A. García de Cortázar y Ruiz de
   Aguirre/R. Teja Casuso (ed.), Monjes y monasterios hispanos en la edad
   media. Aguilar de Campos 2006, p. 255–288.

J.A. McNamara, Sisters in Arms. Catholic Nuns Through Two Millennia.
   Cambridge 1996.

C. Potts. Monastic Revival and Regional Identity in Early Normandy.
   Woodbridge 1997.

V. Ramseyer, The Transformation of a Religious Landscape. Medieval Southern
   Italy 850–1150. Ithaca, NY 2006.

A. Rabin, Courtly Habits: Monastic Women's Legal Literacy in Early
   Anglo-Saxon England, in V. Blanton/V. O'Mara/P. Stoop (ed.), Nuns'
   Literacies in Medieval Europe: The Kansas City Dialogue. Turnhout 2015,
   p. 289–305.

C.T. Reidel, Monastic Reform and Lay Religion in Aethelwold's Winchester.
   Unpublished doctoral dissertation, Boston College 2015.

J. Riyeff, Saint Æthelwold of Winchester, The Old English Rule of Saint
   Benedict, with Related Old English Texts. Collegeville, MN 2017.

E. Sackur, Die Cluniacenser in ihrer kirchlichen und allgemeingeschichtlichen
   Wirksamkeit bis zur Mitte des elften Jahrhunderts, 2 vols. Halle a.d. Saale
   1892–1894.

M.M. Schaefer, Women in Pastoral Office. The Story of Santa Prassede, Rome.
   Oxford 2013.

K. Schmid, Kloster Hirsau und seine Stifter. Freiburg im Breisgau 1959.

G. TELLENBACH, Die westliche Kirche vom 10. bis zum frühen 12. Jahrhundert. Göttingen 1988.

F. TINTI, Benedictine Reform and Pastoral Care in Late Anglo-Saxon England, Early Medieval Europe 23 (2015), p. 229–251.

S. VANDERPUTTEN, Reconsidering Religious Migration and its Impact. The Problem of 'Irish Reform Monks' in Tenth-Century Lotharingia, Revue d'histoire ecclésiastique 113 (2018), p. 588–618.

S. VANDERPUTTEN, Monastic Reform from the Tenth to the Early Twelfth Century, in A. BEACH/I. COCHELIN (ed.), The Cambridge History of Medieval Monasticism in the Latin West, 2 vols. Cambridge 2020, p. 599–617.

A. WAGNER, Gorze au XIe siècle. Contribution à l'histoire du monachisme bénédictin dans l'Empire. Turnhout 1996.

S. WEBER, Iren auf dem Kontinent: Das Leben des Marianus Scottus von Regensburg und die Anfänge der irischen "Schottenklöster". Heidelberg 2010.

J. WOLLASCH, Mönchtum des Mittelalters zwischen Kirche und Welt. Munich 1973.

J. WOLLASCH, Konventsstärke und Armensorge in mittelalterlichen Klöstern. Zeugnisse und Fragen, Saeculum 39 (1988), p. 184–199.

J. WOLLASCH, Cluny – Licht der Welt. Aufstieg und Niedergang der klösterlichen Gemeinschaft, Zurich 1996.

B.A.E. YORKE, Nunneries and the Anglo-Saxon Royal Houses. London 2003.

3.5 The Conversion of the World

S. AIRLIE, The Anxiety of Sanctity: St. Gerald of Aurillac and his Maker, The Journal of Ecclesiastical History 43 (1992), p. 372–395.

R. BALZARETTI, Men and Sex in Tenth-Century Italy, in D.M. HADLEY (ed.), Masculinity in Medieval Europe. London 1999, p. 143–159.

A.J.A. BIJSTERVELD, Do ut des: Gift Giving, memoria, and Conflict Management in the Medieval Low Countries. Hilversum 2007.

C.B. BOUCHARD, Sword, Miter and Cloister. Nobility and the Church in Burgundy, 980–1198. Ithaca, NY 1987.

F. BOUGARD, Le crédit dans l'Occident du haut Moyen Age: Documentation et pratique, in J.P. DEVROEY/L. FELLER/R. LE JAN (ed.), Les élites et la richesse au haut Moyen Age. Turnhout 2010, p. 439–478.

A.-M. BULTOT-VERLEYSEN, Le dossier de saint Géraud d'Aurillac, Francia 22 (1995), p. 173–206.

G. CONSTABLE, Monasteries, Rural Churches and the cura animarum in the Early Middle Ages, in Cristianizzazione ed organizzazione ecclesiastica delle campagne nell'alto medioevo. Espansione e resistenze, 2 vols. Spoleto 1982, vol. 1, p. 349–389.

C. CUBITT, Archbishop Dunstan: A Prophet in Politics?, in J. BARROW/A. WAREHAM (ed.), Myth, Rulership, Church and Charters. Aldershot 2008, p. 145–166.

M. Davide, L'economia monastica dei secoli X e XI tra agricoltura e credito, in M. Bottazzi/P. Buffo/C. Ciccopiedi/L. Furbetta/T. Granier (ed.), La società monastica nei secoli VI–XII: Sentieri di ricerca. Trieste 2016, p. 401–424.

M. De Jong, Charlemagne's Church, in J.E. Story (ed.), Charlemagne: Empire and Society. Manchester 2005, p. 103–135.

C. Duhamel-Amado, Le "miles conuersus et fundator": De Guillaume de Gellone à Pons de Léras, in M. Lauwers (ed.), Guerriers et moines. Conversion et sainteté aristocratiques dans l'occident médiéval (IXe–XIIe siècle). Antibes 2002, p. 419–427.

F. Felten, Wie adelig waren Kanonissenstifte (und andere Konvente) im frühen und hohen Mittelalter?, in I. Crusius (ed.), Vita religiosa sanctimonialium: Norm und Praxis des weiblichen religiösen Lebens vom 6. bis zum 13. Jahrhundert. Korb 2005, p. 93–162.

V. Gazeau, Normannia monastica. 1: Princes normands et abbés bénédictins (Xe–XIIe siècle). 2: Prosopographie des abbés bénédictins (Xe–XIIe siècle), 2 vols. Turnhout 2007.

D. Iogna-Prat (2002a), La place idéale du laïc à Cluny (v. 930–v. 1150), d'une morale statutaire à une éthique absolue?, in M. Lauwers (ed.), Guerriers et moines. Conversion et sainteté aristocratiques dans l'occident médiéval (IXe–XIIe siècle). Antibes 2002, p. 291–316.

D. Iogna-Prat (2002b), La "Vita Geraldi" d'Odon de Cluny: Un texte fondateur?, in M. Lauwers (ed.), Guerriers et moines. Conversion et sainteté aristocratiques dans l'Occident médiéval (IXe–XIIe siècle). Antibes 2002, p. 143–155.

K.J. Leyser, Rule and Conflict in an Early Medieval Society: Ottonian Saxony. London 1979.

F. Mazel, La noblesse et l'Église en Provence, fin Xe–début XIVe siècle: L'exemple des familles d'Agoult-Simiane, de Baux et de Marseille. Paris 2002.

J. Nelson, Monks, Secular Men and Masculinity, c. 900, in D.M. Hadley (ed.), Masculinity in Medieval Europe. London 1999, p. 254–272.

Ottone III e Romualdo di Ravenna. Impero monasteri e santi asceti. Negarine di S. Pietro in Cariano 2003.

R. Rappmann/A. Zettler, Die Reichenauer Mönchsgemeinschaft und ihr Totengedenken im frühen Mittelalter, Sigmaringen 1998.

A.J. Romig, Be a Perfect Man: Christian Masculinity and the Carolingian Aristocracy. Philadelphia, PA 2017.

I. Rosé, Construire une société seigneuriale. Itinéraire et ecclésiologie de l'abbé Odon de Cluny (fin IXe–milieu du Xe siècle). Turnhout 2008.

I. Rosé, Commutatio. Le vocabulaire de l'échange chrétien au haut Moyen Age, in J.P. Devroey/L. Feller/R. Le Jan (ed.), Les élites et la richesse au haut Moyen Age. Turnhout 2010, p. 113–138.

R. Savigni, Les laïcs dans l'ecclésiologie carolingienne: Normes statutaires et idéal de "conversion", in M. Lauwers (ed.), Guerriers et moines. Conversion et sainteté aristocratiques dans l'occident médiéval (IXe–XIIe siècle). Antibes 2002, p. 41–92.

R. Stephenson, The Politics of Language. Byrthferth, Aelfric, and the Multilingual Identity of the Benedictine Reform. Toronto 2015.

R. Stone, Masculinity Without Conflict: Noblemen in Eighth- and Ninth-Century Francia, in J.H. Arnold/S. Brady (ed.), What is Masculinity? Historical Dynamics from Antiquity to the Contemporary World. Basingstoke 2011, p. 76–93.

L. Trân-Duc, Herluin, fondateur de l'abbaye du Bec: La fabrique d'un saint à l'époque de la réforme de l'église, in J. Barrow/F. Delivré/V. Gazeau (ed.), Autour de Lanfranc (1010–2010). Caen 2015, p. 227–240.

S. Vanderputten, Monks, Knights, and the Enactment of Competing Social Realities in Eleventh- and Early-Twelfth-Century Flanders, Speculum 84 (2009), p. 582–612.

S. Vanderputten, A Compromised Inheritance. Monastic Discourse and the Politics of Property Exchange in Early-Twelfth-Century Flanders, The Journal of Ecclesiastical History 61 (2010), p. 229–251.

S. Vanderputten, Communities of Practice and Emotional Aspects of Loyalty in Reformist Circles of the Tenth and Eleventh Centuries, in J. Sonntag/C. Zermatten (ed.), Loyalty in the Middle Ages. Ideal and Practice of a Cross-Social Value. Turnhout 2015, p. 279–303.

S. Vanderputten, The Dignity of Our Bodies and the Salvation of Our Souls. Scandal, Purity, and the Pursuit of Unity in Late Tenth-Century Monasticism, in S. Esders/S. Greer/A. Hicklin (ed.), Using and Not Using the Past after the Carolingian Empire, c. 900–c. 1050. Abingdon 2020, p. 262–281.

A. Wilkin, Communautés bénédictines et environnement économique, IXe–XIIe siècles. Réflexions sur les tendances historiographiques de l'analyse du temporel monastique, in S. Vanderputten/B. Meijns (ed.), Ecclesia in medio nationis. Reflections on the Study of Monasticism in the Central Middle Ages/Réflexions sur l'étude du monachisme au Moyen Age Central. Leuven 2011. p. 101–150.

J. Wollasch, Wer waren die Mönche von Cluny vom 10. bis zum 12. Jahrhundert?, in R. Lejeune (ed.), Clio et son regard. Mélanges d'histoire de l'art et d'archéologie offerts à Jacques Stiennon à l'occasion de ses 25 ans d'enseignement à l'Université de Liège. Liège 1982, p. 663–678.

3.6 Cluniac and Other Nebulas

H. Atsma/J. Vezin, Gestion de la mémoire à l'époque de saint Hugues (1049–1109): La genèse paléographique et codicologique du plus ancien cartulaire de l'abbaye de Cluny, Histoire et archives 7 (2000), p. 5–29.

S. Barret, La mémoire et l'écrit: L'abbaye de Cluny et ses archives (Xe–XVIIIe siècle). Münster 2004.

A. Baud, Cluny. La Maior ecclesia – 1088 (?)-1130. Expression monumentale de l'Ecclesia cluniacensis, in J. Jarnut/M. Wemhoff (ed.), Vom Umbruch

zur Erneuerung? Das 11. und beginnende 12. Jahrhundert. Positionen der
Forschung. Munich 2006, p. 219–230.

J. Burton, Monastic and Religious Orders in Britain, 1000–1300. Cambridge
1994.

G. Constable (2010a), Cluniac Reform in the Eleventh Century, in The Abbey of
Cluny. A Collection of Essays to Mark the Eleven-Hundredth Anniversary of
its Foundation. Münster 2010, p. 81–111.

G. Constable (2010b), Cluny and the Investiture Controversy, in The Abbey of
Cluny. A Collection of Essays to Mark the Eleven-Hundredth Anniversary of
its Foundation. Münster, 2010, p. 179–190.

H.E.J. Cowdrey, William I's Relationship with Cluny Further Considered, in The
Crusades and Latin Monasticism, 11th–12th Centuries. Aldershot 1999,
art. VIII, p. 1–14.

E. De Valous, Le monachisme clunisien des origines au XVe siècle. Vie
intérieure des monastères et organisation de l'ordre. 2 vols. Paris 1970
(second edition).

J. Harris, Building Heaven on Earth: Cluny as locus sanctissimus in the
Eleventh Century, in S. Boynton/I. Cochelin (ed.), From Dead of Night
to End of Day: The Medieval Customs of Cluny/Du cœur de la nuit à la
fin du jour: Les coutumes clunisiennes au Moyen Age. Turnhout 2005,
p. 131–151.

D. Iogna-Prat, Agni immaculati. Recherches sur les sources hagiographiques
relatives à saint Maieul de Cluny (954–994). Paris 1988.

D. Iogna-Prat, La confection des cartulaires et l'historiographie à Cluny
(XIe–XIIe siècles), in O. Guyotjeannin/L. Morelle/M. Parisse (ed.), Les
cartulaires. Actes de la table ronde organisée par l'Ecole Nationale des
Chartes 1991. Paris 1993, p. 27–44.

D. Iogna-Prat, Les lieux de mémoire du Cluny médiéval (v. 940–v. 1200), in
P. Henriet/A.-M. Legras (ed.), Au cloître et dans le monde. Femmes,
hommes et sociétés (IXe–XVe siècle). Mélanges en l'honneur de Paulette
l'Hermite-Leclercq. Paris 2000, p. 103–117.

H. Jakobs, Der Adel in der Klosterreform von St. Blasien. Cologne 1968.

J.F. Lemarignier, L'exemption monastique et les origines de la réforme
grégorienne, in A Cluny: Congrès scientifique. Dijon 1950, p. 288–340.

U. Longo, Riti e agiografia. L'istituzione della commemoratio omnium fidelium
defunctorum nelle Vitae di Odilone di Cluny, Bullettino dell'Istituto storico
italiano per il medio evo 103 (2000/2001), p. 163–200.

C.M. Malone, Saint-Bénigne de Dijon en l'an mil, totius Galliae basilicis
mirabilior: Interprétation politique, liturgique et théologique. Brepols 2009.

L.C. Pick, Rethinking Cluny in Spain, Journal of Medieval Iberian Studies 5
(2013), p. 1–17.

D.W. Poeck, Cluniacensis Ecclesia. Der cluniacensische Klosterverband (10.-12.
Jahrhundert). Munich 1998.

P. Racinet, L'expansion de Cluny sous Hugues Ier de Semur, in Le
gouvernement d'Hugues de Semur à Cluny. Cluny 1990, p. 93–131.

B.H. Rosenwein, Cluny's Immunities in the Tenth and Eleventh Centuries:
Images and Narratives, in G. Constable/G. Melville/J. Oberste (ed.),

Die Cluniazenser in ihrem politisch-sozialen Umfeld. Münster 1998,
p. 145–163.

B.H. Rosenwein, Negotiating Space: Power, Restraint, and Privileges of
Immunity in Early Medieval Europe. Manchester 1999.

K. Schreiner, Hirsau und Hirsauer Reform. Lebens- und Verfassungsformen
einer Reformbewegung, in U. Faust/F. Quarthal (ed.), Die
Reformverbände und Kongregationen der Benediktiner im deutschen
Sprachraum. St. Ottilien 1999, p. 89–124.

J. Semmler, Die Klosterreform von Siegburg. Ihre Ausbreitung und ihr
Reformprogramm im 11. und 12. Jahrhundert. Bonn 1959.

S. Vanderputten, A Time of Great Confusion. Second-Generation
Cluniac Reformers and Resistance to Centralization in the County of
Flanders (Circa 1125–45), Revue d'histoire ecclésiastique 102 (2007),
p. 47–75.

S. Vanderputten, Imagining Religious Leadership in the Middle Ages: Richard
of Saint-Vanne and the Politics of Reform. Ithaca, NY 2015.

S. Vanderputten, Imagining Early Cluny in Abbatial Biographies, in S. Bruce
and S. Vanderputten (ed.), A Companion to the Abbey of Cluny in the
Middle Ages, Leiden (forthcoming).

E.M. Wischermann, Marcigny-Sur-Loire. Gründungs- u. Frühgeschichte des 1.
Cluniacenserinnenpriorates (1055–1150). Munich 1986.

J. Wollasch, Hugues Ier abbé de Cluny et la mémoire des morts, in Le
gouvernement d'Hugues de Semur à Cluny. Cluny 1990, p. 75–92.

J. Wollasch, Cluny und Deutschland, Studien und Mitteilungen zur Geschichte
des Benediktinerordens und seiner Zweige 103 (1992), p. 7–32.

3.7 The 'Quest for the Primitive'

C. Andenna, La costruzione dell'identità nella vita religiosa. L'esempio degli
agostiniani e dei carmelitani, in E. Filippini/G. Andenna (ed.), Religiosità
e civiltà – identità delle forme religiose. Milan 2011, p. 65–101.

U. Andermann, Die unsittlichen und disziplinlosen Kanonissen. Ein
Topos und seine Hintergründe, aufgezeigt an Beispielen sächsischer
Frauenstifte (11.-13. Jahrhundert), Westfälische Zeitschrift 146 (1996),
p. 39–63.

N. Bériou/P. Josserand (ed.), Prier et combattre: Dictionnaire européen des
ordres militaires au Moyen Age. Paris 2009.

C. Berman, The Cistercian Evolution: The Invention of a Religious Order in
Twelfth-Century Europe. Philadelphia, PA 2000.

S. Bonde/C. Maines, Saint-Jean-des-Vignes in Soissons. Approaches to its
Architecture, Archaeology and History. Turnhout 2003.

J.E. Burton/K. Stöber (ed.), The Regular Canons in the Medieval British Isles.
Turnhout 2011.

C. Caby, Finis eremitarum? Les formes régulières et communautaires de l'érémitisme médiéval, in A. Vauchez (ed.), Ermites de France et d'Italie XIe–XVe siècle. Rome 2003, p. 47–80.

C. Caby, Vies parallèles: Ermites d'Italie et de la France de l'ouest (Xe–XIIe siècle), in J. Dalarun (ed.), Robert d'Arbrissel et la vie religieuse dans l'ouest de la France. Turnhout 2004, p. 11–24.

N. Cantor, The Crisis of Western Monasticism, 1050–1130, American Historical Review 66 (1960–1961), p. 47–67.

D. Carraz/E. Dehoux (ed.), Images et ornements autour des ordres militaires au Moyen Age. Culture visuelle et culte des saints (France, Espagne du Nord, Italie). Toulouse 2016.

G. Constable, Moderation and Restraint in Ascetic Practices in the Middle Ages, in Culture and Spirituality in Medieval Europe. Aldershot 1996, art. X, p. 315–327.

N. D'Acunto, La rete monastico-eremitica di Pier Damiani e quella di Fonte Avellana, in N. D'Acunto (ed.), Dinamiche istituzionali delle reti monastiche e canonicali nell'Italia dei secoli X–XII. Negarine di S. Pietro in Cariano 2007, p. 133–156.

N. D'Acunto (ed.), Fonte Avellana nel secolo di Pier Damiani. Negarine di S. Pietro in Cariano 2008.

N. D'Acunto, Monachesimo camaldolese e monachesimo "riformatore" nel secolo XI, in C. Caby/P. Licciardello (ed.), Camaldoli e l'ordine camaldolese dalle origini alla fine del XV secolo. Cesena 2014, p. 21–38.

F.J. Felten, Zwischen Berufung und Amt: Norbert von Xanten und seinesgleichen im ersten Viertel des 12. Jahrhunderts, in G. Andenna/M. Breitenstein/G. Melville (ed.), Charisma und religiöse Gemeinschaften im Mittelalter. Münster 2005, p. 103–149.

I.C. Ferreira Fernandes (ed.), As ordens militares. Freires, guerreiros, cavaleiros. Actas do VI encontro sobre ordens militares, 2 vols. Pamela 2012.

C.D. Fonseca, La regola dei Trinitari oltre gli ideali degli ordini religioso-cavallereschi, in G. Rossetti/G. Vitolo (ed.), Medioevo, Mezzogiorno, Mediterraneo. Studi in onore di Mario Del Treppo, 2 vols. Naples 2000, vol. 1, p. 147–159.

R. Gilchrist, Contemplation and Action: The Other Monasticism. London 1995.

H. Grundmann, Religiöse Bewegungen im Mittelalter. Untersuchungen über die geschichtlichen Zusammenhänge zwischen der Ketzerei, den Bettelorden und der religiösen Frauenbewegung im 12. und 13. Jahrhundert und über die geschichtlichen Grundlagen der deutschen Mystik. Berlin 1935 (translated into English as Religious Movements in the Middle Ages: The Historical Links between Heresy, the Mendicant Orders, and the Women's Religious Movement in the Twelfth and Thirteenth Century, with the Historical Foundations of German Mysticism. Notre Dame, IN 1995).

N. Jaspert, Frühformen der geistlichen Ritterorden und die Kreuzzugsbewegung auf der Iberischen Halbinsel, in K. Herbers (ed.), Europa an der Wende vom 11. bis 12. Jahrhundert. Beiträge zu Ehren von Werner Goez. Stuttgart 2001, p. 90–116.

P. Jestice, Wayward Monks and the Religious Revolution of the Eleventh Century. Leiden 1997.

M. LAUWERS, De l'incastellamento à l'inecclesiamento. Monachisme et logiques spatiales du féodalisme, in D. IOGNA-PRAT/M. LAUWERS/F. MAZEL/I. ROSÉ (ed.), Cluny: Les moines et la société au premier âge féodal. Rennes 2013, p. 315–338.

H. LEYSER, Hermits and the New Monasticism: A Study of Religious Communities in Western Europe. New York, NY 1984.

T. LICENCE, Hermits & Recluses in English Society 950–1200. Oxford 2011.

U. LONGO, La riforma della Chiesa tra Pier Damiani a Bernardo di Chiaravalle. Un concetto da declinare al plurale, in M. BOTAZZI/P. BUFFO/C. CICCOPIEDI et al. (ed.), La società monastica nei secoli VI–XII: Sentieri di ricerca. Trieste 2016, p. 113–132.

A. LUTTREL/H.J. NICHOLSON (ed.), Hospitaller Women in the Middle Ages. Aldershot 2006.

J. LYON, Otto of Freising's Tyrants: Church Advocates and Noble Lordship in the Long Twelfth Century, in D.C. MENGEL/L. WOLVERTON (ed.), Christianity and Culture in the Middle Ages: Essays to Honor John Van Engen. South Bend, IN 2015, p. 141–167.

L.E. MANCIA, Emotional Monasticism. Affective Piety in the Eleventh-Century Monastery of John of Fécamp. Manchester 2019.

D. MARCOMBE, Leper Knights: The Order of St. Lazarus of Jerusalem in England, c. 1150–1544. Woodbridge 2003.

L.H. McAVOY (ed.), Anchoritic Traditions in Medieval Europe. Woodbridge 2010.

B. MEIJNS, L'ordre canonial dans le comté de Flandre depuis l'époque mérovingienne jusqu'à 1155: Typologie, chronologie et constants de l'histoire de fondation et de réforme, Revue d'histoire ecclésiastique 97 (2002), p. 5–58.

B. MEIJNS, Hirsau dans la plaine côtière flamande? Les Guatinenses, les évêques de Thérouanne et la réforme de l'Eglise sous Grégoire VII (1073–1085), in B.-M. TOCK/J. RIDER (ed.), Le diocèse de Thérouanne au Moyen Age, special issue of Mémoires de la commission départementale d'histoire et d'archeologie du Pas-de-Calais 39 (2010), p. 81–97.

G. MELVILLE, Stephan von Obazine: Begründung und Überwindung charismatischer Führung, in Frommer Eifer und methodischer Betrieb: Beiträge zum mittelalterlichen Mönchtum. Cologne 2014, p. 85–101.

E. MENESTÒ (ed.), Eremitismo e habitat rupestre. Spoleto 2015.

K. O'BRIEN O'KEEFFE, Stealing Obedience. Narratives of Agency and Identity in Later Anglo-Saxon England. Toronto 2012.

J.M. POWELL, Innocent III, the Trinitarians, and the Renewal of the Church, 1198–1200, in G. CIPPOLONE (ed.), La liberazione dei "captivi" tra Cristianità e Islam. Oltre la crociata e il Giha'd: Tolleranza e servizio umanitario. Vatican City 2000, p. 245–254.

M. PARISSE (ed.), Les chanoines réguliers. Emergence et expansion (XIe–XIIIe siècles). Saint-Etienne 2009.

J.-M. SANSTERRE, Le monachisme bénédictin d'Italie et les bénédictins italiens en France face au renouveau de l'érémitisme à la fin du Xe et au XIe siècle, in A. VAUCHEZ (ed.), Ermites de France et d'Italie XIe–XVe siècle. Rome 2003, p. 29–46.

J. Sᴀʀɴᴏᴡsᴋʏ, Der deutsche Orden. Munich 2007.

J. Sᴀʀɴᴏᴡsᴋʏ, Die Johanniter. Munich 2011.

L. Sᴄʜɴᴇɪᴅᴇʀ, De l'horizon impérial aux sociétés locales: Patrimoine monastique, spatialisation des pouvoirs et mnémotopie autour de Saint-Sauveur d'Aniane (782–1006), in D. Iᴏɢɴᴀ-Pʀᴀᴛ/M. Lᴀᴜᴡᴇʀs/F. Mᴀᴢᴇʟ/I. Rᴏsᴇ́ (ed.), Cluny: Les moines et la société au premier âge féodal. Rennes 2013, p. 339–390.

K. Sʏᴋᴇs, Inventing Sempringham. Gilbert of Sempringham and the Origins of the Role of the Master. Berlin 2011.

K. Tʜᴏᴍᴘsᴏɴ, The Monks of Tiron. A Monastic Community and Religious Reform in the Twelfth Century. Cambridge 2014.

B.-M. Tᴏᴄᴋ, Un réformateur ordinaire de la vie monastique: Raoul, abbé de Vaucelles (1132–1151), in J. Bᴀʀʀᴏᴡ/F. Dᴇʟɪᴠʀᴇ́/V. Gᴀᴢᴇᴀᴜ (ed.), Autour de Lanfranc (1010–2010). Caen 2015, p. 253–262.

S. Vᴀɴᴅᴇʀᴘᴜᴛᴛᴇɴ, Crises of Cenobitism: Abbatial Leadership and Monastic Competition in Late Eleventh-Century Flanders, The English Historical Review 127 (2012), p. 259–284.

S. Vᴀɴᴅᴇʀᴘᴜᴛᴛᴇɴ, Custom and Identity at Le Bec, in B. Pᴏʜʟ/L.L. Gᴀᴛʜᴀʜᴀɴ (ed.), A Companion to the Abbey of Le Bec in the Central Middle Ages (11th–13th Centuries). Leiden 2017, p. 228–247.

J. Vᴀɴ Eɴɢᴇɴ, The Crisis of Cenobitism Reconsidered: Benedictine Monasticism in the Years 1050–1150, Speculum 61 (1986), p. 269–304.

Y. Vᴇʏʀᴇɴᴄʜᴇ, Identité canoniale et modèles monastiques. Le cas des coutumes de Saint-Ruf, in S. Exᴄᴏꜰꜰᴏɴ/D.-O. Hᴜʀᴇʟ/A. Pᴇᴛᴇʀs-Cᴜsᴛᴏᴛ (ed.), Interactions, emprunts, confrontations chez les religieux: Antiquité tardive-fin du XIXe siècle. Saint-Etienne 2016, p. 163–184.

C. Wᴇsᴛ, Monks, Aristocrats, and Justice: Twelfth-Century Monastic Advocacy in a European Perspective, Speculum 92 (2017), 372–404 (debated at http://www.themedievalacademyblog.org/a-response-to-west-charles-monks-aristocrats-and-justice-twelfth-century-monastic-advocacy-in-a-european-perspective/, accessed 15 June 2019).

S. Zᴜᴄᴄʜɪɴɪ, "Vecchio" e "nuovo" monachesimo a cavallo tra il primo ed il secondo millennio, in Riforma o restaurazione? La cristianità nel passaggio dal primo al secondo millennio. Persistenze e novità. Negarine di S. Pietro in Cariano 2006, p. 83–100.

4 Later Medieval Monasticisms

4.1 Transformations in Monastic Governance

A. Bᴀᴜᴅɪɴ/A. Gʀᴇ́ʟᴏɪs (ed.), Le temps long de Clairvaux. Nouvelles recherches, nouvelles perspectives (XIIe–XXIe siècle). Paris 2016.

A.I. Bᴇᴀᴄʜ, The Trauma of Monastic Reform: Community and Conflict in Twelfth-Century Germany. Cambridge 2017.

J. Belaen, Abbots, Confraternities, and Monastic Mobility. A 'Cluniac Nebula' in the Ecclesiastical Province of Reims (c. 1100–1131), in S. Vanderputten (ed.), Abbots and Abbesses as a Human Resource in the Ninth- to Twelfth-Century West. Zürich 2018, p. 119–143.

R.F. Berkhofer, Day of Reckoning: Power and Accountability in Medieval France. Philadelphia, PA 2004.

G. Cariboni, 'No One Can Serve Two Masters': Abbots and Arch-Abbots in the Monastic Networks at the End of the Eleventh Century, The Journal of Medieval Monastic Studies 2 (2013), p. 39–74.

G. Constable (2010a), Cluniac Administration and Administrators in the Twelfth Century, in The Abbey of Cluny. A Collection of Essays to Mark the Eleven-Hundredth Anniversary of its Foundation. Münster 2010, p. 339–360.

G. Constable (2010b), Commemoration and Confraternity at Cluny During the Abbacy of Peter the Venerable, in The Abbey of Cluny. A Collection of Essays to Mark the Eleven-Hundredth Anniversary of its Foundation. Münster 2010, p. 313–338.

F. Cygler, Das Generalkapitel im hohen Mittelalter. Cisterzienser, Prämonstratenser, Kartäuser und Cluniazenser. Münster 2001.

N. D'Acunto, Monachesimo camaldolese e monachesimo riformatore, in C. Caby/P.L. Licciardello (ed.), Camaldoli e l'ordine camaldolese dalle origini alla fine del XV secolo. Cesena 2014, p. 21–38.

N. Deflou-Leca, Réforme et réseaux de dépendances dans le monachisme post-carolingien (Xe-XIe siècles), in D. Iogna-Prat/M. Lauwers/F. Mazel/I. Rosé (ed.), Cluny: Les moines et la société au premier âge féodal. Rennes 2013, p. 53–63.

Ecrire son histoire. Les communautés régulières face à leur passé. Saint-Etienne 2006.

F. Felten, Waren die Zisterzienser frauenfeindlich? Die Zisterzienser und die religiöse Frauenbewegung im 12. und frühen 13. Jahrhundert. Versuch einer Bestandsaufnahme der Forschung seit 1980, in F. Felten/W. Rösener (ed.), Norm und Realität: Kontinuität und Wandel der Zisterzienser im Mittelalter. Berlin 2009, p. 179–223.

C. Holdsworth, The Affiliation of Savigny, in M.L. Dutton/D.M. La Corte/P. Lockey ed., Truth as Gift: Studies in Honor of John R. Sommerfeldt. Kalamazoo, MI 2004, p. 43–88.

L. Jégou, Evêques et moines à l'époque de Lanfranc: L'émancipation monastique en débat, in J. Barrow/F. Delivré/V. Gazeau (ed.), Autour de Lanfranc (1010–2010). Caen 2015, p. 263–278.

B. Krings, Zum Ordensrecht der Prämonstratenser bis zur Mitte des 12. Jahrhunderts, Analecta Praemonstratensia 76 (2000), p. 9–28.

S. Lecouteux, Réseaux de confraternité et histoire des bibliothèques. L'exemple de l'abbaye bénédictine de la Trinité de Fécamp. Unpublished doctoral dissertation, Université de Caen 2015.

G. Melville, Zur Semantik von 'ordo' im Religiosentum der ersten Hälfte des 12. Jahrhunderts: Lucius II., seine Bulle vom 19. Mai 1144, und der 'Orden'

der Prämonstratenser, in I. Crusius/H. Flachenecker (ed.), Studien zum
Prämonstratenserorden. Göttingen 2003, p. 201–224.
G. Melville, Regeln-Consuetudines-Texte-Statuten. Positionen für eine
Typologie des normativen Schrifttums religiöser Gemeinschaften im
Mittelalter, in C. Andenna/G. Melville (ed.), Regulae – Consuetudines –
Statuta: Studi sulle fonti normative degli ordini religiosi nei secoli centrali
del Medioevo. Münster 2005, p. 5–38.
G. Melville, Brückenschlag zur zweiten Generation. Die kritische Phase
der Institutionalisierung mittelalterlicher Orden, in J. Rogg (ed.),
Religiöse Ordnungsvorstellungen und Frömmigkeitspraxis im Hoch- und
Spätmittelalter. Korb 2008, p. 77–98.
A. Miegel, Kooperation, Vernetzung, Erneuerung. Das benediktinische
Verbrüderungs- und Memorialwesen vom 12. bis 15. Jahrhundert.
Ostfildern 2014.
S. Patzold, Die monastischen Reformen in Süddeutschland am Beispiel
Hirsaus, Schaffhausens und St. Blasiens, in C. Stiegemann/M. Wemhoff
(ed.), Canossa 1077 – Erschütterung der Welt. Geschichte, Kunst und
Kultur am Aufgang der Romanik, 2 vols. Munich 2006, vol. 1, p. 199–208.
B. Pohl/S. Vanderputten, Fécamp, Cluny and the Invention of Traditions in
the Later Eleventh Century, The Journal of Medieval Monastic Studies 5
(2016), p. 1–41.
B. Pohl, The Problem of Cluniac Exemption, in S. Bruce/S. Vanderputten
(ed.), A Companion to the Medieval Abbey of Cluny, Leiden (forthcoming).
C.M. Reglero de la Fuente, La Reforma Gregoriana y la introducción del
rito romano, in J.A. Escudero (ed.), La Iglesia en la Historia de España.
Madrid 2014, p. 317–326.
L. Roach, Forging Memory in an Age of Iron: False Documents and Institutional
Memory around the Year 1000 (forthcoming).
B.H. Rosenwein/T. Head/S. Farmer, Monks and Their Enemies: A Comparative
Approach, Speculum 66 (1991), p. 764–796.
B. Tutsch, Studien zur Rezeptionsgeschichte der Consuetudines Ulrichs von
Cluny. Münster 1998.
S. Vanderputten, The 1131 General Chapter of Benedictine Abbots
Reconsidered, The Journal of Ecclesiastical History 66 (2015), p. 715–734.
S. Vanderputten/J. Belaen, An Attempted 'Reform' of the General Chapter
of Benedictine Abbots in the Late 1160s, Revue Mabillon 27 (2016),
p. 23–47.
S. Vanderputten, 'I Would be Rather Pleased if the World Were to be Rid of
Monks'. Resistance to Cluniac Integration in Late Eleventh- and Early
Twelfth-Century France, Journal of Medieval History (forthcoming).
C. Waddell, The Myth of Cistercian Origins: C.H. Berman and the
Manuscript Sources, Cîteaux: Commentarii Cistercienses 51 (2000),
p. 299–386.
S. Weinfurter, Norbert von Xanten und die Entstehung des
Prämonstratenserordens, in S. Weinfurter (ed.), Gelebte Ordnung –
Gedachte Ordnung. Ausgewählte Beiträge zu König, Kirche und Reich.
Ostfildern 2005, p. 65–94.

4.2 Monastic Experiences in the Long Twelfth Century

C. Andenna, Zu den Hospitälern der norditalienischen Regularkanoniker im 12. und 13. Jahrhundert. Einige Beispiele aus der 'Ecclesia Mortariensis', in L. Clemens/A. Haverkamp/R. Kunert (ed.), Formen der Armenfürsorge in hoch- und spätmittelalterlichen Zentren nördlich und südlich der Alpen. Trier 2011, p. 15–36.

A.I. Beach, Women as Scribes. Book Production and Monastic Reform in Twelfth-Century Bavaria. Oxford 2003.

A. Benvenuti, Cellanae et reclusae dans l'Italie médiévale. Modèles sociaux et comportements religieux, in I. Heullant-Donnat/J. Claustre/E. Lusset (ed.), Enfermements. Le cloître et la prison, VIe-XVIIIe siècle. Paris 2011, p. 249–260.

C.H. Berman, Women and Monasticism in Medieval Europe: Sisters and Patrons of the Cistercian Reform. Kalamazoo, MI 2002.

C.H. Berman, The White Nuns. Cistercian Abbeys for Women in Medieval France. Philadelphia, PA 2018.

M. Breitenstein, Das Noviziat im hohen Mittelalter: Zur Organisation des Eintritts bei den Cluniazensern, Cisterziensern und Franziskanern. Berlin 2008.

C.W. Bynum, Jesus as Mother: Studies in the Spirituality of the High Middle Ages. Berkeley, CA 1982.

C. Caby, Les moines et la dîme (XIe–XIIIe siècle). Construction, enjeux et évolutions d'un débat polymorphe, in M. Lauwers (ed.), La dîme dans l'Occident médiéval. Prélèvement seigneurial, église et territoires. Turnhout 2012, p. 361–401.

G. Cariboni, Frauenklöster der lombardischen Städtelandschaft (11.-13. Jahrhundert), in F.J. Felten/H. Müller/H. Ochs (ed.), Landschaft(en). Begriffe – Formen – Implikatione. Stuttgart 2012, p. 391–411.

G. Cariboni/N. D'Acunto (ed.), Costruzione identitaria e spazi sociali. Spoleto 2017.

I. Cochelin, Downplayed or Silenced: Authorial Voices Behind Customaries and Customs (Eighth–Eleventh c.), in K. Pansters/A. Plunkett-Latimer (ed.), Shaping Stability. The Normation and Formation of Religious Life in the Middle Ages. Turnhout 2016, p. 158–181.

G. Constable, Renewal and Reform in Religious Life: Concepts and Realities, in R.L. Benson/G. Constable/C. Dana (ed.), Renaissance and Renewal in the Twelfth Century. Oxford 1982, p. 37–67.

G. Constable, The Reformation of the Twelfth Century. Cambridge 1996.

T. Coomans, Cistercian Architecture or Architecture of the Cistercians?, in M. Birkedal Bruun (ed.), The Cambridge Companion to the Cistercian Order. Cambridge 2013, p. 151–169.

L.-A. Dannenberg, Das Recht der Religiosen in der Kanonistik des 12. und 13. Jahrhunderts. Berlin 2008.

C. De Miramon, Embrasser l'état monastique à l'âge adulte (1050–1200). Etude sur la conversion tardive, Annales 54 (1999), p. 825–850.

K. Elm/M. Parisse (ed.), Doppelklöster und andere Formen der Symbiose männlicher und weiblicher Religiosen im Mittelalter. Berlin 1992.

T. Falmagne, Les Cisterciens et les nouvelles formes d'organisation des florilèges aux 12e et 13e siècles, Archivum latinitatis medii aevi 55 (1997), p. 73–176.

F. Felten, Der Zisterzienserorden und die Frauen, in C. Kleinjung (ed.), Vita religiosa sanctimonialium: Norm und Praxis des weiblichen religiösen Lebens vom 6. bis zum 13. Jahrhundert. Korb 2011, p. 199–274.

J. France, Separate but Equal: Cistercian Lay Brothers 1120–1350. Collegeville, MN 2012.

R. Gilchrist, Gender and Material Culture. The Archaeology of Religious Women. London 1994.

F.J. Griffiths/J. Hotchin, Women and Men in the Medieval Religious Landscape, in F.J. Griffiths/J. Hotchin (ed.), Partners in Spirit. Women, Men, and Religious Life in Germany 1100–1500. Turnhout 2012, p. 1–46.

F.J. Griffiths, Nuns' Priests' Tales. Men and Salvation in Medieval Women's Monastic Life. Philadelphia, PA 2018.

C. Gunn, Ancrene Wisse. From Pastoral Literature to Vernacular Spirituality. Cardiff 2008.

C. Gunn/L.H. McAvoy (ed.), Medieval Anchorites in Their Communities. Woodbridge 2017.

J. Hotchin, Female Religious Life and the "Cura monialium" in Hirsau Monasticism, 1080 to 1150, in C.J. Mews (ed.), Listen Daughter: The Speculum Virginum and the Formation of Religious Women in the Middle Ages. New York, NY 2001, p. 59–84.

M. Hughes-Edwards, Reading Medieval Anchoritism. Ideology and Spiritual Practices. Cardiff 2012.

E. Jamroziak, Rievaulx Abbey and its Social Context, 1132–1300. Memory, Locality, and Networks. Turnhout 2005.

E. Jamroziak, Survival and Success on Medieval Borders: Cistercian Houses in Medieval Scotland and Pomerania from the Twelfth to Late Fourteenth Century. Turnhout 2011.

E.L. Jordan, Gender Concerns: Monks, Nuns, and Patronage of the Cistercian Order in the Thirteenth-Century Flanders and Hainaut, Speculum 87 (2012), p. 62–94.

J. Leclercq, The Love of Learning and the Desire for God. New York, NY 1961.

A.E. Lester, Creating Cistercian Nuns: The Women's Religious Movement and its Reform in Thirteenth-Century Champagne. Ithaca, NY 2011.

M. Long, High Medieval Monasteries as Communities of Practice: Approaching Monastic Learning Through Letters, Journal of Religious History 41 (2017), p. 42–59.

C. Lutter (2005a), Geschlecht und Wissen, Norm und Praxis, Lesen und Schreiben: Monastische Reformgemeinschaften im 12. Jahrhundert. Vienna 2005.

C. Lutter (2005b), Klausur zwischen realen Begrenzungen und spirituellen Entwürfen. Handlungsspielräume und Identifikationsmodelle der Admonter Nonnen im 12. Jahrhundert, in E. Vavra (ed.), Virtuelle Räume.

Raumwahrnehmung und Raumvorstellung im Mittelalter. Berlin 2005, p. 305–324.

C.J. MEWS, Negotiating the Boundaries of Gender in Religious Life: Robert of Arbrissel and Hersende, Abelard and Heloise, Viator 37 (2007), p. 113–148.

A. MULDER-BAKKER, Lives of the Anchoresses: The Rise of the Urban Recluse in Medieval Europe. Philadelphia, PA 2005.

M.G. NEWMAN, The Boundaries of Charity. Cistercian Culture and Ecclesiastical Reform, 1098–1180. Stanford, CA 1996.

B. NOELL, Expectation and Unrest among Cistercian Lay Brothers in the Twelfth and Thirteenth Centuries, Journal of Medieval History 32 (2006), p. 253–274.

D.J. REILLY, Art, in M. BIRKEDAL BRUUN (ed.), The Cambridge Companion to the Cistercian Order. Cambridge 2013, p. 125–139.

D.J. REILLY, The Cistercian Reform and the Art of the Book in Twelfth-Century France. Amsterdam 2019.

K.E. SALZER, Vaucelles Abbey: Social, Political, and Ecclesiastical Relationships in the Borderland Region of the Cambrésis, 1131–1300. Turnhout 2017.

E. SCHLOTHEUBER, "Gelehrte Bräute Christi". Geistliche Frauen in der mittelalterlichen Gesellschaft. Tübingen 2018.

Y. SEALE, Well-Behaved Women? Agnès of Baudement and Agnès of Braine as Female Lords and Patrons of the Premonstratensian Order, The Haskins Society Journal 28 (2017), p. 101–118.

G. SIGNORI, Johannes Hertenstain's Translation (1425) of Grimlaicus's Rule for the Anchoresses at Steinertobel near St Gallen, in M. VAN DIJK/R.I.A. NIP (ed.), Saints, Scholars, and Politicians. Gender as a Tool in Medieval Studies. Turnhout 2005, p. 43–63.

W. SIMONS, On the Margins of Religious Life: Hermits and Recluses, Penitents and Tertiairies, Beguines and Beghards, in M. RUBIN/W. SIMONS (ed.), Christianity in Western Europe c. 1000–c. 1500. Cambridge 2009, p. 309–323.

V. SMIRNOVA/M.-A. POLO DE BEAULIEU/J. BERLIOZ (ed.), The Art of Cistercian Persuasion in the Middle Ages and Beyond: Caesarius of Heisterbach's Dialogue on Miracles and its Reception. Leiden 2015.

J. SONNTAG, Klosterleben im Spiegel des Zeichenhaften: Symbolisches Denken und Handeln hochmittelalterlicher Mönche zwischen Dauer und Wandel, Regel und Gewohnheit. Berlin 2008.

4.3 Law, Custom, and the Early Thirteenth-Century Papal Reforms

P.C. ADAMO, New Monks in Old Habits. The Formation of the Caulite Monastic Order, 1193–1267. Toronto 2014.

J.W. BALDWIN, Paris et Rome en 1215: Les réformes du IVe Concile de Latran, Journal des Savants (1997), p. 99–124.

J. Belaen, Was Benedictine Monasticism Conservative? Evidence from
the Sermon Collection of Jacques de Furnes, Abbot of Saint-Bertin
(1230–1237), Revue belge de philologie et d'histoire 95 (2017),
p. 131–160.

U. Berlière, Les chapitres généraux de l'ordre de Saint Benoît avant le IVe
concile de Latran (1215), Revue bénédictine 8 (1891), p. 255–264.

C.B. Bouchard, Holy Entrepreneurs: Cistercians, Knights, and Economic
Exchange in Twelfth-Century Burgundy. Ithaca, NY 1991.

A. Boureau, Prout moris est iure, les moines et la question de la coutume
(XIIe–XIIIe siècles), Revue historique 303 (2001), p. 363–402.

C. Cappuccio, Die päpstlichen Subdiakone als Mittel der Kommunikation
zwischen Rom und der Lombardei (1198–1216), in C. Ulrich (ed.), Dialog
und Dialogizität: Interdisziplinär, interkulturell, international. Munich
2017, p. 216–232.

C.R. Cheney, Episcopal Visitation of Monasteries in the Thirteenth Century.
Manchester 1931.

A.J. Davis, The Holy Bureaucrat. Eudes Rigaud and Religious Reform in
Thirteenth-Century Normandy. Ithaca, NY 2006.

S. Excoffon, Une abbaye en Dauphiné aux XIIe et XIIIe siècles: Chalais avant
son rattachment à la Grande-Chartreuse, Revue Mabillon 69 (1997),
p. 115–154.

L. Falkenstein, La papauté et les abbayes françaises aux XIe et XIIe siècles:
Exemption et protection apostolique. Paris 1997.

F.J. Felten, Die Kurie und die Reformen im Prämonstratenserorden im hohen
und späten Mittelalter, in I. Crusius/H. Flachenecker (ed.), Studien zum
Prämonstratenserorden. Göttingen 2003, p. 349–398.

F.J. Felten (2011a), Gregor IX. Als Reformer von Orden und Klöstern, in Gregorio
IX e gli ordini Mendicanti. Spoleto 2011, p. 3–71.

F. Felten (2011b), Der Zisterzienserorden und die Frauen, in K. Kleinjung (ed.),
Vita religiosa sanctimonialium: Norm und Praxis des weiblichen religiösen
Lebens vom 6. bis zum 13. Jahrhundert. Korb 2011, p. 199–274.

J. Johrendt/H. Müller (ed.), Rom und die Regionen. Studien zur
Homogenisierung der lateinischen Kirche im Hochmittelalter. Berlin 2012.

E.L. Jordan, Shared Rule, Separate Practice? Assessing Benedictine Economic
Activities in Flanders during the Thirteenth Century, Revue bénédictine 115
(2005), p. 187–204.

B. Krings, Die Statuten des Prämonstratenserordens von 1244/46 und ihre
Überarbeitung im Jahre 1279, Analecta Praemonstratensia 83 (2007),
p. 5–127.

M. Maccarrone, Le costituzioni del IV Concilio Lateranense sui religiosi,
in R. Lambertini (ed.), Nuovi studi su Innocenzo III. Rome 1995,
p. 1–46.

W. Maleczek, Gregor IX. als Kanonist und als Gesetzgeber religiöser Orden,
in Gregorio IX e gli ordini Mendicanti. Spoleto 2011, p. 123–194.

G. Melville, Die cluniazensische Reformatio tam in capite quam in membris.
Institutioneller Wandel zwischen Anpassung und Bewahrung, in
J. Miethke (ed.), Sozialer Wandel im Mittelalter. Wahrnehmungsformen,

Erklärungsmuster, Regelungsmechanismen. Sigmaringen 1994,
p. 249–297.

F. Neiske, Reform oder Kodifizierung? Päpstliche Statuten für Cluny im 13.
Jahrhundert, Archivum Historiae Pontificiae 26 (1988), p. 71–118.

J. Oberste, Visitation und Ordensorganisation. Formen sozialer Normierung,
Kontrolle und Kommunikation bei Cisterziensern, Prämonstratensern und
Cluniazensern (12.-frühes 14. Jahrhundert). Münster 1996.

W.A. Pantin, The General and Provincial Chapters of the English Black Monks,
1215–1540, Transactions of the Royal Historical Society 10 (1927), p. 195–263.

P. Racinet, Les maisons de l'Ordre de Cluny au Moyen Age: Evolution et
permanence d'un ancien ordre bénédictin au nord de Paris. Louvain 1990.

C. Reglero, Cluny en España. Los prioratos de la provincia y sus redes sociales
(1073–ca. 1270). Madrid 2008.

H.-J. Schmidt, Iuxta morem Cisterciensium. Päpstliche Anweisungen Zur
kommunikativen Koordination von Klöstern (13. Jahrhundert), in
C. Andenna/ G. Blennemann/K. Herbers/G. Melville (ed.), Die
Ordnung der Kommunikation und die Kommunikation der Ordnungen.
2. Zentralität: Papstum und Orden im Europa des 12. und 13. Jahrhunderts.
Stuttgart 2013, p. 145–168.

T.W. Smith, Pope Honorius III, the Military Orders and the Financing of the Fifth
Crusade: A Culture of Papal Preference?, in J. Schenk/M. Carr (ed.), The
Military Orders: Volume 6.1, Culture and Conflict in the Mediterranean
World. London 2017, p. 54–61.

4.4 Emergence and Integration of the Mendicants

F. Andrews, The Other Friars: Carmelite, Augustinian, Sack and Pied Friars in
the Middle Ages. Woodbridge 2006.

A. Benvenuti Papi, "In domo bighittarum seu viduarium": Pubblica assistenza
e marginalità femminile nella Firenze medievale, in E. Cristiano/E.
Salvatori (ed.), Città e servizi sociali nell'Italia dei secoli XII-XV. Pistoia
1990, p. 325–353.

N. Bériou/J. Chiffoleau (ed.), Economie et religion: L'expérience des ordres
mendiants (XIIIe–XVe siècle). Lyon 2009.

R.B. Brooke, Early Franciscan Government: Elias to Bonaventure. Cambridge
2004.

C. Bruzelius, Preaching, Building, and Burying: Friars in the Medieval City.
New Haven, CT 2014.

G.T. Colesanti/B. Garí/N. Jornet-Benito (ed.), Clarisas y dominicas. Modelos
de implantación, filiación, promoción y devoción en la Península Ibérica,
Cerdeña, Nápoles y Sicilia. Florence 2017 (e-book: http://digital.casalini.
it/9788864536767).

F. Conti, Witchcraft, Superstition, and Observant Franciscan Preachers: Pastoral
Approach and Intellectual Debate in Renaissance Milan. Turnhout 2015.

F. Cygler, Zur institutionellen Symbolizität der dominikanischen Verfassung.
  Versuch einer Deutung, in G. Melville (ed.), Institutionalität und
  Symbolisierung. Cologne 2001, p. 409–424.

J. Dalarun, François d'Assise: Écrits, vies, témoignages, 2 vols. Paris 2010.

M.-M. De Cevins/L. Viallet (ed.), L'économie des couvents mendiants
  en Europe centrale: Bohême, Hongrie, Pologne, v. 1220–v. 1550.
  Rennes 2018.

M.-L. Ehrenschwendtner, Die Bildung der Dominikanerinnen in
  Süddeutschland vom 13. bis 15. Jahrhundert. Stuttgart 2004.

S.L. Field, New Light on the 1230s: History, Hagiography, and Thomas of
  Celano's The Life of Our Blessed Father Francis, Franciscan Studies 74
  (2016), p. 239–248.

F. Garcia-Serrano, The Friars and Their Influence in Medieval Spain.
  Amsterdam 2018.

N. Holder (ed.), The Friaries of Medieval London: From Foundation to
  Dissolution. Woodbridge 2017.

C. Jäggi, Frauenklöster im Spätmittelalter: Die Kirchen der Klarissen und
  Dominkanerinnen im 13. und 14. Jahrhundert. Petersberg 2006.

A. Jotischky, The Carmelites and Antiquity: Mendicants and Their Pasts in the
  Middle Ages. Oxford 2002.

L. Knox, Creating Clare of Assisi: Female Franciscan Identities in Later Medieval
  Italy. Leiden 2008.

A.-J. Lahaye, Spiritual Renewal and Changing Landscapes: The Mendicant
  Orders in Ireland, Thirteenth-Sixteenth Century, in J. Lyttleton/M. Stout
  (ed.), Church and Settlement of Ireland. Dublin 2018, p. 119–141.

C. Linde (ed.), Making and Breaking the Rules: Discussion, Implementation,
  and Consequences of Dominican Legislation. Oxford 2018.

F.J. Mapelli, L'amministrazione francescana di Inghilterra e Francia: Personale
  di governo e strutture dell'Ordine fino al Concilio di Vienne (1311).
  Rome 2003.

G. Melville/J. Oberste (ed.), Die Bettelorden im Aufbau: Beiträge zu
  Institutionalisierungsprozessen im mittelalterlichen Religiosentum.
  Münster 1999.

G. Melville, System Rationality and the Dominican Success in the Middle
  Ages, in M. Robson/J. Röhrkasten (ed.), Franciscan Organisation in the
  Mendicant Context. Berlin 2010, p. 377–388.

C.M. Mooney, Clare of Assisi and the Thirteenth-Century Church: Religious
  Women, Rules, and Resistance. Philadelphia, PA 2016.

A. Müller, Bettelmönche in islamischer Fremde. Münster 2002.

S.M. Neidhardt, Autonomie im Gehorsam: Die dominikanische Observanz in
  Selbstzeugnissen geistlicher Frauen des Spätmittelalters. Berlin 2017.

P. Nold, Pope John XXII and His Franciscan Cardinal: Bertrand de la Tour and
  the Apostolic Poverty Controversy. Oxford 2003.

B. Rano, Augustinian Origins, Charism, and Spirituality. Villanova 1994.

M. Robson/J. Röhrkasten (ed.), Franciscan Organisation in the Mendicant
  Context: Formal and Informal Structures of the Friars' Lives and Ministry in
  the Middle Ages. Berlin 2010.

M. Robson (ed.), The Cambridge Companion to Francis of Assisi. Cambridge 2012.

B. Roest, A History of Franciscan Education (c. 1210–1517). Leiden 2000.

B. Roest, Order and Disorder: The Poor Clares Between Foundation and Reform. Leiden 2013.

B. Roest/J. Uphoff (ed.), Religious Orders and Religious Identity Formation, ca. 1420–1620: Discourses and Strategies of Observance and Pastoral Engagement. Leiden 2016.

B. Romhányi, Mendicant Networks and Population in a European Perspective, in G. Jaritz/K.G. Szende (ed.), Medieval East Central Europe in a Comparative Perspective: From Frontier Zones to Lands in Focus. London 2016, p. 99–122.

N. Şenocak, The Poor and the Perfect: The Rise of Learning in the Franciscan Order, 1209–1310. Ithaca, NY 2012.

R. Sickert, Wenn Klosterbrüder zu Jahrmarktsbrüdern werden: Studien zur Wahrnehmung der Franziskaner und Dominikaner im 13. Jahrhundert. Berlin 2006.

N.I. Tsougarakis, The Latin Religious Orders in Medieval Greece, 1204–1500. Turnhout 2012.

A. Vauchez, François d'Assise: Entre histoire et mémoire. Paris 2009.

R. Vose, Dominicans, Muslims, and Jews in the Medieval Crown of Aragon. Cambridge 2009.

A. Wesjohann, Flüchtigkeit und Bewahrung des Charisma oder: War der heilige Dominikus etwa auch ein Charismatiker?, in G. Andenna/M. Breiteinstein/G. Melville (ed.), Charisma und religiöse Gemeinschaften im Mittelalter. Münster 2005, p. 227–260.

A. Wesjohann, Mendikantische Gründungserzählungen im 13. und 14. Jahrhundert: Mythen als Element institutioneller Eigengeschichtsschreibung der mittelalterlichen Franziskaner, Dominikaner und Augustiner-Eremiten. Münster 2012.

4.5 'Semi-religious' Movements in the Later Middle Ages

M.P. Alberzoni, Die Humiliaten zwischen Legende und Wirklichkeit, Mitteilungen des Instituts für Österreichische Geschichtsforschung 107 (1999), p. 324–353.

G. Andreozzi, Il terzo ordine regolare di San Francesco nella sua storia e nelle sue leggi, 3 vols. Rome 1993–1995.

F. Andrews, The Early Humilitati. Cambridge 1999.

A. Bartolomei Romagnoli/E. Paoli/P. Piatti (ed.), Angeliche Visioni. Veronica da Binasco nella Milano del Rinascimento. Florence 2016.

L. Böhringer/J. Kolpacoff Deane/H. Van Engen (ed.), Labels and Libels: Naming Beguines in Northern Medieval Europe. Turnhout 2014.

L. Böhringer, Merging into Clergy: Beguine Self-Promotion in Cologne in the Thirteenth and Fourteenth Centuries, in L. Böhringer/J. Kolpacoff

Deane/H. Van Engen (ed.), Labels and Libels: Naming Beguines in Northern Medieval Europe. Turnhout 2014, p. 151–186.

L. Braguier, Servantes de Dieu: Les *beatas* de la couronne de Castille (1450–1600). Rennes 2019.

G. Cariboni, Gregorio IX e la nascita delle 'Sorores penitentes' di Santa Maria Maddalena 'in Alemannia', Annali dell'Istituto storico italo-germanico in Trento 25 (1999), p. 11–44.

G. Casagrande, Il movimento penitenziale francescano nel dibattito storiografico degli ultimi 25 anni, in L. Temperini (ed.), Santi e santità nel movimento penitenziale francescano dal Duecento al Cinquecento. Rome 1998, p. 351–389.

D.E.H. De Boer/I. Kwiatowski (ed.), Die Devotio Moderna: Sozialer und kultureller Transfer (1350–1580), 2 vols. Münster 2013.

J. De Vries, The Proper Beguine's Interaction with the Outside World: Some Beguine Rules from the Late Medieval Low Countries, in K. Pansters/A.G. Plunkett-Latimer (ed.), Shaping Stability. The Normation and Formation of Religious Life in the Middle Ages. Turnhout 2016, p. 137–152.

K. Elm, Vita regularis sine regula. Bedeutung, Rechtsstellung und Selbstverständnis des mittelalterlichen und frühneuzeitlichen Semireligiosentums, in E. Müller-Luckner/F. Šmahel (ed.), Häresie und vorzeitige Reformation im Spätmittelalter. Munich 1998, p. 239–273.

K. Goudriaan, Piety in Practice and Print. Essay on the Late Medieval Religious Landscape. Hilversum 2016.

H. Joldersma, "Alternative Spiritual Exercises for Weaker Minds"? Vernacular Religious Song in the Lives of Women of the Devotio moderna, Church History and Religious Culture 88 (2008), p. 371–393.

M. Lehmijoki-Gardner, Writing Religious Rules as an Interactive Process: Dominican Penitent Women and the Making of their 'Regula', Speculum 79 (2004), p. 660–687.

M. Lehmijoki-Gardner, Dominican Penitent Women. New York, NY 2005.

E.M. Makowski, "A Pernicious Sort of Woman": Quasi-Religious Women and Canon Lawyers in the Later Middle Ages. Washington, DC 2005.

A. More, Institutionalizing Penitential Life in Later Medieval and Early Modern Europe: Third Orders, Rules and Canonical Legitimacy, Church History 83 (2014), p. 297–323.

A. More, Fictive Orders and Feminine Religious Identities, 1200–1600. Oxford 2018.

Les mouvances laïques des ordres religieux. Saint-Etienne 1996.

D.I. Nieto-Isabel, Overlapping Networks. Beguins, Franciscans, and Poor Clares at the Crossroads of a Shared Spirituality, in G.T. Colesanti/B. Garí/N. Jornet-Benito (ed.), Clarisas y dominicas. Modelos de implantación, filiación, promoción y devoción en la Península Ibérica, Cerdeña, Nápoles y Sicilia. Florence 2017, p. 429–448.

M. Reichstein, Das Beginenwesen in Deutschland: Studien und Katalog. Berlin 2001.

B. Schmidt, "Infideles et perversae feminae": Das Beginen-Bild in der Kirchen-
und Konziliengeschichtsschreibung, in J. Voigt/B. Schmidt/M.A. Sorace
(ed.), Das Beginenwesen in Spätmittelalter und Früher Neuzeit. Stuttgart
2015, p. 317–330.

W. Simons, Cities of Ladies: Beguine Communities in the Medieval Low
Countries 1200–1565. Philadelphia PA 2001.

W. Simons, In Praise of Faithful Women: Count Robert of Flanders's Defense of
Beguines against the Clementine Decree Cum de quibusdam mulieribus
(ca. 1318–1320), in D.C. Mengel/L.A. Wolverton (ed.), Christianity and
Culture in the Middle Ages: Essays to Honor John Van Engen. Notre Dame,
IN 2015, p. 331–352 and 353–357.

T. Stabler Miller, The Beguines of Medieval Paris. Gender, Patronage, and
Spiritual Authority. Philadelphia, PA 2014.

N. Staubach (ed.), Kirchenreform von unten. Gerhard Zerbolt von Zutphen und
die Brüder vom gemeinsamen Leben. Frankfurt am Main 2005.

N. Terpstra, Lay Confraternities and Civic Religion in Renaissance Bologna.
Cambridge 1995.

R.T.M. Van Dijk/R.H.F. Hofman/M. Van den Berg (ed.), Salome
Sticken (1369–1449) en de oorsprong van de Moderne Devotie.
Hilversum 2015.

H. Van Engen, De derde orde van Sint-Franciscus in het middeleeuwse bisdom
Utrecht. Een bijdrage tot de institutionele geschiedenis van de Moderne
Devotie. Hilversum 2006.

J. Van Engen, Friar Johannes Nyder on Laypeople Living as Religious
in the World, in F.J. Felten/N. Jaspert (ed.), Vita Religiosa im
Mittelalter. Festschrift für Kaspar Elm zum 70. Geburtstag. Berlin 2004,
p. 583–615.

J. Van Engen, Sisters and Brothers of the Common Life: The Devotio Moderna
and the World of the Later Middle Ages. Philadelphia, PA 2008.

M. Van Luijk, Bruiden van Christus. De tweede religieuze vrouwenbeweging in
Leiden en Zwolle, 1380–1580. Zutphen 2004.

A. Vauchez (ed.), Ermites de France et d'Italie (XIe–XVe siècle). Rome 2003.

J. Voigt, Beginen im Spätmittelalter. Frauenfrömmigkeit in Thüringen und im
Reich. Cologne 2012.

S. Von Heusinger, Johannes Mulberg OP († 1414): Ein Leben im Spannungsfeld
von Dominikanerobservanz und Beginenstreit. Berlin 2000.

M. Wehrli-Johns, Voraussetzungen und Perspektiven mittelalterlicher
Laienfrömmigkeit seit Innozenz III. Eine Auseinandersetzung mit
Herbert Grundmanns "Religiösen Bewegungen", Mitteilungen des
Instituts für Österreichische Geschichtsforschung 104 (1996),
p. 286–307.

M. Wehrli-Johns, Das mittelalterliche Beginentum. Religiöse Frauenbewegung
oder Sozialidee der Scholastik, in M. Wehrli-Johns/C. Opitz (ed.),
Fromme Frauen oder Ketzerinnen? Leben und Verfolgung der Beginen im
Mittelalter. Freiburg im Breisgau 1998, p. 25–51.

4.6 Late Medieval Challenges and Experiences

N. Bériou/M. Morard/D. Nebbiai-Dalla Guarda (ed.), Entre stabilité et itinérance: Livres et culture des ordres mendiants, XIIIe–XVe siècle. Turnhout 2014.

F.X. Bischof/M. Thurner (ed.), Die benediktinische Klosterreform im 15. Jahrhundert. Berlin 2013.

C. Caby, De l'érémitisme rural au monachisme urbain: Les Camaldules en Italie à la fin du Moyen Age. Rome 1999.

R. Cahill, The Sequestration of the Hessian Monasteries, in B.A. Kümin (ed.), Reformations Old and New: Essays on the Socio-economic Impact of Religious Change, c. 1470–1630. Aldershot 1996, p. 39–56.

J.G. Clark/K.E. Bush, Monastic preaching, c. 1350–c. 1545, in A. Beach/I. Cochelin (ed.), The Cambridge History of Medieval Monasticism in the Latin West, 2 vols. Cambridge 2020, p. 1125–1139.

H. Dewez, Une simplicité trompeuse: Le compte manorial monastique (Angleterre, xiiie–xive siècle), in O. Mattéoni/P. Beck (ed.), Classer, dire, compter: Discipline du chiffre et fabrique d'une norme comptable à la fin du Moyen Age. Paris 2015, p. 153–170.

K. Elm (ed.), Reformbemühungen und Observanzbestrebungen im spätmittelalterlichen Ordenswesen. Berlin 1989.

K. Elm, Decline and Renewal of the Religious Orders in the Late Middle Ages: Current Research and Research Agendas, in K. Elm/J. Mixson (ed.), Religious Life Between Jerusalem, the Desert, and the World: Selected Essays. Leiden 2016, p. 138–188.

S. Excoffon, Un ordre et sa disparition. Les monastères Chalaisiens de la fin du XIIe au début du XIVe siècle, Provence historique 51 (2001), p. 265–281.

F.J. Felten, Die Ordensreformen Benedikts XII. unter institutionsgeschichtlichem Aspekt, in G. Melville (ed.), Institutionen und Geschichte. Theoretische Aspekte und mittelalterliche Befunde. Cologne 1992, p. 369–435.

S. Fritsch, Das Refektorium im Jahreskreis. Norm und Praxis des Essens in Klöstern des 14. Jahrhunderts. Vienna 2008.

G. Geltner, The Making of Medieval Antifraternalism. Polemic, Violence, Deviance, and Remembrance. Oxford 2012.

O.P. Grell (ed.), The Scandinavian Reformation: From Evangelical Movement to Institutionalisation of Reform. Cambridge 1995.

J.F. Hamburger, Nuns as Artists: The Visual Culture of a Medieval Convent. Berkeley, CA 1997.

J.F. Hamburger/R. Suckale (ed.), Krone und Schleier: Kunst aus mittelalterlichen Frauenklöstern. Munich 2005.

M. Heale, The Abbots and Priors of Late Medieval and Reformation England. Oxford 2016.

J. Hotchin, Reformatrices and Their Books: Religious Women and Reading Networks in Fifteenth-Century Germany, in C.J. Mews/J.N. Crossley (ed.), Communities of Learning: Networks and the Shaping of Intellectual Identity in Europe, 1100–1500. Turnhout 2011, p. 251–291.

U. Israel, Reform durch Mönche aus der Ferne. Das Beispiel der Benediktinerabtei Subiaco, in U. Israel (ed.), Vita communis und ethnische Vielfalt. Berlin 2006, p. 157–178.

C.T. Jones, Ruling the Spirit: Women, Liturgy, and Dominican Reform in Late Medieval Germany. Philadelphia, PA 2018.

M. Kaartinen, Religious Life and English Culture in the Reformation. Basingstoke 2002.

R.L. Kendrick, Celestial Sirens: Nuns and their Music in Early Modern Milan. Oxford 1996.

J. Kerr, Monastic Hospitality: The Benedictines in England, c. 1070–c. 1250. Woodbridge 2007.

P. King, The Cistercian Order 1200–1600, in M. Bruun (ed.), The Cambridge Companion to the Cistercian Order. Cambridge 2013, p. 38–49.

S. Kristjánsdóttir/I. Larsson/P.A. Asen, The Icelandic Medieval Monastic Garden - Did it Exist?, Scandinavian Journal of History 39 (2014), p. 560–579.

J.-M. Le Gall, Les moines au temps des réformes: France, 1480–1560. Seyssel 2001.

F.D. Logan, Runaway Religious in Medieval England, c. 1240–1540. Cambridge 1996.

E. Lusset, Crime, châtiment et grâce dans les monastères au Moyen Age (XIIe–XVe siècle). Turnhout 2017.

E.M. Makowski, Canon Law and Cloistered Women: Periculoso and its Commentators, 1298–1545. Washington, DC 1997.

U. Mersch, Soziale Dimensionen visueller Kommunikation in hoch- und spätmittelalterlichen Frauenkommunitäten. Göttingen 2012.

J.D. Mixson, Poverty's Proprietors: Ownership and Mortal Sin at the Origins of the Observant Movement. Leiden 2009.

J. Mixson/B. Roest (ed.), A Companion to Observant Reform in the Late Middle Ages and Beyond. Leiden 2015.

K. Pansters (ed.), The Carthusians in the Low Countries: Studies in Monastic History and Heritage. Leuven 2014.

F. Perez Rodriguez, Los monasterios premonstratenses en los reinos occidentales de la Península Ibérica, in Entre el claustro y el mundo. Canónigos regulares y monjes premonstratenses en la Edad Media. Aguilar de Campóo 2009, p. 165–205.

P. Racinet, Crises et renouveaux. Les monastères Clunisiens à la fin du Moyen Age (XIIIe–XVIe siècles). De la Flandre au Berry et comparaisons méridionales. Arras 1997.

C. Rey, L'entreprise archivistique de Jean de Cirey, abbé de Cîteaux (1476–1501). Le dossier documentaire de la seigneurie de Villars en Côte-d'Or, Bulletin du centre d'études médiévales d'Auxerre 14 (2010) (http://cem.revues.org/index11638.html, accessed 14 March 2018).

B. Roest/J. Uphoff (ed.), Religious orders and Religious Identity Formation, ca. 1420–1620. Discourse and Strategies of Observance and Pastoral Engagement. Leiden 2016.

H. Rüthing, Die Kartäuser und die spätmittelalterlichen Ordensreformen, in K. Elm (ed.), Reformbemühungen und Observanzbestrebungen im spätmittelalterlichen Ordenswesen. Berlin 1989, p. 35–58.

R.L.J. Shaw, The Celestine Monks of France, c. 1350–1450. Observant Reform in an Age of Schism, Council and War. Amsterdam 2018.

A. Schlechter/F.S. Pelgen (ed.), Johannes Trithemius (1462–1516): Benediktiner, Humanist und Kirchenreformer. Koblenz 2016.

A. Sohn/L. Verger (ed.), Die regulierten Kollegien im Europa des Mittelalters und der Renaissance/Les collèges réguliers en Europe au Moyen Age et à la Renaissance. Bochum 2012.

L. Sönke (ed.), Bücher, Bibliotheken, und Schriftkultur der Kartäuser. Stuttgart 2002.

V.G. Spear, Leadership in Medieval English Nunneries. Woodbridge 2005.

S. Steckel, Satirical Depictions of Monastic Life, in I. Cochelin/A. Beach (ed.), The Cambridge History of Medieval Monasticism in the Latin World. Cambridge 2020, p. 1154–1170.

K. Stöber, Late Medieval Monasteries and Their Patrons: England and Wales, c. 1300–1540. Woodbridge 2007.

Studies in St. Birgitta and the Brigittine Order, 2 vols. Salzburg 1993.

J. Van Engen, Multiple Options: The World of the Fifteenth-Century Church, Church History 77 (2008), p. 257–284.

L. Viallet, Les sens de l'observance. Enquête sur les réformes franciscaines. Berlin 2014.

C. Zermatten, Reform Endeavors and the Development of Congregations: Regulating Diversity Within the Carmelite Order, K. Pansters/A. Plunkett-Latimer (ed.), Shaping Stability. The Normation and Formation of Religious Life in the Middle Ages. Turnhout 2016, p. 245–261.

Index of People

https://doi.org/10.1515/9783110543780-004

Index of Authors

https://doi.org/10.1515/9783110543780-005

Index of Places and Concepts

https://doi.org/10.1515/9783110543780-006

Oldenbourg Grundriss der Geschichte

Herausgegeben von Lothar Gall, Karl-Joachim Hölkeskamp und Steffen Patzold

https://doi.org/10.1515/9783110543780-007

Band 13
Dieter Langewiesche
Europa zwischen Restauration und Revolution
1815–1849
5. Aufl. 2007. 261 S., 4 Karten.
ISBN 978-3-486-49734-2

Band 14
Lothar Gall
Europa auf dem Weg in die Moderne
1850–1890
5. Aufl. 2009. 332 S., 4 Karten
ISBN 978-3-486-58718-0

Band 15
Gregor Schöllgen/Friedrich Kießling
Das Zeitalter des Imperialismus
5., überarb. u. erw. Aufl. 2009. 326 S.
ISBN 978-3-486-58868-2

Band 16
Eberhard Kolb/Dirk Schumann
Die Weimarer Republik
8., aktualis. u. erw. Aufl. 2012. 349 S.,
1 Karte
ISBN 978-3-486-71267-4

Band 17
Klaus Hildebrand
Das Dritte Reich
7., durchges. Aufl. 2009. 474 S., 1 Karte
ISBN 978-3-486-59200-9

Band 18
Jost Dülffer
Europa im Ost-West-Konflikt 1945–1991
2004. 304 S., 2 Karten
ISBN 978-3-486-49105-0

Band 19
Rudolf Morsey
Die Bundesrepublik Deutschland
Entstehung und Entwicklung bis 1969
5., durchges. Aufl. 2007. 343 S.
ISBN 978-3-486-58319-9

Band 19a
Andreas Rödder
Die Bundesrepublik Deutschland
1969–1990
2003. 330 S., 2 Karten
ISBN 978-3-486-56697-0

Band 20
Hermann Weber
Die DDR 1945–1990
5., aktual. Aufl. 2011. 384 S.
ISBN 978-3-486-70440-2

Band 21
Horst Möller
Europa zwischen den Weltkriegen
1998. 278 S.
ISBN 978-3-486-52321-8

Band 22
Peter Schreiner
Byzanz
4., aktual. Aufl. 2011. 340 S., 2 Karten
ISBN 978-3-486-70271-2

Band 23
Hanns J. Prem
Geschichte Altamerikas
2., völlig überarb. Aufl. 2008. 386 S.,
5 Karten
ISBN 978-3-486-53032-2

Band 24
Tilman Nagel
Die islamische Welt bis 1500
1998. 312 S.
ISBN 978-3-486-53011-7

Band 25
Hans J. Nissen
Geschichte Alt-Vorderasiens
2., überarb. u. erw. Aufl. 2012. 309 S.,
4 Karten
ISBN 978-3-486-59223-8

Band 26
Helwig Schmidt-Glintzer
Geschichte Chinas bis zur mongolischen
Eroberung 250 v. Chr.–1279 n. Chr.
1999. 235 S., 7 Karten
ISBN 978-3-486-56402-0

Band 27
Leonhard Harding
Geschichte Afrikas im 19. und 20.
Jahrhundert
2., durchges. Aufl. 2006. 272 S., 4 Karten
ISBN 978-3-486-57746-4

Band 28
Willi Paul Adams
Die USA vor 1900
2. Aufl. 2009. 294 S.
ISBN 978-3-486-58940-5

Band 29
Willi Paul Adams
Die USA im 20. Jahrhundert
2. Aufl., aktual. u. erg. v. Manfred Berg 2008.
302 S.
ISBN 978-3-486-56466-0

Band 30
Klaus Kreiser
Der Osmanische Staat 1300–1922
2., aktual. Aufl. 2008. 262 S., 4 Karten
ISBN 978-3-486-58588-9

Band 31
Manfred Hildermeier
Die Sowjetunion 1917–1991
3. überarb. und akt. Aufl. 2016. XXX S.
ISBN 978-3-486-71848-5

Band 32
Peter Wende
Großbritannien 1500–2000
2001. 234 S., 1 Karte
ISBN 978-3-486-56180-7

Band 33
Christoph Schmidt
Russische Geschichte 1547–1917
2. Aufl. 2009. 261 S., 1 Karte
ISBN 978-3-486-58721-0

Band 34
Hermann Kulke
Indische Geschichte bis 1750
2005. 275 S., 12 Karten
ISBN 978-3-486-55741-1

Band 35
Sabine Dabringhaus
Geschichte Chinas 1279–1949
3. akt. und überarb. Aufl. 2015.
324 S.
ISBN 978-3-486-78112-0

Band 36
Gerhard Krebs
Das moderne Japan 1868–1952
2009. 249 S.
ISBN 978-3-486-55894-4

Band 37
Manfred Clauss
Geschichte des alten Israel
2009. 259 S., 6 Karten
ISBN 978-3-486-55927-9

Band 38
Joachim von Puttkamer
Ostmitteleuropa im 19. und 20.
Jahrhundert
2010. 353 S., 4 Karten
ISBN 978-3-486-58169-0

Band 39
Alfred Kohler
Von der Reformation zum Westfälischen
Frieden
2011. 253 S.
ISBN 978-3-486-59803-2

Band 40
Jürgen Lütt
Das moderne Indien 1498 bis 2004
2012. 272 S., 3 Karten
ISBN 978-3-486-58161-4

Band 41
Andreas Fahrmeir
Europa zwischen Restauration, Reform und
Revolution 1815–1850
2012. 228 S.
ISBN 978-3-486-70939-1

Band 42
Manfred Berg
Geschichte der USA
2013. 233 S.
ISBN 978-3-486-70482-2

Band 43
Ian Wood
Europe in Late Antiquity
2020. ca. 288 S.
ISBN 978-3-11-035264-1

Band 44
Klaus Mühlhahn
Die Volksrepublik China 2017. 324 S.
ISBN 978-3-11-035530-7

Band 45
Jorg Echternkamp
Das Dritte Reich. Diktatur, Volksgemeinschaft,
Krieg
2018. 344 S., 2 Karten
ISBN 978-3-486-75569-5

Band 46
Christoph Ulf/Erich Kistler
Die Entstehung Griechenlands
2019. 328 S., 26 Abb.
ISBN 978-3-486-52991-3

Band 47
Steven Vanderputten
Medieval Monasticisms
2020. 294 S.
ISBN 978-3-11-054377-3